New Regionalisms in the Global Political Economy

D0139872

'This collection brings together a series of outstanding analyses of the different facets of the latest wave of regionalism and regionalization. The general theme of the book, that regionalization and regionalism must be examined in the context of globalization and the changing nature of the global political economy, serves to knit the chapters together into a coherent whole. Certainly, anyone wanting to understand the new wave of regionalism could have no better place to start than this insightful volume.'

Professor Richard Stubbs, *McMaster University*

Following the financial crises in large parts of the world at the end of the twentieth century, regionalisms in the global political economy have evolved in a number of interesting ways. This book seeks to bring together the leading scholars in the field to provide cutting-edge analyses of contemporary regions and regionalist projects.

New Regionalisms in the Global Political Economy provides an innovative integration of theoretical considerations with sophisticated and detailed analyses of a wide range of case studies from across the world – from Africa, Asia, Latin America, Europe and the South Pacific. The chapters consider systematically the relationship between globalisation, financial crises and regional projects. In combination, the contributions to this volume facilitate the widest possible base within the literature for a truly comparative study of contemporary regionalism.

Shaun Breslin is Reader in Politics and Principal Research Fellow in the Centre for the Study of Globalisation and Regionalisation at the University of Warwick. **Christopher W. Hughes** is Senior Research Fellow, Centre for the Study of Globalisation and Regionalisation, University of Warwick. **Nicola Phillips** is Lecturer in Politics and International Studies at the University of Warwick. **Ben Rosamond** is Senior Lecturer in Politics and International Studies at the University of Warwick.

Routledge/Warwick studies in globalisation

Edited by Richard Higgott and published in association with the Centre for the Study of Globalisation and Regionalisation, University of Warwick

What is globalisation and does it matter? How can we measure it? What are its policy implications? The Centre for the Study of Globalisation and Regionalisation at the University of Warwick is an international site for the study of key questions such as these in the theory and practice of globalisation and regionalisation. Its agenda is avowedly inter-disciplinary. The work of the Centre will be showcased in this new series.

This series comprises two strands:

Warwick Studies in Globalisation addresses the needs of students and teachers, and the titles will be published in hardback and paperback. Titles include:

Globalisation and the Asia-Pacific
Contested territories
Edited by Kris Olds, Peter Dicken, Philip F. Kelly, Lily Kong and Henry Wai-chung Yeung

Regulating the Global Information Society
Edited by Christopher Marsden

Banking on Knowledge
The genesis of the global development network
Edited by Diane Stone

Historical Materialism and Globalisation
Essays on continuity and change
Edited by Hazel Smith and Mark Rupert

Civil Society and Global Finance
Edited by Jan Aart Scholte with Albrecht Schnabel

Towards a Global Polity
Edited by Morten Ougaard and Richard Higgott

New Regionalisms in the Global Political Economy
Edited by Shaun Breslin, Christopher W. Hughes, Nicola Phillips and Ben Rosamond

Routledge/Warwick Studies in Globalisation is a forum for innovative new research intended for a high-level specialist readership, and the titles will be available in hardback only. Titles include:

New Regionalisms in the Global Political Economy

Edited by
Shaun Breslin, Christopher W.
Hughes, Nicola Phillips and Ben
Rosamond

LONDON AND NEW YORK

First published 2002
by Routledge
11 New Fetter Lane, London EC4P 4EE

Simultaneously published in the USA and Canada
by Routledge
29 West 35th Street, New York, NY 10001

Routledge is an imprint of the Taylor & Francis Group

Typeset in Baskerville by M Rules
Printed and bound in Great Britain by
St Edmundsbury Press, Bury St Edmunds, Suffolk

British Library Cataloguing in Publication Data
A catalogue record for this book is available from the British Library

Library of Congress Cataloging in Publication Data
A catalog record for this book has been requested

ISBN 0–415–27767–1 (hbk)
ISBN 0–415–27768–X (pbk)

Contents

Notes on contributors

Amitav Acharya is Deputy Director and Professor of the Institute of Defence and Strategic Studies at Nanyang Technological University in Singapore.

Andreas Bieler is Lecturer in Politics at the University of Nottingham.

Morten Bøås is Research Fellow at the Centre for Development and the Environment in Oslo.

Paul Bowles is Professor of Economics at the University of Northern British Columbia.

Shaun Breslin is Reader in Politics and Principal Research Fellow in the Centre for the Study of Globalisation and Regionalisation at the University of Warwick.

Stuart Harris is Professor and Convenor of the Northeast Asia Program in the Research School of Pacific and Asian Studies at the Australian National University.

Björn Hettne is Professor in the Department of Peace Development Research at Goteborg University.

Richard Higgott is Professor of International Political Economy and Director of the Centre for the Study of Globalisation and Regionalisation at the University of Warwick.

Peter J. Katzenstein is Walter S. Carpenter Professor of International Studies at Cornell University.

Simon Lee is Lecturer in Politics at the University of Hull.

Yoko Ogashiwa is Associate Professor of International Relations at Hiroshima University.

Nicola Phillips is Lecturer in Politics and International Studies at the University of Warwick.

Ben Rosamond is Senior Lecturer in Politics and International Studies at the University of Warwick.

Timothy M. Shaw is Professor of Commonwealth Governance and Development and Director of the Institute of Commonwealth Studies in London.

Fredrik Söderbaum is a Ph.D. candidate at the Department of Peace and Development Research, Göteborg University (Padrigu).

Ian Taylor is Lecturer in the Department of Political and Administrative Studies, University of Botswana.

Helen Wallace is Director of the Robert Schuman Centre for Advanced Studies At the European University Institute in Florence.

Acknowledgements

This volume had its origins in a conference held at the University of Warwick in September 1999. The conference was supported by grants from the Japan Foundation, and the Argentinean Embassy in the UK, and we gratefully acknowledge their support. All research in the Centre for the Study of Globalisation and Regionalisation is funded by the UK Economic and Social Research Council, and we gratefully acknowledge their support in funding the conference, and the research programme of the Centre in general. Some of the chapters in this volume first appeared in a special edition of *New Political Economy* (5:3, December 2000), and we thank the publisher Taylor & Francis, whose website can be found at <http://www.tandf.co.uk>, for allowing us to reprint them here.

Abbreviations

ACP	Africa, the Caribbean and the Pacific
ADB	Asian Development Bank
AEC	African Economic Community
AERC	African Economic Research Consortium
AFTA	ASEAN Free Trade Area
ANCERTA	Australia–New Zealand Free Trade Area
ANZUS	Australia New Zealand United States Security Treaty
AOSIS	Alliance of Small Island States
APEC	Asia Pacific Economic Cooperation
ARF	ASEAN Regional Forum
ASEAN	Association of South East Asian Nations
ASEM	Asia–Europe Meeting
Bist-ec	Bangladesh, India, Sri Lanka, Thailand – Economic Cooperation Forum
CAN	Community of Andean Nations
CEAL	Congress of Latin American Businessmen
CEC	Commission for Environmental Cooperation
CENTO	Central Treaty Organization
CFSP	Common Foreign and Security Policy
CIS	Commonwealth of Independent States
CITES	Conventions on International Trade in Endangered Species
CMC	Common Market Council (within Mercosur)
COMESA	Common Market of Eastern and Southern Africa
COP	Conference of the Parties (of the Framework Convention on Climate Change)
CSBMs	Confidence- and Security-Building Measures
CSCAP	Council for Security Cooperation in Asia Pacific
CSCE	Conference on Security and Cooperation in Europe
DCs	Developed Countries
DG	Directorate General (of the European Commission)
DTI	Department of Trade and Industry
EAEC	East Asian Economic Caucus
EC	European Community
ECA	Economic Commission for Africa

ECOMOG	The Economic Community of West African States Monitoring Group
ECOWAS	Economic Community of West African States
EEC	European Economic Community
EMAS	Environmental management and auditing
EMEAP	Executive Meeting of East Asia and Pacific Central Banks
EMU	Economic and Monetary Union
EPA	Environmental Protection Agency
EPZ	Export Processing Zone
ESCAP	Economic and Social Commission for Asia and the Pacific
ESPRIT	European Strategic Programme for Research and Development in Information Technology
ETSI	European Telecommunications Standardisation Institute
EU	European Union
EUREKA	European Research Co-ordinating Agency
EVSL	Early Voluntary Sector Liberalization
FCCC	Framework Convention on Climate Change
FDI	Foreign direct investment
FLS	Front line states (in Africa)
FPÖ	Austrian Freedom Party
FTAA	Free Trade Area of the Americas
GA	Austrian Green Party
GATT	General Agreement on Tariffs and Trade
GCC	Gulf Cooperation Council
GDP	Gross domestic policy
GEAR	Growth, Employment and Reconstruction Plan
GMC	Grupo Mercado Comun (Mercosur Common Market Group)
GNP	Gross national product
IFIs	International financial institutions
IGAD	Inter-Governmental Authority on Development
IMF	International Monetary Fund
IPE	International Political Economy
IR	International Relations
ISI	Import substituting industrialisation
LDCs	Less developed countries
LO	Swedish Trade Union Confederation
MAI	Multilateral Agreement on Investment
Mercosur	Common Market of the South (Mercado Comun del Sur)
MITI	Ministry of International Trade and Industry (Japan)
MNCs	Multinational corporations
NAFTA	North American Free Trade Agreement
NATO	North Atlantic Treaty Organization
NGOs	Non-governmental organisations
NICs	Newly industrialised countries
NIEO	New International Economic Order
NRT	New regionalism theory
NTBs	Non-tariff barriers
NZFAR	*New Zealand Foreign Affairs Review*

OAS	Organization of American States
OAU	Organisation of African Unity
OECD	Organisation for Economic Cooperation and Development
OECS	Organization of East Caribbean States
OSCE	Organisation on Security and Cooperation in Europe
ÖVP	Austrian People's Party
PAFTA	Pacific Free Trade Area
PALM	Japan–South Pacific Forum Summit Meeting
PE	Political Economy
PECC	Pacific Economic Cooperation Council
PIM	*Pacific Islands Monthly*
PKOs	Peace-keeping operations
RACE	Research and development in advanced communications technologies in Europe
R&D	Research and development
RDP	Reconstruction and Development Programme
RMA	Revolution in military affairs
SAA	South African Airways
SADC	Southern African Development Community
SADCC	Southern African Development Coordination Conference
SAFTA	South American Free Trade Area
SAP	Swedish Social Democratic Labour Party
SARIPS	Southern African Regional Institute for Policy Studies
SARRC	South Asian Association for Regional Co-operation
SDI	Spatial development initiative (South Africa)
SEATO	South East Asia Treaty Organization
SMEs	Small and medium-sized enterprises
SPC	South Pacific Commission
SPEC	South Pacific Bureau for Economic Co-operation
SPF	South Pacific Forum
SPÖ	Austrian Socialist Party
SPREP	South Pacific Regional Environment Programme
TAC	Treaty of Amity and Cooperation
TCO	Swedish Confederation of Professional Employees
TNCs	Transnational corporations
UK	United Kingdom
UN	United Nations
UNCED	UN Conference on Environment and Development
UNDP	United Nations Development Programme
UNEP	United Nations Environment Programme
UNICE	Union of Industrial and Employers' Confederation of Europe
UNISA	University of South Africa
US	United States
USSR	Union of Soviet Socialist Republics
VAT	Value Added Tax
VÖI	Austrian Federation of Industrialists
WTO	World Trade Organisation

1 Regions in comparative perspective

Shaun Breslin, Richard Higgott and Ben Rosamond[1]

(global)

F IS R11

The study of regions, regionalism and regionalization has once again come to prominence.[2] Not since the 1970s has the analysis of regional integration been so conspicuous (see Fawcett and Hurrell, 1995; Gamble and Payne, 1996; Mansfield and Milner, 1997; Coleman and Underhill, 1998; Grugel and Hout, 1998; Hettne *et al.*, 1999, 2000a, 2000b, 2000c). This has much to do with the emergence and in some cases resurgence of regional projects in the 1980s and 1990s. Scholarly attention in the United States was given a shot in the arm by the much-discussed creation of the North American Free Trade Agreement (NAFTA). In South America, MERCOSUR was created in 1991. ASEAN (the Association of South East Asian Nations) became more assertive in Asia during the 1990s, and 1989 saw the birth of Asia Pacific Economic Cooperation (APEC). Meanwhile the Southern African Development Community (SADC) became a focal point for stabilization and regeneration following the end of apartheid. Most prominently, the European Union's (EU) single market programme intensified economic and political integration in western Europe from the mid-1980s, a process which continued with the remarkable achievement of monetary integration among a majority of member states by the end of the 1990s.

This book is in part designed as a stock-taking exercise of various conceptual and theoretical approaches to regionalism from the broad subfield of international political economy. It takes as its immediate reference point the prospects for regionalism and its study in the wake of the financial crises that began in Asia in the second half of 1997. This directs attention not only to the extent to which regionalism remains a viable policy option for states in an increasingly globalized economy, but also to the issue of whether there are particular templates to which the growth of formal regional integration necessarily corresponds. The book also has the wider brief of thinking about how regionalism is theorized and whether meaningful comparative study is a plausible academic enterprise.

This chapter introduces this collection by placing the contemporary study of regionalism into context. It argues that the study of regionalism has occurred in two waves. The first of these began to gather pace as a subfield of International Relations from the late 1950s and the second, as indicated above, emerged in the context of the IPE from the late 1980s. By first casting our gaze back to the first wave, we show how both the scholarly and 'real world' practices of regionalism shifted between the two periods. We then move on to explore the particular challenges to both theory and practice posed by the recent financial crises, before exploring the prospects for the emergence of a genuinely comparative political economy of regionalism.

The study of regionalism: the first wave

Early debates about regionalism emerged from three primary sources. The first was a political-normative question about the sustainability of the nation-state as a vehicle for effective and peaceful human governance. The second was the growth and gradual formalization of the social sciences, particularly in the United States. The third, of course, was the appearance of regional integration schemes. Of these the most discussed emerged in the 1950s in western Europe with the European Coal and Steel Community, the abortive European Defence Community and the eventual European Economic Community. The spread of decolonization in the post-war period had also seen the genesis of (now defunct) bodies such as the East African Common Market, but it was Europe that became the intellectual laboratory for the study of regionalism.

Integration theorists led by Ernst Haas (1958, 1964) and Leon Lindberg (1966) drew inspiration from two sources. From the work of Karl Deutsch (Deutsch *et al.*, 1957), they inherited an interest in developing a social science of post-national community building that emphasized rigour over excessive normativity or idealism. From the earlier functionalism of David Mitrany (1966), they acquired an interest in the role of functional and technocratic imperatives in laying the basis for new forms of authority. However, there were significant departures from these two sources of inspiration. Mitrany's functionalism had argued that rational governance could be achieved only by total open-mindedness when it came to devising forms and levels of governance to meet changing human welfare needs. Mitrany was therefore certainly not a theorist of *regionalism*. Confining new functional institutions to a territorial region would infringe his basic idea that form should follow function. The neofunctionalists, led by Haas, in contrast saw functional 'spillovers' leading to economic and (ultimately) political integration occurring on a territorial basis. In addition, whereas Deutch's concept of security communities anticipated increasing transactions leading to ultimate comity between states, Haas *et al.* theorized the transcendence of the states system rather than its survival. Finally, neofunctionalist theory saw the processes of economic and political integration being driven by the actions of rational actors, be they supranational institutions or self-regarding producer groups.

Haas, Lindberg and others such as Philippe Schmitter (1971; Haas and Schmitter 1964), Stuart Scheingold (Lindberg and Scheingold, 1970) and Joseph Nye (1968, 1971) used the European experience as a basis for the production of generalizations about the prospects for regional integration elsewhere. As it developed through the 1960s and early 1970s this form of integration theory became a model of impeccable rationalist social science. Work on regional integration inspired by the Haasian model and its variants became highly prominent in well-established US journals such as *International Organization* and added a degree of the-oretical solemnity to new European outlets such as the *Journal of Common Market Studies*. The emphasis on functional pressures, growing interdependence and the significance of non-state actors stood in sharp contrast to the dominant orthodoxy of realism in American International Relations and in many ways laid some of the ground for the development of contemporary international political economy (IPE).

That said, by the mid-1970s this first wave of regional integration scholarship seemed to have run out of steam. The publication of Haas' devastating *The Obsolescence of Regional Integration Theory* (Haas, 1975) seemed to indicate not only that neofunctionalism had run aground, but that the very idea of producing theo-retical models of *regionalism* was deeply misconceived. There seemed to be two major problems with the project of integration theory. First, the expectation that the European experience would be replicated elsewhere seemed to have been scuppered. Ambitious analogous projects such as the Latin American Free Trade Area had failed, and there seemed to be little momentum among elites to engage in regionalist enterprises. Second, Haas acknowledged that in the European case integration theories had largely underestimated the role of national governments and the pervasiveness of nationalist sentiment. This had been underscored empir-ically by the behaviour of 'dramatic actors' such as President de Gaulle. Rather than being anomalous or recidivist, the engagement of Gaullism with European integration also shifted the overall policy style of the European Communities into an altogether more intergovernmentalist direction (Wallace, 1996). Indeed, as Stanley Hoffmann (1966) noted, the game of European integration was compli-cated further by the domestic politics of the member states as well as their distinctive alignments in the international system (see also Hansen, 1969).

The dissolution of 'integration theory' was not simply a consequence of the dis-crepancies between theoretical predictions and empirical 'reality'. In addition, neofunctionalism was marginalized by the emerging distaste for grand predictive social scientific theories (Moravcsik, 1998) and the development of interest in 'interdependence'. The latter became a partial rallying-point for the nascent sub-discipline of international political economy (Katzenstein *et al.*, 1998; see also Caporaso, 1978). This also led many erstwhile students of integration to take sides in the dominant neo-realist neo-liberal debates that characterized international relations in the 1970s and 1980s (Higgott, 1993).

The seemingly dramatic revival of European integration that accompanied the emergence of the single market programme in the mid-1980s produced a partial revival of neofunctionalist theorizing. The evidence of an activist European Commission under Jacques Delors seemed to offer an empirical reinstatement of the neofunctionalist idea of supranational activism. Meanwhile the single market was suggestive of a number of spillovers into social policy, economic and monetary union, and political integration more generally (Tranholm-Mikkelsen, 1991). Meanwhile, scholars of various persuasions became interested in applying new sophisticated forms of federalist theory to the European experience while norma-tive political theorists and legal theorists began to apply their tools to the 'new'

European Community (see, e.g. Sbragia, 1992; Brown, 1994; Shaw and More, 1995).

Yet, if anything, these developments underscored the distinctive nature of regional integration in Europe. Indeed, the growth and increasing sophistication of conceptual work on European integration and supranational governance reinforced this point. The complex nature of the Community's decision-making processes drew attention away from International Relations paradigms towards a mixture of classic Laswellian political science and new forms of policy analysis (Hix, 1999). Others found state-centric accounts integration inherently unsatisfying either because they clung to outdated quasi-realist state fetishism (Rosamond, 2000) or because they could not possibly capture the 'everyday' regulatory complexity of the European policy process (Wincott, 1995). This is not to say that IR-derived work did not penetrate the European studies community – far from it. Indeed, Moravcsik's influential and much-discussed analysis of European integration (Moravcsik, 1998) grew out of neo-liberal institutionalist scholarship. While placing states and national executives at the centre of its analysis, Moravcsik's 'liberal intergovernmentalism' emphasized the significance of domestic variables upon national preference formation and the two-level game character of international negotiation.

In that regard it resembled other emerging work on extra-European regional integration. The *relance* of European integration occurred more or less simultaneously with the appearance of regional free trade areas elsewhere. The appearance of regional integration schemes in North and South America, the Asia Pacific and Southern Africa (to name but the most prominent) was suggestive of a new regionalized world order, although the form that this took and the power configurations that were significant varied from account to account. For some, the world order would be triadic, with Europe, the US and East Asia as the nodal points. Others imagined the emergence of regions corresponding to civilizational orders (Huntington, 1998).

The temptation to see linkages between (and thus comparability among) the various forms of regionalism came from the supposition that they were driven by similar external forces. Two in particular stood out: the radically revised geopolitical security structure that followed the end of the Cold War and the growth of globalization. The former loosened up the possibilities of trans-border activity and interstate exchange while the latter contributed to the questioning of relations founded on the premise of national territory and added fuel to IPE's concern with the fuzziness of the distinction between the 'domestic' and the 'international'.

Regionalism after the financial crisis

The financial crises of the late 1990s may not have marked a watershed in the study of regionalism, but they did provoke a number of key issues for analysts of regional and global economic management that might have been less obvious in the heady 'emerging market' days of the early 1990s. This sense of curiosity was perhaps most acute among scholars of regional processes in Asia. In spite of the hype that accompanied their development prior to 1997, both APEC and ASEAN seemed incapable of delivering short-term palliative responses to the regional financial crisis. This posed serious questions about their very efficacy as emergent modes of regional organization in Asia and the Asia Pacific. This reading was further justified by the abortive Japanese initiative to establish an Asian Monetary Fund in the wake of the crises. The collapse of this plan in the face of US opposition highlighted the fragility of Asian regional projects. On the face of it, these seemed dependent on the hegemonic blessing of the US and any momentum from within was apparently constrained by the pivotal position of Japan between the US and the rest of Asia.

On the other hand, there is a powerful argument that the crises cleared the way for much clearer thinking about regionalism in Asia. Thus, in the longer term the crises may have pushed states to think again about how best to build a regional order that is capable of preventing financial crises (or at least competent to deal effectively with those crises when they arise). For example, discussions over the creation of a network of currency swaps and other financial arrangements arising from Asian Development Bank meetings in May 2000 may represent a new approach to regional co-operation. In the longer term these could lead to what Dieter (2000) has called 'a new monetary regionalism'. This would be consistent with the view that monetary integration in Europe has been stimulated by a collective will to deal with the potentially ruinous consequences of internationally mobile capital (Verdun, 2000).

Even if such initiatives amount to nought, the negotiations at least refer to a growing regional self-definition of 'East Asia' as a valid economic space with a discernible political voice. Analytically, this suggests that such policy initiatives do not simply arise as rational (functional) spillovers from financial integration. Rather they depend upon emergent senses of collective identity that frame the ways in which elites respond to exogenous shocks. This highlights the centrality of two important variables in the study of regionalism that we earlier identified as largely absent from first-wave theorizing: the idea of regional identities and the catalytic challenges posed by external challenge.

The development of the idea of 'East Asia', as opposed to the idea of 'Southeast Asia' writ small or the 'Asia Pacific' writ large is a reasonably long-standing process in which insiders and outsiders are identified (Higgott and Stubbs, 1995). The attempt to assert a particular conception of 'Asia' is again evident in the recent debates about monetary regional co-operation where the in-group consists of the ASEAN states, plus China, South Korea and Japan. This 'Asia' also corresponds to the Asian side of the Asia–Europe Meeting (ASEM) process. In effect, it represents a widening of the membership of the East Asian Economic Caucus that emerged, in spite of stiff resistance from the US, within APEC in the 1990s.

To reiterate, that discussions on monetary regionalism in East Asia may come to nothing is less relevant than the fact that they are taking place. They are an important sign of one of the longer term consequences of the financial crises on Asian regionalism: the emergence of a will on the part of regional policy elites to take greater control of financial affairs at a regional level than previously. Initiatives to build a regional monetary order are specifically inspired by a desire on the part of regional policy communities not to be exposed again to compulsory adjustment measures imposed by the international financial institutions. In Asia these institutions were perceived as imposing largely western/developed world perspectives on how states should organize (or more precisely *not* organize) their economies (Bello, 1999b).

At a more general level, the crises in Asia allow us to think about the potential roles that nascent regional organizations play as mediating layers of governance between the nation-state and global financial institutions. In the Asian case this may involve the deflection of dominant western ideologies, preferences and economic models that are bound up with the philosophies and actions of the international financial institutions. In Europe, one purpose of such a mediating layer may involve the (perceived) protection of the 'European social model' against the assimilating tendencies of deregulated American capitalism (Hay and Rosamond, 2002). As Peter Katzenstein puts it in his contribution to this volume: 'Because they often mediate between national and global effects, as in the story of Goldilocks, they are neither too hot, nor too cold, but just right' (p. 104).

Moreover, if we move beyond Asia to consider the subsequent financial crises in Russia and Latin America, the relationship becomes clearer still. All told, the post-1997 crises brought into question some rather cherished assumptions about the global economy. There was sharpened interrogation of the benefits of globalization and specifically the utility of the 'Washington Consensus' (Williamson, 1990) as a way for developing countries to deal with economic adjustment in general and financial deregulation in particular.

These specific observations lead us to identify three broad issues that contemporary students of regionalism need to address. First, how do international/global-level variables (investment flows, prevailing ideological orthodoxies, the development of other regional groupings and developments in the major international financial institutions and the WTO) affect the incentive structures of member states of regional organizations?

Second, there is the issue of the relationship between domestic politics and the policies of member states within given regional organizations. By domestic politics is meant both the complex of government–society relations and the cultural configuration of domestic political economies. In Helen Milner's (1992, 1998) account state elites find themselves in a two-level game. Demands for regional outcomes emerge from powerful domestic forces. The supply of such outcomes is the product of international bargains, the consequences of which feed back into the processes of domestic politics. This line of questioning offers one way in which the importance of states can be acknowledged without resorting to the unitary conceptions of states that prevailed for so long in much US International Relations scholarship. It is a strategy that also treats intergovernmental exchange in terms that go beyond traditional conceptions of diplomacy.

Third, there would seem to be ample space for the development of both rationalist and constructivist approaches in relation to regional integration (Hurrell, 1995a). Constructivists have posed serious challenges to the way in which IR has thought about interstate interaction. Moreover, they treat institutions (such as regular forums for regional dialogue) as 'social' venues rather than capsules in which rational action takes place. Therefore, various forms of constructivism ask us to contemplate the relationship between institutionalized interaction and the emergence of regional identities and interests. The constructivist literature remains on the thin side, though there has been something of a breakthrough into the study of European integration (Christiansen *et al.*, 2001). Rationalists need not follow well-worn state-centric paths. Strategic action by state actors may still be important, but it is increasingly imperative to place this within an analysis of complexes of actors and institutional venues that conspire (and several levels of analysis) to influence the development of regionalism.

At the same time, tried, trusted and 'believed to be efficient' approaches to institutional design and strategic action are likely to be popular with governmental actors. We would expect them to be repeated, as rationalists might suggest, in the behaviour of states at the regional level. It is for this reason that the networking style of political relationships practised within the boundaries of many Asian states found their way throughout the 1990s into the political relationships that, as with ASEAN, developed at the regional level (Acharya, 1997a).

The interest that this volume expresses in the impact of financial crises takes us somewhat beyond thinking about the structures of global financial governance. It also poses questions about the role of domestic politics in the relationship between wider multilateral and regional processes of governance under conditions of globalization. The 'bringing in' of the domestic and the global into the analysis of regionalism reflects a marked departure from much first wave work. In addition, earlier work often saw regionalism as a defensive mechanism to reduce dependence on the international economy. Many scholars of the new regionalism see it as a way of securing greater competitive access to global markets as opposed to securing regional autarchy. Most recognize that in practice regionalism is rather more multifaceted and multidimensional than in the past. States now engage in any number of overlapping regional endeavours without sensing that there may be contradictions in such a process.

That said, there is no doubt that the defensive legacies of the earlier phase remain. The reconsideration of regional arrangements, especially of the kind discussed here by Bowles and Phillips, reflect a growing scepticism among political elites in developing states about the benefits of the unregulated nature of contemporary global capitalism. It is not just a case of finding regional solutions to economic crises, but a questioning of the advantages of pursuing unfettered neoliberal strategies *per se*.

However, this does not imply that there is growing regional resistance to all elements of the globalization process. Indeed, there is the very serious question of the extent to which regional organizations act as a spur to global economic liberalization. An obvious example here is APEC's commitment to an 'open regionalism' approach founded on a promise of unilateral liberalization of member state economies. In the case of APEC, the regional project was designed to facilitate wider global processes and could be read as a means of preventing the emergence of a specific 'East Asian' regionalism. Indeed, the major spur to APEC in the early 1990s was the desire by its 'Caucasian' members to use it as a stick with which to beat the EU into finalizing the Uruguay Round.

We should also consider the changing rationale for joining (or forming) regional organizations for many developing states. On one level, the formal criteria established for membership by organizations such as the EU forces policy changes on aspirant members. In the very process of liberalizing to meet EU standards, these economies become more open to the global economy in general. In such cases regionalism may be seen as a pathway to globalization.

On another level, decisions made to forge closer regional economic relations may also have wider global implications. In this regard Bowles shows that there is a key distinction between current and old explanations for regional projects. Rather than building (or joining) regional arrangements to enhance independence from the global economy, many developing states now see regionalism as a measure to ensure continued participation in it (Chapter 6). This type of north–south regionalism – predicated on the extension of neo-liberal economic paradigms into the developing world – may be understood as a means by which developing states might consciously increase their dependence on investment and markets in developed cores (Grugel and Hout, 1998), while at the same time enhancing their regional voice in the wider global economic dialogue.

As these decisions are made to harness the economic benefits of international trade and investment, this suggests a symbiotic process where responses to globalization can lead to the promotion of regional projects, and the regions themselves can simultaneously promote globalization. Regionalism can be simultaneously a response to and a dynamic behind globalization. In short, we are dealing with mutually reinforcing and co-constitutive rather than contending processes. As Morten Bøås argues (Chapter 4), regimes are not barriers to globalization, but rather 'in-betweens': 'the regional project is both part of and a facilitator of globalization, and a regional counter-governance layer in the world political economy' (p. 63).

There is much more to the study of regions than economic integration alone. Nevertheless, the relationship between regions and neo-liberal paradigms and economic policies lies at the heart of many of the new assessments of regionalism and regionalization. Not surprisingly, it is also one of the key themes that emerges from this collection of chapters. As yet, there are no clear conclusions. As both Bowles and Phillips suggest here, financial crises have raised question marks over the acceptability of financial deregulation in particular and economic liberalization more generally as the best routes to development. Whether this is one, two or three steps back after two steps forward towards liberalization more generally remains less than clear. Both Latin American and East Asian responses suggest a move towards defensive regional organizations that provide some level of regulation.

This is occurring partly in response to recent heightened negative perceptions of the 'Anglo-American' model of development. But it is also a response to the perceived defects and injustices attendant upon IMF and World Bank imposed solutions to financial crises. For some the policy response of the global institutions has been interpreted as a politically inspired attempt to force countries away from 'developmental statist' pathways. As *The Economist* put it, 'The International Monetary Fund is so unpopular in East Asia that it now has an entire economic crisis named after it' (*The Economist*, 13 May 2000: 109–110).

Comparative regionalism

The prospects for the theory and practice of regionalism in the wake of financial crises provided a key rationale for collecting together the chapters in this volume. A second stimulus was an interest in providing a forum for comparative analyses of regional processes. This is not a new problem for students of regional integration, but it is one we argue that still requires careful thought and development. Two particular issues spring to mind: the relationship between 'area studies' and studies of regionalism and the more specific question of the quasi-hegemonic status of 'EU studies' in the analysis of regional processes.

Area studies and comparative regionalism

Despite a marked growth in work on regionalism in recent years, the literature comparing regional projects remains stubbornly small. Most detailed analyses examine individual regional processes that attempt to place the case study at hand in a wider comparative context. Such work is often lopsided, and is influenced theoretically and empirically by the concerns of US academicians. Studies of comparative regionalism in the US are likely to focus on comparisons of NAFTA with the EU and increasingly with APEC. Indeed, a considerable interest in explaining why Asian regionalism was 'different' emerged in the 1990s. There is very little comparative discussion of the problems and prospects for regionalism in Africa and the Middle East. Yet, surprisingly in a US context (given geographic proximity and proposals for a pan-American free trade area) there is very little work on regional processes in Latin America.

There are a few exceptions. Vellinga's edited collection (Vellinga, 1999) takes Asia, Europe and Latin America as the focus of comparison. The key variable for the unit of comparison in this work is responses to globalization. The edited volume by Mansfield and Milner (1997) concentrates on explanations for both regional deepening and institutional variation. Meanwhile, Gamble and Payne (1996) have sought to set the agenda for cross-case regional research within the 'new political economy' (Gamble, 1995), a project carried a stage further by Hook and Kearns (1999) who focus on regionalism in 'non-core' states. Grugel and Hout (1998) focus on regionalisms across north–south boundaries. The work of Mattli treats regional integration as 'the process of internalizing externalities that cross borders within a group of countries' (1999: 199), a definition which enables comparison across time as well as space.[3]

Following Anthony Payne (1998), we suggest that both area studies and the study of regionalism would benefit from more studies of regional processes that focus on areas other than Europe and North America. This starting point gives us the potential benefit of bringing together the merits of two sub-disciplines that combine the theory building of students of regionalism with the richer empirical work in area studies that is able to identify historical and political specificities. The chapters in this volume grow out of that aspiration.

Political scientists have long recognized the virtues of careful comparative analysis. It is the best device we have for both testing theoretical propositions and applying new readings to particular case studies. The case studies gathered here have been conducted by scholars who, in disciplinary terms, are most usually characterized as international political economists, but who also possess detailed area studies knowledge.

Other chapters in this collection also offer a route into comparative analysis. Morten Bøås identifies a series of common variables and assesses their effects on different areas. Amitav Acharya (see also Acharya, 1997b) develops a distinction between sovereignty-bound and intrusive forms of regionalism. This helps him to assess the nature of the relationship between regionalism and post-Westphalian world order. Often juxtaposition masquerades as comparison. It is not enough to place two objects alongside one another and identify that they are different. The EU is different from regional organizations in Asia. Yes, of course – but so what? If a valid comparison is to be made, then – in these cases – the disjuncture of temporal stages of development need to be taken into account. Perhaps this means that the appropriate comparison is between European and Asian regionalism at similar stages of development.

Simple comparison in the here and now would quite quickly yield the claim that unlike the EU, Asian regionalism is compromised by deep ideational conflicts, by residual Cold War divisions, by memories of war and occupation, by vastly different levels of development among component member states, by radically different indigenous models of political economy, by the ambitions of competing regional powers, and by the strategic ambitions of the United States. Moreover, there are clearly rival regional projects and multiple voices of regions in contemporary Asia, whereas the EU is now unequivocally the dominant regional organization in Europe. But of course, this characterization of Asia could easily have been applied to Europe at the end of the Second World War.

This is not to say that Europe's present is Asia's future (Higgott, 1998). For the comparativist there are significant consequences, such as identifying those variables that are likely to yield different outcomes. The key question is whether comparison is a valid enterprise. On the other hand, the principles of good comparison when applied should be able to tell us whether we are engaged in an act of folly. The idea that Europe *circa* 1950 and Asia *circa* 2000 may be at similar stages of development may be an outlandish generalization and could be shown to be such by theorists who might challenge the very idea of uniform patterns of development, and by area specialists who might identify insurmountable contextual specificities in each region. Thus William Wallace (1994) all but argues that European regional integration should not be compared to other regional projects. The specific geopolitical, local, historical and ideational context of the late 1940s and early 1950s yielded a very particular and peculiar model of regional institution building in western Europe that simply cannot provide a template for the analysis of other regional projects. Nor is it valid for policy-makers elsewhere to judge their regional enterprises with reference to the contemporary and historical EU.

Two qualifications may be in order. First, an IPE frame of reference offers comparative study at a slightly higher level of abstraction. Therefore, meaningful questions can be asked about *inter alia* regional projects as a response to the replacement of national markets by international or global markets; regionalism as a response to the internationalization of the division of labour and production; and regionalism as a response to the strengthening of multinational and private policy-making structures. Asking how authoritative actors respond, albeit at different times, to common challenges forces us to isolate the major variables and explain how they interact.

Second, the very fact that policy-makers (rightly or wrongly) conceptualize regionalism with reference to the European model is in itself an important reason for scholars to explore the possibilities of comparison – if only to show that we are not dealing with functionally equivalent entities. It is clear that policy learning and the politics of emulation (or in many cases the politics of avoidance) are major features of current deliberations about regionalism. Most obviously, the time lag between European developments and the construction of regional orders elsewhere has meant that region-building elites have had the opportunity to learn from the EU's experience, to emulate specific attributes of the European experience and, more often, to avoid replication (Hurrell, 1995a). The less institutionalized approach that is emerging in Asia seems to represent a deliberate choice to avoid the perceived 'cartesian' legal formalism of the EU.

EU studies and comparative regional studies

The spectre of the EU and the European experience of regionalism loomed large in the preceding paragraphs. Ironically, it is probably fair to say that the EU as an exercise in regional integration is one of the major obstacles to the development of analytical and theoretical studies of regional integration. For example, the characterization of Asian and Latin American regionalisms as 'loose' or 'informal' reflects a teleological prejudice informed by the assumption that 'progress' in regional organization is defined in terms of EU-style institutionalization.

This need not necessarily be a methodological problem. To undertake comparison, we need to have something with which to compare. However, the dominance of the EU in regional studies raises three difficulties. First, as Helen Wallace notes (Chapter 9), '[t]oo much of the discussion of Europe and Europeanization has been conducted as if somehow Europe were closed off from the wider international arena' (p. 137). Perhaps understandably, given the immense complexity of the EU as a system of economic governance, specialists in 'EU studies' have been reluctant to raise their gaze to think about the broader global and regional processes of which European integration is a part and to which it contributes. Indeed, as Wallace notes, the EU fixation of European integration studies often neglects the wider processes of political and economic reconstruction that have characterized the continent since 1989 (see also Wallace, 2000).

The second problem emerges from the claim (or more often the latent assumption) that EU represents *the* paradigmatic case of regionalism. It provides too strong a point of comparison against which all other regional projects are judged. The comparative question is rarely turned on its head. If the EU and APEC are compared, emphasis is almost always on why APEC is different rather than vice versa. This dominance of the EU in our scholarly mental maps also imposes an understanding of regionalism as being bound up with formal institutionalization. To equate mature regionalism with the creation of supranational bodies equivalent to the European Commission, the European Parliament and the European Court of Justice automatically prejudices any conclusions we might wish to make about the emergence of a world order based on regional organizations. It thus side-steps some of the perhaps more profound political economy questions that should lie at the heart of contemporary analyses.

The final problem emerges from the increasing professionalization of EU studies as a distinct sub-disciplinary domain in the political sciences. It has its own conference circuit, a number of established journals (at least six in English alone),[4] national and international professional associations and its own internal discourses. Energies and activities are concentrated within that community. It is a little dangerous to claim that professional advancement for scholars is solely dependent upon success within the EU studies community (especially in the US where, for instrumental reasons, leading analysts of the EU tend increasingly to seek to establish a wider political science identity for themselves – Pollack, 2001).[5] Yet there can be little doubt that entire academic careers can be spent in researching and teaching the EU. Of course, the Union's longevity, its institutional complexity and its policy reach mean that it is considerably more than an international organization. Indeed, it is now routine to characterize the EU as a political system rather than as a project of regional integration. For writers like Simon Hix, this means that the EU should be studied as a political system using the established tools of political science (Hix, 1999). The side effect, runs the argument, is the profound devaluation of the theoretical toolkit of 'International Relations' (Hix, 1994). This is an extreme position in the debate (for a critique see Rosamond, 2000: ch. 7), but it does raise the issue of whether the EU is actually an instance of integration, and thus of regionalism, at all. The gauntlet thrown down by Hix is the assertion that since most self-interested actors within the EU polity do not operate with questions of integration and region building at the forefront of their calculus, then neither should we as analysts of their behaviour.

Hix's position is not an appeal for narrow area studies, but an argument against not only comparative regionalism but also the utility of 'international studies' as a parent discipline for the study of the EU. Against this, we would argue that the confinement of the analysis of regionalism to a distinct disciplinary domain creates an unhelpful barrier between 'International Relations' and 'political science' that threatens to cordon off EU studies from innovative theoretical developments in areas such as IPE. As Simon Lee shows (Chapter 11, this volume), the conceptual tools of international political economy can tell us a lot about the ways in which the EU's policy-making processes are beginning to pan out at the commencement of the twenty-first century.

Varieties of regional integration

Notwithstanding the preceding discussion, there is a widespread assumption in some areas that in order to be 'proper' regionalism, a degree of EU-style institutionalism should be in place. This emphasis on institutional regionalism proceeding through a mixture of intergovernmental dialogue and treaty revision is at the heart of the now classic model of economic integration developed forty years ago by Bela Balassa (1962). Balassa used the term 'economic integration' to refer to the creation of formal co-operation between states and the progressive movement towards a free trade area, a customs union, a common market, monetary union and finally total economic integration. This view of regionalism is at the heart of much of the existent comparative literature, and its teleological, progressive reasoning also informed the neofunctionalist version of integration theory (Webb, 1983). Despite widespread scepticism about the virtues of unidirectional models of modernization in the social sciences, the staged model of Balassa still frames quite a lot of discussion, even among those who eschew trade as the key spillover dynamic (Dieter, 2000).

At one level, this reading of regionalism is statist, seeing as it does advances in regionalism as driven by the formal sanction of intergovernmental bargains. But at another level it raises central questions about the relationship between politics and economics, between states and markets and between formal and informal authority. In the models of Balassa and Haas, the integration of economies at a certain level (say, a free trade area) would create functional pressures for the deepening of economic integration (in this case a customs union, which in turn would generate an overriding rationale in favour of the development of a common market). But, as economic integration deepened, so authority and regulatory capacity would also have to drift to the regional level.

But also at the heart of this way of thinking is an issue that has become central to second-wave deliberations about regionalism. This is the relationship between what William Wallace (1990) has called formal and informal integration. The former refers to integration led by the formal authority of governmental actors through agreement or treaty. The latter is integration led by the *de facto* emergence of transnational space among private market actors (see also Higgott, 1998). The key issue is the 'chicken and egg' question of whether formal precedes informal integration or vice versa. This helps us to break out of the teleological shackles of the first wave and may help us to move our focus to different types of regional response to more specialized issue-specific questions.

This connects to an issue of terminology: the distinction between regionalism and regionalization. It is becoming increasingly accepted that *regionalism* refers to those state-led projects of co-operation that emerge as a result of intergovernmental dialogues and treaties. Regionalization refers to those processes of integration which 'come from markets, from private trade and investment flows, and from the policies and decisions of companies' (Hurrell, 1995a: 334) rather than as a result of the predetermined plans of national or local governments. This distinction opens up more possibilities for studying processes of regional integration in those parts of the world where more formalized, EU-style regional organizations are absent.

However, in our attempts to advance comparative research, we would insert three important caveats. The first is that the notion of the boundary or perimeter of a region may, by default or by design, be fuzzy. It may often be the case that there is no treaty which stipulates membership of a regional order. As such there is less need to exercise pedantic definitional thinking about the parameters of a 'region' than is often the case in 'regional' literature – it is processes rather than just the outcomes that are important here. A similar definitional relaxation can be made in the relationship between regionalization and globalization. These are not mutually exclusive processes. Failure to recognize the dialectic between globalization and regionalization can mean that we might impose a regional level of analysis on something that is actually global. Or perhaps more correctly, we should make sure that we consider the salience of extra-regional relations whenever we are considering regionalization. As suggested above, this was one of the principal deficiencies of first-wave integration theory.

A good negative example is found in the work of Kent Calder (1996). Calder's assessment of the rise of inter-Asian trade concludes that the biggest victim of this regionalization is what he calls 'globalism'. The increase in intra-regional trade means a decrease in reliance on the extra-region, and in particular, the US. But in large part, the growth in intra-regional trade is the consequence of the fragmentation of production across national boundaries. With components produced in factories across the region, the trade component in the production of a single commodity increases dramatically. The final good produced as a result of this intra-regional trade still has to be sold somewhere; and still, as much as ever, the US remains the major market for these goods. Is this regionalization or globalization? The dichotomy clearly does not help. The answer is both: the processes of developing regional production networks are themselves driven by global processes and are contingent on global markets. Close regional economic integration both results from and further drives globalization.

The second caveat concerns how we map both economic and political space. Care should be taken to avoid strict national or sovereign parameters when identifying regionalization. In addition to looking for a correlation between the national state and regional membership, we should also examine the wider groups and classes of actors that are involved in processes of integration. The fusion of transnational class alliances that integrate elites, but not usually the wider populations of a given country, is the key here. Nowhere is this better illustrated than in the context of the development of APEC where there is a clear disjuncture between the enthusiasm for the process among regional corporate and bureaucratic elite and the disinterest, if not hostility, of the wider communities in many of the member states. This kind of argument is given a neo-Gramscian spin in this volume in Chapter 10 by Andreas Bieler on Europe and Chapter 13 by Ian Taylor on Southern Africa.

Similarly, we need to think about the increasing importance of the emergence of sub-national and cross-national economic (if not yet political or social) space. Where economic regionalization is occurring, it is often at the sub-national, transnational level: across the Franco–Spanish border, along the Maputo corridor, across the US–Mexican border, across the Yellow Sea and so on. Sovereign boundary demarcation, as we have known throughout history, is not automatically a guide to the parameters of economic interaction. Helen Wallace makes a similar point (Chapter 9, this volume) which locates its discussion of European regionalism in a broader historical perspective.

For obvious reasons, assessments of 'region' invariably focus on integration at the expense of the possible counterfactual process: fragmentation (if not disintegration). As sub-national areas or sectors become externally oriented or integrated – as part of emerging transnational economic space – we should ask more often how they subsequently relate the configuration of national political space. Bernard and Ravenhill (1995) explore the relationship between Singapore and Export Processing Zones (EPZs) in Malaysia. They comment that foreign subsidiaries in the EPZs were more integrated with Singapore's free trade industrial sector than with 'local' industry. The case of the EPZs is particularly pertinent. In many parts of the world, developing states have created technology zones, special economic zones, export processing zones and so on to tie these sub-national areas into wider regional or global economies. In many cases they are purposely designed to foster cross-border integration – and in the process contribute to the disaggregation of domestic *national* economies.

This brings us to the third qualification which relates to the false dichotomy question. Charles Oman argues that the 'principal macroeconomic force shaping those dynamics and driving "globalization" . . . is the ongoing development, formidable competitive strength, and spread . . . of post-Taylorist "flexible" approaches to the organization of production within and between firms' (Oman, 1999: 36). One unfortunate problem of regional analysis over the past few years is that some observers have taken such judgements on technical and economic change and extrapolated from them into the socio-political sphere in a manner for which the evidence is, at best, flimsy. Nowhere is this better illustrated than in what is often called the 'hyperglobalist' literature (Held *et al.*, 1999) which sees the demise of the significance of state actors and state borders in the creation of what Kenichi Ohmae (1995) has labelled 'region states'. This marginalizes the role of the state in processes of regional restructuring because it imagines the state as nothing other than the victim of cross-border processes.

The teleology of the 'hyperglobalization' thesis, therefore, runs the risk of misconstruing how economic space is politically and socially (re)constructed. At the very least, economic regionalization is facilitated by the development of infrastructural links (an area, we maintain, in which there is much research to be done). On a more basic level, economic regionalization requires governments to sanction the relaxation of barriers to trade and investment, or more proactively, to facilitate the provision of incentives to investment and trade sponsorship. Thus, it is not to privilege state-led or *de jure* regionalization as the dominant variable. Rather it is to identify the manner in which it relates to the processes of *de facto* market-led regionalization – the relationship between regionalism as a state-led project and regionalization as a process.

Towards a new political economy and new regionalism?

The preceding caveats suggest not only the dangers of making simplistic assumptions; they actually indicate potentially more fruitful areas for future research on regional processes. As we suggested at the beginning of this introduction, there is an increased scholarly interest in regionalization that is not in all instances keeping pace with the changing understandings of its practice on the ground. This is especially true in the analysis of East Asia where regionalization is perhaps a more obvious focus of research than regionalism. More generally, regionalization remains an under-studied phenomenon. That said, and by way of conclusion to this chapter and introduction to the rest of this volume, it is possible to pull together some emerging themes from scholars in this dynamic and evolving field of enquiry.

Most obviously, new regionalisms are defined in rejection of the old; 'old' in terms of both theory and practice. We spent some time thinking about old – or, as we put it, 'first-wave' – theories of regionalism precisely so that differences might be identified. At the level of practice, the key feature of the 'new' is the sheer number of formal regional arrangements. There are few countries that are not members of at least one regional organization and most are members of more than one. This upsurge in regional activity may be explained in several ways.

First, the end of bipolarity has removed the significance of Cold War perceptions and divisions. Second (and related), the United States no longer adopts an antithetical position towards regional co-operation. Put more properly, the US is no longer hostile to certain forms of regional organization that either include the US as a member or promote an agenda reflecting neo-liberal views conducive to American thinking. In this regard, the increased adoption of varieties of domestic neo-liberal policies should be seen as a third explanatory variable for explaining new regional initiatives. Notably, the promotion of export growth strategies has promoted the reality of increased economic regionalization. For both Shaw and Bowles in this volume, this is the way in which the new regionalism comes to be embodied effectively in the South (and it is in the South that we should look for our analyses of regionalism more than in the past). A fourth explanation is to be found in the declining Westphalian system and the decreasing significance of territorial borders in an era of a more globalized economy (Scholte, 2000). The need to either respond to globalization or, for Bowles, the need to *participate* in the global economy is a driving factor for governments, both weak and strong.

A further spur to new thinking has been frustration with the dominance of intergovernmentalist explanations that emanate from much theorizing, and in particular the stubborn dominance of hegemonic stability theory in much US-based literature. This exasperation is evident in Gamble and Payne's (1996) call for a new political economy approach to studying regionalism. An understanding that state actors are but one set of key agents among potentially many is at the heart of newer approaches.

Timothy M. Shaw's study of Africa (Chapter 12, this volume) is premised on the idea that moving away from this old statist approach is the defining characteristic of the 'new regionalisms'. First-wave theorizing tended to polarize debate between state-centric perspectives and those that more or less wrote states out of the equation. Newer perspectives recognize the complex cocktail of state actors, interstate and global institutions and non-state actors (especially multinational corporations, emerging civil society organizations and NGOs) that have an effect upon regional outcomes. Of course, the balance in importance of these actors varies on a case-to-case basis. Indeed, Hettne and Soderbaum here warn against the danger of trying to find a 'one size fits all' explanation. The world is complex and we should only try to find complex answers. To this long list of potentially important actors we should add sub-national and local authorities. Often these actors are found playing increasingly active roles in developing both formal regionalism and informal economic regionalization. In many cases, these local state actors operate on their own initiative and at times their preferences conflict markedly with those of national governments (Breslin, 2000).

Another key feature of the new regionalism in both form and approach is the significance of coexistent multiple forms of region. This is not a desperately novel observation. Indeed, similar thinking lay at the heart of Mitrany's rejection of politically inspired regions and the need instead for 'form' to 'follow function' in debates over the Tennessee Valley Authority in the 1930s. Mitrany's advocacy of flexibility in the construction of post-national forms of governance foresaw a quite variegated pattern of authority and socio-economic management. Indeed, Mitrany (1965) was particularly scathing in his criticism of territorially bound regional organizations such as the European Community. Nevertheless, as Bowles argues here, it is multiple forms of *regionalism* that is striking about the contemporary period and which bears some resemblance to the variegated pattern of governance forms that writers like Mitrany envisaged (and in his case advocated).

A number of crucial issues emerge for students of regionalism in the current period. On one level, we see the involvement of key states in a number of different regional projects, notably the US as a key node in both NAFTA and APEC. In other cases, we see different organizations based on functional responsibility in the same broadly defined geographic area. One example is the distinct but overlapping memberships of NATO, the Council of Europe and the European Union as suppliers of security in Europe. Even if we take a single issue – say, economic integration built around trade and investment links – then numerous levels of both formal regionalism and informal regionalization can be identified. A good example is the Mexico–Tijuana micro-region that not only exists alongside the larger NAFTA, but whose development has in many ways been facilitated by the very creation of NAFTA. Similarly, cross-border micro-regionalism in Europe (e.g. between

France and Spain) has been read as a consequence of higher levels of formal regionalism in the broader EU. The authority and efficacy of national governments in dealing with trans-boundary issues has been transformed, some would say undermined, by a dual movement. This has been both 'upwards' and 'downwards'. It results in the transfer of some fields of national sovereignty to the EU and the concomitant dismantling of national borders as barriers to inter-EU trade. Indeed, institutional changes at the EU level, as well as new communication technologies and the development of transportation, have encouraged the formation of regional networks based on common interests in terms of economic development (Morata, 1997).

The closer economic relationship between New Zealand and Australia is another example of dual processes of regional integration. So indeed is the existence of ASEAN, with its renewed emphasis on free trade in the development of an Asian Free Trade Area, and APEC which has its own 'open regionalism' agenda. Indeed, the Asian example provides a number of interesting insights. Macro-level economic regionalization in East Asia is proceeding through different overlapping micro-regional processes, yet this micro-regional integration is itself driven by, even reliant on, globalization. Thus we need to consider not only the relationship between the regional and the global, but also the relationship between different regions; different in terms of levels (perhaps defined best in terms of size) and also in forms (in terms of functions).

Conclusion

We have attempted to illustrate the manner in which the theory and practice of regionalism and regionalization is in a state of dynamic evolution. There are continuities in the study of these processes in the contemporary era with research on integration from thirty to forty years ago that we identified as the first wave of theorizing. But we have also suggested that there are significant theoretical advances, especially to the extent that the contemporary literature is much less state-centric, has a much greater recognition of the importance of politics and recognizes the degree to which the 'idea of region' is socially constructed.

These innovations are a reflection of advances in theorizing. They also represent a response to the manner in which regionalism as both a quantitative and qualitative important factor in global politics has developed over the time since the first wave theorists were writing. The increasing salience of regions has enhanced our understanding of these processes but, at the same time, made it difficult to augment much of our general explanatory ability – generalization being the hallmark of theorizing. In part this has been explained by the dominance of the EU as the principal observable enterprise in regionalism in the post-war period and the manner in which it has skewed the development of regional integration theory. But, as we have suggested, the evolution of other, invariably less formalized processes of regionalism and regionalization in other parts of the world is theoretically underspecified because of the way in which these developments have been juxtaposed against the European experience.

Notes

1 This chapter is a revised version of Shaun Breslin and Richard Higgott's 'Studying regions: learning from the old, constructing the new', *New Political Economy* 5(3), 2000.

2 These are deeply ambiguous terms. More often than not these are obvious contiguous geographical units, though it is not axiomatic that this should always be the case. The contiguity question makes the identification of regions manageable, but it does not negate the fact that they are conscious socio-political constructions and hence open to political contest. We do think it is important, however, to distinguish between the *de facto*, market-driven nature of the evolution of 'regionalization' and the *de jure*, state-driven nature of 'regionalism'.

3 Other good recent examples of work on regionalism include special issues of *Third World Quarterly* 20(5), 1999 and *Politeia* 17(3), 1998.

4 *Journal of Common Market Studies, Journal of European Public Policy, Journal of European Integration, European Foreign Affairs Review, European Union Politics* and *Current Politics and Economics in Europe*.

5 We do not have space to argue this point through; suffice it to say that the trajectory of EU studies in the US is closely related to (1) the rise of rational choice as the dominant paradigm in political science, and (2) the declining legitimacy of 'area studies' as a route to career advancement (see Rosamond, 2001).

2 Regionalism and the emerging world order

Sovereignty, autonomy, identity

Amitav Acharya

Introduction

Two momentous events of the late twentieth century have underscored both the potential and the pitfalls of regionalism in shaping world order in the new millennium. The crisis over Kosovo hastened the decline of Westphalian sovereignty in the interstate system. The financial meltdown in Asia around mid-1997 highlighted the challenge to sovereignty in the global economy. In Kosovo, a regional alliance, NATO, led a successful assault against sovereignty after it had paralysed the UN's hand in the crisis. The Asian crisis, on the other hand, indicated that regional institutions (in this case ASEAN) which stick to the principle of absolute sovereignty (and its corollary, the principle of non-interference) are poorly equipped to offer security against the onslaught of globalization.

I argue in this chapter that regionalism and regional institutions are increasingly being challenged and conditioned by the sovereignty-modifying effects of globalization and – for the lack of a better term – 'humanitarian intervention'. Regionalism is becoming, and facing the pressure to become, less sovereignty-bound, in the sense of going against the norms of non-interference and non-intervention that had underpinned the Westphalian international system. Furthermore, intrusive regionalism is providing a new basis of regional identity building, especially in Europe, but also in parts of the Third World. Where regional identity during the Cold War had been defined, functionally speaking, in the process of organizing collective defence against external threats, it could now be constructed on the basis of a shared commitment to intrusive action in promoting human rights and democracy and coping with the challenges of economic globalization.

In developing this central argument, this chapter seeks to perform two functions. The first is to provide a brief intellectual history of regionalism in world politics. The purpose of this exercise is not just to identify the main forms of regional organization that have emerged in the post-Second World War period, but also to examine the underlying linkage between regionalism and sovereignty.

The second aim is to explain some of the key trends in regionalism which may have a crucial bearing on world order in the early twenty-first century. The discussion will focus on the changes in the traditional functions of regionalism and the emergence of what has been called 'new regionalism'. The latter became a popular construct in the late 1980s and early 1990s by drawing attention to the informal, non-hegemonic, comprehensive and multi-dimensional nature of newly emerging regional interactions and processes. (Hettne and Inotai, 1994). Yet even with new regionalism, I argue, the task of redefining the theory and practice of regionalism remains incomplete. Perhaps the most significant trend in regionalism today is its 'intrusive' nature. No discussion of the emerging world order at the beginning of the twenty-first century can be complete without considering the cooperative and conflict-causing potential of intrusive regionalism. This will be highlighted in the final section of the chapter, with particular reference to political and strategic elements of intrusive regionalism.

Sovereignty and regionalism after the Second World War

In the early part of the post-Second World War period, the role of regionalism in the international system could be best described as a bulwark of sovereignty, the founding principle of the modern state system. This was especially true of the three major regional organizations whose primary goal was to control interstate conflicts, such as the Organization of American States (OAS), the League of Arab States and the Organization of African Unity (OAU). At the same time, conceptions of regionalism that threatened to dilute the sovereignty and autonomy of state actors found little support in the international society, especially in the Third World.

For example, some of the earliest proposals about regionalism in international relations envisioned a system of geo-strategic blocs existing as the spheres of influence of the world's leading powers, and contributing towards a global balance of power.[1] Walter Lippmann, for example, identified four such possible regional systems: an Atlantic system managed by the US and the USSR; a Russian system, a Chinese system and eventually an Indian system. Within such hegemonic regional systems, 'the preponderance of a great power was to be recognized; each small power was to accept the protection of the great power in whose region it found itself, and was to forgo the right to form alliances with any extra-regional power' (Bull, 1977: 222–3). Winston Churchill similarly envisaged a number of regional systems as part of the proposed world organization (UN), including in Europe, Asia Minor, Scandinavia, Danubia, the Balkans and the Far East (Churchill, 1950: 711–12). George Liska, an academic, advised small states to develop regional groupings by 'cluster[ing] around the local Great Power' and surrendering to its 'stronger hands the chief responsibility for organizing regional security' (Liska, 1973: 236). These frameworks were precursors to the superpower-led regional military alliances in the Third World.

While the newer entrants to the international system found in regionalism an important foreign policy tool, this was primarily to protect their sovereignty and autonomy from great power meddling. Regionalism was also viewed by the Third World states as a means of collective economic and political self-reliance.[2] At a time when much of Asia, Africa and the Middle East was still under colonial rule, the

OAU and the Arab League functioned more as 'the instrument of national independence rather than of regional integration' (Miller, 1973: 58). The concern with
sovereignty also ensured the ultimate rejection by the majority of Third World countries of superpower-led regional military alliances. Alliances such as the South East
Asia Treaty Organization (SEATO) and the Central Treaty Organization (CENTO)
were at odds with the political aspirations of a non-aligned Third World community
whose members saw in such alliances dangers to their new-found sovereignty.

While the superpower-led regional security organizations faltered in the Third
World, the more multipurpose regional groups managed to secure a place within
the UN system as legitimate mechanisms for the pacific settlement of disputes
between states. This role had been conceded by the so-called 'universalists' (pro-
ponents of a strong and overarching UN with an exclusive role in peace and
security) with some reluctance. While drafting the UN charter at the San Francisco
conference, the 'regionalists' (led by representatives from Latin America and the
Middle East) argued that geographic neighbours would have a better understanding of local disputes and that they would also be better placed to provide prompt
assistance to victims of conflict and aggression (Etzioni, 1970). Despite concerns
that regional organizations might compete with and dilute the authority of the UN,
the 'universalists' (led by the great powers invested with a Security Council veto
power) agreed to a compromise which gave regional organizations a secondary
(point of first contact) role in managing regional conflicts (see Padelford, 1954:
203–16; Haas, 1956: 238–63; Claude, 1963: ch. 6; Wilcox, 1965: 789–811). But as
long as regional organizations remained subject to the norms of the UN-based collective security framework, they remained essentially sovereignty-bound. The
primary purpose of collective security, after all, was to protect state sovereignty
from external encroachment. The charter of all the major regional groupings in
the world enshrined the key UN norm of non-interference in the internal affairs of
states. In the case of the OAU, this norm, complementing an agreement on the
non-violability of post-colonial frontiers, ensured a modicum of interstate peace in
a regional system of weak and internally vulnerable states (Jackson and Roseberg,
1982: 194–208).

As the collective security role of the UN became bogged down in the Cold War,
the limitations of the conflict-regulative role of regionalism also became increasingly apparent, largely due to the constraints imposed by the non-interference
doctrine. While regional institutions could be credited with limited success in keeping conflicts localized and isolated from superpower intervention, they failed
(especially in dealing with intrastate conflicts, the most common form of Third
World conflict in which sovereignty issues were more salient' (Nye, 1971).[3]

The second half of the Cold War was marked by the decline of the OAS, the
OAU and the Arab League, and the emergence of sub-regional frameworks for
security. These included, among others, the Association of Southeast Asian Nations
(ASEAN), the Gulf Cooperation Council (GCC), the Economic Community of
West African States (ECOWAS) and the Contadora Group. Like their larger predecessors, these groupings were oriented towards a conflict-control role. Some of
them, especially ASEAN, made an important contribution to peacemaking in

regional conflicts (Brown, 1986; Tow, 1990). But these groupings also remained bound by the principle of sovereignty and non-interference. Indeed, it was the latter norm which ensured the success of both the ASEAN and the GCC in ensuring collective regime security, even as the region which they were part of remained strategically polarized (the GCC vs. Iran, and ASEAN vs. Vietnam) (Acharya, 1991: 143–64).

In the late 1950s, a different framework of regionalism had emerged in Western Europe. Though not strictly with a security function, it had promised to go 'beyond the nation-state' and to enable states to overcome the security dilemma associated with it. This conception of regionalism found its most sophisticated expression in regional integration theory, an intellectual high point of post-war liberal institutionalism (Nye, 1988: 239). The sovereignty-eroding potential of this form of regionalism (which I call *integrative* regionalism) was captured from a neofunctionalist standpoint by Ernst Haas, who defined integration as 'a process whereby political actors in several distinct national settings are persuaded to shift their loyalties, expectations, and political activities towards a new centre, whose institutions possess or demand jurisdiction over the pre-existing national states' (Haas, 1968: 16). Karl Deutsch, a transactionalist, was more explicit in recognizing the potential of integrative regionalism to overcome the sovereignty trap and the security dilemma. He defined regional integration as the attainment, within a territory, of a 'sense of community' and of institutions and practices strong enough and widespread enough to assure, for a 'long' time, dependable expectations of 'peaceful change' among its population (Deutsch *et al.*, 1957). Deutsch envisaged two such kinds of 'security communities': an 'amalgamated' variety, in which the political units transferred their claim to sovereignty to a new centre, and a 'pluralistic' variety, in which war would no longer be accepted as a legitimate means of problem-solving among nominally sovereign states.

But the fortunes of integration theory rose and fell with the European Economic Community (which later became the European Community and still later the European Union). Integrationists were accused by their critics of overestimating the durability of West European integration. The taming of sovereignty and nationalism in post-war Western Europe, they argued, was but a temporary phenomenon, explained by the shared experience of a highly destructive war. Even if the EC could turn France and Germany into being part of a pluralistic security community, it failed to offer a collective response to several key external challenges, especially the Middle East oil crisis and the American technological challenge. Even the integration theorists themselves found their hopes for an early demise of the national state to have been premature. The relationship between regional integration and transregional economic and technological interdependence, they conceded, was too uncertain and 'turbulent' to justify the earlier view of the former as an incremental or linear process. Against this backdrop, regional integration theory was pronounced 'obsolescent' and the hitherto academic fascination with the subject was replaced by a similar degree of theoretical enthusiasm about international interdependence (which would still later give way to interest in globalization) (Haas, 1975).[4]

Outside of Europe, integrative models of regionalism fared even less well. While several sub-regional economic groups in the Third World sought to self-consciously emulate the EEC, none succeeded in achieving a comparable level of market centralization and trade creation. Neither could they realize the 'spillover' effect of economic cooperation in producing agreement on security issues. In general, regional economic integration in the Third World proved to be 'much more rudimentary than in Europe, more obscure in purpose and uncertain in content' (Gordon, 1961: 245). Sovereignty, in this case newly achieved, proved to be an even more severe obstacle in the Third World than in the West. Regional economic groups which proliferated in Africa and Latin America in the 1960s and 1970s were to ultimately 'founder on the reefs of distrust, non cooperation and parochial nationalism' (Duffy and Feld, 1980: 497).

The transition from sovereignty-bound regionalism

The foregoing analysis shows that none of the three main forms of regional organization in the post-war period (superpower-led regional alliances, regional conflict control organizations and regional economic groupings) was able to escape the sovereignty trap. The EEC was a limited exception. West Europe accepted, but failed to carry it to its logical conclusion, its sovereignty-eroding form of regionalism. The Third World rejected it much more completely. Yet a slow and tentative transition from sovereignty-bound regionalism did take hold during the final phase of the Cold War and was considerably accelerated after, but not necessarily by, its end. Several developments contributed to this transition. For the purpose of this chapter, four are especially noteworthy, and a brief examination of these developments would show that progress towards sovereignty-freeing regionalism has been neither decisive nor linear.

The first was the incremental success of the Conference on Security and Cooperation in Europe (CSCE, which later became an Organization, or OSCE). During the 1980s, the CSCE developed and began to implement an extensive menu of Confidence- and Security-Building Measures (CSBMs), including transparency and constraining measures and verification procedures that crossed the bounds of non-interference in the internal affairs of states. More importantly, the CSCE successfully incorporated human rights issues into the regional confidence-building agenda, thereby setting norms that would regulate the internal as well as external political behaviour of states (Zelikow, 1992: 26). This aspect of the CSCE also distinguished it from the other major regional groupings (such as the OAS, OAU and the Arab League) which, as mentioned earlier, had a minimal role in the regulation of internal conflicts within their member states.

As the Cold War came to a close, the CSCE model acquired greater legitimacy and appeal. The CSCE's contribution to ending the Cold War generated early hopes that balance-of-power approaches to security, the chief rationale for regional alliances, would be replaced by common and cooperative regional security frameworks in the New World Order. Proposals for CSCE-style regional security mechanisms for Asia and the Middle East surfaced, but implementing these proposals proved to be highly difficult, because of the challenge they posed to sovereignty concerns. Despite renewed expectation that regional organizations in the Third World might now be able to assume a more important role in global peace and security (and thereby help to take some of the burden off the UN) (Acharya, 1995a), the former continued to suffer from a host of organizational and political problems.[5] When faced with an explosion of internal conflicts, Third World countries remained reluctant to abandon the non-interference principle to permit collective regional intervention (MacFarlane and Weiss, 1992: 31).

But the CSCE model did have an impact on the character of regional alliances. With the swift demise of the Warsaw Pact, the remaining Cold War regional alliance, NATO, was seen to be heading towards acute obsolescence. 'Permanent alliances of states with on-going common interests, such as NATO,' argued Samuel Huntington, 'are likely to give way to ad hoc temporary coalitions assembled for particular purposes, such as . . . in the Gulf crisis' (Huntington, 1990: 190). This fear of obsolescence would drive NATO to reorient itself in ways that would not only ensure its continued relevance, but also add considerable momentum to the transition from sovereignty-bound regionalism in the international system (to be explained in the next section of the chapter).

A second development contributing to the transformation of regionalism was the revival of the EU's integrative ambitions. While the CSCE was developing security mechanisms that would encompass the whole of Europe, the EU was making its transition to a single market. It is true that West European supranationalism faced old difficulties, especially in developing a full-fledged monetary union. Far more daunting were challenges to the development of a common foreign and defence policy framework. Its failure to deal unitedly and effectively with the crisis in the former Yugoslavia highlighted the limits of a spillover from low politics to issues of high politics, as envisaged by the neofunctionalists. Yet the EC's progress is a major milestone in the long struggle against sovereignty-freeing regionalism in Europe.

But the West European brand of integrative regionalism was no longer being regarded as a possible universal model for regional economic cooperation. Outside of Europe, the most important examples of regional integration resulted not so much through formal bureaucracy-driven trade liberalization as from a 'market-driven' process of transnational production (and in the case of Africa, not through grand schemes for an African Economic Community, but from transnational linkages along the 'informal sector'). The so-called 'growth triangles' or 'natural economic territories' of Northeast and Southeast Asia, in which factors of production – land, capital, technology and labour – for a single product could be derived from, and located within, several national territories, constituted some of the clearest examples of such *regionalization without regionalism*. But they too did not, and could not, bypass state authority and regulation as entirely as initially expected by many observers (Acharya, 1995b: 173–85). On the other hand, the Asia Pacific Economic Cooperation (APEC) grouping, the first formal intergovernmental organization dedicated to trade liberalization in the Asia Pacific region, remained strictly sovereignty-bound. Espousing the principle of 'soft' regionalism, APEC would be kept by its Asian members as a 'consultative mechanism', rather than being developed into an 'economic community' (as initially advocated by Australia) (Acharya, 1997a). In a region where the regionalization of production and the globalization of finance (both with inherent sovereignty-defying tendencies) were moving far ahead of regional institution building, the sovereignty-bound nature of APEC would explain its weak response to the Asian economic crisis.

A third factor explaining the erosion of sovereignty in regional organizations has been well captured by the concept of 'new regionalism' outlined in a study published by Hettne and Inotai in 1994. The difference between 'old' and 'new' regionalism lies in three areas: the multipolar context of the latter (as opposed to the bipolar context of old regionalism); the dominant role of hegemonic actors (regionalism from 'outside' and 'above') in the creation of old regionalism as opposed to the 'autonomous' nature of new regionalism (from 'within' and 'below'), and the comprehensiveness and multidimensional nature of new regionalism as opposed to the narrow and specific focus of the old (Hettne and Inotai, 1994). Of these, the last aspect deserves particular notice. In contrast to the early post-Cold War period, regionalism could no longer be associated with a set of relatively narrow security (whether as a dispute-settlement mechanism, or as a framework for defence against a common threat in the interstate system) and economic (such as a framework of capitalist trade liberalization) goals.

For example, during the 1980s, pressure was mounting on Third World regional groups to deal with an increasingly wider menu of issues, including the challenges posed by their debt burden, the crisis in the world trading regime and environmental degradation (see e.g. Mathews, 1994: 287; Dewitt and Acharya, 1995). Serious doubts about the future of the liberal international economic order led to a revival of interest in regional economic integration in the Third World in the late 1980s and early 1990s. This included ASEAN's decision in 1992 to create a regional free trade area, and the emergence of two new trade groupings in South America (the Mercosur group including Argentina, Brazil, Paraguay and Uruguay, created in 1991, and the Group of Three including Mexico, Venezuela and Colombia, established in 1994) (*The Economist*, 18 July 1994: 47). While old problems associated with regional integration in the developing world remained, especially the difficulty of ensuring an equitable distribution of benefits, the advent of these new regional structures required a shift from sovereignty-bound thinking and approach.

Moreover, the expanding scope of regionalist tasks entailed a corresponding broadening of regionalist actors. Intergovernmental policy coordination, the main traditional tool of sovereignty-bound regionalism, was being joined by a rapid proliferation of regionally based transnational social and cultural networks addressing human rights, democracy, environment and social justice issues. For example, the existence of a regional civil society in the Nordic region could be credited with the security policies of governments in the region during the Cold War which differed markedly from the hard-line postures of the NATO alliance (Hettne and Inotai, 1994: 3). In Southeast Asia, protests organized by Thai NGOs against the illegal logging activities of Thai companies in neighbouring Cambodia and Burma attested to increasing cooperation among regional NGOs (Acharya, 1995c). The emergence of nascent regional civil societies around the world was thus a further blow to sovereignty-bound regionalism.

A fourth development affecting the latter was the collapse of bipolarity. For neorealists, this meant a possible return to more traditional forms of regional rivalry, long suppressed by the superpower 'overlay' (to use Barry Buzan's term) (Mearsheimer, 1990: 5–55; Buzan, 1991a: 167–89). But the end of the Cold War also created the need for devising new principles and ways to organize regional interactions. While neorealists focused on how multipolarity might redefine regional power alignments, constructivist thinking set out to explore how new forms of regional identity building might be emerging on the basis of shared norms and values, a process which might lead to a redefinition of 'regionness'.

During the Cold War, the process of building regional identity found its most concrete expression in frameworks for collective defence against external threats, as was the case in the transatlantic world, or in efforts to organize a common political front against superpower meddling, as in the case of much of the Third World. Without the Berlin Wall and the Soviet threat, Western regionalism (transatlantic and the West European) turned to new ways to define regional identity in Europe. Championing the 'Western' concepts of market capitalism, human rights and liberal democracy, NATO and the EU offered the post-communist states of Eastern Europe an irresistible chance to join, or 'rejoin', the West by acquiring membership in them (Wallace, 1995: 205). In this process, the aspiring members were made to accept, perhaps despite their occasional reluctance, norms of regional conduct specified by NATO and the EU which had become progressively less sovereignty-bound. Moreover, the process of regional identity building around human rights and liberal democracy could not be meaningful unless the relevant regional groups also developed monitoring and enforcement mechanisms, both political, economic and military. In so doing, European regionalism assumed an increasingly intrusive character.

Such processes did not, however, occur outside of Europe. The only other regional organization to have undertaken significant membership expansion after the Cold War was ASEAN. ASEAN undertook the project of constructing 'One Southeast Asia' by gradually bringing into its fold Vietnam (its former adversary) as well as Laos, Burma and Cambodia (the induction of the latter in 1999 completed the process) (Acharya, 2000). But in contrast to Europe, the expansion of ASEAN did not impose any requirement on the prospective members to respect human rights and democracy (though commitment to market capitalism was asked for). Instead, ASEAN chose to dismiss international protests against its decision to grant membership to Burma's highly repressive regime under the pretext of its 'constructive engagement' policy, which itself reflected ASEAN's long-standing commitment to non-interference in the domestic affairs of states (Burma's internal political make-up was of no valid concern to ASEAN). The expansion of ASEAN involved the extension of the so-called 'ASEAN Way'. The latter was defined not only in opposition to European-style regionalism featuring formal bureaucratic structures and legalistic decision-making procedures, it also required strict respect for the norm of non-interference (as outlined in ASEAN's Treaty of Amity and Cooperation).

Moreover, the ASEAN Way reflected some of the illiberal underpinning of the 'Asian values' construct, which had stressed the importance of a communitarian ethic ('society over the self') in explaining the region's economic dynamism. Both the ASEAN Way (explicitly) and Asian values (somewhat more implicitly) constituted the basis of a good deal of Asian thinking about regionalism, including the role of the ASEAN Regional Forum and APEC, which stayed away from any policy initiative that would significantly intrude into the domestic political affairs of its members. Moreover, APEC's sponsorship by Australia and the fear of its possible domination by the US prompted Malaysia to propose an alternative framework of East Asian regionalism (Higgott and Stubbs, 1995: 516–35). Known as the East Asian Economic Caucus (EAEC, whose membership would exclude all the Western members of APEC including Australia, Canada and the US), this regional construct sought not only to build on the existing production networks in Eastern Asia, but also to draw upon the 'Asianness' of its members, including their shared commitment to Asian values.

Intrusive regionalism: possibilities and limits

After over fifty years, regionalism has come a long way from its initial pro-sovereignty predisposition. The transition may be described as one towards 'intrusive regionalism'. To understand the nature of intrusive regionalism, it is useful to compare it with integrative regionalism of the kind envisaged by the regional integration theorists in the context of the EEC. The former, though sovereignty-freeing, was not sovereignty-defying. The original model of integrative regionalism was based on the consent and active participation of member states. Regional integration described how states are persuaded to make *voluntary* concessions on sovereignty in order to realize collective goals. Today's intrusive regionalism, on the other hand, is not always based on consent (although it can be).[6] It is also distinguished by a coercive element. While the early development of integrative regionalism in West Europe relied on economic interdependence, political association and functional transactions, intrusive regionalism relies, ultimately, on the practice of humanitarian intervention, as illustrated in the case of NATO's action against Serbia.

Although intrusive regionalism drew some of its conceptual justification from post-Cold War UN humanitarian intervention missions (Weiss and Campbell, 1991; Scheffer, 1992; Pease and Forsythe, 1993), especially those in northern Iraq and Somalia, credit must be given, for reasons described earlier, to the CSCE/OSCE as the true inventor of intrusive regionalism. It was then the task of NATO, desperately seeking a way out of obsolescence, to steal the show (and the idea) from the OSCE.[7] With far superior resources and a military command structure, NATO could practise humanitarian intervention much more forcefully than the OSCE. The OSCE's role as the teacher of norms should not, however, be overlooked at a time of its alleged obsolescence and the transatlantic euphoria over NATO's 'victory' over Serbia.

Outside of Europe, intrusive regionalism has made more limited progress, the significance of which should not be dismissed, however. Regional confidence-building and preventive diplomacy mechanisms, which are by their very nature sovereignty-eroding, have been advocated and tried by Asia Pacific, Middle Eastern and Latin American regional multilateral institutions. In Asia, the fledgling ASEAN Regional Forum has developed a set of largely non-intrusive CBSMs. To be sure, neither the ARF nor any other Third World regional organization has come even close to the truly intrusive OSCE-style CBMs. But somewhat greater progress has been made on the political front. Through a number of recent initiatives beginning with the 'Santiago Commitment to Democracy and the Renewal of the Inter-American System', the OAS has developed new norms and practices to prevent democratic breakdowns.[8] Even the normally sovereignty-bound OAU has progressively recognized the need for addressing internal conflicts, including those dealing with human rights violations.[9] It recently adopted a policy framework to isolate regimes that come to office through military coups. In Southeast Asia, however, a proposal by the then Malaysian deputy prime minister Anwar Ibrahim for 'constructive intervention' (through wholly non-military means, however) failed to attract broad support in 1996 (Acharya, 1997b). Asia and the Middle East also remain major exceptions to the establishment of regional human rights monitoring bodies, a key form of intrusive regionalism, although ASEAN is reportedly considering proposals for such a body.

The case of ASEAN deserves special attention because it is here that the tension between intrusive regionalism and sovereignty has been most pronounced. While sovereignty concerns prevailed over constructive intervention by ASEAN in the political arena, the grouping, facing international criticism of its weak response to the Asian economic crisis, may no longer be able to resist calls for rethinking its doctrine of non-interference in the economic arena.

The Asian crisis brought home to the ASEAN members the dangers of the doctrine when confronting the challenges of economic globalization. When the crisis broke out, critics of non-interference argued that had ASEAN been not so tightly bound by it, Thailand, the first ASEAN country to go under, could have been issued with a more timely warning about its worsening economic condition. In the wake of the crisis, the foreign minister of Thailand argued for a policy of 'flexible engagement' (later termed 'enhanced interaction'), which would allow a 'peer review' of the members' economic policies (Thailand also claimed a right to criticize Burma's human rights record under this framework) (Acharya, 1999: 1–29). While the political aspects of this proposal were rejected by ASEAN, the grouping has taken the first tentative steps towards intrusive regionalism by establishing a regional financial and macro-economic surveillance process ('ASEAN Surveillance Process', as opposed to 'ASEAN Surveillance Mechanism', which had been advocated by the US but was rejected by ASEAN for being too intrusive). Moreover, ASEAN members have faced increasing demands to move beyond the ASEAN Way of informality and *ad hoc*-ism, and to develop more concrete institutional mechanisms and 'rule-based transparency in governance' to deal with future economic meltdowns (Acharya, 1999: 19–20).

Intrusive regionalism could affect global peace and security in several ways. The practice of intrusive regionalism could give rise to new and more robust forms of collective identity, expressed through a deepening and widening of multilateral political and security institutions and approaches. This is happening in Europe and, to a lesser extent, in Latin America. The norms of intrusive regionalism could also lead to the development of more mature 'security communities' in Southeast Asia and the Southern Cone (Hurrell, 1998: 260). In Europe, the norms of intrusive regionalism have created the basis of a wider democratic security community that is already extending beyond the EU. ASEAN remains an illiberal security community, but the advent of intrusive economic regionalism, if backed by incremental democratization, could make ASEAN stronger and more durable (Acharya, 1998: 198–227).

Caution should, however, be expressed about the pacific effects of intrusive regionalism. In Southeast Asia, the hitherto lack of intrusive regionalism has actually promoted regional order. In the Gulf, however, deviation from the doctrine of non-interference in the post-1990 period (especially in the Qatari case) has led to a weakening of regional order (Barnett and Gause, 1998: 184–5). Intrusive regionalism carried out without a collective purpose and without a set of agreed norms, criteria and modalities of collective action may prove highly destabilizing.

Moreover, intrusive regionalism has the potential to fuel inter-regional discord. A case in point is the conflict between ASEAN and the European Union over the former's policy of 'constructive engagement' of Burma. A regional collective identity developed around the norms of intrusive regionalism could also breed exceptionalism and exclusionism. The danger of this happening in Europe has been highlighted by Tony Smith:

> were the European project to achieve its political goals, it would also entail, not just economic exclusion, but also cultural differentiation and with it the possibility of cultural and racial exclusion. The forging of a deep continental cultural identity to support political unification may well require an ideology of European cultural exclusiveness.
>
> (Smith, 1992: 76)

Conclusion

Regionalism has been a defender of sovereignty in the past, especially in the Third World. Today, globalization and changing international norms concerning humanitarian intervention are turning regionalism from being a bulwark of sovereignty into a building block of an intrusive world order. New forms of regional identity built around intrusive regionalism could become important stepping stones to a post-Westphalian world order in the twenty-first century.

Around the globe, intrusive regionalism is being practised through a variety of means. In the economic sphere, macro-economic surveillance and financial monitoring have been added to the classical trade liberalization agenda and market-driven regional investment coordination. In the political sphere, the instruments of intrusive regionalism include the development and mutual obser-vance of norms against human rights abuses and democratic breakdowns (as in Africa and Latin America, but not in the Middle East and Asia), the development of regional human rights bodies (again, the Middle East and Asia are exceptions here), and mechanisms of humanitarian military intervention (only NATO so far, although whether NATO will develop an out-of-area humanitarian intervention role is by no means certain).

The transition to intrusive regionalism remains far from complete or linear. This chapter has highlighted the positive aspects of intrusive regionalism, especially its role in fostering human rights and democracy and promoting the ideal of common and cooperative security. But its dangers and limitations also deserve attention. The international community remains, and will remain for the foresee-able future, ambivalent about it. Such ambivalence will persist if intrusive regionalism involves too much coercion and military intervention. Without appro-priate multilateral norms to guide it, intrusive regionalism could lead to both intra-regional polarization and inter-regional conflict.

Intrusive regionalism also contributes to North–South tensions, with the South seeing in it a new form of Western domination. The Third World recognizes the potential of regionalism as a whole to foster a greater decentralization and democ-ratization of global institutions and regimes, but it remains largely unwilling and unable to follow European models and practices of intrusive regionalism. In the economic sphere, intrusive regionalism may prove to be an indispensable tool for Third World countries in dealing more effectively with globalization. In the polit-ical sphere, however, sovereignty-bound regionalism will remain more popular in the Third World as a counter to the intrusive globalism and regionalism of the West (recognizing, however, that the Third World countries may not always be able to separate regionalism in the economic arena from the political). Against this backdrop, prospects for world order will be affected by a clash between two forms of regionalism: intrusive and sovereignty-bound, the former shaping the values, identities and foreign policy behaviour of the West, while the latter characterizes much of the rest. Reconciling the norms and practices of the two regionalisms is one of the most serious tasks for the international community in the coming decades.

Notes

1 The genesis of this idea could be traced, ironically, to the Draft Treaty of Mutual Assistance prepared by the League's committee on the Reduction of Armaments in 1923, though it was never approved by the League's membership.
2 In an earlier article I characterized this conception of regionalism as 'autonomous' regionalism, to be contrasted with the 'hegemonic' regionalism associated with the Cold War alliances (see Acharya, 1992: 7–21). This distinction, however, dealt primar-ily with the regionalism of the state; this chapter also recognizes the role of transnational social movements in creating what critical theorists would call 'counter-hegemonic' regional coalitions.
3 For a study of the constraints on regional organizations in regulating internal conflict, see Miller (1967: 582–600).

4 Some scholars have argued that while integration became obsolete, integration studies did not. Puchala (1984: 198) points out that integration studies remained 'relevant, alive, well, and quite vibrant' because its 'earlier curiosities about international collaboration via transnational processes within settings of interdependence have become central concerns of International Relations'.

5 This problem was highlighted in the ECOWAS operation in Liberia which was dominated by Nigerian troops and financial support. ECOWAS as an organization was able to provide only $3 million out of the total US $50 million operation, with the remainder coming mostly from Nigeria. Nigerian dominance was resented by most of ECOMOG's French-speaking members as well as Ghana. See *The Economist Foreign Report*, 18 July 1991: 6–7.

6 In an earlier article I defined intrusive regionalism as a framework that 'calls for closer interaction among members of a regional group, including mutual receptivity to early warnings about domestic developments with transnational consequences, and cooperation against such commonly faced dangers even though such cooperation may intrude into the domestic affairs of member states' (Acharya, 1999: 1–29).

7 The extent to which the principles and practices of the OSCE have been 'embedded' in other European multilateral institutions, especially NATO, is described in Adler (1998: 143–7).

8 The OAS foreign ministers in a joint declaration at Santiago in June 1991 stressed their 'uncompromising commitment to the defense of democracy' and to renew the OAS as 'the political forum for dialogue, understanding, and cooperation among all countries in the hemisphere' (Andersen, 1994: 2; see also Farer, 1996: 1–25).

9 The development of African mechanisms to 'prevent or at any rate to resolve, any conflict situation that arises on the continent . . . especially in the area of internal conflicts' is outlined in OAU (1992: 9).

3 Theorising the rise of regionness

Björn Hettne and Fredrik Söderbaum

Introduction

For more than a decade, regionalism has now 'been brought back in' to international studies, after some time of almost complete neglect.[1] The 'new regionalism' began to emerge in the mid-1980s in the context of the comprehensive structural transformation of the global system. Similar to the 'old regionalism' which began in the 1950s and stagnated in the 1970s, the new wave must be understood in its historical context. That is, it needs to be related to the structural transformation of the world, *inter alia*, including (1) the move from bipolarity towards a multipolar or perhaps tripolar structure, with a new division of power and new division of labour; (2) the relative decline of American hegemony in combination with a more permissive attitude on the part of the USA towards regionalism; (3) the erosion of the Westphalian nation-state system and the growth of interdependence and 'globalisation', and (4) the changed attitudes towards (neo-liberal) economic development and political systems in the developing countries, as well as in the post-communist countries (see de Melo and Panagariya, 1993; Fawcett and Hurrell, 1995; Gamble and Payne, 1996; Hettne and Soderbaum, 1998a; Hettne *et al.*, 1999, 2000a, 2000b, 2000c; Böås *et al.*, 1999b; and Kearns, 1999).

The 'new regionalism' is a truly worldwide phenomenon that is taking place in more areas of the world than ever before. Today's regionalism is extroverted rather than introverted, which reflects the deeper interdependence of today's global political economy and the intriguing relationship between globalisation and regionalisation. It should also be noted that the 'new regionalism' is simultaneously linked with domestic factors, sometimes challenging the nation-state while at other times strengthening it. Thus the renewed trend of regionalism is a complex process of change simultaneously involving state as well as non-state actors, and occurring as a result of global, regional, national and local level forces. It is not possible to state which level is dominant, because actors and processes interact at the various levels and their relative importance differs in time and space.

In spite of the recent mushrooming of research in this academic field, the overall puzzle to explain, understand, predict and prescribe the emergence, dynamics and consolidation of regionalisation – i.e. rising regionness – in world politics remains only partly resolved. This is, in our view, mainly explained by the lack of adequate theory. Our ambition in this chapter is therefore to move towards a more coherent construction of a New Regionalism Theory (NRT), built around the core concept of 'regionness', indicating the multidimensional result of the process of regionalisation of a particular geographic area.[2] The concept of regionness – ranging from regional space, regional complex, regional society, regional community to region–state – is outlined and suggested as a comparative analytical tool for understanding the construction and consolidation of regions and the formation of relevant actors in a historical and multidimensional perspective. To some extent the five levels express a certain evolutionary logic, but there is, for sure, nothing deterministic with the rise of regionness.

It may still be somewhat premature to outline a theory of the 'new regionalism' in full, but it should be possible to say what we should expect from it. A theory of the 'new regionalism' cannot be about emerging regions only. It has to be a theory about the world order in transformation and the emergence of a multi-level pattern of governance. The NRT has to explain the world order that makes processes of regionalisation possible, or even necessary, and the world order that may result from new regionalisms in interaction. Note the plural. Analysts of the renewed trend of regionalisation emphasise that there are many regionalisms and regionalisation processes, i.e. different regional projects and different types of regional activities.

The world order approach does not prevent a particular focus on the regions, which is important both for empirical and normative reasons. Empirical because we do not yet know enough about the emerging regional formations, normative because the point is to question some consequences of globalisation and discuss the possibility of a 'return of the political' in the form of regionalism. Somewhat ironically, there is increasing agreement even among 'globalists' that some 'regulation' is needed in the world political economy; the question is how, by whom and for whom.

This chapter is structured in two main parts. The first elaborates on some meta-theoretical points of departure while the second contains an in-depth analysis of the five levels of regionness.

Before moving on, some conceptual clarifications are necessary. 'Regionalism' refers to the general phenomenon under study, i.e. the 'new' or 'second wave of regionalism' arising more or less all over the world today. In the analytical, operational sense it refers to the current ideology of regionalism, i.e. the urge for a regionalist order, either in a particular geographical area or as a type of world order. Regionalism in this particular sense is usually associated with a programme and strategy, and may lead to formal institution building. 'Regionalisation' denotes the (empirical) process that leads to patterns of cooperation, integration, complementarity and convergence within a particular cross-national geographical space. It is important to distinguish formal regionalism (as ideology and programme) from the process of regionalisation. In Europe there is, for example, a strong anti-regionalist ideology in the form of neo-nationalism which does not necessarily prevent regionalisation on the ground from taking place. In our view, the empirical study of regionalisation has been neglected due to excessive focus on regionalist projects and regionalism as ideology. Regionalisation implies increasing 'region-ness'. Thus the latter concept is a way to investigate the state of regionalisation in various dimensions and contexts and to compare various situations.

Meta-theoretical postulates

We should briefly describe our meta-theoretical points of departures: (1) global social theory, (2) social constructivism, and (3) comparative regional studies.

Global social theory

Since the 'new regionalism' is closely linked to global structural change and glob-alisation, it cannot be understood merely from the point of view of the single region in question. What we are looking for specifically is global theory that takes regional peculiarities into consideration (Hettne and Soderbaum, 1999). This is not only motivated by the need to understand particular regions, because to better understand society in general is also to better understand a particular region. Good theory makes sense of ongoing events; it explains where we are, how we got there and where we are going (without necessarily being able to forecast everything on the way). Good theory also makes it possible to act in order to improve our sit-uation, but since we are not all sitting in the same boat, it also differentiates between different we-categories and facilitates a dialogue between different world-views and standpoints.

Global social theory means a comprehensive social science that abandons state-centrism in an ontologically fundamental sense. Social processes must be analysed delinked from national space. As emphasised by the late Susan Strange (1999), it is not our job to defend or excuse the 'Westfailure system'. Somewhat simplistically we speak in favour of a marriage between certain strands in development theory and international political economy (IPE), or rather political economy (PE), since 'international' no longer needs mentioning. Such a merger may ultimately strengthen an emerging 'new' or 'critical political economy', dealing with histori-cal power structures, emphasising contradictions in them, as well as change and transformation expressed in normative terms (i.e. development) (Murphy and Tooze, 1991; Hettne, 1995; Cox with Sinclair, 1996) .This much-needed focus on history is an escape from unchanging transhistorical theory, artificially imposed on an ever-changing reality, and characterising what is still mainstream international theory (i.e. IR and IPE).

Global social theory must go beyond the mystifications of the concept of glob-alisation, distinguishing the new aspects from the old and specifying what concrete dimensions are involved and how they are related, *if* they are related. Globalisation cannot just be taken for granted, neither should the privilege of defining the phe-nomenon be left to the ideological 'globalists'.

Global social theory, furthermore, has to come to terms with the micro–macro relation since the distinction between 'international' and 'domestic' is being tran-scended. Conventionally, analysts within the field of IR/IPE and international economics have been concerned mainly with the 'big' processes of macro-regionalism, primarily in and between the three core regions – Europe, North America and Asia Pacific – often focusing on EU, NAFTA and APEC, or other regional organisations such as ASEAN, Mercosur, SADC and ECOWAS and so on. In other academic disciplines, such as geography, cultural studies, regional and urban planning and so on, the main focus has been placed first and foremost on sub-national regions but also on cross-border (micro)regions, such as the Euro-regions, growth polygons, growth triangles and development corridors in Asia, North America and Africa, as well as the micro-states such as Singapore and Hong Kong (Ohmae, 1995; Keating and Loughlin, 1997). In line with our effort to contribute to a comprehensive, interdisciplinary, historically based international social science, we seek to integrate the macro and the micro perspectives rather than separate them, which has been the case up until now. In essence, one of the innovative features of the NRT is, at least in our own minds, the ambition to bridge the rift between macro-regionalism and micro-regionalism. Another aspiration is to emphasise the reality of regionalisation behind the fetishism of formal regional organisations.

Social constructivism

Social constructivism constitutes another of our meta-theoretical building blocks. It 'provides a theoretically rich and promising way of conceptualising the interaction between material incentives, inter-subjective structures, and the identity and interests of the actors' (Hurrell, 1995b: 72). Instead of focusing solely on material incentives, constructivists emphasise the importance of shared knowledge, learning, ideational forces, and normative and institutional structures. They claim that understanding intersubjective structures allows us to trace the ways in which interests and identities change over time and new forms of cooperation and community can emerge. It represents a sociological approach to systemic theory, which in turn is based on the fact that political communities are not exogenously given but constructed by historically contingent interactions.

The relevance in this context would of course be that social constructivism draws particular attention to how regions are socially constructed and also consolidated. The region constitutes an open process, and can only be defined *post factum*. Regions are social constructions, and to observe and describe regionalisation is also to participate in the construction of regions. Since there are no given regions, there are no given regionalist interests either, but the interests and identities are shaped in the process of interaction and intersubjective understanding. But no interaction is possible without some shared interests to start with (Smith, 1997: 185). Regionalisation is a process. The relevance of 'hard structuralism' is limited in such a situation. We agree with Alexander Wendt (1992: 395) that 'structure has no existence or causal power apart from process'. 'Structuralism' has thus to be transcended, and in order to understand structural change we must move from structure to agency, actors, visions and strategies. In accordance with social constructivism more generally, the NRT seeks to address the fact that agency, and particularly the role of often previously excluded transnational actors, is an under-researched field in the study of regionalisation.

Similarly to neo-liberal institutionalists, social constructivists share the idea that norms and beliefs may shape behaviour, but contrary to the former rationalist/neo-utilitarian view, actors' interests, motives, ideas and identities are not exogenously given but socially constructed by *reflective* actors, capable of adapting to challenges imposed by the actions of others and changing contexts. From this perspective, agency is often motivated and explained by ideas, identity and learning.

Comparative studies

Most studies of regionalisation have been case studies of a single region, with emphasis on those variables that the particular theoretical approach perceives as most important in explaining the outcome. Scholars have often tried to draw lessons from the cases, but little genuine comparative analysis has been undertaken in the 'new regionalism' to date (although there is now an increase of comparative studies in the field).

Comparative studies have been heavily criticised by area specialists, postmodernists and others, who emphasise cultural relativism and the importance of a deep multidisciplinary knowledge of various contexts and people. Part of this critique seems to hold true, particularly the emphasis that the comparative method is ultimately based on the same logic as the experimental method. Consequently, comparative analysis should be used with care in the social sciences. On the other hand, we believe that comparative analysis helps to guard against ethnocentric bias and culture-bound interpretations that can arise in a too contextualised specialisation. Since theory necessarily relies on some generalisations, comparative analysis is also crucial for theory building.

We perceive a middle ground between context and area studies on the one hand and 'hard' social science as reflected in the use of 'laborative' comparisons on the other – i.e. what has been referred to as the 'eclectic center' of comparative studies (Axline, 1994; Payne, 1998).[3] By this combination we hope to avoid the devil of exaggerated contextualisation and the deep blue sea of general theory. A useful way of overcoming whatever tensions there may exist between 'globalism' and 'localism' is to focus on comparative regional studies within a globalised framework; i.e. to look upon a particular region in a world of regions, together constituting an emerging world order marked by regional peculiarities.

Theorising regionness

The concept of 'region' is obviously fundamental to regional analysis. The main task of identifying regions implies making judgements about the degree to which a particular area in various respects constitutes a distinct entity, which may be distinguished as a relatively coherent territorial subsystem (in contrast with non-territorial subsystems) from the rest of the global system.[4]

It is conventionally held that a region minimally refers to a limited number of states linked together by a geographical relationship and by a degree of mutual interdependence. However, in an effort to transcend state-centrism and the fixation on regional organisations rather than the processes of regionalisation, the NRT does not view regions as simple aggregations of 'states'. Depending on how 'region' is defined, the regional frontier may very well cut through a particular state's territory, positioning some parts of the state within the emerging region and others outside. It could, for instance, be argued that some parts of China, mainly the coastal areas, form part of an East Asian regionalisation process while mainland China does not. A less dramatic example is the well-consolidated nation-state of Sweden where, nevertheless, the eastern part turns 'Baltic', while the western turns 'Atlantic' and the southern 'Continental'. Furthermore, what is referred to as a region with regard to economic relations may not always be a relevant delimitation seen from, for instance, a political or a cultural perspective. Particularly at the less advanced levels of regionness and with regard to the outer boundaries, which tend to be the most blurred, it is necessary to maintain eclectic and flexible definitions of regions.

When different processes of regionalisation in various fields and at various levels intensify and converge within the same geographical area, the cohesiveness and thereby the distinctiveness of the region in the making increases. The NRT seeks to describe this process of regionalisation in terms of levels of 'regionness' (i.e. the process whereby a geographical area is transformed from a passive object to an active subject, capable of articulating the transnational interests of the emerging region). Regionness thus implies that a region can be a region 'more or less'. The level of regionness can both increase and decrease.

Given the excessive attention received in the literature, both old and new, it is important to conceive regional organisation as a second order phenomenon, compared to processes that underlie regionalisation in a particular geographical area, which should be seen as a 'region in the making'. Becoming rather than being is thus what is focused upon in this context.

Since regions are political and social projects, devised by human actors in order to protect or transform existing structures, they may, like nation-state projects before them, fail. Regions can be disrupted from within and from without by the same forces that build them up. Since a region can be constructed it can also be deconstructed, ideationally as well as materially (Adler and Barnett, 1998b: 58). Integration and disintegration go hand in hand (albeit at different levels), and at each stage there is the possibility of spill-back. Other processes such as globalisation, nation building and fragmentation may dominate, possibly in combination with more negative forms of regional scenarios than the particular forms of regionalization outlined in this chapter, (e.g. hostile regional 'fortresses' or 'open', neo-liberal regions serving as temporary 'stepping-stones' to multilateralism). Thus we do not deny a normative element in NRT.[5]

In spite of the pluralistic and often heterogeneous nature of contemporary regionalisation and the fact that sometimes there is a decreasing level of regionness in certain parts of the world, we take seriously that after a process of regionalisation has begun, it appears as if different logics begin to develop, expressing a certain evolutionary or irreversible logic. In our view, mainstream theories in the field do not adequately explain such multidimensional increase and later consolidation of the processes of regionalisation. We agree with Andrew Hurrell in that although a 'stage-theory' approach to understanding regionalism may be somewhat theoretically unsatisfying, it is historically very plausible and it has a great deal to offer in sharpening our understanding of the moves towards increasing regionalization in many parts of the world (Hurrell, 1995b: 73).

Mostly when we speak of regions we actually mean regions in the making. There are no 'natural' or 'given' regions, but these are created and re-created in the process of global transformation. Regionness can be understood in analogy with concepts such as 'stateness' and 'nationness'. The regionalisation process can be intentional or non-intentional, and may proceed unevenly along the various dimensions of the 'new regionalism' (i.e. economics, politics, culture, security, etc.). Needless to say, there are also different forms of regionness in different regions. In what follows we will describe five generalised levels of regionness, which may be said to define a particular region in terms of regional coherence and community.

Regional space

Although the importance of geographical contiguity must not be exaggerated, the NRT is founded on the fact that (almost by definition) a functioning society cannot exist separated from territory. That is, a region is firmly rooted in territorial space: a group of people living in a geographically bounded community, controlling a certain set of natural resources, and united through a certain set of cultural values and common bonds of social order forged by history.

First of all one can therefore identify a potential region as a primarily geographical unit, delimited by more or less natural physical barriers and marked by ecological characteristics: 'Europe from the Atlantic to the Urals', North America, the Southern cone of South America, 'Africa South of Sahara', Central Asia, or 'the Indian subcontinent'. In the earliest history of such an area, people presumably lived in small, isolated communities with little contact. This first level of regionness may therefore be referred to as a 'proto-region', or a 'pre-regional zone', since there is no organised international/world society in this situation.

However, some translocal relations are bound to develop rather early. Premodern exchange systems tend to be based on symbolic kinship bonds rather than expectations associated with market behaviour. Premarket transactions, which Karl Polanyi (1944) referred to as 'embedded', contained an important element of diplomacy and the creation of trust between isolated communities experiencing occasional 'encounters'. In order to further regionalise, a particular territory must necessarily experience increasing interaction and more frequent contact between human communities, which after living as 'isolated' groupings are moving towards some kind of translocal relationship, giving rise to a regional social system or what we will call 'regional complex'.

Regional complex

Increased social contacts and transactions between previously more isolated groups – the creation of a social system – facilitate some sort of regionness, albeit on a low level. The creation of Latin Christendom between 800 and 1200, which also implied the birth of a European identity, is a case in point (Bartlett, 1993). Such early relations of interdependence also constitute a regional complex and indicate the real starting point for the regionalisation process (Buzan, 1991b).

The emergence of a regional complex thus implies ever-widening translocal relations – positive and/or negative – between human groups and influences between cultures ('little traditions'). It is reasonable to assume that regional identities may be historically deep-seated. Hence it is necessary to take a longer historical perspective than simply the nation-building period, for example, the Westphalian era in European and international history (i.e. the establishment of a global state system). This is of particular importance in the South where the state system is much more recent, feeble and often quite artificial. It is quite likely in many parts of the world that an erosion or reorganisation of nation-states will strengthen regional identity. This may happen in Europe as well.

The creation of states – state formation and nation building – leads to a consolidation of national territories which for a time (the Westphalian era of Europe) implies a more inward orientation, and usually means a temporary decline in the level of regionness, which has a counterpart in the post-colonial creation of states in Latin America during the nineteenth century and in Asia and Africa after the Second World War. The collective memory of a more widespread identity, albeit confined to a relatively small elite, dissipates. The territorial states by definition monopolise all external relations and decide who are friend or foe, which implies a discouragement of whatever regional consciousness there may be. The existing social relations in a nation-state system may very well be hostile and completely lacking in cooperation. In fact this is a defining feature of a nation-state system according to the dominant theoretical school in IR. The people of the separate 'nation-states' are not likely to have much knowledge of or mutual trust in each other, much less a shared identity. When the states relax their 'inward-orientedness' and become more open to external relations, the degree of transnational contact may increase dramatically, which may trigger a process of further regionalisation in various fields.

In security terms the region at this level is best understood as a 'conflict formation' or a 'regional (in)security complex', in which the constituent units, as far as their own security is concerned, are dependent on each other as well as on the overall stability of the regional system (Buzan *et al.*, 1998). The region, just like the larger international system of which it forms a part, can therefore on this level of regionness be described as 'anarchic', with territorial states as the only relevant actors. The classic case of such a regional order is nineteenth-century Europe. At this low level of regionness, a balance of power, or some kind of 'concert', is the sole security guarantee for the states constituting the system. This is a rather primitive security mechanism. We could therefore talk of a 'primitive' region, exemplified by the Balkans today, and as far as political security is concerned (in spite of a relatively high degree of economic regionalisation) by East Asia.

Similarly to security matters, the political economy of development may be understood as 'anarchic', implying that there exists no transnational welfare mechanism which can ensure a functioning regional economic system. In Europe this is the legacy of the mercantilism associated with nation building, which in the Third World has its counterpart in the dependency/economic nationalism syndrome. The patterns of economic interdependencies tend to be exploitative rather than cooperative and mutually reinforcing, often resulting in hostile protectionism, trade wars, beggar-thy-neighbour policies, relative gain-seeking and various strategies to isolate the 'national' economies from the negative effects of the larger regional (and of course global) economic system of which they form a part, while at the same time trying to exploit the opportunities of the same system(s). The actors may also look towards the larger external system rather than the region. There is no shared sense of 'sitting in the same boat'. Exchanges and economic interactions are unstable, short-sighted and based on self-interest rather than expectations of economic reciprocity, social communication and mutual trust. This economic behaviour is inherent in the ideology of globalism.

Regional society

This is where the crucial regionalisation process develops and intensifies, in the sense that a number of different actors, apart from states, appear on different societal levels and move towards transcendence of national space, making use of a more rule-based pattern of relations. The dynamics at this stage implies the emergence of a variety of processes of communication and interaction between a multitude of state and non-state actors and along several dimensions, economic as well as political and cultural, i.e. multidimensional regionalisation. This rise in intensity, scope and width of regionalisation may come about through formalised regional cooperation or more spontaneously.

In the case of more formally organised cooperation, the region is defined by the members of the regional organisation in question. In most conventional analyses this is the only region acknowledged as such. This more organised region, which we look upon as a second order phenomenon, could be called the 'formal' or *de jure* region. In order to assess the relevance and future potential of a particular regional organisation, it should be possible to relate the 'formal region' to the 'real region', which has to be defined in terms of potentialities, *de facto* regionalisation, convergencies and through other, less precise criteria (Oman, 1994; Mittelman, 1999).

This level of regionness may be referred to as a regional form of 'international society' of cooperating states, as used in the English School, but (and this is the major difference) not confined simply to state relations (Bull, 1977). With lower degrees of regionness, the regional dynamics is often dominated by a state-centric logic, but increasing interdependence and relaxed inward orientation, which is typical of this level of regionness, give rise to a complex interaction between many types of actors. Here we include the wide range of 'non-state', transnational actors:

private businesses and firms, transnational corporations (TNCs), NGOs, social movements and other types of social networks formed on the basis of professional, ideological, ethnic or religious ties, which contribute to the formation of a transnational regional economy and regional civil society.

It is important to recognise that the relationships and strengths of the 'formal' and the 'real' region, between state and non-state actors, differ in time and space. The crucial question is therefore to understand how the region is constructed in the interplay between various types of state, market and civil society actors in various regional spaces. Rising regionness does not mean that the so-called nation-states are becoming obsolete or disappearing, but rather that they are undergoing major restructuring in the context of regionalisation (and globalisation) and the complex interplay of state–market–society relations. Increasing regionalisation also means that they end up as semi-independent parts of larger regional political societies. One helpful way of conceiving the ongoing restructuring of the nation-state and the new governance structures is to understand the Westphalian state as a 'bundle' of functions, loyalties and identities, some of which in the new global situation are becoming delinked from the state level and associated with other political levels, shaping a multilayered political landscape in which other actors than the state are also gaining strength.

Various dimensions of regionalisms and regionalisations occur at different spatial levels of regions, which to a large extent are all related to one another (and therefore must be understood within the same analytical framework). We should therefore explicitly integrate 'micro-regions' and micro-regionalisms into the analysis. Micro-regionalism is related to macro-regionalism in the way that the larger regionalisation (and globalisation) processes create possibilities for smaller economically dynamic sub-national or transnational regions to gain direct access to the larger regional economic system, often bypassing the nation-state and the national capital, and sometimes even as an alternative or in opposition to the challenged state and to formal state regionalisms.

There is a diverse pattern of micro-regions in the world today. The Euro-regions are well-known examples which must be understood in their particular European context. As illustrated by concepts such as growth polygons, growth triangles, development corridors, spatial development initiatives and cross-border regions, most micro-regions in other parts of the world are often state-assisted with a weak degree of institutionalisation while at the same time being private sector-led and market-driven, thus involving a high degree of interactions initiated by non-state actors and interpersonal transnational networks (e.g. diasporas, ethnic or family networks, religious ties, etc.) (Bøås and Hveem, forthcoming).

In order to further regionalise, the great diversity of processes at various levels (i.e. macro-micro) and in various sectors must to an increasing extent become mutually reinforcing and evolve in a complementary and mutually reinforcing rather than competitive and diverging direction. The increasing and widening relationships between the formal and the real region lead to an institutionalisation of cognitive structures and a gradual deepening of mutual trust and responsiveness. Formal organisations and social institutions play a crucial role in this process leading towards community and region building.

Regional community

The fourth level of regionness refers to the process whereby the region increasingly turns into an active subject with a distinct identity, institutionalised or informal actor capability, legitimacy and structure of decision-making, in relation with a more or less responsive regional civil society, transcending the old state borders. It implies a convergence and compatibility of ideas, organisations and processes within a particular region.

In security terms, to continue this line of argument, the reference is to 'security community' and its recent rediscovery (Adler and Barnett, 1998a), which means that the level of regionness achieved makes it inconceivable to solve conflicts by violent means, between as well as within former states. With regard to development, the regional sphere is not merely reduced to a 'market', but there exist also regional mechanisms that can offset the polarisation effects inherent in the market and ensure social security, regional balance and welfare, with similar albeit still embryonic functions as in the old states.

A regional community is characterised by a mutually reinforcing relationship between the 'formal' region, defined by the community of states, and the 'real' region, in which a transnationalised regional civil society also has a role to play. The regional civil society may emerge spontaneously from 'below', but is ultimately dependent on enduring (formal and informal) institutions and 'regimes' that facilitate and promote security, welfare, social communication and convergence of values, norms, identities and actions throughout the region.

The micro-regions do not disappear at this stage. On the contrary, they often flourish and become a permanent feature of the larger region, thus contributing to the diversity and increasing level of cross-border relations within the macro-region. A dense pattern of micro-regions is gradually emerging, and as these become more dynamic and stronger, they also contribute to increased relations between the various micro-regions. At such high levels of regionness, the pattern of micro-regions will not have different visions from the larger macro-region, but will relate to it in a mutually reinforcing manner.

A regional collective identity has emerged and the relations are characterised by mutual trust driven by social learning. As Adler and Barnett correctly surmise:

> Learning increases the knowledge that individuals in states have not just about each others' purposes and intentions but also of each others' interpretations of society, politics, economics, and culture; to the extent that these interpretations are increasingly shared and disseminated across national borders, the stage has been laid for the development of a regional collective identity.
>
> (Adler and Barnett, 1998b: 54)

With increasing levels of regional community, the dividing line between the separate (and often artificial) national communities within the region gradually disappears and differentiation is increasingly between those within from those outside the (macro) region. The region can in this sense be the organising basis for relationships within the region and define the relations to the rest of the world (Hurrell, 1995b). This implies a radical shift away from how the world has been organised in the Westphalian era. However, just like nation-states, all regions are to a certain extent 'imagined', subjectively defined and cognitive constructions. In order to be successful, regionalisation necessitates a certain degree of compatibility of culture, identity and fundamental values.

A shared cultural tradition – an inherent regional civil society – in a particular region is often of importance here, particularly for more informal forms of regionalisation. However, it must be remembered that culture is not given, but continuously created and re-created. The defining element is rather the multi-dimensional and voluntary quality of regional interaction, and the societal characteristics indicating an emerging regional community. Some examples are the Nordic group of countries and perhaps North America (gradually including Mexico). On their way are the Southern Cone of South America and (at least the original) members of ASEAN. The established community spirit may be negatively affected by opportunistic and politically motivated inclusion of new unprepared members, such as the surprising cooptation of the Democratic Republic of Congo into SADC. In such cases the formal region is acting without regard for the real region which may in fact hamper the regionalisation process.

Region-state

In the still rather hypothetical and perhaps unlikely fifth level of regionness, the processes shaping the 'formal' and 'real' region are similar, but by no means identical, to state formation and nation building. The ultimate outcome could be a region-state, which in terms of scope and cultural heterogeneity may be compared to the classical empires. A region-state must be distinguished from a nation-state. It will never aspire to that degree of homogeneity and sovereignty of the Westphalian type of state, and therefore a regionalised order cannot be regarded simply as Westphalianism with fewer units (Bull, 1977: 266).

As there are many types of nation-states, there will also be different types of region-states. Furthermore, the political logic of regionalisation is somewhat different compared to a nation-state. Homogenisation within a region cannot (as in the nation-state) imply cultural standardisation in accordance with one specific ethnic model, but rather compatibility between differences within a pluralist culture. World regions are per definition multicultural and heterogeneous. Region-states cannot therefore be based on force, which would imply that they sooner or later explode from within, as illustrated by the Soviet empire and some large and complex African states.

In terms of political order, a region-state constitutes a voluntary evolution of a group of formerly sovereign national communities into a new form of political entity, where sovereignty is pooled for the best of all, and which is radically more democratic than other 'international' polities. National interests may prevail but do not necessarily become identical with nation-states. Moreover, authority, power and decision-making are not centralised but layered, decentralised to the local, micro-regional, national and macro-regional/supranational levels. This is basically the idea of the EU as outlined in the Maastricht Treaty. The three pillars – market integration, external security and internal security – together with the social dimension, implying a European form of more or less regulated welfare capitalism, do cover the essential functions of an organised political community or a region-state. There is no doubt whatsoever that relations between these functions – theorised in the form of 'spill over effects' in the old regionalism – will appear sooner or later as a matter of course. For regions other than Europe this may be far into the future, but should by no means be ruled out. Stranger things have happened in history. Besides, we do not suggest repetitions of a European path, simply that the decreasing nation-state capacity will give room for a multi-level governance structure, where the regional level for historical and pragmatic reasons will play a significant role. Thus we assume that some kind of equilibrium between the levels of governance will appear before a 'region-state' in the stronger ('Orwellian') sense of the word takes shape.

Conclusion

It may be safely said that the New Regionalism is here to stay. Few areas of the world are still not organised into regional formations, but the reasons for forming regions, the actual forms this process will take and the role of various types of actors will show a varying pattern of regionalisation. The dynamics of regionalisation and particularly its consolidation into increasing levels of regionness is still in search of theory. If we have made but a small contribution to this, we have succeeded in our effort.

We started out discussing some meta-theoretical postulates, the most important being that in the present world order, *relevant social science theory is global social theory*, and therefore theorising the rise of regionness must form part of that. The regional level will be increasingly important but it may not necessarily predominate. Rather, the world system will operate on many levels. A number of important questions will have to be handled on the global level; the nation-state will not disappear but its functions and organisation will change. Under the nation-state there will emerge an increasingly large number of collective identities reasserting themselves on various levels of the world system. Thus the future is multilayered, but the regional dimension will remain crucial and worthy of continued research.

Since globalisation is the main contemporary challenge, many regionalisation processes and experiments are initiated from quite different starting points in terms of regionness. Globalisation and regionalisation processes are closely related and interact under different conditions, creating a variety of pathways of regionalisation, and by implication also leading to different regionalisms.

The social constructivist approach was also mentioned as one theoretical building block for the construction of the NRT, bearing in mind that regions are large 'imagined communities' and that regionalisation is carried out by many different actors. We have thus emphasized the fact that the actors behind regionalist projects are not only states, but a large number of different types of institutions, organisations and movements and non-state actors, such as domestic firms, transnational corporations, NGOs and other types of social networks and social movements. Together they contribute to the formation of a ('real') transnational regional economy and civil society. It appears that economic, social and cultural networks are developing more quickly than the formal political cooperation at the regional level. We therefore need detailed empirical (comparative case) studies on the strength and relationship between various types of state, market and civil society induced processes of regionalisation in the various phases of the process. Are there typical sequences (or 'spillovers') in these regionalisation processes?

The comparative approach was finally seen as one important step towards theory, and a framework based on the concept of regionness was built for that purpose. The five levels of regionness – regional space, regional complex, regional society, regional community and finally region-state – may express a certain evolutionary logic. However, the idea is not to suggest a stage theory, because there is nothing deterministic or inherently evolutionary about the emergence, spread and consolidation of regionalisation. As was made clear above, we do not anticipate a single path or detailed 'series of stages' that are (exactly) the same for all regions and that must be passed in order for higher levels of regionness to occur.

The concept of regionness is heuristic; it constitutes a natural history of regionalisation, which makes it easier to pinpoint the specificities of real world regionalisations. Between regionness and theory there is a need for comparative research based on issues which are significant for theory building in that they refer to the constitutive elements of each 'natural history phase of regionalisation'.

In the era of globalisation, new larger structures beyond the state are obviously preferable to political regression into micro-polities. However, an all-encompassing global organisation is simply premature, and therefore the region-based territorial order – 'regional multilateralism' – seems to possess a stability and equality that a completely globalised order, assuming that this is at all a possibility, would lack (Hettne *et al.*, 1999). A regionalised world order will still be hierarchic, and the way to horizontalise this order and create 'regional multilateralism' is for the peripheral regions to increase their level of 'regionness' through security and development regionalisms. Since regionalisation is a response to specific challenges related to globalisation, the driving factor may differ depending on the specific encounter between various social forces and actors, and the particular level of regionness at hand. Thus if trade agreements and market harmonisation represent the major task in one case, regional conflict resolution or ecological crisis management may be the predominant issues in others.

Notes

1 This chapter is a revised version of our contribution to the special issue of *New Political Economy* 4 (4).
2 In effect we seek to move from what is known as the New Regionalism Approach

(NRA) towards the NRT, using the concept of regionness as the building block. The NRA was one of the main analytical tools used within the UNU/WIDER research project on *The New Regionalism*. See Hettne and Söderbaum, 1998a; Hettne *et al.* 1999, 2000a, 2000b, 2000c; Schulz *et al.* (2001).

3 See also the special issues of *World Politics*, The role of theory in comparative politics. A symposium', 48(1), 1995, and 'The future of regional studies', *Africa Today* 44(2), 1997.

4 As a consequence of our ambition to move towards a more coherent theoretical construct, it should be noted that the present version of regionness differs slightly compared with previous formulations made by Hettne, and Hettne and Söderbaum. See Hettne, 1993, 1999; Hettne and Söderbaum, 1998b.

5 We are sympathetic towards a recent approach developed by Adler and Barnett (1998a). The similarities and differences between our two approaches are further elaborated upon in our article in the special issue of *New Political Economy* (4). Some differences that ought to be mentioned here are: (1) Adler and Barnett start from a system of states, whereas our idea of NRT may be applied also to historical periods that precede (and proceed) the state system; (2) compared to Adler and Barnett, we are inclined to argue that the NRT is less state-centric, less 'formal', and more explicitly includes the agency of non-state actors and transnational forces; (3) whereas Adler and Barnett claim that security communities do not have to be geographically contiguous and tied to geographical space, territoriality as a basis for community is basic to our approach; (4) Adler and Barnett are concerned with non-war communities and 'negative peace', whereas the NRT is founded on that security, peace, and the political economy of development and culture should be integrated within the same analytical framework, thus emphasising their intrinsic relationship rather than differences; (5) although Adler and Barnett certainly recognise the phenomenon, the NRT framework is more 'global' in nature and explicitly takes into consideration that regionalisation is taking shape within the overall context of globalisation, i.e. regions are constructed not only through the inside-out but also through the outside-in.

4 The trade–environment nexus and the potential of regional trade institutions

Morten Bøås

Introduction – the regional potential?

The popularity of regional arrangements in some circles is built largely on the perception that such arrangements will help resolve collective action problems on the global level.[1] The argument is that in areas where the 'tragedy of commons' and the 'problem of big numbers' are notorious, global negotiations are often inefficient, and the implementation of agreements once agreed ineffective. One reason lies in the difficulty of aggregating the interests of a great number of actors into a common policy position. Another lies in supervising implementation. As such, advocates of state-led formal regionalism often argue that the regional level may aggregate individual national policy positions on to a joint position *vis-à-vis* third parties and thus facilitate both the establishment and the implementation of global multilateral agreement.

In order to try to assess such an argument, this chapter will look at how three organisations for regional co-operation – the Association for Southeast Asian Nations (ASEAN), the European Union (EU) and the North American Free Trade Agreement (NAFTA) – deal with the trade–environment nexus both internally and externally. The argument put forward here is that there is no necessity that the establishment of various layers of regional governance in the world political economy will enhance the possibility of common global policy within this specific issue-area. That said, the establishment of regional governance layers could facilitate joint positions with respect to regional third parties and/or to global negotiations. However, for this to happen the states that constitute a region must reach common agreement on what their position within an issue-area such as the trade–environment nexus actually should be. As we will see from the analysis of ASEAN, the EU and NAFTA, this is most often much easier said than done. Even the most institutionalised regional scheme in the world, the EU, has huge problems in coming to terms with this issue-area internally. In fact, of these three regional schemes the one with the most coherent external position – ASEAN – is also the one least likely to promote global governance within this issue-area. The reason is that all ASEAN member countries resist the trade–environment linkage.

Governance and the trade–environment nexus

Governance may be seen as a social function aimed at making collective choices with respect to matters of common concern for a specific group of people (Young, 1995). Regional governance is thus the set of social functions concerned with making collective choices among people delineated by geographical proximity and other shared notions of sameness. It takes place within an international region delimited by some sort of geographical proximity.[2] As such, regional governance is concerned with the regime that constitutes the set of fundamental rules for the organisation of the regional public realm, and not only with regional intergovernmental institutions in the narrow sense. Both regional governance and regional intergovernmental institutions refer to goal-oriented activities and systems of rule, but whereas regional intergovernmental institutions suggests constituted policies backed by formal authority, regional governance refers to activities backed up by shared goals that may or may not derive from legal and formal authority (Rosenau, 1992). Regional governance clearly embraces regional intergovernmental institutions, but it also subsumes non-governmental institutions operating within the public realm.

As a system of rule, regional governance is therefore as dependent on intersubjective meanings as on formally sanctioned constitutions and charters: it will only work if it is accepted by the majority (or at least by the most powerful actors within the regional system). Subsequently, regional governance is equivalent to the management of regime structures for the purpose of enhancing the legitimacy of the regional public realm. Thus, regional governance and actual regional policy-making are both separated and interwoven entities. Good regional governance not only ensures the legitimacy of the regime that governs the regional public realm, it also confers legitimacy on the actual regional decision-makers.[3] The question, then, concerns the actual potential for regional governance of the trade–environment nexus.

One obvious challenge is that there is neither academic nor political consensus as to the necessity of linking trade and environment policies. Scholars have argued that unrestricted international exchange of goods and services will cause severe environmental degradation (Lang and Hines, 1993), that trade instruments do not provide an appropriate mechanism for environmental protection (Anderson and Blackhurst, 1992), or that trade barriers will be, at most, a second best way of reducing environmental degradation (Dean, 1992). There is also an abundance of charges that linking environment considerations to trade policy is an implicit protectionist measure. For instance, it has been argued that 'the trade/environment area has an above average risk of being exploited by special interest groups to their own benefit at the expense of the general interest. More specifically, the risk is that traditional protectionist groups will manipulate environmental concerns in order to reduce competition from imports' (Anderson and Blackhurst, 1992: 20–1).

This chapter makes no a priori assumption with regard to the inherent nature of the tension between trade and environment: there is no inherent logic, economic or other, that generally determines whether trade liberalisation (deregulation) and environment protection (regulation) stand in conflict or are reconcilable. Trade liberalisation may damage the environment by giving governments incentives to relax environmental policies (deregulation) in order to give their producers a competitive edge. However, one may also point to reasons why the effectiveness of environmental deregulation may be low or even reversed. Through processes of environmental regulation economic actors may adopt strategic behaviour in dealing with political and institutional factors. By allowing for strategic behaviour by and interaction among producers, the incentives for the government to keep environmental standards could be reversed.

The general trend, however, is that deregulation as either decreasing the field of legal regulation or as replacing public regulation (e.g. command-control) with other means and methods (e.g. market-based incentives) is on the rise (Bándi, 1996). Both in the United States and in the EU new schemes of environmental protection have been introduced which are designed to encourage collaboration between state and market. These new schemes tend to favour the use of market forces over traditional command-control approaches to environmental protection. The name of the game for environmental protection in the new millennium seems to be 'environmental protection through deregulation'; in other words, another type of environmental governance than the one prescribed by the command/control approach.[4]

In practice, different regional arrangements have taken different positions on this issue. The fifteen countries that constitute the EU have formally agreed on the necessity of linking trade and environment within the multilateral framework of the World Trade Organisation (WTO). In NAFTA, trade and environment are linked, at least partly, through the NAFTA side agreement on the environment. The ASEAN member countries have expressed outspoken resistance against such linkages. Thus the remainder of this chapter is dedicated to an attempt to document how nation-states through regional trade institutions such as ASEAN, the EU and NAFTA have tried to respond to the challenges that the trade–environment nexus represents to them. The idea is that such documentation can help to clarify the real potential (if any) of regional trade institutions within the trade–environment nexus.

The trade–environment nexus: the regional response

ASEAN

For many developing countries and/or newly industrialising countries the main objective of regionalism is to recapture collective autonomy in relation to the EU and the United States, and to begin to organise a competitive response to the Japanese challenge (Streek and Schmitter, 1991). The objective behind the establishment of ASEAN is however somewhat different. As an international institution ASEAN was originally established in 1967 and today comprises Brunei, Indonesia, Malaysia, the Philippines, Singapore, Thailand, Vietnam, Laos and Myanmar.[5] ASEAN's primary objectives are to promote security, economic growth, and social and cultural development in the sub-region. Historically, political and military security were the most important aspects of the ASEAN agenda and constituted the main factors behind its establishment. It was formed as a deliberate political act, as a bulwark against what was perceived to be the spread of world communism in the sub-region. 'Not only were internal threats more pressing, but mutual co-operation against transborder movement of communist guerrillas, including intelligence-sharing, mutual extradition treaties, and joint border patrols and counter-insurgency operations served as an important basis for intra-ASEAN solidarity' (Acharya, 1998).

As recently as the late 1980s Thai and Vietnamese forces clashed on the Cambodian border. Its ASEAN partners and the West backed Thailand, while Hanoi was supported by the former Soviet Union.[6] However, the end of the Cold War has completely changed this part of Asia's geopolitics. ASEAN, which used to look at the regional security framework as a defence mechanism against external and internal communist threats (present or perceived), is currently adopting a broader perception of it that includes economic and environmental components as well. Following the completion of the Uruguay Round, the initiative to form the Asia-Pacific Economic Cooperation (APEC) Forum, and unilateral liberalisation in a growing number of ASEAN countries, ASEAN ministers agreed in September 1995 to accelerate its plan to create a regional trade bloc with a combined market of 420 million consumers by 2003. It was agreed to increase the number of items with tariff rates reduced to between zero to 5 per cent by 2000, and to give members of ASEAN Free trade Area (AFTA) concessions in the service sector more favourable than those agreed in the WTO (Yue, 1998).[7] The decision came as a response to an initiative taken by Brunei and Singapore which were afraid that ASEAN would be left behind by other regional trade groupings: 'AFTA must move faster than other free-trade areas. I have therefore proposed at the ASEAN ministerial meeting last month that we advance the time frame for the realisation of AFTA to the year 2000' (Bolkiah, 1995).[8]

The accelerated pace of AFTA's development both in scope and depth contrasts with the patchy start to the regional free trade zone. It is therefore reasonable to assume that the acceleration is a response to competition from other foreign regional schemes, reflecting at the same time a new perception of economic security. The main concern of the ASEAN countries is to keep the competitive edge, which has helped them carve out substantial shares of the world market.

ASEAN and the environment

ASEAN has developed a Strategic Plan of Action on the Environment, which among other elements aims to strengthen the legal and institutional capacity to implement international environmental agreements, and to harmonise ambient air and river water quality standards. The association has also developed an ASEAN Co-operation Plan on Transboundary Pollution that covers the programme areas of transboundary atmospheric pollution, transboundary ship-borne pollution, and transboundary movement of hazardous waste between member countries.

ASEAN's concern for the environment of its member countries has grown lately, but ASEAN governments still appear to believe that too much emphasis on environmental issues and policies could dampen the region's economic development. Environmental concerns are therefore directed towards problems directly affecting living conditions and population health, not towards broader environmental issues such as global warming and biodiversity. In light of the recent financial crisis in the ASEAN countries, considerable political will is necessary to mitigate further serious degradation of the natural resource base. The presence of such a will can be questioned. Nationally, all ASEAN countries have formally enacted various environmental laws and regulations, but the institutional capacity for developing, implementing and particularly for enforcing environmental measures is still limited. The Indonesian forest fires that annually spew smoke over neighbouring Malaysia and Singapore illustrate the enforcement problem. This is clearly a regional issue that ASEAN should have addressed, but when the smoke spews over its member countries ASEAN as a regional institution keeps its head down. So far, ASEAN environment ministers have primarily used ASEAN as a chair for co-ordinating environmental policy positions on the international agenda and to demand stronger commitment from the Western countries towards the global environment and the Rio Earth Summit Declaration.

Sooner or later the ASEAN countries will have to face considerable environmental challenges because Asia is the most polluted and environmentally degraded region in the world.

> During the past 30 years, Asia has lost half its forest cover, and with it countless unique animal and plant species. A third of its agricultural land has been degraded. Fish stocks have fallen by 50 per cent. No other region has as many heavily polluted cities, and its rivers and lakes are among the world's most polluted. In short, Asia's environment has been under attack. While rapid economic development has created dynamism and wealth, Asia has at the same time become dirtier, less ecological diverse, and more environmentally vulnerable.
>
> (ADB, 1997: 199)

In itself this is not a big surprise. The environment suffered during the industrialisation of Western Europe, North America and Japan as well, but because Asia's economic transformation has taken place faster than anywhere else, the environmental impact seems to be worse.[9] Furthermore, Asian policy-makers ignored the environmental impact of rapid growth for too long. Concern about the environment was not a priority, rather, the mentality was one of 'grow now, clean up later'. When the governments finally got going, the environmental regulations they adopted were ineffectively designed and not well implemented. The imposed environmental standards were often neither monitored nor enforced. In short, as the example with the Indonesian forest fires illustrates, several of these governments seem to lack the institutional capacity and/or political willingness to enforce their own standards. As the governments' political will to confront these issues can be questioned, one could argue that further trade liberalisation may exacerbate the environmental problems because environmental costs are not being sufficiently internalised. They are not reflected in the prices for goods and services. The importance placed on attracting foreign direct investments may also increase the pressure for resource extraction from pristine natural ecosystems and mitigate attempts to introduce higher environmental standards.

At least in the short to medium term, a greater emphasis on environmental concerns and increased opportunities to promote convergence with trade issues would appear to be largely dependent on pressure from abroad, on TNC policies, and on the growth of civil society, including further democratisation in the ASEAN countries. Promotion of civil society depends *inter alia* on the role of NGOs, and their record to date appears at best mixed (Eccleston and Potter, 1996).

Like other developing/newly industrialising countries the ASEAN countries are faced with the possibility that more stringent environmental standards can not only make their products less competitive, but could also be used as a non-tariff barrier against them. Such scenarios are in particular threatening for the ASEAN countries because economic growth in these countries occurred simultaneously with stagnant and not increased intra-ASEAN trade. Rather, it was concurrent with a tremendous increase in trade with non-ASEAN countries (Azis, 1996). The guiding economic principle of the ASEAN countries has traditionally been to seek economic growth through improved competitiveness in global markets, and not by giving preferential access to other ASEAN member countries.

The two most commonly cited environmental standards in trade are product standards related to production methods and eco-labelling. These are particularly important for the ASEAN countries because about 60 per cent of the value of their manufacturing exports originates in sectors with potentially significant environmental impacts. Product standards can reduce market access because they may be formulated in such a way that domestic industries find it easier to conform to them. Eco-labelling is in principle voluntary. The intention is to give consumers the ability to express their demand for environmental conservation by buying environmentally friendly products. Nevertheless, eco-labelling can also be biased against imported products.

So far, the main response from ASEAN to these challenges has been to argue with force that issue-areas such as the trade–environment nexus should not be included on the WTO agenda. Their argument is that they are not and never have been at the heart of the GATT agreement. In the WTO debate on the trade–environment nexus ASEAN has accused Western powers such as the EU and the United States of hypocrisy, claiming that the attempt to raise environmental standards in other countries is not motivated by environmental concerns, but by increased unemployment and the desire to blame this problem on unsound exploitation of the environment by trading partners such as the ASEAN countries. For example, the ASEAN reaction to Western criticism of forest degradation in Indonesia and Malaysia has come in the form of counter arguments such as 'it seems odd that the argument put forth by DCs often refers to the compulsion to safeguard the global environment (ozone layer), the present quality of which has been thoroughly affected by DC's past production and present consumption' (Aziz, 1996: 311). In other words, ASEAN's main argument against what ASEAN interprets as Western insistence on uniform environmental standards is that Western countries grew rich by polluting the global environment, but now these countries want to force the expenses from this development strategy on newly industrialising countries as well. ASEAN acknowledges that it is quite likely that in the years to come various environmental issues in the ASEAN countries will be brought by the region's trading partners into the trade policy debate. None the less, ASEAN's response is that this is just too bizarre. According to ASEAN, trade is not, and never has been, the cause of environmental problems. Subsequently, trade sanctions cannot and will not affect the root cause of such problems. ASEAN admits that its member countries should try to do more to protect their local environments, but not because they have to comply with demands made by trading partners. National environmental policies and standards are an integrated part of a country's national development strategy. External attempts to influence such policies and standards are equivalent to infringements of the national sovereignty of the ASEAN countries.[10]

The core of the ASEAN position is that national competitiveness is the single most important concern for trade, and not global commons like ozone depletion, climate change or endangered species. The trade–environment nexus is therefore regarded by ASEAN as a reflection of the West's 'export of ideology', which if forced upon them could diminish their economic growth and subsequently place in jeopardy the legitimacy of the political regimes in the ASEAN region. At the heart of the matter is therefore also the (in)famous debate about universality: one either interprets the right to development and affluence as a prerequisite for environmental awareness (e.g. 'grow now, clean up later') as ASEAN contends, or believes that today the opposite is the correct strategy (as ASEAN believes that the West thinks).

The question is what kind of implications these differences will have for the economic (and political) relationship between ASEAN and both its individual trading partners and other regional and global trading arrangements as well. At worst, the trade relations between ASEAN and other countries/multilateral trading arrangements could be constantly threatened by tension and conflict. At best, some sort of compromise will be reached as the WTO settles down to start working again on all the issues that became clouded with tear-gas at the Seattle meeting in late 1999. However, so far, the achievements of the trade–environment nexus within the context of the WTO have been small.

NAFTA

The implementation of NAFTA in January 1994 created a free trade area comprising Canada, Mexico and the United States. This agreement created the world's largest free trade zone, stretching from the Yukon to the Yucatan, with a combined gross national product of approximately $6 trillion. NAFTA is in fact a novelty in the history of regionalisation because it contemplates virtually complete free trade (in ten to fifteen years) between two highly developed countries and one developing country, where the latter receives no special and differentiated treatment apart from different time frames for the implementation of some measures.

The NAFTA treaty includes provisions similar to those found in GATT/WTO regarding most favoured nation treatment, national treatment, rules of origin and customs procedures. According to the agreement the three countries are to eliminate prohibitions and quantitative restrictions applied at the border, such as quotas and import licences. In addition, NAFTA includes provisions designed to reduce barriers to trade in services. These provisions remove significant investment barriers, ensure basic protection for NAFTA investors, provide a mechanism to resolve disputes between investors and NAFTA countries and set out certain basic protection for intellectual property rights.

Supporters of NAFTA have pointed to the treaty's environmental virtues (Esty, 1994). It is a fact that in the NAFTA preamble the signatories make commitments not only to environmental protection, but also to the promotion of sustainable development. The main elements in the side agreement are the Commission for Environmental Co-operation and the Dispute Settlement Mechanism. During the negotiations between the three countries important differences surfaced. Both the Canadian and the Mexican drafts proposed a weaker commission than the US, in which the Commission's secretariat would be less independent of ministerial control (Kelly, 1993). The US preferred a more powerful institution, with greater independence and less subject to national control. With respect to the Mexican position, it reflected both political tradition as well as fear of losing national control.

> If such an institution frequently would issue complaints, recommendations and demands, the Mexicans would end up in a response situation where much time, energy and resources would end up being directed towards responding to allegations and recommendations forwarded by the commission.
>
> (Brænden, 1996)

The outcome of the negotiations was a trinational Commission for Environmental Co-operation (CEC), which provides for the parties a structure to study issues, form working groups and solve problems of common concern. The following bodies constitute the commission: the Council, the Secretariat and the Joint Public Advisory Committee. The environmental ministers of the three parties constitute the Council, and it is supported by a full-time permanent and independent secretariat. The Council has the power to appoint arbitration panels, if it is requested by one or more of the parties, in order to investigate complaints on persistent patterns of non-compliance with environmental laws. The Secretariat has the power to independently prepare reports for the Council, but the most important function of the Secretariat is that it can decide whether complaints from NGOs or individuals should be submitted to the parties with the request of a response. Five representatives of civil society make up a joint advisory committee from each country. This committee is supposed to advise the Council on any matter within the scope of the agreement.

It is quite clear that on the whole it was US preferences that prevailed during the negotiations. The Secretariat was granted independent capacity to investigate issues of environmental concern between the parties, and the Commission was also granted more independent power than Mexico preferred.

The differences between the concerned parties were pretty much the same as above with respect to the issue of trade sanctions. The US position was that sanctions were to be allowed for persistent and unjustifiable patterns of non-enforcement of a country's environmental laws. If the Council or the parties themselves were unable to solve the dispute, NAFTA benefits could be suspended. The Mexican position on enforcement was that if a country systematically failed to enforce domestic law in order to attract or retain investment, the other member countries could request that the state against which the allegations were made should make a full report to the Council. The Council could then recommend further action. Trade sanctions were not contemplated in the Mexican position. The heaviest sanction advocated by the Mexicans was to make the Council's recommendations public unless otherwise agreed by the parties (*Inside US Special Trade Report*, 21 May 1993). With respect to the Canadian position, their point of departure in the negotiations was to oppose the incorporation of trade sanctions in the side agreement. According to Saunders (1994), Canada's insistence on the avoidance of trade sanctions was rooted in a long-standing distrust of US willingness to use trade sanctions for protectionist ends, but the Canadian Prime Minister Brian Mulroney also argued publicly that trade sanctions were antithetical to the philosophy of free trade agreements. In an effort to break the impasse in the negotiations that had been created by the different national positions, Canada proposed that fines against governments could serve as an alternative to trade sanctions as an enforcement measure. However, such a solution would have created legal problems in the US,[11] and Mexico rejected the proposal as a clear and undesired infringement of national sovereignty. In the end, therefore, the negotiations ended with the establishment of a dispute settlement mechanism which is supposed to ensure that the parties effectively enforce their domestic environmental laws. In the NAFTA side agreement, found to have a persistent pattern of failure to effectively enforce their environmental laws are required to correct the problem (e.g. to implement the recommendations from the Council). If the accused party does not implement the recommendations, the Council can impose a fine of up to $20 million in the first year. If the party complained against still refuses to act on the complaint or to pay the fine, it will be liable to trade sanctions or, in the case of Canada, the decision may be enforced against the government in court. The dispute settlement mechanism is, however, a complex and long process that must be initiated by the governments (through the ministers in the Commission), and there are many hurdles to jump before the process reaches the dispute panel stage.

The dispute settlement procedure[12]

1   consultation on whether there has been a persistent failure to effectively enforce environmental laws;

2   special session of the Council;
3   convening of an arbitration panel;
4   presenting an initial and final report to the panel;
5   making an action plan;
6   if non-agreement with the action plan, approval by the panel or fines;
7   if continued non-compliance NAFTA benefits are suspended.

The test for potential sanctions is whether there is a 'persistent pattern' of failure to enforce effectively domestic environmental laws.[13] It may prove very difficult to prove that this is the case, but this is also the element that makes NAFTA a unique international agreement.

> Under the Environmental Agreement, NAFTA parties are committed to enforcing their domestic environmental laws. This is the first time such commitments have been made in an international agreement, and the Agreement creates mechanisms to ensure that they are carried through.
>
> (Carol Browner, Administrator EPA,
> NAFTA Testimony, 10 November 1993)

In the end, therefore, the US succeeded in its efforts to establish trade sanctions as the last deterrent against persistent non-enforcement of environmental laws. But the final solution was broadened to include fines in the case of Canada as opposed to trade sanctions in the case of Mexico and the US.

Canada's successful resistance against trade sanctions may be interpreted in three interwoven ways:

1   The *raison d'état* behind the side agreement was environmental problems at the US–Mexican border.
2   Canada already had the Free Trade Agreement with the US, and wanted NAFTA for strategic reasons.
3   The US has much more confidence in the Canadian legal system than in the Mexican courts.

None of these arguments really favoured too much pressure on Canada from the US. The side agreement was directed towards Mexico, and not Canada.

Another example often put forward by NAFTA protagonists is NAFTA's treatment of trade obligations imposed by international environmental agreements. A number of environmental treaties require nations to restrict or prohibit trade in harmful goods, but NAFTA provides that trade obligations set out in a limited and specified number of international treaties 'shall prevail' over any inconsistencies in NAFTA.[14] Although NAFTA supporters claim that this provision affirms the supremacy of international environmental agreements, not all measures taken pursuant to international environmental obligations 'shall prevail' over NAFTA obligations. Rather, it seems that such measures will survive NAFTA scrutiny only 'provided that where a Party has a choice among equally effective and reasonably available means of complying with such obligations, the Party chooses the alternative that is the least inconsistent with the other provisions of this agreement' (NAFTA, supra note 115, art. 104 [1]).

This language seems to follow closely the 'least trade restrictive' interpretation given to the term 'necessary' found in the Article XX exemption clause of the GATT,[15] and moreover, this provision contrasts sharply with NAFTA's treatment of pre-existing tax conventions, the provisions of which expressly and unconditionally take precedence over any inconsistent NAFTA provisions.

Another formal exception with NAFTA is that it addresses the question of 'pollution havens'. In response to concern that a NAFTA party might lower its environmental standards to attract foreign investments, NAFTA provides that 'a Party should not waive or otherwise derogate from domestic environmental measures to encourage foreign investment'.[16]

However, a nation that believes another party is lowering its environmental standards to encourage foreign direct investment and thereby failing to honour the NAFTA provision quoted above cannot utilise the formal NAFTA dispute settlement process to resolve this issue. Instead, the nation can only request consultations with the allegedly offending nation with a view to avoiding any encouragement of foreign direct investment though relaxation of environmental measures.

There is truth in the claim made by NAFTA supporters that the agreement represents a new and fresh regional approach towards the trade–environment nexus, but it is also obvious that there are several weaknesses in NAFTA. Questions concerned with legitimacy can be raised. For instance, the side agreement did not define clearly the actual relation between trade and environment. Only the dispute mechanism procedure is set up with qualification procedure: the problem must have a trade nexus. And as this definition is very likely to be interpreted differently, the question of how legitimate the NAFTA partners think the trade–environment linkage really is is lurking around the corner. The side agreement was an American invention directed against Mexico, which Mexico was not able to resist during the negotiation, but the fact that definitions and procedures are unclear entail that capable agents have sufficient space to try to influence the functioning of the institution. As long as actors have different motivations for linking and/or accepting linkages in agreements, the fruitfulness of the trade–environment nexus in terms of its contribution to sustainable development can be overrated if we do not have a proper understanding of why the nexus was initiated and for what strategic purposes. Therefore, it is perhaps true that the fact that the trade–environment relation remained unspecified is a good illustration of the strong symbolic aspects of the side agreement (Brænden, 1996). However, in politics symbols are not unimportant, and NAFTA's role as an example of co-operative regionalisation (although highly asymmetrical) across the former North–South divide is important within a trade–environment debate which quite often seems to re-create the 'new international economic order' cleavages of the 1970s between developed and developing countries.

The European Union

The case of the EU is somewhat distinct compared to the two other regional arrangements that are analysed in this chapter. The EU is the regional arrangement with the broadest mandate, it has a wider range of legal instruments at its disposal than have other regional arrangements, and in contrast to ASEAN and NAFTA it is a truly global actor. It is the world's largest trading bloc, and the sheer size of its market gives it incomparable potential influence on both international trade policies and international environmental policies (Bretherton and Vogler, 1999). Given the high level of institutionalisation, it thus reflects the 'hardest' regional project and provides therefore an interesting 'ideal' case of the opportunities for and constraints to governance at the regional level.

The search for European unity and governance is driven by two competing visions. These are based on the notion that competitiveness requires constant-wide approaches, but they lead to opposite results. The first idea holds that market forces should operate on a continental basis, and subsequently the process of European integration should provide greater access to third parties. The second idea assumes that in terms of intervention and rules, the social-environmental dimension should operate similarly. This leads to a Europe that is more protectionist and closed to outsiders (Lawrence, 1994b; Sideri, 1997).

The point is that the EU as an avant-garde of regionalisation with considerable economic clout has forced the rest of the world to conform increasingly to its standards, to reduce their barrier to EU exports and to seek lower entry barriers for their products in the EU market by concluding special associational agreements with it or, where possible, to join it. However, this is just one dimension of the EU picture. The EU, as the most institutionalised example so far of regional socio-economic governance, shows that trade represents just one part of a much more complex and dynamic economic system constructed by the interaction of services, technology, advanced and integrated public infrastructures and corporate cross-border networking strategies.

European-based companies rather than simply seeking exports and economies of scale, are developing Euro-wide delivery systems, corporate alliances, production networks and electronic marketplaces. The profound restructuring they are carrying out involves seeking customised, in-depth interactions with clients, suppliers and partners through an expanding gamut of networking strategies, many of which have a strong information and advanced communication content. In this they are supported by Community programmes such as RACE, ESPRIT, EUREKA, Erasmus and Comet, and institutions like ETSI (European Telecommunications Standardisation Institute) (Sideri, 1997: 55).

Economic competitiveness (trade) was highly instrumental in the formation of the European Economic Community in 1957, and whereas other objectives such as environmental protection have gained currency, competitiveness is still of primary importance in the EU. At the same time there has been some recognition of the necessity to integrate trade/competitiveness issues and environmental concerns. The Single European Act as well as the Treaty on the European Union explicitly state the principle of environmental policy integration and introduce the notion that there need not be a trade-off between seeking a higher level of environmental protection and creating internationally competitive economic structures in Europe. This is also the central message of the Fifth Environmental Action Programme. The 1993 Commission *White Paper on Growth, Competitiveness and Employment* discussed the notion of a 'double dividend', for example, the integration of environmental protection with economic growth through a reform of the tax system and support of the environmental technology sector. The 1996 Communication on Trade and Environment discussed the compatibility of environmental protection measures with the expansion of liberal trading relations on a global scale (under the GATT/WTO). However, these ideas have so far not been translated into policy, and competitiveness and environmental policies continue to be pursued along separate tracks. There has been much environmental rhetoric but little systematic effort at analysing and responding to the links between competitiveness and environmental protection at the EU level.

At the EU level, globalisation has coincided with greater calls for subsidiarity as a number of member states have become disenchanted with the increased centralisation of policy-making at the EU level. At the same time, the adoption of sustainability as a goal in EU policy-making has led to calls for 'shared responsibility' (through the Fifth Environmental Action Programme). In principle, subsidiarity and shared responsibility could mean a more decentralised type of decision-making with a greater participation from and co-operation among all relevant actors, which could be compatible with both environmental and competitiveness objectives. However, claims have been made that instead these concerns with the appropriate level of policy-making are leading to both re-nationalisation and deregulation, with a disproportionate influence from industry, referring to competitiveness issues as a reason for less stringent action. For instance, in 1993 the influential European Round Table of Industrialists[17] called for significant changes to the extent and nature of the European regulatory framework as part of their plan to restore European competitiveness. Furthermore, this way of thinking was echoed in communication from the Commission. In a speech in 1994, Bernard Delogu, a leading DG XI official in charge of environmental auditing and control of industrial installations, stated that future European environmental legislation would be strongly influenced by the concept of market forces and less dependent on command and control regulation.[18]

The driving force behind the shift from command-control (regulation) to market forces (deregulation) was concern in the EU about the erosion of European competitiveness.[19] In April 1994, the British and German governments set up a group of business leaders as part of an effort to curb the effects of what was perceived as over-regulation in the EU. In spring 1995, this group called on the Commission to scrap the Directive on Dangerous Substances, revise the Drinking Water Directive and amend proposals for Integrated Pollution Prevention and Control (Grant, 1996). Furthermore, the alliance established between Britain and Germany continued to press for further deregulation at the Corfu European Summit. At this summit, Britain supported Germany's request for the establishment of a group of businessmen and civil servants in order to examine whether the EU and national legislation was imposing unnecessary burdens on companies. With a mandate from the summit to examine national and EU-wide legislation and their effects on competitiveness and job creation and to recommend how regulations could be abolished or simplified, the committee went to work.

Its conclusions were presented to the Cannes Summit in June 1995. It did not call for widespread deregulation. Nevertheless, it did state that regulatory frameworks must be reviewed if competitiveness and employment objectives were to be achieved, and hence environmental and other regulations were identified as creating additional burdens for companies. In short, the argument was that the 'playing field needed levelling'. However, the Commission defended the benefits of regulation with the argument that 'a good regulatory framework sets out the [limits] within which the businessman knows he can operate freely' (*Financial Times*, 23 June 1995).

In other words, whereas claims that 'shared responsibility' leads deregulation and a disproportionate influence from industry are unsubstantiated, questions do arise about the future of environmental protection in the EU in a context of increased economic globalisation and political struggles over the EU's governance structures. It has, for instance, been suggested that with respect to the question of environmental deregulation in Europe firms are applying the game of competition in two different arenas: the policy area and the competitive arena.

> A firm's ability to influence the outcomes in the regulatory arena depends on its position in the competitive arenas; symmetrically, its competitive position depends, [in] the medium and long run, on its ability to secure advantages on the policy arena, so that the two chessboards interact with each other in a complex way.
>
> (Brusco *et al.*, 1996: 133)

However, a firm is not just any firm, and evidence from the EU seems to suggest that, in general, the balance of the advantage in both arenas is with the larger firm, although the difference is more marked in the policy arena than in the competitive arena (Grant, 1996). Larger firms have better access to and greater possibilities to influence the agenda of environmental deregulation in the EU whereas the competitiveness of smaller firms is likely to be more adversely affected by existing and proposed regulations. Large firms are (de)regulation makers, small firms are (de)regulation takers (Lévèque, 1996).

Another contested area for deregulation is the transport sector and EU policies regarding governance of the transport–environment nexus. The main problem is that both from a legal and historical perspective, European transport policies were designed to serve the objective of European integration, and not environmental protection. The environmental dimension must therefore try to find its niche within the generic objective of European/market integration (Hey, 1997). Thus, until recently, taxes on road transport have been treated by the EU mainly as a harmonisation problem. The building of a common European transport market entailed liberalisation of intra-EU transport and a step-by-step opening of national markets for non-resident hauliers (cabotage). This created tension between member states with high vehicle taxes, no direct charges for road use and an attractive internal transport market (particularly in Germany). On the other side stood those whose national hauliers were expected to gain the main profits from the opening of markets. This group comprised the Netherlands, Belgium and Denmark. For instance, the Dutch hauliers are among the most efficient in Europe and, in addition, they enjoyed lower tax burdens than did their German competitors. This made the German government, and in particular the Ministry of Transport (which is traditionally considered to have a close relationship wirh the national hauliers' association) block any further step towards the opening of markets as long as there was no agreement on parallel harmonisation measures. Germany insisted on the harmonisation of annual vehicle taxes at a high level, and argued for the introduction of road-user charges built on the principle of territoriality. As a consequence of the German position, charges would have to be paid where the infrastructure was actually used and not only in a vehicle's home country. Apart from fiscal motivations and Germany's obvious will to defend its national road transport industry, in order to sustain and strengthen its position the German government also argued strongly that high taxes were needed in order to ensure that road transport contributed to the total infrastructural and environmental costs. This conflict was resolved in a political compromise in June 1993. The outcome was an agreement around a framework of stepwise deregulation of cabotage until 1998 (see Council Regulation 3118/93), the introduction of minimum levels for vehicle taxes and the introduction of new road-user charges in the Benelux countries, Denmark and Germany (see Eurovignette, Council Directive 93/98). In line with the general spirit of the European Community a compromise was reached about which nobody was extremely thrilled, but which also nobody disliked enough to keep the issue as a top priority on their EU agenda.

In sum, we can say that the system of regionalised governance that is emerging in Europe is both unique and uniquely complex. To some extent the member states seem to become semi-sovereign entities, but on the other side no evidence at hand seems to suggest that they will disappear. The outcome is a complex system of regionalised governance in which the Community's supranational institutions have to share power with national as well as international, transnational and sub-national institutions. Such a system of governance has its strengths – it facilitates the kind of political compromise described above, but it also has its obvious weaknesses. The main one is a profound absence of hierarchy and monopoly among a wide range of players – nations, classes, sectors and firms – of different but uncertain status. The EU is without doubt the regional arrangement with the broadest mandate, with the widest range of legal instruments at its disposal and the highest level of institutionalisation, but it is also clear that even though the EU can be used as a showcase for the opportunities for governance at the regional level, it has not managed to sort out the multitude of constraints against regional governance. The trade–environment nexus is still unsolved within the EU, and the discussion on the compatibility of environmental protection measures with the expansion of liberal trading relations under the supervision of GATT/WTO has not been translated into policy. In short, both the internal and the external dimensions of the trade–environmental nexus continue to be pursued along separate tracks in the EU.

Conclusion – the potential of regional trade institutions?

ASEAN, NAFTA and the EU may be interpreted as kinds of regional governance layers in a globalised world political economy that try to deal with the challenges posed for national actors by the general deregulation of public control over the economy. However, no evidence suggests that they represent a firm barrier against globalisation. On the contrary, they should rather be seen as in-betweens: the regional project is both a part of and a facilitator of globalisation, and a regional counter-governance layer in the world political economy. In other words, no general answer may be offered to the question of whether they can constitute a regional governance basis on which global co-operation can be built. The potential is present (as indicated by the NAFTA experience), but whether we will actually be able to reap these benefits is another matter entirely. This will depend on the actors involved in the regional project, and how they perceive their situation and their contextual relationship to other regional arrangements. It is not just one uniform approach to the trade–environment nexus, but a whole range of approaches. What kind of approach different regions choose is influenced by their various historical trajectories and how the participants involved perceive their socio-economic situation. The legitimacy of the political regimes that constitute ASEAN is built on economic growth. Subsequently, the ASEAN countries are afraid that the trade–environment nexus may constitute an effective barrier against continued ASEAN penetration of overseas markets. ASEAN has therefore argued with force that issues such as the trade–environment nexus should not be included on the WTO agenda. In NAFTA, the trade–environment nexus is formally integrated through the side agreement, but we also saw how the various actors involved in that process clearly had different motivations for linking and/or accepting linkages in the agreement. These differences may decrease the legitimacy of the trade–environment linkage in NAFTA. Even in the EU – the avant-garde of formal regionalisation – the opportunities for governance at the regional level with respect to the trade–environment nexus have not yet materialised. The 15 EU countries have formally agreed to link trade and environment, but the quite advanced generic discussion on the compatibility of environmental protection measures with the expansion of liberal trading relations under the supervision of GATT/WTO has not been translated into policy. The question is: Does this evidence suggest that the idea about a regional governance layer is a 'bridge too far'?

Not necessarily. At least, not if we accept that national governance of interwoven issue-areas such as the trade–environment nexus under the spell of globalisation is more or less impossible. If this is the situation we are faced with, we are in need of new efficient, effective and legitimate governance structures in which some kind of reconciliation of the trade–environment nexus can be embedded. Thus, even though all of the three regional projects under scrutiny here seem to have both efficiency problems and legitimacy problems it is also difficult to envision the emergence of other more viable governance alternatives than the regional layer. In other words, the best bet for reconciliation of the trade–environment nexus in the age of globalisation is most probably the emergence of various regional governance layers. However, in order for such a development to emerge, the various regional projects in place around the globe must sort out their problems connected to the regional governance triangular *problematique* of efficiency, effectiveness and legitimacy. It is only through effective and legitimate regional co-ordination of national policies that the regional layer can emerge as an efficient and viable governance alternative in between the national and the global level.

Notes

1 Comments from the editors, and from Benedicte Bull, Morten Nordskag and Jonas Vevatne are highly appreciated.
2 A geographically based definition is not unproblematic because the borderline of a region may look different depending on whether geographic proximity, economic relations or political co-operation is used as the principal defining criterion. The delimitation of a region is not always determined by geography alone, and geography is not by necessity an objective criterion; it is just as much a social construct (see Keith and Pile, 1993; Ohlson, 1993; Neumann, 1996).
3 For a more elaborate argument about the relationship between governance, the public realm and the state–civil society nexus see Bøås, 1998.
4 This does not necessarily imply that environmental protection will be harmed, but it will change the political-economic context of environmental protection.
5 Vietnam joined ASEAN on 28 July 1995. Cambodia was supposed to join together with Myanmar and Laos in July 1997, but after the *coup d'état* by Hun Sen on the 5 July 1997 ASEAN had to postpone Cambodia's induction into the regional grouping for one year.
6 Thailand and Vietnam's respective traditional backing of the royalist movement and Hun Sen's communist party is one reason why the new Cambodian crisis that surfaced on 5 July 1997 was so painful for ASEAN. Instead of celebrating Southeast Asian harmony and unity by the enlargement of ASEAN to ten countries by induction of Cambodia, Laos and Myanmar, Cambodian membership had to be postponed, and it was feared that the situation could escalate to renewed tension between Thailand and Vietnam. In other words, one feared that the situation could turn the clock back to the regional geopolitics of the Cold War.
7 In November 1999, ASEAN decided to advance the target date for zero tariffs in ASEAN from 2015 to 2010, and since January 2000 almost 90 per cent of goods traded within ASEAN are subject to tariffs of less than 5 per cent (see Severino, 1999).
8 Sultan Hassan Bolkiah, opening address to the ASEAN trade and economic ministers meeting, Brunei, September 1995.
9 This is however not an argument in favour of slow or zero growth. Slow economic growth does not guarantee a better environment. The environmental problems are just as huge in slow-growing South Asia as in fast-growing Southeast Asia. The environmental degradation in Eastern Europe is another rejoinder that the relationship between growth rates and the environment is ambiguous at best.
10 Rules listed in any multilateral environmental agreement that ASEAN countries have agreed to join are another matter however. The ASEAN view is that these should be adhered to even if such agreements have trade provisions.

11 Of the three countries concerned it is only in Canada that it is possible to use domestic courts to enforce fines by an international body.

12 See Brænden (1996) and part five of the *North American Free Trade Agreement Side Accord on the Environment,* articles 22–36.

13 'Persistent patterns' means a sustained or recurring course of action or inaction beginning after the day of entry of the agreement. See art. 45 (1).

14 NAFTA supra note 115, art. 104. This provision applies to CITES, the Montreal Protocol and the Basel Convention on the Control of Transboundary Movement of Hazardous Waste and Their Disposal.

15 This provision also imposes new requirements and new trade disciplines on parties to these international environmental agreements.

16 NAFTA, supra note 115, art. 2103. During the NAFTA negotiations the three parties considered, but finally could not agree on stronger language. The Canadians had urged the use of the mandatory verb 'shall' rather than the hortatory 'should'; this suggestion was rejected by the Bush administration.

17 This round table is made up of the chief executives of leading European companies.

18 The EU's schemes for eco-labelling and environmental management and auditing (EMAS) are examples of this trend. See *European Chemical News,* 20 June 1994.

19 For instance, the report of the 'Five Wise Men' in November 1994 argued that any export-led recovery had to be coupled with more deregulation (see Grant, 1996).

5 Governance after financial crisis

South American perspectives on the reformulation of regionalism

Nicola Phillips

With the recent financial crises in Asia, Russia and Brazil, the resurgence of debate on the 'management' of globalisation has thrown into doubt a number of the 'certainties' which policy-makers constructed to deal with the 'uncertainties' of a post-Cold War, globalising world order. These 'certainties' centred around the dominance of the Washington Consensus, the euphoria of 'globalisation' and the heralding of an inexorable march towards a truly 'global' economy, and the notion of the 'information age' and the 'digital revolution' which eliminated cumbersome national boundaries and 'shrunk' the world into something approximating a 'global village'. Academic and policy debate, bored with the monotony (and inaccuracy) of this 'hyper-globalisation' discourse and, perhaps, with contesting yet again the alleged disappearance of the state, has turned of late towards a 'restructuring' agenda: of, for example, the financial architecture, the regulatory role of the national state, global markets, multilateral institutions, and crucially, the conceptual foundations of our understanding of International Political Economy (IPE).

Neo-classical economists' stubborn refusal to treat social and political variables as anything other than exogenous to the mainstream of market activity has been challenged by a growing intellectual preoccupation among international political economists (and other social scientists) with the normative connotations of the particular configuration of economic and political power implied by the term 'globalisation'.[1] This emerging normative agenda found particular expression in responses to the crises of market fundamentalism occasioned by the financial turbulence of 1997 to 1999. The 'no-alternative' rhetoric of globalisation appears to have given way to a more nuanced understanding of processes of global change, and, moreover, of the socio-political consequences of the 'commodification' of economic and social relations. Most importantly, the financial crises propelled a renewed emphasis on the agency of state and non-state actors in directing, managing, perhaps mitigating the impact of the specific types of global economic activity that dominated the 1990s. In short, there appears to be a rethinking of development models and policy principles underway, as well as the institutional configurations associated with them.

So where and how does regionalism fit into this picture? This chapter focuses on the ways in which financial crisis has altered conceptions and forms of regionalism in the global political economy, and thus compels a change in our theoretical understandings not only of regionalist dynamics but also of 'governance' in the broader sense.[2] To this end, my aim is to look through a South American lens at the central issues involved in the reformulation of regionalism. I propose to do this by setting out a series of three interconnected responses to the question of where regionalism fits into a 'post-globalisation' (Cox, 1993), 'post-Washington Consensus' (Stiglitz, 1998) reconsideration of key structures, development models and policy issues. These are considered in turn in successive sections of the chapter.

The first of the three is that the financial crises, by propelling an important 'globalisation backlash' (Helleiner, 1996; see also Strange, 1986), contributed to significant shifts in the articulated interests of states and the policy agendas through which these interests are pursued. Given, as we will see, that regionalism is inherently a project driven by states and a significant means by which some measure of policy latitude threatened by globalisation might be salvaged, there is a persuasive argument to be made that the domestic impact of recent global trends will necessarily involve a redefinition of the bases of regionalism in various parts of the world. In addition, if the central foundations on which contemporary regional arrangements are constructed are challenged, modified, or torn down, then it seems reasonable to expect, supported by recent evidence, that the nature of the resulting regional projects will undergo a consequent and related process of change.

The second idea focuses on the articulation (or not) of regional responses to financial volatility. As yet, the literature on financial crisis has tended to focus on the implications of turmoil for 'regions' – especially with reference to such phenomena as 'contagion' – with little sustained attention to the impact on regional *projects*. There is a generalised assumption, though, that recent instability has generated a 'relegitimation of the containment effects of neo-regional arrangements' (Bach and Hveem, 1998). This is an attractive proposition given the somewhat pitiful prospects for individual countries to respond in meaningful fashion to financial crisis in view of its scale in various regions. The idea of imposing capital controls, for example, intuitively seems more viable in the context of a concerted effort among various players, at least some of whom might hold sufficient 'structural power' to have some sort of significant impact on outcomes. The wisdom holds, furthermore, that if regionalism is assumed to capitalise on commonalities of interests among member states, the notion of collective responses to global instability similarly will be informed by a convergence of 'interests' reflective of common circumstances.

Nevertheless, evidence from various regions does not bear out unequivocally the contention that collective responses to volatility in the global capitalist economy are desired or indeed viable. Contrary to the apparent consensus that the crises will act to strengthen regionalism, developments in South America and elsewhere[3] appear to suggest that *in the short term* possibilities for collective action are weakened and regional projects are as likely to fragment as coalesce. However, from a longer term perspective, it seems probable that the consequences of this process of change will favour the articulation of stronger regional identification, which may well lead to an important redefinition of the nature and patterns of contemporary regionalism.

Of late, perhaps since the Mexican crisis, the neo-liberal 'credibility' effect of regionalism has become less relevant than its importance as a means of shoring up national economies against the crisis-generating nature of global capitalism. For many, therefore, the most pertinent function of regional integration will be increasingly its defensive potential against the vagaries of global capitalism on the one hand, and its importance as a mechanism for collective action on the other. In the context of current shifts in approaches to globalisation, the question is how some sort of reconstituted regionalism will relate to broader 'global' trends.

This leads into the third idea about how regionalism is implicated in recent global instability. The final part of the chapter offers some preliminary thoughts on the implications of these trends for current imaginings of the future of global governance. A 'regionalisation' of the 'post-globalisation' world order potentially undermines the central principles of global liberalisation which depend crucially on the now threadbare idea of 'convergence'. The progressive articulation of regional difference, as well as the 'regionalisation' of policy agendas, generates important questions about the future trajectory of 'governance'. Moreover, to conceive of world order in regionalist terms of a future 'triadic' structure of global governance is problematic, principally in its neglect of the regional trends identified in the bulk of this chapter. The resulting dynamic in the global political economy is thus more likely to be one of tension between the forces of regionalism and globalism than one of mutual reinforcement in which global and regionalist governance serve the same global ends.

States, interests and regional alliances

Along with the long-standing debate in mainstream globalisation theory over the 'retreat' of the state (Ohmae, 1995: Strange, 1996) versus its rehabilitation in new areas of competence and authority (see Boyer and Drache, 1996; Evans, 1997; Scholte, 1997; Weiss, 1998; Zysman, 1996), mainstream theories of regionalism remain somewhat ambivalent about the significance of national states in a range of regional arrangements. The recent confluence of currents in comparative politics, which call for a more rigorous understanding of the complexity of state–society interactions in conditions of 'structured privilege', and currents in IPE, which emphasise the 'transnationalisation' of political activity and the diffusion of power away from its exclusive concentration in the structures of national states, have provided useful avenues for theorising the politics of regionalist governance (Payne, 2000: 202). An important strand of the research agenda on regionalism in recent years has been the concern with regionalist 'governance' which, for good reason, takes as its principal laboratory the European Union. The concern with supranationalism and the attractive notion of 'multilevel governance' (Marks *et al.*, 1996) have generated a theoretical movement away from traditional Westphalian understandings of states and sovereignty. Under conditions of globalisation, states have lost or surrendered a significant degree of policy-making latitude as a result of the compression of time and space, the primacy of global (especially financial) markets and the increasing salience of transnational power structures and non-state forms of authority. As is now well-understood, however, these arguments are not incompatible with more 'national' perspectives on the state which emphasise its continuing monopoly over political legitimacy and its continuing centrality in policy management and the arbitration of social conflict.

Ideas about the 'pooling' of sovereignty at the regional level often fall into the same trap as arguments that equate globalisation with the disappearance of states. From a 'global' perspective, regionalism constitutes a transnationalisation of economic and political activity, which implies the transcendence of state boundaries in the interests of ensuring cooperation and reducing the potential for conflict, of whatever description, between geographically (and perhaps culturally) proximate partners. From a 'bottom-up' perspective, the formation of a regional bloc is concerned with various dimensions of state-building. The rationale for regionalism is invariably that there are common goals which can best be pursued in concert with other states or actors. Rather than implying a loss of 'statehood', regional arrangements allow not only for the elaboration of appropriate responses to the pressures of global liberalisation (Hirst and Thompson, 1996: 149–51), but also for the maintenance of some degree of 'discretion' in the management of domestic policy issues and the salvaging of effectiveness in specific policy areas. The 'regionalisation' of social or industrial policy, for example, or the regional negotiation of policy in sensitive areas such as agriculture or automobile industries, permit governments to attempt to reconcile in some constructive way priorities peculiar to the 'national' (and perhaps 'regional') setting with the internationalisation of economic activity under conditions of market globalisation.

Whether or not we choose to focus on the multi-level governance structures of the EU, then, we are drawn to Payne and Gamble's definition of regionalism as a 'state-led or states-led project' which remains crucially 'statist' in its various manifestations, as distinct from the social *process* implied by the term 'globalisation' (Payne and Gamble, 1996: 2). Thus the 'globalisation and the state' debate differs from questions about the national state in regionalism, the latter departing from the notion that regionalism is a specific policy *project* propelled and directed by states, notwithstanding complex relationships with non-state agency and the emergence of increasingly complex notions and structures of governance. The momentum of regionalism relies on 'palpable' manifestations of state action (treaties, trade agreements, formal and informal institutionalisation, intergovernmental decisions) which are in many respects lacking from contemporary manifestations of 'globalisation'. Regionalism must necessarily be understood as a constructed product of human agency (Mace and Bélanger, 1999: 1). In this sense, the regional dimensions of structural change have long been something of an inconvenience for the less reflexive of 'globalisers' who used the hegemonic discourse of globalisation to dispense with any meaningful notion of a national state.

South American regionalism is notable for the extent to which states occupy, almost exclusively, the epicentre of the regionalist project. The transfer of political authority from national governmental structures to specialist policy communities and the supranational structures of the EU find few parallels in the Mercosur.[4] In the same way as South American politics remain inconveniently statist for those who wish to proclaim a decisive shift in the location of political power towards non-state sites of authority, regionalism bears the imprint of this particular centralised type of state–society interaction. The Mercosur is not entirely without institutions, but its institutional structure is wholly intergovernmental rather than supranational. The two intergovernmental bodies created by the Treaty of Asunción – the Common Market Council (CMC) and the Common Market Group (GMC) – are composed (in the case of the former) of the foreign and (usually) economy ministers of each member country and (in the case of the latter) of representatives of the foreign ministries, economy ministries and central banks. Virtually without exception presidential meetings and negotiations dominated the major summits between Mercosur countries in the 1990s. Apart from the small bureaucracy of 'Mercocrats' which makes up the Administrative Secretariat, the integration process in Mercosur is handled by groups of officials in the relevant ministries in each of the member countries. Therefore, the technocratic teams remain located at national level rather than at supranational level as in the EU. They remain politically accountable to their respective governments and responsive to other state agencies (especially those concerned with economic policy), provincial governments and business interests (Hirst, 1995: 4–6).

Business interests remain under-represented in the Mercosur, notwithstanding the formation of the Economic and Social Consultative Forum in 1994 and important advances in cooperation between national business communities in the late 1990s. The preference has remained for informal bargaining channels and lobbying activities as opposed to further regional institutionalisation that would give more formal expression to business interests. As a result, business interests are articulated in regional negotiations through the structures of the states. That trade union input which exists is similarly mediated by national governmental structures. Other actors, such as political parties, small firms and social movements, remain to date of relatively marginal importance in the formal structures and operations of the Mercosur. As such, the South American case currently conforms far more closely with the arguments of the 'intergovernmentalist' camp in the literature on EU regionalism (Hoffmann, 1982; Moravcsik, 1993) than the neofunctionalist emphasis on supranationalism or the 'decisional reallocation' of multi-level governance approaches.

So where does all this lead us? First, to the conclusion that regionalist projects (and perhaps especially the South American) remain dominated by state actors and, by extension, the interests of states at a given historical moment. (The extent and ways in which the states can be seen as an aggregation of interests, and the dynamics that we observe in the construction of what eventually become the 'interests' of states, require empirical elaboration on the basis of individual cases). Second, to the particular historical moment in which global, regional and domestic orders are currently situated. The financial crises of 1997 to 1999 propelled a questioning of the dominant global orthodoxy in a variety of ways. One of these concerns policy choice, in which the most important agents remain national governments and state actors. The process of rethinking central tenets of development models necessarily involves reconfigurations of political and economic power, which consequently propel reassessments of participation in the global political economy and the construction of regional orders. It is significant that national states are central to both of these mutually constitutive processes: the rethinking of policy ideas privileges a rethinking of the parameters of state action, state authority and state responsibility, which feeds into a state(s)-led project of change at the regional level.

Given that the latest 'wave' of regionalism was constructed to complement and reinforce neo-liberal reform processes (notably in Latin America), it is reasonable to expect that the questioning of the fundamentals of neo-liberalism will be reflected in the nature of regionalist projects. While the extent of this questioning should not be exaggerated, it is evident that the zealous commitment to neo-liberal restructuring in the early 1990s had been superseded by the end of the decade by an awareness among policy elites and societies in the affected countries that adherence to a strict set of policy measures had not generated a solid basis for growth and development, nor for the continued dynamism of global capitalism. The disillusion occasioned by burgeoning social dislocations – consequent upon shifts in employment structures and tax burdens – combined with a marked resentment of both private financial agents and IMF-Treasury elites in the aftermath of financial crisis to produce a generalised backlash against globalisation, of which trends in South America form part (Higgott and Phillips, 2000).

The result was the emergence of a genuine (though to date less than concrete) debate in policy and academic circles on potential means of 'governing' globalisation and of making good the notion of the 'social market'. At the 1999 and 2000 meetings of the World Economic Forum and G7 summits, much was made of the apparent trade-off between international competitiveness and the social and political priorities of democratic systems (*International Herald Tribune*, 5 February 1999; *Financial Times*, 27 April 1999). Privatisation and deregulation in welfare provision, especially, were recognised to have contributed to rising levels of domestic inequalities, and the 'logic' of international restructuring to have fed into an increasingly painful differentiation between rich and poor countries. Social injustice came during this time to be associated with the absence of effective economic regulation, or at the very least with the process of deregulation which most countries were engaged in engineering for much of the 1990s. By the end of the decade there were increasing but still muted calls, some emanating from the discipline of economics, to recognise the negative correlation between social stability and 'purist' forms of neo-liberal globalisation (Krugman, 1999; Rodrik, 1997). As a result, the objectives of market economics were seen to stand in need of re-evaluation as much as the functioning of the market economy itself.

'Reform fatigue' (Edwards, 1997: 102) became entrenched among Latin American electorates over the course of the 1990s. The politics of the spate of presidential elections at the end of the decade demonstrated that, while public opinion stopped short of condemning the fundamentals of the economic model, support had become notably contingent on governments' commitment to mediating the socially deleterious effects of global liberalisation. What was needed, Latin Americans argued, was a novel approach to economic and social governance which displays flexibility and imagination – 'intelligent solutions', in short, 'even if they don't feature in Economics textbooks' (Rodarte, 1998; see also *El Cronista* (Argentina), 25 August 1998). Current evidence accordingly suggests that the future trajectory of policy in South America will reflect a trend away from 'automatic pilot' market strategies towards more active policies of the types enshrined in the Asian 'developmental state' model and advocated in Latin America by a growing number of governmental, societal and media voices.

This condemnation of the 'stateless market' points to a (re-)recognition (in policy intellectual circles) of the institutional and social embeddedness of markets as well as the ways in which the functioning of domestic and global markets depends on the generation of political consent (Polanyi, 1944; Ruggie, 1995). The presence of highly mobile international capital and processes of commercial and financial liberalisation proved over the 1990s to be socially unworkable in emerging economies which are not possessed of the sorts of domestic compensatory mechanisms found in the industrialised countries (Garrett, 1998). In some cases, notably Venezuela, traditional antagonisms to the Anglo-American neo-liberal agenda and resistance to 'globalisation' became increasingly pronounced. There and elsewhere, this scepticism prompted echoes in some quarters of pre-globalisation, pre-reform arguments that developing countries are neither ready for nor suited to globalisation (*El Nacional* (Venezuela), 8 October 1998; *Excelsior* (Mexico), 7 October 1998).

The Southern Cone countries did not at this time exhibit such strong insertion into a generalised 'globalisation backlash', but certainly exhibited a concern for genuine policy change, notably a re-empowerment of the state in a 'globalised' market environment which has found only inadequate ways, if any, of dealing with the social and institutional dislocations it generates. With financial instability, old reservations resurfaced about both the absence of effective regulation of capital and of mechanisms for correcting market failures. At a policy level, the 'dangers' of openness to globalised finance and the observation of global contagion revitalised neo-Keynesian ideas about the role of the domestic economy in producing growth. Long-term growth projects based entirely on the vitalisation of the external sector, particularly in places like Argentina where the external sector still accounts for less than 10 per cent of GDP, were gradually (or not so gradually) losing currency among policy elites. Political climates at the end of the 1990s were dominated by heightened awareness of the social responsibilities of governments, propelled by rising levels of popular mobilisation (in countries like Chile), increasingly salient social inequities (such as in Brazil) and persistently high levels of unemployment (most obviously in Argentina).

Whether these processes of re-evaluation will yield significant results remains to be seen. The observation that the financial crises propelled a scrutiny of neo-liberal models does not mean that neo-liberalism will be discarded as the dominant policy paradigm. Clearly the hands of policy elites in the majority of South American countries remain tied by IMF agreements and the need to appease sources of investment and external finance. Concrete alternative policy agendas have yet to be articulated convincingly by domestic policy elites. It is, however, significant that even among prominent international political economists the espousal of unorthodox strategies by prominent international economists is much less uncommon than in the pre-Thai devaluation days: calls for capital controls being the most obvious example.

The implications for regionalism, in this light, are twofold. The first is that these changes in the constituent bases of regionalist projects (policy ideas and state interests) are likely, in ways which vary across regions and projects, to alter the nature of regionalism and the uses to which it is put. While financial crisis may not have weakened support for free(r) trade, it prompted a questioning of the 'one-size-fits-all' policy formula, and consequently may strengthen articulations of regional 'identity' informed by political and socio-economic realities rather than by a globalised set of values and policy prescriptions captured under the banner of 'Anglo-American neo-liberalism'. This reconstitution may well take a shape which introduces elements of a more explicitly 'defensive' strategy in response to the pressures of multilateralism and globalism. While this is highly unlikely to translate directly into open protectionism, key departures from the principles of unfettered competition or complete deregulation, for example, seem to be strong possibilities. In short, the compulsion to conform with the minutiae of the 'globalised' neo-liberal policy package appears increasingly diluted by a concern to find policy strategies appropriate to specific historical-institutional and economic settings, and to implement policies to offset the raft of economic and political dislocations occasioned by global liberalisation.

The second implication is that the only viable means by which genuine policy change might be achieved is through collective action at the regional level. In the same ways that one of the primary functions of regionalism in the heyday of neo-liberalism was to 'lock in' policy reform, future directions of policy change are likely of necessity to rely on the same mechanisms of regional collective action to increase the costs of deviation and also to construct political legitimation for a particular policy agenda. Moreover, however, the particular configuration of economic, institutional and political capacity resulting from the most recent period of capitalist instability necessitates collective action as the only means by which a range of public goods might be provided by governments. These arguments are elaborated in the next section.

Regional collective action: coalescence or fragmentation?

The suggestion, therefore, is that given the 'backlash' against unfettered globalisation, some 'regionalisation' of policy ideas seems likely as policy solutions sensitive to specifically local difficulties are sought, putting paid (yet again) to the notion of 'convergence' on a single, globalised set of values and policy principles. Meaningful policy change, however, is not easy and, moreover, does not come cheap. The capitalist world economy remains dominated by integrated trade and capital flows, unregulated financial markets and technological dynamism. Moreover, development strategies remain dependent on external capital resources, particularly in the aftermath of currency collapse. Political impetus for policy change in response to what we might call the 'globalisation of inequity' has a high price tag, especially in the absence of strong capital inflows or in the presence of strong capital outflows. As a result, incentives for collective action are heightened as countries seek to maximise the international credibility of whichever policy responses are politically expedient in a given situation.

It is here that our arguments about regionalism come into play. Given the difficulties associated with international cooperation in broader terms (Milner, 1997), and in light of the relatively insignificant role that Latin American countries (and developing countries generally) play in international cooperation for the provision of public goods, regional collaboration may well retain its utility as a credibility-maximising and legitimacy-generating mechanism by which countries can pursue sets of similar goals in a globalising, currently volatile, international economy. As policy elites start to rethink their role in providing those collective goods associated with mitigating the worst impacts of socio-economic dislocation – and indeed what those collective goods might be – the regional dimensions of that provision become decisive. And if states in Latin America (and other developing countries) are more concerned, for a variety of reasons, with the elimination or management of 'public bads' rather than the provision of collective goods (Phillips and Higgott, 1999), then the regional dimension is all the more salient given the limitations on the political, institutional and economic capacities of these states to engage in this type of public policy. Finally, collective action is necessitated by the prior existence of a regional bloc and the need to maintain a balance of competitiveness. When this balance is disturbed by financial crisis or unilateral policy innovation, we can hypothesise that the maintenance of a regional project depends on collective action between states.

If, for example, South American countries are concerned to construct a model which is more socially responsive and politically sensitive, the options for funding such a shift in public policy are largely limited to increasing or restructuring taxation. Tax structures have important implications for balances of external competitiveness. Changes in the domestic distribution of tax burdens, especially in the presence of such structural imbalances as those which exist in the aftermath of precipitous devaluation, induce changes in the relative competitiveness of domestic industrial and external sectors. In the presence of a regional bloc, not only are perceptions of such competitive (dis)advantages heightened, especially in countries which are very significantly dependent on regional markets, but also pressures for reciprocal coordination between member countries are likely to emerge. For this reason policy initiatives which affect external competitiveness generally will flounder in the absence of collaboration. Both economic and political objectives may be seen to demand collective *regional* action in key areas of policy change. Increasingly loud calls from Argentina for policy harmonisation in a range of areas respond directly to these considerations. Similar arguments apply to the introduction of social charters, or to labour flexibilisation initiatives.

Another illustration of this point may be found in the debates on regional currencies propelled by experiences of financial volatility at the end of the 1990s and the annihilation during this time of most forms of semi-fixed exchange rate regimes. The notion of some sort of triadic currency order – centred on regions currently structured around the dollar, euro and yen – has been floated frequently in discussions on the creation of a new 'global financial architecture' (see Eichengreen, 1999; Ocampo, 1999; United Nations, 199). Developments in South America in the aftermath of the Brazilian devaluation reflected these debates. Although virtually a lone voice, Argentina's spirited defence of its currency, which is fully convertible to the dollar in a currency board arrangement established in 1991, was based on calls from government and some business elites for both the creation of a common Mercosur currency and/or the dollarisation of the Latin American region as a whole.[5]

However, the possibilities for European-style monetary union in South America would appear still to be limited. Although the notion of a 'little Maastricht' for the Mercosur gained considerable ground over the course of 1999 and the first part of 2000, the Brazilians for the foreseeable future are likely to be unwilling to abandon the benefits of a floating exchange rate (Bulmer-Thomas, 1999). Dollarisation, given the concessions it implies to the United States (and indeed its inauspicious start in countries like Ecuador), can be largely ruled out of future scenarios. Moreover, although Argentine preferences might find some resonance with Mexican business, for example (Beddoes, 1999: 8–13), the likelihood that such a project would find even swampy ground in South America is diminished by precisely those factors which complicate the generation of collective responses to financial crisis. Despite the arguments for regional collective action outlined above, present evidence indicates that this can be only a long-term scenario, for two reasons. The first is that at present the Mercosur is not equipped to 'carry' the sort of integration that significant policy innovation might require. Its minimal level of institutionalisation and its slow progress on key (and basic) economic issues – such as trade in services, government procurement, intellectual property, competition policy, harmonisation of customs procedures and exchange rate coordination – prompt scepticism about its capacity as a *modus operandi* for collective action.

The second and related issue is that the divergence between member countries for much of the late 1990s was far more pronounced than convergence. Key differences in economic structures and policy orientations (notwithstanding a general commitment to an economic development model which privileges open markets) generated significant tensions between Argentina and Brazil especially, not only on immediate policy issues but also on visions of the future of the regional project. These tensions were exacerbated by the Brazilian devaluation of early 1999, and led to a marked atomisation of policy responses rather than increased coordination and cooperation. Superficial short-run collective responses – seen in the frenzy of summit meetings with the IMF, rhetorical commitments to 'support' from the US government, bail-out packages and twenty-four-hour hotlines between Mercosur presidents – only thinly disguised increased regional atomisation as governments formulated responses most suited to particular national situations. The tension between Argentina and Brazil and the exigencies of responding to domestic instability pushed the regional agenda on to the back burner. While the Argentine government was calling for dollarisation and macro-economic policy harmonisation, Brazilian elites were concerned with more specifically national priorities of dealing with the impact on prices and interest rates, and, no less important, in trying to salvage the fortunes of the beleaguered President Cardoso, rescue the reform agenda, and bring the belligerence of the provincial governments under some semblance of centralised control.

Furthermore, as *The Economist* recently put it, 'weak presidents make weak diplomacy' (*The Economist*, 14 August 1999). Given, as we have seen, that the Mercosur has to date been propelled by presidential summitry, it should come as no surprise that the fragility of the positions of both Cardoso and Menem in 1999 would have at least a 'stalling' effect on the regional agenda. As it turned out, the effect was to heighten hostility and generate the most profound crisis yet in the Mercosur. Brazil announced in February 2000, after plentiful rumours to the effect, that it was taking Argentina to the WTO to resolve a dispute over textiles exports (*Financial Times*, 16 February 2000). Former Argentine Economy Minister Cavallo called in August 1999 for a 'suspension' of the Mercosur while countries engaged in nationally defined damage limitation exercises,[6] and it was subsequently reported in early 2000 that the option of abandoning the Mercosur had been tabled before the Brazilian government (*Mecropress News Agency*, 8 February 2000, <www.mecropress.com>). Despite the limited house-room that such proposals were afforded, and despite the expressions of steadfast commitment from all governments and the subsequent flurry of new (and on the whole insubstantial) 'pacts', the significance of the *questioning* of the continued existence of the Mercosur should not be underestimated.

The short-term pattern thus indicates a fragmentation of the existing consensus, greater dissociation between Mercosur countries and the pursuit of increasingly individualistic policy agendas rather than an enhancement of collective priorities. Optimistic accounts of the 'strengthening' of regionalism thus overlook important short-term dynamics of regional collective action, complicated by ongoing political wranglings within member countries, particularly between government and industry in Argentina. While we can accept that regionalism is a political project responsive to the manifold effects of global structural change – whether these are seen to be social degeneration, societal disarticulation, the profusion of new and traditional inequities, the disempowerment of developing countries, and so on – the inclusion of financial crisis in the picture alters the ways in which we understand collective action through regional cooperation. The limitations of the regional project itself indicate that the transformation of South American regionalism into a genuine theatre for collective action and policy innovation is likely to occur only in the much longer term.

However, and crucially, these sub-regional dynamics cannot be treated in isolation from the process of hemispheric integration under negotiation since the 1994 Summit of the Americas in Miami. The notion of a Free Trade Area of the Americas (FTAA) has to date been secondary in importance (and vitality) to the development of sub-regional units and the vigorous pursuit of a patchwork of bilateral deals. It seems clear that the future of the FTAA will be determined by the interaction of the northern and southern hegemons. Given the divisive congressional politics in the United States which have denied fast-track negotiating authority to the executive branch, Brazil retains its status as 'veto player' in the hemispheric negotiations. From the start, Brazil's interest in the Mercosur stemmed in large part from traditional tensions with the US and from the potentially 'threatening' creation of the NAFTA. The resulting focus of Brazilian attention on consolidating its role as sub-regional hegemon led to the proposition in 1994 of the idea of a South American Free Trade Area (SAFTA) as a collective negotiating platform in the FTAA negotiations, and as an alternative to the US's preferred country-by-country negotiating strategy. This has shifted of late to an emphasis on the expansion of the Mercosur to other South American countries but not, crucially, to the further institutionalisation of the regional arrangement nor to significant macro-economic policy harmonisation between member countries. Brazilian opposition to these sorts of developments remains pronounced, but its commitment to opposing US negotiating strategies underlines its preferences for the expansion and reinforcement of the South American bloc. Current emphasis in the Mercosur on negotiations with the EU further dilutes the hemispheric agenda. On specific policy matters, the US is seen to be promoting provisions which go beyond those agreed during the Uruguay Round, while Brazil's preference in the short term is to consolidate the measures agreed in the WTO (see Bouzas, 1999; Grugel and de Almeida Medeiros, 1999; Wrobel, 1998). Similarly, Brazil and most other South American countries are concerned principally with trade issues, while the US's objectives are more focused on 'newer' issues such as services, intellectual property rights, competition policy, government procurement and environmental and labour standards.

Put this picture together with the fall-out from the Brazilian devaluation, as well as the 'backlash' resulting from the failure of the IMF and the US government to handle effectively the impending crisis over the second half of 1998, and the prospects for the successful negotiation of a meaningful FTAA by 2005 appear complicated. The rethinking of neo-liberalism is likely to entrench long-standing differences between Brazil and the United States in approaches to economic management. As we have seen, the climate at the end of the 1990s favoured an expansion of governments' regulatory and managerial roles and capacities, tendencies already well established in Brazilian preferences for strategic trade policies active industrial policy, and state-led development. Experiences of financial volatility are likely not only to have strengthened the southern countries' existing desire to negotiate as a coherent bloc rather than as spokes around a hub, thereby generating enhanced potential for collective action, but also to accentuate the divergences between the north and south of the Americas.

Perhaps paradoxically, therefore, it is possible that the hostilities between Mercosur countries which complicate the generation of regional collective action will be diluted in the longer run by the greater oppositions between the north and south of the hemisphere, especially in the area of policy responses to globalisation and in the area of hemispheric integration. The nascent lineaments of a genuine regional identity that goes beyond the loose economic bloc, at present absent from the Mercosur, emerge most strongly in the context of the relationship with the United States and NAFTA. Brazil's unbending preference for sub-regional integration as opposed to a US-led hemispheric initiative has led to a situation in which each new move by the US has pushed Brazil closer to its sub-regional commitments (Soares de Lima, 1999: 136). When combined with the increased importance of regional collective action, for reasons of internal and external competitiveness and the requirements of policy change, the long-term scenario would appear to be one in which the regionalisation of a distinct form of South American capitalist organisation is a strong tendency. While collaboration within these 'smaller' regional constructions is far from uncomplicated by problems associated with collective action, as well as the limitations on the capacities of the Mercosur at the present time, it appears that these are the lines along which South American and hemispheric regionalism will be 'rethought'.

Global and regionalist governance

So, in conclusion, what does all this tell us about the future of regionalism in a 'post-Washington Consensus' era? The complexity of the relationship between globalism, regionalism and the myriad other levels of political and economic activity is not captured in now sterile assessments of whether open regionalism can in fact be open and whether regional blocs work to the detriment of multilateralism (Mansfield and Milner, 1999). Regionalism itself constitutes an element of an increasingly complex system of governance operating at a variety of levels in which questions about public goods, welfare, economic organisation and political participation are addressed. The re-accommodation of globalism and regionalism, as the principal structural consequence of the financial crises, therefore has its roots in key governance issues.

What is curious and telling, in this vein, is that these two levels of governance continue to be treated more or less in isolation from each other. In a recent volume on 'the political economy of world economic governance', for example, the regional dimensions of the future of governance are neglected almost entirely, and mentioned only twice (on separate pages) in connection with the regional currencies debate (Michie and Grieve Smith, 1999). While most analyses of regionalism offer insights into its relationship with multilateralism or globalisation, very little of the global governance debate focuses on regionalism itself, beyond some appreciation of a 'regional' (for which read 'triadic') approach to the restructuring of the global financial architecture. Furthermore, the treatment of regionalism remains excessively 'aggregated'. Discussions of the relationship between globalism and regionalism suffer not only from their static qualities but also from a propensity to treat 'regionalism' as a homogenous phenomenon. Payne's illustration of the diversity of forms of regionalist governance – multi-level governance in the EU, 'hub-and-spoke governance' in North America and what he calls 'pre-governance' in Asia (which might, incidentally, apply usefully also to South America) – highlights that simplistic conceptions of a single relationship between something called 'regionalism' and something called 'globalism' are analytically and empirically problematic (Payne, 2000: 211–15).

These inadequacies in contemporary understandings of 'regional governance' are reflected in debates on the future structures and governance of the global political economy. Most obviously, the notion that the restructuring of the financial architecture will be undertaken with a strongly 'regional' bent is flawed, or at best unreflective of the regional and domestic dynamics which would inform such a project. Not only does it underestimate the variety of social forces that need to be incorporated into analyses of governance and the plethora of 'levels' at which sites of authority are located, it also misconceives the dynamics of regionalism in the 'aftermath' (or else temporary lull) of financial crisis in various parts of the world. The resulting assumptions guiding debates at the start of the new decade are thus dubious.

First, the projected division of the world into a triadic structure paints lines of connection between 'regions', countries and actors which appear erroneous. While they make some (limited) sense in terms of currency arrangements, they have little coherence when we consider other dimensions of convergence and conflict in the global political economy. In the area of policy ideas, for example, there is some significant convergence between East Asia and Europe, and, crucially now, South America. The closer identification by South American government elites with key policy debates of the European 'centre-left' governments is exacerbated by the continuing insistence by the US government and associated international institutions on a deepening of neo-liberal stringency. This is reflected, furthermore, in a smattering of calls in South American countries for the establishment of closer relations with Europe in preference to the United States (*La Nación* (Argentina), 16 May 1999), as well as in the current political negotiations for EU–Mercosur trade agreements. The arrows of 'cooperation' thus point in directions not immediately consistent with a global triad of 'regional' constructions. While Europe's proposals for the construction of 'monetary zones' as a means of containing financial volatility are broadly supported in East Asia and received sympathetically in South America, it is far from clear that these might correspond to a structure of 'regionalist governance' in the wider sense capable of transcending increasing tensions in the 'regions' of the Americas and the Asia Pacific.

Second, the idea of a triadic structure takes no account of the emerging importance of sub-regional identification as the apparently strongest basis for the future trajectory of regionalism. We have seen that the dynamics of South American regionalism do not augur well for anything more than a loose network of 'hemispheric' relationships, if in fact an FTAA does come to any sort of fruition. Similar trends may be observed in the fragmentation of APEC. Perspectives on regionalist governance from a 'globalist' perspective do not sit well with considerations of *specific* domestic and regional dynamics which inform emerging structures of governance.

In this vein, and third, the 'globalisation backlash' has sharpened tensions between the more and less developed countries – seen clearly in the Seattle meetings of the World Trade Organisation in late 1999 – which are neglected by these globalist imaginings of new regionalist governance. Given that the most prominent trend of recent years has been the globalisation of inequity, the financial crises generated resurgent perceptions of structures of 'disadvantage' in the global political economy. Moral hazard, for example, shifted the liabilities of financial markets and the impact of their behaviour to those 'emerging' markets targeted by speculative capital. And the impact of massive capital flight exacerbated pronounced social dislocations in developing countries occasioned by global neo-liberalism. The reactions against inequity and disadvantage, therefore, are significantly bound up with power relations in the global political economy, and would be most likely to militate against cooperation at the levels suggested by ideas of triadic governance, especially in the Americas. As we have seen at various points in the discussion, emerging patterns of 'spoke–spoke' relationships are potentially of equal utility to (if not greater than) 'hub–spoke' interactions. If regionalism is strengthened as a means by which global polarisation might best be addressed, the notion of triadic governance structures is anachronistic to the sharpened appreciations, including in South America, of the prejudicial dimensions of the globalist project.

Notes

1 The working understanding of 'globalisation' employed here refers to the progressive integration, liberalisation, deregulation and privatisation of the international economy and its constituent parts. Thus it refers to the dominant policy and economic understandings of the term, without ignoring the complexity of its contemporary usage.

2 Rosenau's recent definition of 'governance' seems to have become the standard understanding of the term. He refers to 'spheres of authority at all levels of human activity . . . that amount to systems of rule in which goals are pursued through the exercise of control' (Rosenau, 1997: 145).

3 For comparative perspectives on the impact of crisis on APEC and other Asian regional groupings, see Beeson, 1999; Ahmed and Ghoshal, 1999; Berger, 1999.

4 The Mercado Común del Sur (Southern Common Market), established in 1991 by Argentina, Brazil, Paraguay and Uruguay. Chile and Bolivia are associate members.

5 See e.g. 'Menem forces dollar plan to top of political agenda in Argentina', *Financial Times*, 27 January 1999; 'No more peso?', *The Economist*, 23 January 1999; 'A Yankee currency for Argentina?', *International Herald Tribune*, 4 February 1999; 'El largo camino hacia la desaparición del peso', *El Economista* (Argentina), 14 May 1999.

6 'Mercosul: Cavallo sugere interrupção', news bulletin from Agência Estado (Brazil), 6 August 1999, <http: //www.agestado.com.br>.

6 Regionalism and development after(?) the global financial crises

Paul Bowles

F30 0 16
F15 F21 0 19

Introduction

Regionalism as an economic policy choice of governments was prone to periods of fashion throughout the twentieth century.[1] The last decade of the century undoubtedly marked one of its more popular phases with fully 90 per cent of the countries which are members of the World Trade Organization (WTO) also belonging to at least one regional trading arrangement. This latest rise in the popularity of regionalism has been widespread, and has been evident in countries at different levels of economic development and with varying levels of previous involvement with regional economic integration schemes.

This chapter focuses on the appeal of regionalism, in the form of regional economic integration schemes, to developing countries in the 1990s, and analyses the impact of the recent global financial crises on this appeal in the twenty-first century. As background to this, the next section considers the causal factors underlying the re-emergence of regionalism as an attractive policy choice for developing countries. As will be shown, there are significant differences between the economic motives for regionalism since the mid-1980s and those of earlier decades. Regionalism has, in fact, been associated with a variety of development strategies; what characterizes the 'new regionalism' is the combination of regionalism with the adoption of neo-liberal development strategies.

Just as the 'new regionalism' was taking hold, the international economic system was rocked by a series of financial crises, starting with some European countries in 1992, overtaking Mexico in 1994, and exploding spectacularly in Asia in 1997 before moving on to Russia and Brazil. The third section of the chapter provides a (limited) review of the competing explanations of the financial crises and of the proposals for preventing their recurrence through a redesign of the 'international financial architecture'.

The financial crises have led to significant changes in the policy agenda of many countries, especially in the so-called emerging (developing) economies, and of the international financial institutions (IFIs) with international financial stability now much higher on the agenda. The fourth section of the chapter analyses the effects of the crises and the changed policy agenda on the prospects for the new regionalism. To provide some empirical content to this discussion, the analysis of the fourth section draws upon the post-crisis experience of two of the most prominent developing country regional economic arrangements, namely the Mercosur and the ASEAN Free Trade Area (AFTA).

The concluding section is more speculative in nature and looks at some of the obstacles that must be overcome before it can be concluded that the regionalism of the 1990s will remain a feature of the international political economy in the twenty-first century.

Regionalism and development strategies: an overview

Regionalism has had a chequered history as an economic policy choice. Its popularity at the end of the twentieth century was the latest turn in a much longer process. As Lawrence has argued :

> the shift towards regionalism [in the 1980s and 1990s] is the third such wave in this century, but the forces driving the current developments are radically different from the previous waves. Unlike the episode of the 1930s, the current initiatives have all been presented as efforts to facilitate their members' participation in the world economy rather than their withdrawal from it. Unlike those in the 1950s and 1960s, the initiatives involving developing countries are part of a strategy to liberalize and open up their economies to implement export- and foreign-investment-led strategies rather than import substitution policies.
>
> (Lawrence, 1994a: 366)

The regionalism of the 1980s and 1990s is therefore to be distinguished from previous rounds both by its content and its motives. As Lawrence suggests, for developing countries a central feature has been the shift towards the adoption of neo-liberal economic policies and away from the more inward-looking import substitution policies of the 1950s and 1960s. Yet, as Lawrence also notes, regionalism has been used in both periods but to serve different ends; regionalism, it seems, can be applied flexibly and can be used with quite different development strategies.

Development discourse in the immediate post-war decades centred on the need for developing countries to gain a more equal share of the benefits of international economic interaction. It was premised on the need for North–South transfers through official development assistance as a means of closing the 'dual gaps' of savings and foreign exchange and for the countries of the South to industrialize using various protectionist tools. 'Free Trade' was rejected on the basis that the structure of world trade was such that the division of labour between industrial and developing countries relegated the latter to being the predominant suppliers of primary products (although this increasingly broke down as developing countries became the sites for the new international division of labour based on labour-intensive manufacturing exports). At the international level, concern over the deteriorating terms of trade for primary products was evident and calls for commodity price stabilization schemes heard. The demands of the new international economic order advanced by developing countries included more control over multinational corporations (MNCs) and the regulation of technology transfer to ensure that developing countries benefited more from MNCs' operations. A complementary policy to these demands at the international level were South–South regional trading agreements, especially popular in the 1960s, premised on the need to have sufficiently large internal markets for developing countries to pursue import substituting industrialization (ISI) strategies. Such agreements typically involved high external tariffs and assorted market sharing – and industry sharing – arrangements between member countries.[2] Added to these economic motives were political motives as well; as Ghatak notes, 'one of the major reasons for setting up such trading blocks is political. Regional co-ordination among the LDCs is supposed to provide them with a greater bargaining power in their economic and political relationships with the DCs' (1978: 303).

Development theory in the 1950s and 1960s was therefore premised on the need for an activist state, an activism demanded not only by the requirements of domestic resource mobilization but also by the structural impediments to growth which the international capitalist economy imposed on developing countries and which only interventionist and protectionist policies could overcome. Regionalism could be adapted to meet these ends, although its fate in this particular incarnation was tied to that of the ISI. As ISI ran out of steam towards the end of the 1960s so did the appeal of regionalism.

The counter-revolution in economic thinking and the rise of neo-liberalism had dramatically changed the nature of development discourse by the 1980s. The case for state activism and protectionist policies came under sustained assault in many countries led by the core industrial countries. This change at the ideological level was reinforced by the increasing awareness of the differences in development outcomes. In particular, the high costs of the ISI strategy in terms of support for domestically protected producers and the declining growth potential of the ISI strategy appeared in stark contrast to the rapid export-led growth of countries located in East Asia. The rapid growth of East Asian countries was interpreted by the new dominant paradigm as evidence that the structural impediments facing developing countries – and which formed the basis of dependency theory and ISI strategies – had been greatly exaggerated and that the key to growth lay in domestic policy choices rather than changes in the international trading system. The increasing differentiation between developing countries led many to announce 'the end of the Third World' and the end of development theory (Harris, 1987; Lall, 1980; Leys, 1996). It would be more accurate to describe this latter process as the dominance of neo-liberalism as development theory, a theory in which countries differed in their endowments rather than in their structural relationship to the world economy. All countries were seen as operating according to the same economic laws and therefore a separate 'development economics' was not required.

The rise of neo-liberalism in the core countries was matched by the changing intellectual attitudes of the international financial institutions (IFIs) and was reflected in their shift to policy-based lending as a response to the international debt crisis of the early 1980s. As Bhagwati notes, 'the macroeconomic crisis of the 1980s . . . fed the movement to microeconomic reforms' (1992: 15). The remedy to the international debt crisis was seen not in changing the rules of the international economy but in adjusting national economic development strategies. The East Asian economies' experience, later deified as the 'East Asian miracle', figured prominently in the recipe for success, namely, low government spending, high investment in infrastructure and human capital, and 'getting prices right' to encourage the tradable goods sector. This recipe became part of the new orthodoxy and formed the basis of the standard structural adjustment package implemented in country after country in Central and Latin America, in sub-Saharan Africa and later in the transitional economies of Eastern Europe. No matter that the interpretation of East Asia's success was contested and that the results of the policy were, to say the least, disappointing; the orthodox development strategy for the 1980s and 1990s was clear (Amsden, 1989; Rodrik, 1995; Wade, 1990).

The spur to adopt the neo-liberal development approach came for many countries as a result of either positive policy choice or by the design of the Bretton Woods institutions through stabilization and structural adjustment programmes. Both sources relied on the international debt crisis, and the consequent need for developing countries to generate increased export earnings, the deflationary state of the international economy in the early 1980s notwithstanding. Thus the ideological triumph of neo-liberalism in the West and in the IFIs was mirrored by policy changes in developing countries either through embracing that neo-liberalism with some enthusiasm (as in many Latin American countries), through a begrudging and contested acceptance (as in many Southeast Asian countries) or through an imposed necessity (as in many sub-Saharan African countries).

It was argued that such a development strategy would require both finance and technology; in short, it would require the rehabilitation of the multinational corporation. Foreign Direct Investment (FDI) based export-led growth therefore became respectable and was embraced with various degrees of enthusiasm by policy-makers in developing countries. As part of the new 'market-friendly' approach to development, restrictions of the activities and requirements placed upon MNCs were reduced as developing countries sought to attract increasing amounts of scarce global FDI to their shores. From the Caribbean to Mauritius to China, MNCs were courted as the harbingers of development.[3]

Coincidentally, just as developing countries were courting FDI, MNCs themselves were searching for lower cost production sites. Flushed with this embrace of foreign private capital, developing countries also began to liberalize capital accounts, allowing free convertibility and opening 'emerging' bond and equity markets to foreign purchasers. During the period 1992 to 1997, FDI inflows for all developing countries averaged US$100.2bn per annum; during the same period, foreign portfolio investment inflows into developing countries averaged US$63.3bn per annum (UNCTAD, 1998: 15).

The new international division of labour based on the production of labour-intensive manufacturers in developing countries can be dated from the mid-1970s as a response to the structural crisis in industrial countries. However, the largest increases in FDI were not to come for another decade. The increase in FDI flows in the mid-1980s partly resulted from the opportunities provided by the liberalization in developing countries themselves, and partly as a result of the exchange rate readjustments initiated by the US and Japan as an attempt to solve the macroeconomic imbalances between the two countries. The Plaza Accord which led to a significant appreciation of the yen fuelled Japanese MNCs' investments in developing Asia. FDI from the US and the EU also surged during this period as core countries MNCs' competitive strategies moved towards the creation of regional networks. In the 1990s FDI continued to rise rapidly, especially inflows into developing countries, as shown in Table 6.1.

Table 6.1 FDI inflows by host region, 1986–1997 (US$bn)

Host region	1986–1991 (annual average)	1992	1993	1994	1995	1996	1997
World	159.3	175.8	217.6	243.0	331.2	337.6	400.5
Developed Countries	129.6	120.3	138.9	141.5	211.5	195.4	233.1
Developing Countries	29.1	51.1	72.5	95.6	105.5	129.8	148.9

Source: UNCTAD, *World Investment Report 1998: Trends and Determinants* (United Nations, 1998), p. 361.

Private capital flows, both long and short term, increasingly outpaced official development assistance flows and the latter became more focused by donors on poverty alleviation in the poorest countries.[4] The economic stimulus given by aid was simply too small, as aid flow stagnated to play the role envisaged for it in the immediate post-war decades. Industrialization in the periphery, the increasing differentiation between developing countries and the success of the NICs changed the development landscape. The structural inequities which were emphasized in much of the development theory of the 1960s and 1970s slipped in importance in the newly dominant paradigm, and developing countries were seen more in regional terms – with the largest problems being those of sub-Saharan Africa – than in structural terms.

This account of the change in the direction of development theory and the rise of neoliberalism is perhaps well known. But why did regionalism re-emerge during the same period as a preferred policy choice of many developing countries? How did this transformation in the popularity of regionalism for developing countries occur in the mid-1980s and 1990s, and how has it been used in conjunction with the wider move towards neoliberalism as a development strategy? This is indeed a good question because there is nothing inherent in the neoliberal approach, which would suggest that regional economic integration arrangements are necessary to its success. Indeed, there has been significant debate between neoliberal economists about the desirability of regional arrangements at all, with some arguing that they detract from the cause of global free trade. Furthermore, although there is plenty of policy advice from the IFIs in terms of liberalization, forming regional trading blocs does not constitute one of the recommendations. Why then, in the absence of strong theoretical reasoning or policy advice from the IFIs, did regionalism among developing countries emerge and form part of their liberalization programmes?

The example of the further integration of the EU and the conversion of the US in favour of regionalism may have been important in lending legitimacy to regionalism, but these, in themselves, are insufficient to explain its widespread appeal for developing countries; something else is needed. Regionalism, I argue, was an attractive proposition for many developing countries in this new environment for at least two reasons. First, in a number of ways, regional economic agreements increased the ability of developing countries to attract FDI. Second, regional initiatives offered the possibility of adopting a step-by-step approach to liberalization which would permit some of the adjustment costs of, and political obstacles to, liberalization to be reduced.

With respect to FDI flows, a central component of the neoliberal development strategy was, as noted above, the attraction of FDI to promote export-led growth (and also to enable privatization to take place). Regional groupings of developing countries offered the possibility of attracting such capital inflows since a group of countries acting together might offer a more attractive package than a single country.[5] Small countries were at a relative disadvantage since the modern production process functions at multiple levels of the commodity chain; a group of countries which could offer not only labour but also some level of industrial and managerial capability would better suit MNC production objectives as well as offering larger markets.[6] Offering an attractive package to MNCs became an imperative since, the large increase in the supply of FDI notwithstanding, the demand for such flows increased dramatically as not only the 'traditional' developing countries sought more FDI but they were joined by China and the transitional economies of the former Soviet bloc. Countries fearing investment diversion therefore sought to form regional economic units as a way of maintaining their attractiveness for both the production and sales of MNCs.

Regional groupings also offered greater credibility than individual country commitment to the security of private investment. This was important because although communication and transportation costs have fallen rapidly with the onset of the information technology revolution, enforcement costs have not (Epstein, 1994). The rapid increase in cross-border FDI flows had little by way of a regulatory framework and institutions to support it. For the past decade, institutional mechanisms have therefore been sought to facilitate and regulate these flows. By the end of 1997, 1513 bilateral investment treaties had been signed involving 169 countries. Of the 153 such treaties signed in 1997, 28 per cent were between developed and developing countries, 27 per cent were between developing countries, and 20 per cent were between developed countries and transition economies (UNCTAD, 1998: 59). Regional agreements offered another way to signal to foreign investors that the move towards investor-friendly neoliberal policies was permanent since the costs of reneging on them were significantly increased. The desire to increase credibility with foreign investors has taken a variety of institutional forms in developing countries, from granting independence to central banks to the willingness of some developing countries to unilaterally adopt the provisions of the Multilateral Agreement on Investment (MAI) at the time of its negotiation by the OECD. Signing on to regional liberalization initiatives provided one more institutional signal.

The adoption of a neoliberal development strategy might be expected to encounter opposition. This would come not simply from marginalized groups such as unskilled workers, public sector workers and the poor, who might – and in many cases did – lose out on the neoliberal policies of privatization, subsidy removal and labour market deregulation. Equally importantly, at least from the point of view of policy elites, was the opposition that might be expected from protected industries which would lose out as part of the liberalization process. Since these industries typically formed powerful political constituencies, a strategy which tempered and ameliorated the costs to these industries was required. Regional trade agreements presented themselves as a liberalization strategy which might meet this requirement since liberalization would be phased, and allowed industries to adjust to the competition from neighbouring countries first before being faced with global competition. This strategy proved successful in mobilizing business support behind regional liberalization initiatives even if some industries would be adversely affected.[7]

Regionalism re-emerged, therefore, as a policy choice for developing countries because it proved useful in implementing neoliberal economic policies.[8] This context also explains some of the particular features which characterized the regionalism of the recent era and which earned it the title of 'new regionalism'. The adjective 'new' refers not only to the temporal dimension, but also to qualitative differences. The appeal of regionalism in the mid-1980s and 1990s for countries was that it allowed them to integrate more fully into the global economy, particularly into global capital flows. Thus, the new regionalism was characterized as an 'open regionalism'. Whether this term actually has any empirical content is debatable, but it is important in indicating the desire of the participants in regional agreements to emphasize that such agreements are seen as complementary to the process of globalization rather than as attempts to replace it.

A second characteristic of the new regionalism is that regional agreements were being formed which encompassed countries at very different levels of per capita GNP and of vastly different economic size. This feature of the new regionalism was recognized as a distinct shift from previous periods. For example, Park observes that 'the current trend towards regionalism involves North–South regional arrangements rather than South–South arrangements which were characteristic of the first wave' (Park, 1995: 23).[9] The role that regionalism played in facilitating FDI flows from Northern capital exporting countries to Southern capital importing countries helps to explain this characteristic of the new regionalism.

A third characteristic has been that regional agreements involving countries spanning the development divide have paid little attention to this divide in policy terms. The structural differences between developing and developed countries which formed the basis of much development theory and debate in the 1950s and

1960s have been viewed as only minimal barriers to free trade agreements between North and South. In NAFTA, for example, Mexico is regarded as needing no special treatment despite opening its economic borders to the largest economic power on earth.[10] In APEC, to take another example, while some statements talk of the development divide this amounts to little in policy terms. The major recognition of differences in developmental status comes in the time required to reach the free trade targets, which are 2010 for developed countries and 2020 for developing countries. In APEC, being a developing country means having a longer time period to reach free trade objectives. Otherwise, the new regionalism is premised on the existence of mutual advantages for both the countries of the North and the South from the liberalization of trade and international capital flows.

A fourth characteristic is that many regional trade agreements including developing countries are, relatively speaking, loosely structured. Typically they have not followed the forms of deeper integration witnessed in the EU or the tight legal structure of the NAFTA. For example, compared to the NAFTA, the Mercosur has no definitions about rules of origin, no mechanisms for resolving conflicts and no sections on foreign investment. The looseness, or vagueness, of many of AFTA's resolutions reflect the operations of the so-called 'ASEAN Way', noted for its lack of formality. New regional arrangements involving developing countries have therefore tended to be looser and more limited agreements reflecting both their newness and the difficulties – in terms of state capacity and the mobilization of political support – associated with implementing such agreements.

To summarize, the new regionalism may said to have the following characteristics:

- FDI-based (typically export-led) growth, underpinned by an ideology of neoliberalism;
- loosely structured;
- supported by business;
- minimizing North–South differences.

Bhagwati, writing in 1992, argued that the new regionalism would be likely to endure because 'it shows many signs of strength and few points of vulnerability' (1992: 16). The question we turn to here is whether the volatility of international capital flows might be one such point of vulnerability. That is, have the global financial crises undermined the basis for the new regionalism as summarized above?

As a first step in analysing this question, I first briefly consider the causes and nature of the financial crises and the response to them by the IFIs and Western governments and organizations.

The financial crises: causes and proposed solutions

The 1990s have witnessed a number of financial crises, with the crisis affecting some of the European countries in 1992 and the Mexican peso crisis of 1994 being precursors of the financial crises which occurred from 1997 onwards in Asia, Russia and Brazil. It is these latter episodes, especially the Asian financial crisis, upon which we focus here. What started as the failure of one bank – Finance One – in one country – Thailand – in July 1997 ended up debunking the 'East Asian miracle', spreading to the most important economy in both 'transition Europe' and in Latin America, and leading to calls for a 'new international financial architecture'. How did this happen?[11]

Several theories have been advanced for the causes of the Asian financial crisis. Two of the most popular are the 'crony capitalism' and 'financial panic' hypotheses (Miller and Zhang, 1999). As MacLean (1999) has argued, the first theory has become widely accepted despite its lack of empirical evidence. It is based on the hypothesis that government – business relations in Asian countries were 'too close' and that, as a result, lending by financial institutions was subject to moral hazard problems. That is, financial institutions acted as if lenders had implicit government guarantees and therefore extended imprudently excessive loans to borrowers. When the borrowers could not repay the loans the weak positions of financial institutions became clear and foreign investors withdrew their money, fearing that they might be faced with non-performing loans. The role of capital inflows in this theory is that they exacerbated the problem by making greater resources available to financial institutions initially, and further exacerbated the problem once the crisis started by the size and swiftness of their withdrawal.[12] However, the behaviour of foreign investors may be described as largely 'rational' and the main causes of the problem – as opposed to exacerbating factors – were financial institutions, which were under-regulated and under-supervised, government–business relations which were too close, and corporations which were operating under poor governance structures.

The 'financial panic' hypothesis argues that the main cause of the financial crises was an irrational panic among speculative investors. The institutional weaknesses of Asian developing countries were all well known for years, risk premiums were relatively low and market forecasts were good. The timing, spread and severity of the crises must therefore be explained primarily in terms of the behaviour of investors who, with self-fulfilling expectations, bet on Thailand having to devalue its currency given its trade deficits. Once Thailand was forced to devalue, this reinforced expectations and investors looked for 'similar' countries. Thus countries with fixed exchange rates, low foreign exchange reserves, trade deficits and high inflows of short-term capital were potential targets for investor panic and currency flight; many became actual targets. Countries with non-transparent financial systems and close government–business relations such as China, Taiwan and India escaped the crisis not because there was less 'cronyism' here but because they did not have high trade deficits, or had large foreign exchange reserves, or had not liberalized their capital accounts to permit large inflows of short-term capital, or – at least in China's case – all three.[13]

While I would argue that the financial panic hypothesis fits the facts best, whatever the relative merit of these two hypotheses, the outcome was that countries had to resort to large bail-outs from the IMF complete with the usual array of austerity measures which plunged many of the countries further into recession (MacLean *et al.*, 1999). The policy packages of the IMF, especially their deflationary impacts, have come in for a great deal of criticism even from mainstream sources. However, rather than focus on those here I want to discuss the longer term issues and, in particular, how it is proposed to prevent future crises through the construction of a 'new international financial architecture'.

As Eichengreen has written, 'reforming the international financial architecture is a game that any number can play. Predictably, there already exists an abundance of proposals' (1999: 79). Some of these proposals have come from the core industrial countries both individually and collectively. The UK, US, French and Canadian governments have all proposed reforms aimed at reducing the risk and impacts of financial crises (Eichengreen, 1999). While they differ in content and emphasis, there are some common elements in the recognition of the need to provide countries experiencing crises with the ability to call on extra credit lines and/or restrict short-term capital flows, for medium-term liberalization of capital accounts in an 'orderly' manner and for longer term policies aimed at increasing financial 'transparency' and improving corporate governance.

Not unsurprisingly, these ideas are also predominant in the G-7 and G-20 proposals for international financial reform (the latter being significant for its inclusion of 'systemically important developing countries'). The emphasis is very much on the need for greater transparency for financial and non-financial institutions in the reporting, accounting and auditing of their international lending and borrowing. These measures are intended to apply in both creditor and debtor countries, and to government as well as the private sector. Various proposals for transparency reporting have also been advanced which include the IMF as well as nation-states. Innovations in bond-issuing and loan-contracting have also been proposed which essentially involve some kind of risk-sharing between borrower and lender in the event of a financial crisis and allow the borrower to defer repayment for a specified period in return for pre-negotiated sums. These arrangements essentially involve reducing the liquidity of short-term lending. However, noticeably absent from all of these proposals is any significant discussion of the need to reduce short-term capital inflows through some form of 'Tobin tax' or through the type of capital import regulations which have been used by Chile and Malaysia. In short, the proposals for the new financial architecture place most emphasis on the need for 'information', 'transparency', and 'surveillance' in line with the 'crony capitalism' explanation of the financial crises. The need for the systematic regulation of international capital flows and for mechanisms to address macro-economic imbalances caused by swings in the currencies of the core countries have been given relatively little weight in comparison.

Given the causes of the crises, and the timidity of the proposed solutions emanating from governments and the IFIs, the task facing emerging developing countries in managing their economies remains, in the era of globalised capital flows, Herculean (for a more activist approach see Blecker, 1999). How regionalism as a development strategy has been affected by this is discussed in the following section.

Regionalism and development strategy after(?) the financial crises

The current combination of regionalism and neoliberal development strategy which characterizes the 'new regionalism' could be challenged by either or both of its components losing popularity. Only if regionalism and neoliberalism remain popular will the regionalism of the mid-1980s/1990s continue into the twenty-first century. At first sight, such a movement may appear improbable, since proposals for new regional arrangements seem to be as popular as ever with Japan recently raising the possibility of forming a Northeast Asian regional grouping and with the South African-led Southern Africa Development Community agreeing in 1998 on a plan to have zero tariffs on 90 per cent of intra-regional trade by 2006 (Dludlu, 1998; MITI, 1999: 46).

However, to analyse the issue more systematically, this section will examine the impact of the global financial crises on the four factors characterizing the new regionalism identified on pages 87–8, namely, the commitment to foreign-investment export-led growth, the loosely structured nature of the arrangements, the support of a pro-liberalization business lobby and the minimization of North–South frictions. This is obviously a large topic and one requiring an empirical approach. To permit this, the scope of the discussion will be restricted to discussing two regional agreements, namely, AFTA and Mercosur. While much attention has been given to the comparative economic performance of the Asian and Latin America 'regions' in the wake of the financial crises (with the emphasis on the relatively better performance of the latter) the focus here is on the (common) implications of the financial crises for 'regionalism'.

The AFTA and the Mercosur both came into existence in the early 1990s. Mercosur was initiated in 1991 between Argentina, Brazil, Paraguay and Uruguay although it did not come into effect until four years later, while AFTA, which initially included the six ASEAN nations, was formed in 1993 (Bowles and MacLean, 1996). Both agreements were designed to reduce regional trade barriers and move towards free regional trade, although Mercosur preferred a customs union (with a common external tariff) while ASEAN went with a Free Trade Area. These two agreements are chosen as suitable for the present discussion given their importance as developing country regional agreements; they are not necessarily representative of all regional agreements but are informative for analysing the position of developing countries.

Foreign investment (and export-led) growth

There has been a clear continuation of the policy of regionalism as a vehicle for attracting FDI in both ASEAN and Mercosur. In fact, the impact of the financial crises has been to stimulate new initiatives in view of the effect which the crises have had on investor confidence in many emerging markets on the one hand, and the increased need for external financing on the other. In both ASEAN and Mercosur we find examples of a recommitment to regionalism as a viable strategy for attracting FDI and integrating into the global economy.

Considering ASEAN first, within three months of the collapse of the *baht*, the Thai deputy foreign minister reported that

> our global view is reflected in our commitment to actively encourage foreign investment in Thailand . . . Although the rapid movement of capital flows has contributed to Thailand's present economic dilemma, we recognise that, with a better regulatory framework in place, we must keep our doors open and promote the cross-border flow of international capital. Only in this way can we achieve greater liberalisation, in turn widening and deepening our potential industrial capacities.
>
> (*Bangkok Post*, 3 October 1997)

The deputy foreign minister then continued by arguing how important Thailand's participation in regional associations such as ASEAN, APEC, the Greater Mekong Sub-region and Bist-ec (the Bangladesh, India, Sri Lanka, Thailand – Economic Cooperation Forum) were to meeting this objective.

The potential role played by regional liberalization as a policy has also been supported by other ASEAN states. As the ASEAN Secretary-General has noted:

> ASEAN leaders have made regional economic integration a primary component of the region's response to the economic troubles that have hit it. They know that ASEAN needs investment for the recovery of its economies, and that a large integrated market can attract investments much more effectively than small, fragmented ones. The economies of scale made possible by larger markets make for more efficient production and marketing. Regional integration fosters competition within the region before regional industries and firms face the inevitable competition brought on by globalization.
>
> (Severinto, 1999)

To support this beyond the level of rhetoric, ASEAN has announced a number of initiatives aimed at providing some substance to this response. For example, the ASEAN economic ministers in December 1998 agreed to a pro-business package which gave additional incentives to foreign investors for a two-year period. Increased FDI was seen as a way out of the crisis (*Agence France Presse*, 12 December 1998). FDI inflows into ASEAN averaged US$14.9bn p.a. between 1990 and 1995 and rose to US$28.96bn in 1996, representing 22.5 per cent of all FDI flows to developing countries; there is no evidence that ASEAN leaders wish to turn their backs on this. Other initiatives include the bringing forward of the AFTA tariff liberalization schedule and the announcement of the ASEAN Industrial Cooperation Scheme by which products manufactured in two or more ASEAN countries can receive AFTA tariff treatment immediately, a benefit that has subsequently been claimed by MNCs from Japan, Europe and the US. The ASEAN Investment Area, which opens up the manufacturing sector to ASEAN producers on national treatment basis, has been announced and, as medium-term measures, the Hanoi

Plan of Action includes capital market development and trade liberalization initiatives for ASEAN to achieve between 1999 and 2004.

ASEAN's continuing faith in foreign investment-led growth as a development strategy and use of regionalism as a mechanism to achieve this is matched by Mercosur leaders' assessment. Argentinean President Menem has justified pursuing Mercosur on the grounds that 'Mercosur has become a magnet for foreign direct investments' which 'increased by 20 per cent from 1997 to 1998 to over $31 billion' (*Telam* (Buenos Aires), 29 June 1999).[14] Furthermore, the continued role of Mercosur as a mechanism for wider liberalization and participation in the global economy is still very much in evidence. Menem has argued that 'there is no doubt in my mind that the upcoming century will be indelibly marked by the move toward a more global economy and the clear tendency toward open regionalism' (Rocasalbas, 1999). Brazilian President Cardoso has argued that 'Mercosur has consolidated itself as the main promoter of the strategy to insert Brazil in the international economic scenario' (Cardoso, 1999), and that regionalization and globalization should be seen as complementary processes. Chile, which has developed close ties with Mercosur, has also shared this view with President Frei, arguing (in July 1998) that 'there is now a new concept of integration, following many years of nationalism that divided us . . . The entire region is characterized by a common economic strategy of opening to the world market. Isolationist policies would today be shortsighted and, frankly, irresponsible' (*Telam* (Buenos Aires), 24 July 1998). As an indication of its continuing desire to pursue regionalism, Mercosur has sought an agreement to establish a free trade area with the Community of Andean Nations (CAN).

The continued attraction of FDI for ASEAN and Mercosur represents not only a continuation of neoliberalism at the ideological level but also a practical judgement that FDI was not the cause of the recent crises.[15] Despite fears of 'firesale FDI' there has been a further bolstering of the position that attracting more FDI is desirable and it is now common to make a distinction between 'good' (i.e. long-term) capital flows and 'bad' (i.e. short-term) capital flows. Even Malaysian Prime Minister Mahathir, the fiercest critic of speculators, accepts this (*Bungei Shunju* (Tokyo), 28 July 1998).

However, beneath the rhetoric of support for regionalism, and notwithstanding the initiatives taken to foster greater integration, it is clear that the financial crises have led to major strains in regional economic relations. In particular, responses to crises have inevitably been based on national strategies, and these have led to increased protectionist pressures and tensions between countries. Tariffs and non-tariff barriers (NTBs) have been used in ASEAN as countries have sought to protect their own industries in times of crisis (Chanwirot, 1998). The Philippines has also argued for a 3 per cent minimum tariff, as opposed to AFTA's official zero tariff goal, to protect its tax revenues (Cahiles-Magkilat, 1999). ASEAN members have also been exploring ways of unilaterally expanding their extra-regional markets to the extent that the ASEAN Secretary-General has cautioned that 'links with developed markets and the global economy must not be forged at ASEAN's expense or as an alternative to it' (Severinto, 1999).

In Mercosur, the two leading economies Brazil and Argentina both suffered recessions in 1999. Intra-regional trade fell by 10 per cent in 1998 and was down a further 20 per cent in the first two months of 1999. The devaluation of the Brazilian *real* in February 1999 put strains on other countries as they feared imports from Brazil. Argentina has responded with a number of NTBs including import licences (Rocha, 1999), and quality certificates for products such as electronics. Brazil has new rules for entry of canned food from Argentina and the problems in reducing the number of commodities on Mercosur's exemption lists have increased. Argentina has enforced anti-dumping measures against Brazilian steel and Brazil has threatened to resort to the WTO, with Mercosur proving ineffective in mediating such disputes. In addition, Mercosur members have entered into bilateral negotiations with other countries breaking the so-called 'four plus one' strategy (Goitia, 1999). For example, Brazil reached agreement with CAN first without its Mercosur partners which it viewed as dragging its feet on the issue (Oliveira, 1999).

Thus, at the level of official discourse, commitment to an open regionalism based on attracting FDI has remained strong and constitutes a part of states' responses to the economic crises emanating from the financial crises. However, beneath this, the economic crises have also placed strains on regional economic cooperation as national responses more firmly rooted in protectionism have been in evidence, and as countries have sought extra-regional markets as ways out of recession. These strains have been evident in both ASEAN and Mercosur and represent a challenge to open regionalism, a challenge brought on by the pressures of recession. There is no doubt, therefore, that currency crises which induce recessions and threaten to unleash competitive devaluations make regionalism more difficult to sustain;[16] the question therefore becomes whether currency crises can be mitigated, a topic to which I now turn.

Loosely structured

The desire of countries to limit the destabilizing impacts of capital flows has resulted in the adoption of various policies designed to achieve this end. Malaysia's capital controls have attracted much attention, as has Chile's requirement that foreign investors place 30 per cent of their investment with the central bank for one year. Argentina requires banks to increase their reserves by 15 per cent every time they receive a deposit as a way of preventing banks with little capital from accepting a lot of short term resources which may be drawn on at any time (Fraga and Oliveira, 1999). The need for increased regulation of short-term capital flows has also led to demands for mechanisms which might increase 'transparency'. These mechanisms have been mooted at the regional level in ASEAN but have proven difficult to implement. ASEAN agreed in late 1997 to set up a surveillance mechanism to assist in crisis identification and prevention. However, Indonesia and Malaysia were wary of the information requirements, although these are supposed to be the same as those required by the IMF.[17] At the ASEAN foreign ministers' meetings in July 1998, Thailand's proposal for a more open debate on domestic issues was quashed (Manibhandu, 1998). There was also some backing away from commitments already made on economic surveillance illustrating the problems of changing the 'ASEAN Way' of 'non-interference'. Thus measures designed to increase transparency at the regional level have proven problematic for ASEAN and may require degrees of regional cooperation which are beyond the desire or capacity of member states to deliver.[18] This same problem is also evident in the evolving debates over exchange rate policies to minimize the risk of currency and financial crises.

The debate over exchange rate policy has been initiated as a result of the view that the financial crises arose as a result of countries pegging their currencies to the US dollar. As this peg became unsustainable, foreign investors quickly sold off their holdings thereby causing a currency crisis which the central banks were unable to combat. Post-crisis debate has therefore centred on preventive measures. Basically, countries are faced with the 'trilemma' of being unable to simultaneously maintain fixed exchange rates, liberalized capital accounts and control of interest rates.[19] IMF prescriptions have been based on giving up control of interest rates but the resulting recessions have robbed this of much credibility. Malaysia has opted for giving up liberalized capital accounts but runs the risk of being cut off from international capital flows, a move which most countries have been reluctant to pursue to any great degree.[20] Exchange rate flexibility would remove from countries the need to defend unsustainable exchange rates but the resulting exchange rate volatility, especially given their propensity for overshooting, makes this an unacceptable option for many countries as well.

The search for a way out of this 'trilemma' has focused mainly on institutional arrangements which might increase the credibility of fixed exchange rate commitments and/or lessen the likelihood of speculative attacks on national currencies. This search for new institutional arrangements has largely involved three options which might be capable of performing this role, namely, currency boards, dollarization and regional currencies. There are some similarities in the debates in Southeast Asia and Latin America on these issues, although there are also differences, with dollarization being more seriously considered in Latin America than in Southeast Asia.[21]

With respect to ASEAN, the attractiveness to policy elites of deeper forms of integration involving a common market and even a single currency have become evident.[22] Other proposals have included plans by ASEAN countries to settle trade using ASEAN currencies rather than the US dollar and also agreeing to try to balance trade between member countries. Malaysia has even suggested moving away from using currencies and increasing barter trade (*Bungei Shunju* (Tokyo), 28 July 1998). Another possibility has been the suggestion of pegging currencies against a trade-weighted currency basket rather than against the US dollar. Such moves have also been welcomed by Japan which is actively seeking to internationalize the yen and increase the yen's use in Asian regional trade. Japanese commentators have therefore argued that 'as the currencies of the countries of Asia were totally dependent upon the dollar, when the dollar ran into a major problem, the Asian countries were affected immediately. Therefore, transforming the yen into some kind of a buffer [to reduce such negative impacts] became an extremely important issue.'[23] Thailand requested that the yen be internationalized as soon as possible after the currency crisis, and Asian central bankers have indicated their interest in a system based on pegging against a basket of currencies including the euro, the dollar and the yen and other trading partners.

The move towards the increasing use of regional currencies to settle intra-ASEAN trade (or the more ambitious use of a single currency) is problematic for at least two reasons. First, the relatively low volume of intra-ASEAN trade makes the use of regional currencies of limited utility in reducing the scope for speculation and, second, requires a higher level of economic cooperation than ASEAN has hitherto been able to achieve (Bayoumi and Mauro, 1999). These problems are perhaps even more evident in Mercosur where the debate over exchange rate policy has moved well beyond the tentative nature of discussion in ASEAN.

The option which caught most attention was Argentina's announcement of its intention to unilaterally move to dollarize its economy. By so doing it would literally eliminate the possibility of a currency crisis by removing any exchange rate to defend. The costs of such a policy are high in that it implies the complete abandonment of monetary sovereignty, but this was apparently a cost that the government was willing to pay in order to gain the potential benefits which might arise from currency certainty. However, more recently, this option seems to have waned as Mercosur has aired its own collective solution, namely, the move towards a single currency. As a prelude to this, Mercosur countries have announced that they will be coordinating macro-economic policies more closely. At the sixteenth Mercosur Summit held in June 1999 the need to coordinate macro-economic policies between member states and avoid unilateral devaluations such as that of Brazil in February were stressed (*Telam* (Buenos Aires), 22 February 1999). Presidents Cardoso (Brazil) and Menem (Argentina) proposed the setting up of a 'small Maastricht' for Mercosur with the eventual aim of moving towards a single currency and an *ad hoc* group to coordinate macro-economic policies was established (Burgueno, 1999). Both countries are also debating fiscal responsibility laws which would complement this coordination by setting legal targets for budget deficits and public borrowing.

In practical terms, such plans would certainly test Mercosur's ability to achieve such a level of policy harmonization and coordination. In addition, tax systems differ widely and Brazil is going ahead with its own VAT plan. The single currency option is also subject to the same problems in Mercosur as for ASEAN, namely, that most investment flows are from outside the region and so speculation between a single currency and other currencies is still possible. Furthermore, none of the Mercosur countries has sufficient credibility to back a single currency.

In both regions, the move to coordinate policies in response to the financial crisis, whether it be for surveillance of capital flows in ASEAN or the more ambitious plans for macro-economic coordination and the possibility of a single currency for Mercosur, represent qualitatively higher degrees of integration and coordination than have been apparent in either bloc in the past. The loosely structured regionalism of the past two decades would have to undergo a significant change if these proposals are to materialize. For this reason, there is good reason to be sceptical whether either regional grouping is capable of achieving such a degree of coordination.

Of course, the exchange rate credibility problem need not be solved by regional means (Eichengreen, 1998). There is no necessary reason why solutions need to be devised at the regional level; NAFTA has been implemented without the adoption of a single currency and has survived the Mexican peso crisis of 1994 without moving in that direction. While it is true that regionalism need not take this deeper form, it seems that leaders are wary of failing to address critical economic issues without a regional dimension for fear of weakening the perceived utility of, and commitment to, regional associations. This commitment has already come under strain because of the economic crisis in many countriesm and we will now turn to a brief examination of whether one key constituency, that of business, has reneged on its enthusiasm for regional liberalization.

Business support

Evidence from Latin America suggests that although particular industrial sectors have been vociferous in calling for protectionism, the broad constituency in favour of continued regional liberalization has survived the financial crisis in Brazil. Thus the Congress of Latin American Businessmen (CEAL) requested greater efforts of economic integration within Mercosur which they argued had made progress in theory but still had far to go in practice (Estado de Sao Paolo, 9 June 1999).

The evidence from ASEAN is, however, more contradictory. The fifty-sixth ASEAN-CCI Council Meeting held in May 1999 reaffirmed its support for AFTA and regional integration, and welcomed the ASEAN Investment Area. However, there were also noticeable words of caution about the wisdom of further liberalization and, indeed, the basis of the neoliberal paradigm. For example, the CCI recommended the adoption of measures to stimulate demand in Asia as a main source of economic growth in addition to export-led strategies to ensure a sustainable economic recovery. Furthermore, they argued that 'lenders should be mindful that over-borrowing is not one-sided and should not be too quick to liquidate companies but should help to ensure the continued survival of viable ASEAN corporations through sound corporate debt restructuring, improved corporate governance, and accountability'.

In terms of the need for increased transparency, the ASEAN-CCI was quick to note that this should begin with more transparency in currency speculation and foreign exchange trading. This includes, the CCI continued, enhancing transparency on the activities of currency traders, hedge fund managers as well as banks dealing with currency trading and curbing the amount of leverage that is allowed for speculative transactions. Perhaps more surprisingly, the ASEAN-CCI concluded that 'as economies in the region are still in the process of restructuring and recovery, the Chamber is not in favour of a new millennium round of trade negotiations at the WTO Ministerial Conference at the end of this year' (Joint Communiqué issues at the fifty-sixth ASEAN-CCI Council Meeting, Rangoon, 27 May 1999).

The questioning of the desirability of a millennium round, especially when such questioning is assured to have virtually no effect, is a strong indication that commitment to trade liberalization among business elites in ASEAN is waning. While other groups in civil society have opposed globalization, the shift in the views of business leaders as a result of the economic crisis signals a potential undermining in the coalition supporting neoliberalism which could also affect the ability to pursue regional initiatives consistent with this policy.

Minimizing differences between North and South

The new regionalism was premised on the existence of mutual advantages for countries of both the North and South from increased economic integration and openness, an underlying shared assumption of the generally positive benefits of free trade, in contrast to development theory of earlier decades and the regionalism which it spawned. Ironically, just as the new regionalism was emerging based on a greater acceptance of the mutual interests of North and South, new frictions were also emerging in the world trade negotiations. As Whalley has noted, the linkage of trade and environment and trade and labour standards 'threatens to revive North–South tensions in the trading system' (Whalley, 1996: 40). The new regionalism notwithstanding, North–South tensions were still evident, and regional groupings continued to have a significant political motive. Have North–South tensions been fuelled by the global financial crises?

The power of international financial markets and of the IFIs, seen as serving the interests of their Northern sponsors, have certainly been subject to much criticism in official and popular circles. In the face of this, regionalism has been seen as a necessary political project to counterbalance the power of Northern interests. This has been clearly expressed by the ASEAN Secretary-General who has argued, in forceful terms, that

> a new world order has not yet arrived, in which the interests are balanced and disputes adjudicated fairly under benign rules that are impartially applied and effectively enforced upon all. It is all too clear that such a utopia remains far from being upon us. Until it arrives, a long, long time from now, if ever, economic power, whether of states or of corporations, will continue to have preponderant advantage. In the face of this, weaker states must band together regionally, strengthening their solidarity and advancing their common interests.
>
> (Severinto, 1999)

The view that the rules of the world trading system are applied unequally has also been expressed in Latin America. Brazilian President Cardoso, for example, has called for reversal of the injustice of the 'asymmetric globalization' processes affecting emerging developing economies. In particular, the faster pace of the liberalization of Latin American markets than of those in industrial countries, with the result that trade growth is much higher in one direction than in the other, has been highlighted (Cardoso, 1999).

Mercosur has therefore been seen as a vital political project enabling Latin American countries to increase their bargaining position with respect to the major economic powers over trade issues. Thus, Mercosur has taken a negotiating position with respect to the US and the EU that all sectors, including agriculture, must be on the table for any trade negotiations. Regional collaboration has also put Mercosur in the position of having both the EU and US vying with each other over completion dates of agreements; the FTAA completion date is set at 2005 and the EU has pushed (unsuccessfully) for an earlier date for the EU–Mercosur accord.

Regionalism as a political response to international power imbalances therefore seems to be of continued importance. The financial crises, and solutions to them, have simply added one more area where developing countries see the need for these imbalances to be addressed. At an EU–Mercosur summit, Chilean President Frei, for example, argued that the world needs 'new institutions that adequately regulate the vast financial flows that characterise the global economy' and called for European countries to ensure that Latin American countries were not marginalized in the process, warning that 'we cannot continue passively contemplating the limitations that financial crises impose on the growth of our countries' (Results of EU-ALC Summit Detailed, Estrategia, Santaigo, 30 June 1999).

The effects of the global financial crises for the four factors identified on pages 87–8 as characterizing the new regionalism are summarized below in Table 6.2 and discussed further in the conclusion.

Table 6.2 Summary of effects of financial crises on support for 'neoliberal regionalism' in ASEAN and Mercosur

Factors underpinning 1980s/1990s regionalism	*Effects of financial crises in ASEAN*	*Effects of financial crises in Mercosur*
FDI funded export-led growth	Enhanced role for FDI at official level; re-emergence of protectionism in practice	Enhanced role for FDI at official level; re-emergence of protectionism in practice
Loosely structured	Challenged by 'transparency' requirements in monitoring capital flows	Challenged by macro-economic coordination and single currency initiatives to reduce currency volatility
Business support	Waning as economic crisis takes hold	Broadly supportive
Minimizing North–South differences	Increased recognition of global power imbalances	Increased recognition of global power imbalances

Conclusion

This chapter has identified the critical factors underlying the re-emergence of regionalism as a popular policy choice for developing countries within the context of the rise of neoliberalism during the past two decades. The comparative analysis of two of the most prominent regional economic arrangements, namely, AFTA and Mercosur, has revealed that the global financial crises have challenged the continuing applicability of some of these factors in important ways. These challenges have come both to neoliberalism as a development strategy and to regionalism as a viable economic project. For example, it has been argued that a loosely constituted regionalism is more difficult to maintain as countries attempt to forge more closely coordinated economic policies at the regional level to insulate themselves from currency crises. The short-term measures required when such crises occur have also inevitably led to the adoption of nationalist economic responses which have strained relations with regional neighbours. The necessary adjustments have also led to a weakening of business support, at least in ASEAN, for further liberalization measures. The barriers to be overcome before regionalism can operate successfully have therefore been raised and the degree of coordination now required may prove difficult for many regional arrangements to sustain.

However, the appeal of foreign investment-led growth as a development strategy appears undiminished to policy-making elites, and the utility of regional arrangements as a magnet for foreign investment is still predominant. In this respect, the new regionalism does exhibit considerable resilience. The desire to regulate short-term capital inflows has not spilled over into any wariness about longer term FDI flows and a core component of the neoliberal development strategy remains intact; the appeal of regionalism as a mechanism to facilitate this strategy also remains strong.

Regionalism has also been bolstered by the perceived need to provide a strong and coordinated response among developing countries to the economic power of the US and the Europeans both bi-regionally and within the context of the next multilateral round of world trade talks. However, this trend is more ambiguous since it is premised on the need to address power imbalances within the international system and, as such, challenges one of the assumptions of the new regionalism, namely, that an open international system provides advantages to countries of both the North and South. Nevertheless, it is more reasonable to describe this challenge as leading to a regionalism which tempers, rather than rejects, neoliberalism. It does raise a potentially interesting historical parallel, however, in that the regionalism of the 1950s and 1960s was spurred in part by the desire of developing countries to insulate themselves from the effects of the business cycles in industrial countries, cycles which were argued to be amplified in the primary commodity-producing developing countries. It will be interesting to see the extent to which a regionalism might emerge in the late 1990s based on the desire of developing countries to insulate themselves from the effects of global capital market instability, an instability which has been particularly acute in emerging developing economies.[24]

At present, therefore, it seems that the factors supporting regionalism as a policy choice have been sufficiently strong to withstand the counter-pressures arising from the global financial crises. Whether this remains the case depends crucially on whether we are indeed 'after' the financial crises or simply in a period of hiatus between crises.

This in turn depends partly on whether a 'new financial architecture' is put in place capable of effectively controlling volatile speculative international capital movements. This would seem an unlikely outcome at present given the assumptions on which the need for a new architecture is based as argued in the section on pages 88–90. It is possible, therefore, that if further crises occur the developing countries of the semi-periphery which embraced regionalism as a policy choice in the wake of the international debt crisis of the early 1980s may yet turn away from regionalism, at least in its current neoliberal form, as a result of the global financial crises of the late 1990s.

Notes

1 I am grateful to Osvaldo Croci and Brian MacLean for comments on this chapter and to SSHRC for financial support.
2 For a similar assessment of the developing countries' motives for entering regional arrangements in the 1960s, see also Jagdish Bhagwati (1992: 10–11) who notes that during this period 'there was an outbreak of FTA proposals in the developing countries as well. While stimulated by the European examples, they were motivated by the altogether different economic rationale formulated by Cooper and Massell, Johnson and Bhagwati. This was that, given any targeted level of import-substituting industrialization, the developing countries, with their small markets, could reduce the cost of this industrialization by exploiting economies of scale through preferential opening of markets with one another. By the end of the 1960s, however, the attempts at forming regional free trade areas and customs unions along these lines had also collapsed.' For examples of South–South regional agreements during this period see Pazos, 1973.
3 See also Rodrik (1999: 37) who argues that 'the attitude of many developing-country policymakers toward DFI has undergone a remarkable turn-around in the last couple of decades, even more so than in the case of exports. Multinational enterprises used to be seen as the emblem of dependency; they have now become the saviours of development. Today's policy literature is filled with extravagant claims about positive spillovers from DFI.'
4 By 1997, official development assistance was 15 per cent of total financial flows to developing countries (see UNCTAD, 1998: 13).
5 This is discussed further below on pages 91–8 for the case of AFTA and the Mercosur.
6 MNCs are therefore attracted to regional trading areas for a variety of reasons. The export orientation of FDI and the incentive to FDI provided by the existence of a large consumer market do vary significantly between countries and regions. See UNCTAD, 1998.
7 Furthermore, as export industries expanded so did their political influence, which further reinforced the pro-liberalization pressures on government. See Busch and Milner (1994) and Bowles and MacLean (1996) for the role played by the ASEAN–CCI in this respect.
8 This was also recognized by the donor countries of the North. For example, Kennes points out that 'one of the key objectives of the EU's development cooperation under the Maastricht Treaty is "the smooth and gradual integration of developing countries into the world economy". It is widely recognised that regional integration forms an essential part of the strategy for achieving this' (1998: 26).
9 The importance of this shift is also emphasized by Robson who argues that the North–South linkage was 'perhaps the single novel feature of the new regionalism in practice' (1993: 340)
10 Tariff elimination is occurring at different rates but these rates are determined by sector rather than by country.
11 This question is answered only in summary fashion here and draws upon the more extended discussion in MacLean *et al.* (1999). For the most comprehensive source, readers are referred to Roubini (n.d.).

12 According to the Ministry of International Trade and Industry, 'private capital flows into the ASEAN 4 and the Republic of Korea, the countries most heavily hit by the crisis, apparently went from a net inflow of US$93.8 billion in 1996 to a net outflow of US$6 billion (estimated value) in 1997, indicating an outflow over a very short period of time of capital equivalent to as much as 10 percent of the GDP of these five countries' (MITI, 1999: 3).

13 Other commentators, such as Bergsten (1998), have also pointed to the role that fluctuations in the US dollar–yen and US dollar–European currency rates played in making the currency pegs utilized by many emerging economies unsustainable. This is a separate hypothesis although complementary to (or, at least, consistent with) the financial panic hypothesis.

14 Menem's assessment receives support from UNCTAD which notes that 'in the case of Mercosur, both Brazil and Argentina have attracted much higher FDI inflows since the constitution of that market in 1995, as, on a smaller scale, has Uruguay which aspires to be the administrative centre of the subregion' (UNCTAD, 1998: 251).

15 This assessment receives some support from an examination of the volatility of international capital flows. UNCTAD reports that 'recent episodes of financial turmoil have focused international attention on the problem of the volatility of private foreign capital flows and the extent to which that volatility creates an unstable environment detrimental to economic development. During the period 1992–1997, commercial bank loans displayed the highest volatility (0.71), as measured by the coefficient of variation, followed by total portfolio investment (0.43) and FDI (0.35)' (UNCTAD, 1998: 14). See also MITI (1999: 20–3) for support for the argument that the currency crises of the 1990s have typically differed from those of the 1980s in their causes, and that high short-term debt ratios and low foreign currency reserves have been important explanatory variables in the 1990s crises.

16 These crises may also induce a reduction in FDI, which would further undermine support for regionalism, if, as Blomstrom and Kokko (1997) argue, the positive effects of regional economic integration on FDI inflows are greatest when accompanied by domestic liberalization and macro-economic stability.

17 The surveillance mechanism is initially to be under the auspices of the Asian Development Bank.

18 At an ASEAN summit meeting in November 1999, it is reported that ASEAN discussed the possibility of having three countries – probably Singapore, Thailand and Vietnam – form a smaller group responsible for responding to emergencies. Such a move is seen as significant in moving away from the non-interventionist and consensus *modus operandi* which has hitherto characterized ASEAN. See 'The other summit: Asia meets in Manila', at <http: //www.stratfor.com/>, 30 November 1999. Whether this possibility will translate into significant change remains to be seen.

19 See MITI (1999: 30–1) for discussion of how this trilemma was handled by the international monetary system in the post-war period.

20 Research by MITI concludes that Japanese MNCs operating in Southeast Asia were significantly affected by foreign exchange losses. As a result they have strong interests in exchange rate stability, and were supportive of many measures to control volatile short-term capital movements. The policy of encouraging longer term FDI but discouraging short-term speculative capital as in the Malaysian case may therefore have a greater chance of success than many critics of the Malaysian policies have suggested (see MITI, 1999: 30).

21 Readers are referred to the collection of papers available at N. Roubini (n.d.), 'What caused Asia's economic and currency crisis?' for a discussion of the relative merits of all of these options. Attention here is focused on the single regional currency option.

22 The prospect of AFTA moving towards a common market was raised by Malaysian Prime Minister Mahathir in October 1997 and quickly endorsed by Thailand. Such an initiative was important for attracting more investment, maintaining economic

cooperation since investors now viewed the region's economies as similar, and providing increased political bargaining power.

23 Hisaya Nara, co-chairman of Keidanren's Financial System Committee at a round table organized by the Keidanren, 16 April 1999, on 'How to promote the internationalization of the yen'.

24 Critics of the neoliberal development strategy have argued that a refashioned regionalism may be a complement to a changed development model, a model more reminiscent of the development strategy of the 1960s. For example, Walden Bello has argued that 'regionalism can become an invaluable adjunct to . . . a process of domestic market-driven growth, but only if both processes are guided not by a perspective of neoliberal integration that will only serve to swamp the region's industries and agriculture by so-called "more efficient" third party producers, but by a vision of regional import-substitution and protected market-integration that gives the region's producers the first opportunity to serve the region's consumers' (Bello, 1999a).

7   Regionalism and Asia

Peter J. Katzenstein

The end of the Cold War has altered fundamentally the way we see the world.[1] The image of bipolarity is no longer useful as a shorthand description. Power politics is now occurring in complex regional contexts that undercut the stark assumption of the international system as unmitigated anarchy. And these regional contexts are making possible a variety of processes that put into question some conventional categories of analysis. The worldwide victory of capitalism blurs stark distinctions between capitalism and socialism and democracy and authoritarianism. Instead it places national political economies in a regional context that is shaped by a variety of processes.

It is relatively easy to state what a world of regions is not: a new world order, an end of history, or a clash of civilizations. Each of these generalizations is easily refuted; for example, by the surge in ethnic cleansing, the rise in ideology and religion, and the prevalence of hybridization processes across civilizations. Going beyond these generalizations we might ask whether world affairs are shaped primarily by state, global or regional effects. Focusing primarily on the effects of different states underlines unduly the heterogeneity of world politics. Conversely, highlighting the effects of global factors emphasizes too much the homogeneous context of world politics. Because they often mediate between national and global effects, regional effects, as in the story of Goldilocks, are neither too hot nor too cold, but just right.

Conceiving of the world in terms of structures is what some analytical perspectives in international relations and the social sciences more generally suggest. Polarity in the international state system and property rights in markets offer powerful examples of structural reasoning. Structures are slow-moving processes. In a world of rapid change we could do worse than trace empirically the effects of processes rather than stipulate analytically the effects of structures. A focus on a world of regions helps us to do so.

Existing explanations of regional orders focus on specific features of international politics: on polarity, on institutional efficiency, and on cultural (ethnic, religious or civilization) divisions. Rooted in realist, liberal and sociological styles of analysis, each approach has considerable strengths in making us understand regional orders as the outcome of balances of power or threat, institutionally and organizationally coordinated policies, and more or less contested identities. But each approach also confronts nagging difficulties. How many poles of power exist in contemporary world politics? How can institutional efficiency be measured? And how can clashing cultural values be integrated analytically with the fact of widespread cultural hybridity?

A world of regions is shaped by economic and social processes of regionalization and by structures of regionalism. Regionalization describes the geographic manifestation of international or global economic processes. Regionalism refers to the political structures that both reflect and shape the strategies of governments, business corporations, and a variety of non-governmental organizations and social movements. The analysis of these two facets of a world of regions requires theoretical eclecticism rather than parsimony in making selective use of the insights of sociological, liberal and realist styles of analysis.

Regions are, among other things, social constructions created through politics. The fact that Italy ended up in the North Atlantic Treaty Organization (NATO) was not 'natural', that is, determined by geography. It was due to an act of political imagination and a subsequent political process. What struck the members of the US Senate as exceedingly odd in the late 1940s today is questioned by no one: the location of a Mediterranean country in the North Atlantic region is both spatial and political. Following Karl Deutsch (1981), we define a region as a group of countries markedly interdependent over a wide range of different dimensions. This pattern of interdependence is often, but not always, indicated by patterns of economic and political transactions and social communications that differentiate groups of countries. Hence regions do not exist only as material objects in the world. They are more than the flow of goods and people across physical space that we may assume to be represented directly and accurately by cartographic depictions. Regions are also social and cognitive constructs that are rooted in political practice. This chapter explores this perspective on Asian regionalism in Section 1.

The effects of the international environment on regions can lead to a relatively open (as in the 1990s) or closed (as in the 1930s) type of regionalism. Regions can be peaceful and rich, or war-prone and poor. They can experience processes of enlargement and set standards for a growing number of polities (as is true of NATO and the EU) or of retraction, as appears possible for ASEAN and APEC in the wake of the Asian financial crisis. Sections 2 and 3 explore these themes with specific reference to Asia and the financial crisis of 1997.

Despite their variability, regional effects are of growing importance in world politics. To the question 'How should one think about international politics after the end of the Cold War?' it is plausible to answer 'as a world of regions'.

Regionalism and Asian collective identities

'Regionalism,' writes Kanishka Jayasuriya, 'is a set of cognitive practices shaped by language and political discourse, which through the creation of concepts, metaphors, analogies, determine how the region is defined; these serve to define the actors who are included (and excluded) within the region and thereby enable the emergence of a regional entity and identity' (Jayasuriya, 1994: 12). In their well-known book *Power and Interdependence*, Keohane and Nye (1977: 165–218) provide a good illustration. They apply their model of complex interdependence to two different bilateral relations: US–Canada and US–Australia. Controlling for a large number of cultural and political similarities, this comparison isolates, among others, differences in the costly effects of geographical distance. In the words of *The Economist*, Australia's problem is self-evident. 'Think of a Canada that had been towed away from where it is, and moored off Africa, and the problems of Australia's physical location becomes clear' (Keohane and Nye, 1977: 166).

Looking for Australia two decades later, salvage crews exploring mooring places off the coast of Africa are likely to come up empty-handed (Byrnes, 1994). Responding to dynamic economic growth in Asia, Opposition leader John Howard appealed to physical and economic geography when he stated that 'there is no doubt that we are incredibly fortunate that our geography has cast us next to the fastest growing region in the world' (Hudson and Stokes, 1997: 146). Geography-as-destiny is an argument in favour of fixed identities, as both the White Australia Policy and Australia's Oriental destiny illustrate.

Other arguments are invoked in the name of multiple identities. Political debate during the past two decades illustrates the process by which Australians are taking their turn to a multiracial and multicultural republic by coping with conflicting collective identities. The symbols of Australia's constitutional and national identities – flag and anthem – are subjects of serious political controversies. Australia is in the process of becoming more Asian but in a very specific manner. 'Without actually becoming Asian,' Gavan McCormack writes, 'Australia is struggling to articulate a regional universalism and to become simultaneously post-European and post-Asian, transcending both its own European racial and cultural heritage and any racially or culturally specific Asia' (McCormack, 1996: 178).

Asian values rather than regional universalism is the message that Singapore's political and cultural identity entrepreneurs are pushing. In contrast to Australia, Singapore's geographical placement in Asia is uncontested. Asia exists as a geographic term. But it is also what Gavan McCormack calls an 'imposed identity: a fantastic ideological construct without racial or cultural meaning . . . paradoxically, the notion of Asia strengthened the farther one moved away from it and receded as one entered into it' (McCormack, 1996: 161). As in the case of Australia, Singapore's forceful articulation of a regionally undefined ideology of Asian values points to the relevance of the perceptual dimension of Asian regionalism.

The government of Singapore has sanctioned think-tanks as legitimate voices of an ideology of Asian values that suits its domestic preoccupation with state building in a multi-ethnic society. In addition, 'think tanks, as discourse managers, are a means to project Asian identities outwards to the West. They articulate concepts about an "Asian Way" and provide intellectual justification for this discourse. In particular, the so-called Singapore School has been vociferous in championing Asian values' (McCormack, 1996: 178).

Which Asian values are to be invoked is a matter of serious disagreement, as is the degree of incompatibility between Asian and Western values. Singapore's stunning success in engineering an ambitious modernization process has given special urgency to policies that insist on the country's uniqueness. Modernization without Westernization offers a way of building a distinctive culture in a multi-ethnic society. During the past thirty years the government has attempted to establish an ideological consensus around the articulation of a tradition, including Asian values, that gives it a legitimate claim to moral leadership. Understanding how traditional Asian values translate into modern life thus is a central preoccupation and source of governmental power.

Classifying the population into four main groups (Chinese, Malay, Indian and Caucasian), for example, disregarded numerous subgroups within these ethnic communities. Eschewing a bottom-up melting-pot, Singapore has adopted a top-down salad bowl approach to manage its ethnic pluralism. Emphasizing Asian values is a possible way of side-stepping both the potentially disintegrative pulls of Chinese, Malay and Indian cultures and the potentially absorptive reach of Western influences. Geographically undefined Asian values are not the temporary expression of the cultural arrogance of one of Asia's miracle economies. Lacking a distinct identity, Asian values offer Singapore's political elites a plausible ideology for building a new state.

Housing policy offers another example. Uprooting virtually the entire population within a generation from very different, traditional settlements into a homogeneous set of Western-style high-rise apartments was a dramatic intrusion of the state into the family, a core of Asian values. Making housing available only to families, trying to arrange for extended family members to live in nearby flats, and giving priority to three-tier generational family groupings are ingenious ways of bringing together old and new traditions of family life. Such policies stand in the service of a new collective identity that can appeal to something modern and Western that is compatible with Asian values, and thus serves to strengthen an emerging collective identity for Singapore.

In language policy the government sought to achieve a similar outcome, quite possibly with less success. Singapore has four accepted languages: English, Mandarin, Malay and Tamil. The government has accepted English as the language of commerce that provides a central pillar for Singapore's economic prosperity. But it insists that schools teach the three mandated mother tongues while their importance has declined in the 1990s. Indians are to learn Tamil in school even though many of them no longer speak it at home. It was therefore no accident that in the early 1990s it was a company from Singapore that offered an advanced videotext system that allowed one to learn a new language phonetically. Technological innovation can help the younger generation to maintain a knowledge of 'their' mother tongue.

Singapore's championing of a specific set of Asian values finds parallels in Malaysia's blunt criticism of mistaken and dangerous Western human rights policies and its outspoken support for a cohesive East Asian community without US or Australian participation. Asian values subordinate individual rights to community obligations, and high growth strategies require strong not weak governments (Gurowitz, 1998: 230–79). For Malaysia the idea of an Asian political community is tied directly to the legitimacy of a soft authoritarian government that is dedicated to a policy of high economic growth and opposed to the growing importance of Western values. In the case of Singapore the leadership seeks to strengthen instead a preferred regional ideology of Asian values that avoids both the homogenization of Westernization and the divisiveness of different ethnic traditions.

Australia's universal regionalism and Singapore's and Malaysia's insistence on the specificities of an Asia that suits their domestic and international needs are flanking the emergence of an Asian Pacific identity that is open to multiple interpretations. The articulation of a specific regional ideology is not simply a ploy of governments seeking to eschew pressures of democratization and liberalization. Regional ideologies that entail specific collective identities are as important for Japan and the United States as they are for Singapore and Malaysia.

The Pacific Rim or Asia Pacific are good illustrations. For a very simple reason they have only a vague geographic referent. 'Definitions of the Pacific,' writes Arif Dirlik, 'are part of the very struggle over the Pacific that they seek to describe' (Dirlik, 1993a: 4). The Pacific community idea, one Australian journalist agrees, is 'a baby whose putative parents are Japanese and American and whose midwife is Australian' (Dirlik, 1993a: 8).

In recent decades Japan's regional ideology has been shaped by Akamatsu's flying geese theory of industrial growth and senescence (Korhonen, 1994). A leading specialist on Japan's relations with Asia, Okita Saburo, was so deeply influenced by Akamatsu's theory that later on he developed the concept of comprehensive security with its emphasis on diplomacy and aid and its rejection of the military means of statecraft. In 1955 Okita became head of the Research Division of the Economic Planning Agency. Following Akamatsu's basic insight, his plan for expanding Japanese exports focused on the unavoidable economic development of Asian economies. If Japan assisted that development process it would dispel animosities, divert attention from dangerous and wasteful political quarrels in Asia, enhance regional growth prospects, and thus create a more stable international environment profitable especially for Japan's highly competitive capital goods sector. This theory of industrial change was based on a conception of Asian regionalism in which governments were directly involved in the flow of trade, investment and aid.

The theory provided a strong intellectual foundation for Japan's Asia policy. In the 1960s Kojima Kiyoshi, Akamatsu's most distinguished and influential student, sought to implement the idea of creating a regional system in the Pacific area that would support the process of regional economic change through which Japan and its Asian neighbours would be indelibly linked. The Pacific Free Trade Area (PAFTA) that Kojima proposed in 1965 encompassed the United States, Canada, Australia and New Zealand. It was to be linked to an integrated region encompassing the Southeast Asian economies. Thus Japan would be connected to both the advanced US economy on whose markets its exports depended vitally, as well as backward Southeast Asia that was destined to absorb Japan's sunset industries.

While a PAFTA was never adopted, the second-track meetings that started in 1969 became a powerful lobby for a market-led integration of a broad Pacific area.

A decade later the then Foreign Minister Okita and Prime Minister Ohira Masayoshi, together with Australian Prime Minister Malcolm Fraser, convened a meeting that led to a non-governmental international seminar (the Pacific Economic Cooperation Conference, PECC). It advanced further a broad, market-based approach to Asia Pacific. PECC embodies a regional idea requiring an economic rather than political language. It reinforces rather than undermines national sovereignty. And it puts economic development and the future ahead of political atonement for past transgressions McCormack, 1996: 153–84).

The United States shares with Japan a strong commitment to Asia Pacific. For the US government that regional designation is not rooted in an old economic theory of region-wide industrial change. Asia Pacific and the Pacific Rim are instead more recent political indications of the strong interest that the US has in a continued involvement in Asian affairs. The US government supported strongly the creation of the Asia Pacific Economic Cooperation Ministerial Conference (APEC). It was inaugurated in Canberra in November 1989 and held its first summit in Seattle in November 1993. With a broad membership APEC supports the policies of economic liberalism that the US has championed throughout the 1980s and 1990s. In the early 1990s intense conflicts between the US and the EU leading to a possible failure of GATT's Uruguay Round and growing trade frictions between the US and Japan made APEC an attractive counter to a rising tide of protectionism. Business and government leaders and their economic advisers saw in Asia's market-based and open regionalism a stepping stone to a liberal, global economic order (Higgott and Stubbs, 1995: 519).

Such a view of Asia Pacific or the Pacific Rim is at odds with that held by many Asian governments. APEC's 1994 commitment to reach full trade liberalization by the year 2020 was, at best, a reluctant acquiescence of most APEC members to the pressures of the United States and Australia. In the aftermath of the Asian financial crisis, lukewarm attitudes cooled further to the point where policy objective and target date may well become, as in the case of Malaysia, merely indicative and non-binding. Many governments in Asia Pacific see market-based integration as a way of retaining government involvement in markets rather than as a process of weakening state institutions in the face of a liberalizing international economy.

Although the United States is becoming part of an emerging Asia-Pacific region in the 1990s, this does not connect in any meaningful way to an embryonic Asian-American identity of a growing segment of US citizens. 'Problems of Asian-American history,' writes Arif Dirlik, 'are also problems in the history of an Asia-Pacific regional formation' (1993b: 305). These problems have centred on one fact. In a Eurocentric Anglo-American culture, Asian-Americans have been viewed as Asian not American. Transpacific ties did not further a recognition of Asian elements in the collective identity of the United States as much as they denied Asians membership of the American political community. For the US to embrace Asia Pacific as a deeply held and meaningful aspect of its collective identity, the domestic politics of multiculturalism, beyond questions of race and Hispanic politics, would also have to politicize fully the strain of Asian-American identity that, to date, remains largely submerged.

Concepts such as Asia Pacific or the Pacific Rim designate a region that Britain traditionally has referred to as Asia or the Far East. The British Foreign Office continues now, as it did at the beginning of the twentieth century, to cover China, Japan, Korea and Mongolia (the 'Far East'), and Australia, New Zealand and a large number of small islands (the 'Pacific') in the Far Eastern and Pacific Department.[2] Britain's unchanging designations reflect political disengagement from Asia and contrast with Singapore's and Malaysia's changing political needs. Asian values and an East Asian community are important symbols for the consolidation of Singapore's and Malaysia's state identity along lines that are neither Western, nor specifically Chinese, Malay or Indian.

As is true of Singapore and Malaysia, neither the United States nor Japan rely on British terminology. Both, however, eschew references to Asian values and an East Asian community. For these two states Asia Pacific or the Pacific Rim are concepts that denote an Asia that is inclusive. These concepts eviscerate the divisions of the Cold War era – the split between East and West, North and South. Asia Pacific and the Pacific Rim have created their own institutionalized language of what Bruce Cumings calls 'rimspeak' (Cumings, 1993). Rimspeak matters, as does the idea of the 'Asia Pacific' that it both reflects and strengthens. Asian collective identities and regionalism refer to political, economic and cultural processes that are creating new relations between places and peoples (Nonini, 1993: 162).

Asian regionalism in international politics

China and Japan are important centres of the new Asian regionalism, but in ways quite different from the regionalism of Japan's Co-Prosperity Sphere of the 1930s and 1940s or George Orwell's nightmarish projection of a tripolar world (Orwell, 1948). While the old regionalism emphasized autarchy and direct rule, the new regionalism relies on interdependence and indirect rule.

Japan's growing role in the nine member states of the Association of Southeast Asian Nations (ASEAN) (Indonesia, Thailand, Malaysia, Philippines, Singapore, Brunei, Vietnam, Burma and Laos) can be traced easily in the areas of trade, aid, investment and technology transfer. In the two decades preceding the realignment of the major international currencies in the Plaza Accord of 1985, Japan accounted for close to half of the total aid and direct foreign investment in the region. The dramatic appreciation of the Yen after 1985 led to a veritable explosion in Japanese investment. Between 1985 and 1989 the total was twice as large as that between 1951 and 1984. The flow of aid also continued to increase as Japan recycled its trade surplus with the region. All governments in Southeast Asia became accustomed to bidding for Japanese investment capital, illustrated by the massive deregulation of their economies and the lucrative incentives they were willing to grant to foreign investors. More importantly, Japan's 'developmental state' became an object of emulation. The establishment of private trading companies and a general commitment by Southeast Asian governments to policies of vigorous export promotion give testimony to the widespread appeal of the Japanese model.

By the early 1990s the growth in Japanese influence in Asia had created widespread unease about the political consequences of intensifying economic relations with Japan. Japan's power was simply too large to be matched in the foreseeable future by any conceivable coalition of Asian states. With the total GNP of ASEAN amounting to no more than 15 per cent of Japan's, any development of a world of self-contained regions in the Northern half of the globe would leave ASEAN's members at the mercy of a Japanese colossus. Most Asian states thus saw in China and the United States useful counterweights to Japan's growing power.

Within a few years after Japan's financial bubble had burst, its anaemic macro-economic performance and a deep crisis in its financial sector had transformed Asia's political landscape. Fear of too much Japanese power in organizing Asia's regional order was transformed into fear of too little Japanese power in dealing with its own economic and financial disorder. If Japan did not travel the road of macro-economic growth and financial stability, how could the rest of Asia? The Asian financial crisis, which so dramatically affected Thailand, Indonesia and South Korea, suggested to many observers that financial stability and economic health would return to Asia only after Japan had made painful adjustments in some of its long-standing policies.

The rapid decline in fear of Japan was also a response to the rise of China in the 1990s. Deng's 'southern trip' in 1992, a change in the statistical estimates of Chinese GDP by international financial institutions such as the IMF and the World Bank, sharp increases in the flow of direct foreign investment, extraordinarily high rates of economic growth, and the government's determined efforts to join GATT and the WTO, all focused attention on China, rather than Japan, as a conceivable rival of the United States a decade or two into the next millennium.

China's reputation as a possible regional hegemon rests on its combination of control of access to the largest untapped market in the world, possession of nuclear weapons and a permanent seat on the UN Security Council. This is not to deny the problems China faces in its relations with Taiwan, Tibet, Japan and the United States. Chinese foreign policy must reconcile a strong unilateralist stance on issues the government perceives to be of great national importance and a weaker multilateralist stance for ongoing diplomatic relations in, for example, the ASEAN Regional Forum (ARF). At the same time China is going through a wrenching process of adjustment in some of its major institutions, including inefficient state-owned enterprises, an oversized central bureaucracy and financial institutions crippled by a mountain of bad debt. The uncertainties inherent in a dual-track foreign policy intersect with the uncertainties of large-scale domestic reform. They combine to make China's neighbours nervous about the regional role that the PRC will play in Asia.

The United States, finally, has been an Asian power with strong interests in and ties to the region throughout the twentieth century. There is no evidence that the US government will alter its traditional stance because of the end of the Cold War. With 100,000 ground troops stationed in East Asia, with the American navy firmly committed to a strong position in Asia, and with the consolidation of US–Japanese security arrangements in the 1980s and 1990s, the United States is likely to remain a first-rate military power in Asia (Katzenstein and Okawara, 1999). Furthermore, since virtually all Asian countries run a substantial trade deficit with Japan and a large trade surplus with the United States, the United States is the economic anchor for national strategies of export-led growth and the integration of the regional economy of Asia Pacific.

In the eyes of many Asian governments an Asia that includes the United States has several advantages. American involvement can diffuse economic and political dependencies on Japan and China with which the smaller Asian states would otherwise have to cope. It provides Japan with the degree of national security that reduces the pressure for a major arms buildup. And it offers China political opportunities for establishing itself as a recognized great power in Asia.

At the threshold of a new millennium, however, the domestic and foreign policies of Japan, China and the United States are also exposed to a number of significant uncertainties. 'For the first time in two centuries Asian countries are in a position to shape their regional system and influence the character of the world system' writes Kenneth Pyle (1997: 6). Currently, Asian regionalism takes two different forms. If measured in terms of purchasing-power-parity GDP, the Japanese and the Chinese economies are of about equal size (Weidenbaum and Hughes, 1996: 95–105, 116–17). But each extends into Asia in different ways. Japanese capitalism is the result of indigenous economic developments and a conscious political strategy orchestrated jointly by government and business elites. Chinese capitalism lacks both an integrated, indigenous political economy and a coherent political strategy. 'Unlike the Japanese,' writes John Kao, 'the Chinese commonwealth has, in computer terms, an "open architecture." It represents access to local resources like information, business connections, raw materials, low labor costs and different business practices . . . In contrast to the Japanese *keiretsu*, the emerging Chinese commonwealth is an interconnected yet potentially open system' (Kao, 1993: 24).

Asian regionalism is an idea whose time has come. Increasing regional cooperation is often invoked as a necessary response to regionalization elsewhere, such as the European Union (EU) or NAFTA. Yet Asian regionalism has yet to be described adequately in terms of formal institutions. In the political norms that inform it and in the political capacity for collective action, the ASEAN Regional Forum (ARF), for example, differs dramatically from its more interventionist European equivalents, the Organisation for Security and Cooperation in Europe (OSCE) and the North Atlantic Treaty Organization (NATO). And the shallow economic integration that is the aim of APEC sets it apart from the deep political integration that characterizes the European Union (EU). Lacking a functional base of binding commitments, ARF and APEC are primarily fora for the discussion of important policy issues, and thus institutions useful for increasing trust. They are designed to strengthen regional economic cooperation only in the long term.

Financial globalization and an Asia in crisis

As with the opening of the Berlin Wall, the end of the Cold War and the peaceful disintegration of the Soviet Union, Asia's financial crisis came unannounced and was largely unanticipated by pundits and politicians, specialists in finance and scholars of Asia (Acharya, 1997a, 1999; Biers, 1998; Goldstein, 1998; Johnson, 1998; Lincoln, 1993; McLeod and Gernaut, 1998; Moon, 1998; Pempel, 1999; Wade, 1998, 1999). A conference sponsored by the Bank of Indonesia and the IMF concluded in November 1996 that 'ASEAN's economic success remains alive and well . . . the region is poised to extend its success into the twenty-first century' (IMF, 1996: 378). In a press conference on 25 April 1997, IMF Managing Director Camdessus remarked that the global economic outlook warranted 'rational exuberance'; and at the spring 1997 meeting, the Interim Committee of the IMF approved a plan to amend the Articles of Agreement to extend the IMF's jurisdiction to cover the movement of capital, thus completing the 'unwritten Chapter' of Bretton Woods, according to Camdessus (IMF, 1997: 129).

IMF policies proved to be inadequate even before the financial crisis hit Asia. Bulgaria's financial meltdown was a dress-rehearsal for what was happening in Asia only a few months later in the latter half of 1997. After years of half-hearted policy reforms by different governments and the IMF, international speculation against the lev forced Bulgaria to surrender its economic sovereignty and accept a currency board as the only plausible avenue in a disastrous situation (Minassian, 1999). Yet as late as spring 1997 IMF officials were celebrating the advantages of policies of liberalization without realizing the potentially disastrous effects of that policy for Bulgaria and other economies lacking the institutional preconditions for financial and economic liberalization.

Just as the end of the Cold War gave a healthy shock to students of national security and spurred a debate that touched on all of the premises of analysis, so debate had begun among students of political economy in the wake of the Asian financial crisis. Before the summer of 1997, even critics of the Asian developmental state model agreed that cosy relations between business and government were important in lowering transaction costs, and thus helping to bring about national growth rates in Asia that were four times higher than the OECD average. But by the end of 1997 economic and business analysts had convinced each other with surprising ease that Asian markets had lacked sophistication, and that banks had lent and business had invested in violation of established prudential principles. Far from lowering transaction costs, lack of transparency and systemic corruption were now judged to be the main impediments to a resumption of economic growth in Asia. This drastic and implausible shift in assessing economic policy led to a very public split between the IMF and the World Bank as well as among specialists in international economics.

The consensus policy, embraced more widely by economists inside than outside of the IMF, held to traditional policy prescriptions in the face of new conditions. Economic contagion became the 1990s' analogue to the 1960s' geo-strategic domino theory. International financial markets can easily lose confidence in the value of national currencies, especially in emerging markets that are exposed to the volatile flows of very liquid capital. When such capital flows out, the ensuing credit crunch can undermine even the trade credits of large corporations and set in motion a downward spiral that chokes off most business activities.

The economic crises in Thailand, Indonesia and South Korea were of very different character. In each, volatile global financial markets intersected with distinctly local political crises. Thailand's was both a macro-economic and a financial crisis. The deficit in its current account stood at 7 per cent of GDP in 1997, suggesting that a timely dose of traditional IMF medicine might have saved the country from its financial meltdown. Despite repeated off-the-record warnings by the IMF and highly public discussions in business journals, the Thai government did not change course. The signs of a looming crisis appeared as early as 1994 when the (central) Bank of Thailand began to examine the crisis of a medium-sized bank, the BBC, which turned into a major financial and political scandal that within a couple of years had seriously undermined the credibility of the central bank and the government suspected of improprieties in what turned out to be a $7bn bail-out. This episode was illustrative of the incompetence, immobilism, indecisiveness and venality of a succession of Thai governments. Chavalit Yongchaiyudh's six-party coalition government which took over in autumn 1996 had arguably the most promising economic and financial team of any of Thailand's elected governments in the 1980s and 1990s. But the traditional logic of Thai politics quickly reasserted itself and left the country unprepared to deal with the financial crisis that unfolded rapidly in the summer of 1997. In the spring of 1997 banks and finance companies were beginning to crack under a growing mountain of bad loans. The first default on foreign loan repayments occurred in February 1997. Rather than shifting losses to the shareholder, the internal politics of the government pointed to an inflationary strategy and massive bail-outs. Within a few months extremely rapid credit growth, even in the non-tradable sector, and high levels of credit denominated in foreign currencies triggered the run on the baht. After the onset of the crisis the economy was immobilized by a political crisis that lasted for four months until a new cabinet finally took over.

In Indonesia the enormous wealth of the Suharto clan had created widespread suspicion and opposition. In contrast to Thailand, a looming succession crisis in the government seemed to threaten the stability of the regime. Chinese businessmen began to lose confidence in the regime and the rupiah as early as 1996, and, according to well-informed sources in Japan's Ministry of Finance, withdrew about $100bn from Indonesia between 1995 and 1997.

American and IMF officials viewed the situation largely in economic categories and insisted on American-style economic reforms. Growing volatility in global capital markets had brought to the surface widespread corruption and a lack of regulatory oversight that, in the interest of investor confidence, needed to be redressed through fundamental institutional reforms and a drastic dose of deflation. Eager to protect the ill-gotten and far-flung assets of his six children and acutely aware of the dangers to the legitimacy of his regime and Indonesia's stability that the crisis had brought about, General Suharto dragged his feet in implementing the reforms on which the IMF insisted.

A leading scholar of Indonesia, Clifford Geertz, worried at the time that Western financial institutions were so fundamentally misreading Javanese culture that they turned a desperate situation into a dangerous one. IMF economists were not aware of cultural expectations that define the goodness of the father by the extent of protection he provides for his spoiled children and that makes insisting on public acknowledgement of mistakes an act of supreme rudeness in a society that prides itself on its civility. Had the IMF behaved differently, Geertz argues, it 'might have gotten what it wanted from the start. But I guess you don't expect that from economists' (Shenon, 1998: A17). The IMF's approach helped push General Suharto to tap into a deep strain of Javanese nationalism. The results were deadly anti-Chinese pogroms and the downfall of the regime.

In 1997 Korea was also undergoing far-reaching institutional and policy changes in a volatile geo-strategic situation on the Korean peninsula. The crisis exploded into the open in the final weeks before the presidential election of December 1997. Rival candidates disavowed the IMF package, which had been put together in record time in November 1997. This undermined further the confidence of international financial markets in Seoul's political capacity for reform.

In the face of sharp increases in dollar-denominated debt burdens, illiquidity and bankruptcy, all three governments guaranteed the assets of creditors and defended national currencies until they had used up virtually all their reserves. This forced the IMF to put together three bail-out packages for a total of $120bn. This stretched the financial and political limits of the Fund without contributing to stabilization of economic conditions in other emerging markets stretching from Russia to Brazil. In addition, the bail-outs undermined the Fund's eroding political support in the US Congress.

The IMF's reform packages differed somewhat in each of the three countries, but at bottom, the IMF sought to effect far-reaching economic and political change in the interest of international liberalization. This required a substantial reorganization of financial markets and ways of doing business as much as the acceptance of foreign partners and the introduction of new accounting rules. Whether and how this imposition of American institutional practices will work remains to be seen. In its first comprehensive assessment of the crisis the World Bank was harshly critical of the high-interest policies that both the IMF and the US government imposed once international investors began to withdraw their liquid assets from national economies that had been all too eager to absorb easily available and inexpensive international credits. With estimated levels of bankruptcy in Indonesia as high as 75 percent, the Bank's chief economist, Joseph Stiglitz, argued that 'you cannot have a country perform with 75 per cent of its firms in bankruptcy' (Sanger, 1998: A20). Compared to Indonesia the chances of success are much greater in South Korea, where President Kim dae Jung is seeking to exploit IMF pressure to further his own agenda of reforming state and society.

Variable national conditions in Thailand, Indonesia and South Korea are not the only factors shaping Asia's financial future. Much will depend on the future course of the financial reform policies adopted by China, Japan and international financial institutions. China's financial system is in a very precarious situation due to a volume of bad debts estimated in excess of 25 per cent of GDP. Financial consolidation is an extremely difficult task at a time in which major institutional changes are transforming radically many sectors of Chinese economy and society.

After years of delay, in 1998 to 1999 the Japanese government moved to a massive rescue effort of its financial sector. The lack of transparency and 'crony capitalism', often cited as the main root of the crisis, extends beyond Japan. International banks, such as Credit Suisse, made substantial profits in the 1990s in assisting Japanese banks in window-dressing their balance sheets and thus concealing from regulatory agencies the true depth of their problems (Tett, 1999: 10).

Inside the US Treasury, the IMF and the World Bank, discussions continue on whether and how to modify the Washington consensus and reform the international financial system. These discussions include issues such as imposing some restraints on capital flows, modifying the lending practices of the Fund and the Bank, re-evaluating the role of regional monetary funds, and reconsidering the suitability of exchange rate regimes, currency boards and policies of 'dollarization' for small open economies (Eichengreen, 1999; Rajan, 1999).

The full implications of the financial crisis for Asian regionalism are complicated and far from clear. Japanese efforts in August 1997 to offer a regional approach to crisis management were half-hearted, given the weakness of the Japanese economy, and were prematurely brushed aside, as IMF and US Treasury officials later acknowledged (Kristof, 1998: A6). Because of its enormous costs, especially for the lower-middle class and the poor, resentments linger. In Malaysia, for example, the government has managed to stay in power with its legitimacy impaired by the deep split between Prime Minister Mahathir Mohamad and his deputy and heir-apparent Anwar Ibrahim and the latter's trial and conviction on what to many Malaysians resembled trumped-up charges. The Malaysian policy of restricting the inflow of short-term capital, anathema to the Washington consensus, appears to have worked remarkably well. In the wake of the financial crisis there are strong political suspicions in Southeast Asia and South Korea that the Washington consensus is little more than an ideological smoke-screen for the determined efforts of US business to go on a shopping spree for Asian financial and industrial assets at bargain basement prices.

The openness of Asian regionalism has two different, closely intertwined sources that are clearly illustrated by Japan: dyadic and systemic vulnerability. First, Japan is embedded in a relationship of dyadic dependence on the United States that creates extraordinary military and economic vulnerabilities. Japan depends on the US navy to patrol the sea lanes through which its imported raw materials and exports flow. Even after diversifying away from the United States for the past two decades, 30 per cent of Japanese exports are still destined for US markets. Military, economic and political dependence thus constrains any Japanese inclination to build an inward-looking Asia. More generally, dyadic and systemic vulnerability affect most other Asian states as much, or more, than Japan.

Second, Japan's systemic vulnerability derives from what Kozo Kato (1998) calls 'global-scope' interdependence, which also constrains the emergence of an inward-looking Asian bloc. Along numerous dimensions of trade, aid, investment and technology transfer, among others, Japan has a more broadly diversified set of economic and political links to both rich and poor countries than does, for example, Germany, which lives internationally inside a European cocoon (Lincoln,

1993: 135; Wan, 1995: 98). The Asian financial crisis illustrates Japan's strong commitment to contribute to the continued functioning of the international system on which its economic prosperity depends so heavily. By September 1998 Japan's level of contribution to the solution of the Asian financial crisis stood at $43bn, about one-third of the total, compared to $12bn for the United States and $7bn for European states, even though the exposure of European banks was comparable to those of Japanese banks (Kristof, 1998: A6). About half of the Japanese credit was committed to credit lines to be disbursed under IMF bail-out plans over which Japan had little direct influence (Kozo Kato, 1998: 2).

The Asian financial crisis illustrates that Asian regionalism was not strong enough to prevent the establishment of beachheads in markets that used to be closed to foreign investors. An IMF-centred, global approach to the regional finan-cial crisis rather than reliance on an Asian-centred, Japanese-led effort revealed the weakness of an exclusive and cohesive East Asian regionalism without US involve-ment. In the immediate aftermath of the crisis the links between Asian regionalism and global financial markets have grown stronger.

On this score the contrast with the Economic and Monetary Union (EMU) is striking. The EMU is driven by political considerations and is on schedule for full operation by the year 2002, when it will contribute to the creation of a regional actor and a regional political economy that is likely to raise the profile of the EU without displacing the role of the dollar as lead currency. In contrast, the Asian financial crisis illuminates, and is likely to advance, a process of regional economic opening rather than political or policy closure.

Conclusion

An open Asian regionalism will encompass the United States politically and eco-nomically. In contrast to the 1930s, the political and economic coalitions prevailing in the United States have no interest in abdicating their influence in various regions. Yet, despite its preponderant international position the United States lacks the resources to be the cornerstone in all of the world's major regions. Instead, the United States acts as a pivot in a number of important regions.

In Asia, this pivot rests on a combination of US military power, economic pres-ence and social appeal that reflects diverse interests and ideologies in the United States and is relevant to important political elites, economic sectors and social strata in Asia. With the end of the Cold War and the withdrawal of most US ground forces from Europe, 100,000 ground troops in East Asia are the main reason why the United States has not returned to its traditional role as a naval power. Compared to Europe and Asia the position of the US territorial economy has probably declined somewhat over the past thirty years. But the competitive position of US corporations in international markets has increased substantially, especially in the past decade. American multinational corporations perform strongly and are often at the cutting edge in the development of new technologies and products. Their full presence in global markets gives American policy-makers a strong incentive to maintain a liberal international economy. Finally, with English as the only universal language, American mass culture has a natural advantage over all of its competitors in disseminating its products on a global scale.

Asia's open regionalism is also important for Europe. Since 1996 the biannual Asia–Europe Meetings (ASEM) of fifteen European and ten Asian heads of state give symbolic expression to the growing importance of regionalization processes and regional structures in world politics. The motivations for these summits differ. They are political for Asian governments seeking to balance against the US pivot on which they so heavily rely, and they are economic for European governments eager to jump-start their lagging economies through improved access to high-growth markets in Asia. Political leaders and journalists at times conceive of ASEM as strengthening the weak third leg of an emerging tripolar regional world in which different blocs will confront each other, as they did in George Orwell's novel *1984*. In light of this chapter's argument this seems highly improbable. Like Asia, Europe is open rather than closed, even though the reason lies less in its external vulnerability to financial shocks, market access and military assistance and more in the liberal character of European polities. Furthermore, differently organized processes of regional enlargement that are now underway in both Asia and Europe will reinforce regional openness rather than closure.

Analyses pointing to the overwhelming power of the US pivot or the emergence of a tripolar world of regional blocs suggest misleading images of the emerging relations among the major states in the Americas, Asia and Europe. Power has too many dimensions to be shrunk to one simple unit as suggested by the metaphor of pivot or blocs. The twenty-first century will be nobody's century: not America's, not Asia's, not Europe's. In an economically more open Asia, Asian relations with the US and Europe will illustrate instead the politics of open regionalism in a more plural world.

Notes

1 This chapter draws on some material previously published. See Katzenstein, 1993, 1997, 2000.
2 Author's personal communications with Helen Wallace, 1999.

8 Asian multilateral institutions and their response to the Asian economic crisis

The regional and global implications

Stuart Harris

The economic crisis that hit East Asia in 1997 had various impacts on Asian regionalist impulses. Important among them was that it enhanced understanding of the region's vulnerability to forces external to the region. It also led to a belief by many inside as well as outside the region that existing regional cooperation arrangements were unable to make an effective contribution to solving the problem. The worst of the crisis now appears to be over. There is a long way to go, of course, but a modest process of recovery is evident. Japan's own economic crisis, significant for the region, also shows some signs of bottoming out, if not yet recovering.

It is not too early to start assessing what these crises meant for Asian regionalism, whether as a defining event in Asia's economic and political development or just another speed bump on the road of regional progress. In this chapter, I look at how Asian regionalism responded to the crisis primarily by considering regional multilateral institutions.[1] Multilateralism has contributed to a sense of region and regional community in Asia, although Asia is seeing the emergence of differing concepts of region: economic, political and security. The tendency has been to dismiss the role of regional multilateralism in Asia generally and its response to the economic crisis. The crisis certainly revealed weaknesses in these processes. In the hubris of the external responses to the crisis, these have been extensively documented – in *The Economist* and elsewhere. Moreover, the future relevance of these institutions has also been questioned.

Undoubtedly, ASEAN (Association of South East Asian Nations) has been weakened. The contribution of the Asia Pacific Economic Cooperation forum (APEC) to crisis management was limited, and one major regional initiative, Japan's regional monetary fund proposal, was opposed by the US, China and others in favour of the US-led global multilateralism of the IMF. Soul-searching is under way in the region. Nevertheless, the early judgements may have been unduly harsh. Although a full assessment needs more time, some things can be said now. Moreover, any rush to judgement needs to bear in mind that the history of Asia–Pacific as a region of independent states is short. Lateral linkages among the regional states were largely non-existent in the aftermath of the Second World War, national building is still far from complete, and those mostly new states started with considerable distrust of the metropolitan powers. This mistrust extended to their institutional constructs including the GATT and the IMF. It is important, therefore, to recognize what regional multilateralism has achieved as well as what it has not. Rather than compare multilateralism in Asia with that elsewhere, the comparison should be with the relatively recent Asian past.

In most discussions of multilateralism, formal institutionalisation is commonly considered necessary, usually to counter problems of free riding. Such needs are less if the time horizons of members are long, gains from cooperation are repetitive and peer pressure is important. If the objective is less than a formal cooperative process of a functional nature, formalized institutions may not be required. Since, in Asia, there has been little institutionalized functional integration– despite ASEAN's efforts – problems of free riding are hardly central.

Addressing Asian regionalism is complex. There is no consensus on what is the region, the concept of region is changing with various geographic sub-regions being encompassed, or excluded. There remain fundamental political and economic differences – Japan, for example, is an advanced economy while China and the Indochina states are at various stages of transformation into 'socialist' market economies. The developing/developed divide is a present although not dominant influence, but important differences remain in some contexts, for example, human resource development and global environmental questions. These various differences have been important but not critical in those regional multilateral institutions that emerged over a period of three decades or so, essentially since ASEAN's creation in 1967.

What is the Asian region?

I shall not rehearse the extensive literature on what constitutes regionalism or a region summarized in the introduction to this volume. We cannot avoid the definitional problem completely, however. Not only is it contested but an important process in Asia has been changing views on, or understandings of, what constitutes the Asian region, for substantive economic and security reasons and for narrower political reasons.

In defining the Asian region, as with any region, various characteristics are important, notably geography, and economic and political/security interdependencies. Geographic proximity and contiguity are important but not defining in Asia. Understandings compete mainly between a wider concept of Asia Pacific, reflected in APEC, which includes North America, and a narrower concept illustrated by the Asian half of the Asia–Europe Meeting (ASEM) which does not include North America (or Australia and New Zealand). Membership of other regional organizations provides limited guidance. Some include outriders; the Economic and Social Commission for Asia and the Pacific (ESCAP), for example, includes Iran and Armenia, the Asian Development Bank (ADB) includes Afghanistan and several CIS states, APEC does include North America and Australia and New Zealand but also Chile, Peru and Russia, and the ASEAN

Regional Forum (ARF) includes India. There are various sub-regions, such as Southeast Asia (ASEAN), ANCERTA (the Australia–New Zealand Free Trade Area), the North America Free Trade Agreement (NAFTA) and non-institutionalized sub-regions, including Northeast Asia, and the China circle encompassing Taiwan and Hong Kong.

Economic interdependencies are important but also not defining. The gradual emergence, autonomously, of economic linkages among the countries of the region and the expectation that these would increase if not hindered became an important motivation for cooperative action leading to semi-formalized processes for facilitating cooperation. In functional terms, until the time of the Asian crisis, both ASEAN and APEC had been trading more intra-regionally: in 1997, 71 per cent of APEC's trade was intra-regional; 19 per cent of ASEAN's trade was intra-regional in the same year. In both cases the growth in intra-regional trade had increased over the previous five years (DFAT, 1998). Intra-regional capital movements have also been growing and, closely associated with this, largely private sector strategic production networks.

A third characteristic is security interdependence. This is a varying influence because of the links between economics and security, the different perceptions of threat and the bilateral allegiances of regional states. Thus economic linkages among states in the region have been encouraged as ways to prevent conflict among states through greater functional interactions. As the region has developed, the security interdependencies have moved in new directions such as towards South Asia and the CIS states, although not yet paralleled by significant economic interdependencies.

A further, less tangible, characteristic deals with what the countries of a region have in common. A number of the countries in the region share common characteristics. These characteristics again can be internally oriented: shared histories, cultures, perceptions, political attitudes, and a sense of regional consciousness; or externally oriented: shared attitudes to others outside of the region.

In addressing these various characteristics, we know that Asian regionalism, like regionalism elsewhere, is a construct: the definition of the region and of Asian regionalism is what the states of the region make of it. Yet the argument is somewhat circular since which are the states of the region is unclear given that there are different ideas of what constitutes the region.

External influences

More generally, the idea of regionalism in Southeast Asia included a post-colonial desire for neutrality in the Cold War and avoidance of involvement in activities of the major powers. The rhetoric included a wish to avoid the adversarial approach perceived among those countries as characteristic of the management of international relations by the major powers. Part of the initial support for regional cooperation processes stemmed from this reaction.

The mix of external factors that subsequently influenced Asian regionalism has included the emergence of regional blocs elsewhere and initially, in particular, the

EU (then the EEC). European trade protection was important in stimulating regional economic cooperation, as were the EC's moves towards a Single Market and the consequent fears of 'fortress Europe', and then the emergence of NAFTA. Subsequently, other regionally oriented motivations have also been important, such as developments in the Cold War and Western human rights pressures. Asia has been and is still being pulled in several directions. The obvious advocate of movement in a narrower direction is Malaysia, but there is wider support for a closer sense of Asian community. At the same time, three offsetting pressures counter this: continuing US links, shifting interdependencies and globalization processes. Although not shared by all to the same degree, maintaining the US presence in the region is an important objective for a number of regional states. Even China's feelings on the subject are ambivalent.

Shifts in interdependencies pose problems for an all-encompassing regionalism. Even for a narrower regionalism, China's shifting interdependencies, for example, pose problems. Although China provides a central geographic link between Northeast and Southeast Asia, it has growing ties in new directions, as well as in developing political and economic (including energy supply) relations in what is now an established sub-regional multilateral grouping, with Russia and central Asia.[2]

The third counter-pressure is globalization. Given that the starting point of the economic crisis was the financial system, that this is the context in which the processes of globalization largely manifest themselves might indicate that regionalism will face special difficulties countering it. This is not totally so, for reasons we elaborate below.

More particularly, there have been regional reactions to the general pressures of globalization, seen as the impact on domestic cultures of international values, including democracy, capitalism and Westernization and to pressures from the West on human rights. The West has again been increasingly cast, not always pejoratively, as the external 'other'. One manifestation was the emergence of 'Asian values', the intellectual arguments being developed by Singapore and endorsed by Malaysia and China in particular, with Dr Mahathir claiming that Asian values were in fact universal but European values were simply European. The basic issue concerned how to balance economic growth and stability. The debate on both sides, however, mixed various arguments, mostly around the use of the values propositions to legitimize authoritarian governmental approaches to governance; hence the strong support given to the values argument by authoritarian regimes.

The economic crisis may have reduced the heat of the debate but is unlikely to disappear as a basic critique, not of economic development since that is not necessarily judged as Western, but of 'Western' values and the excesses perceived to be associated with them.

Multilateralism in Asia

Multilateralism is generally seen as functionally oriented, facilitating the provision of collective or public goods that contribute to economic progress and strategic security. In economic contexts, the need for multilateralism normally arises because norms, rules and standards are required for, among other things, trade, investment, communication, transport and energy supply in which international aspects are dominant. For security, multilateralism is most generally associated with collective security or collective self-defence, but increasingly also for cooperative action on matters such as public health, international crime and the global environment.

Concentrating on functional aspects tends, however, to emphasize the static, and to ignore political and social aspects. Such an approach suggests a view of the state that sees the international system as firmly established, its values and preferences as fixed and its understanding of how the international system does and should operate as unchanging. Yet discussion or dialogue processes may alter preferences, create feelings of shared identity, stimulate the development of norms and encourage cooperative behaviour (Harris, 1994). Such a dynamic element in multilateral arrangements remains important in shaping the approach of countries in the Asia Pacific.[3]

Before asking how the region's multilateral institutions responded to the crisis, I shall look briefly at the earlier achievements of multilateralism in Asia.

Each region of the world has its own historical experiences that shape its perceptions, values and understandings. Asia's regional developments have taken paths differing from those elsewhere. For most of the post-Second World War period, there were important differences, arising from geography, between the north Atlantic and Asia Pacific in how far multilateralism was a feature of the international approach sought in the region. North American literature sometimes generalizes those differences in terms of the states of the Atlantic basin endorsing liberalism and extended deterrence and those of the Pacific basin endorsing international mercantilism and finite deterrence (Kurth, 1989). Like most generalizations, it contains some truth but is increasingly misleading. In particular, it underestimates changes that have taken place in the economic arena, such that it has been argued that in the Asia Pacific, 'Liberalism as a norm is even more strongly emphasized than among GATT members' (Aggarwal, 1993: 1033). It also underestimates differences in the objectives sought in the region through multilateralism.

In the process of providing information, increasing transparency so that the behaviour of neighbours may be monitored, and in economic contexts, reducing transactions costs, regional institutions have reflected but also shaped regional preferences. In reflecting regional preferences, multilateral processes usually direct attention, first, to norms of behaviour, respect for sovereignty, non-aggression and non-interference in the domestic affairs of other members, and second, to the habit of consultation and accommodation, informality, a preference for process, a non-legalistic and non-binding flexible approach and consensus seeking (Snitwongse, 1998: 184).[4] The concomitant shaping influence includes acceptance of diffuse reciprocity and a general sense of give and take neither quantitatively nor time-specific.

Three important characteristics of multilateralism in Asia are, first, that they support, not substitute for, the global multilateral institutions. This point is important both to the assessment of where regional multilateral arrangements fitted during the economic crisis and, as we see below, to the global implications of regionalism.

A second is that weight is placed on semi-official or second-track activities, contrary to experience elsewhere. These constitute research bodies, idea generators and places to propose and discuss, among other things, new norms or standards.

A third characteristic of Asia's approach to multilateralism is its inclusive nature. The interest in bringing within the dialogues those who might be potentially problematic has included China, to the point where at its fifteenth Party Congress in 1997, it adopted multilateralism as a policy and has been generally constructive in its participation in regional security as well as economic meetings. Cambodia, Vietnam and Burma are also examples. There is also considerable interest in bringing North Korea, which already participates in the Council for Security Cooperation in Asia Pacific (CSCAP), a second-track process linked to the ARF, into the official ARF process.

The record to date

What constitute efficient institutional multilateral forms depend on circumstances. A range of motivations was important in stimulating regional multilateral developments. In considering the multilateral efforts, we need to judge them first in terms of their own objectives before looking at the global implications.

'Soft', region-wide institutions are central to Asia's multilateralism. At the regional level, I have suggested that regional multilateralism responded to specific Asian problems and historical experiences – colonialism, nation building and the regional impact of the Cold War – which shaped its choices. Filling the large gaps in understanding the interests and intentions of their regional neighbours and establishing a sense of community was an important goal and consequence of multilateral processes in Asia.

Moreover, an important contribution of multilateralism in Asia Pacific has been to alter the environment within which interactions take place and, in encouraging cognitive learning about the way the world works, to change or reinforce how Asian states wish to pursue their interests and reshape their national objectives. Those influences have also become important in domestic politics. ASEAN and APEC in particular, but also ARF, have been domestically important, making more understandable the choices facing policy-makers, and pressing and legitimizing the liberal trade and investment agendas.

While some norms are supported with guidelines, few rules exist to underpin or buttress them except in ASEAN, in the Treaty of Amity and Cooperation (TAC), and on procedural matters elsewhere; few monitoring or sanctioning mechanisms are in place. The limited efforts at rule-making have been mainly over membership, although decisions there tend still to be made on political grounds.

Multilateralism in Asia has remained informal, gradual and consensual, and is often criticized for its lack of specific reciprocity. Yet, in practice, at the global as well as the regional level, in all but the trade field, diffuse multilateralism is the basis of all multilateralism.

Not all norms have been accepted region-wide but Asian countries have generally agreed on a number of norms. While most attention is usually directed to the norms of preservation of national sovereignty and the principle of non-interference in domestic affairs, others include: the pursuit of prosperity through competitive market mechanisms; the pursuit of economic interdependence to enhance security; the resolution of disputes by peaceful means; and adherence to functional multilateral agreements at the global level.

Provision of public goods associated with economic interdependence and outward-looking market systems, particularly the reduction of transaction costs through availability of information and reduction of non-tariff and other regulatory and procedural barriers to trade and investment, has been an important although less than formalised contribution of multilateralism in Asia.

Asian approaches to multilateralism have reflected their particular security concerns, superpower involvement and a lack of an effective UN collective security system. It will be a long time, however, before common or collective security comes into being in Asia. Multilateralism in the security field will remain a supplement to bilateral relations and will be one feature, with elements of power balancing and with economic interdependence, of security interests and constraints in the region. It will facilitate bilateral relations, however, and help to keep bilateral relations non-threatening.

In global multilateralism, the influence of implicit minilateralism (the dominant influence of a few) has often included large Asian powers (Japan in economic institutions, China in the Security Council). ASEAN, and the Pacific Economic Cooperation Council (PECC)/APEC, however, have at times also been effective in influencing outcomes, if mainly on issues important to them and less important to others (Cambodia) but also on general WTO questions. There are limits to the ability to build regional coalitions for influence in global arenas because of the differing regional interests as, for example, in global trade negotiations, the law of the sea, and ozone layer and carbon dioxide emissions issues. Nevertheless, regional multilateralism has helped smaller countries to balance, with norms and peer pressure, the regional dominance of Indonesia and Japan, to integrate China into the region and to limit US unilateralism.

That regional multilateral dialogues have stimulated cognitive learning has been important in Asia because of the more basic starting point among decolonized Asian countries, and the initial national variability. Such learning helped in the development of ideas behind the open, export-oriented, competitive economies that accounted for Asia's success and will do so again. It has led to learning in the security field, including the links between economic interdependence and security, the issues of economic security themselves and the development of the new security agenda. More generally, a widely held view has developed that cooperative behaviour can be valuable and appropriate in security as well as economic fields, with peer pressure an important influence, and to feelings of shared identity that provide a stimulus to regionalist thinking.

Overall, although largely dialogue processes, regional multilateral processes have gone a long way to establishing a normative framework for the region that covers both the security interdependencies and the economic interdependencies. This may not prevent conflict or avoid all beggar-thy-neighbour policies, but there are grounds for believing it has made important contributions in both directions.

The response to the economic crisis

If these achievements are accepted as coming from Asia's multilateral regionalism, will their future potentialities be limited as a result of the regional economic crisis? If the belief remains that the future of the multilateral institutions is limited, will the crisis lead to major changes? I look at four of the existing arrangements: ASEAN, ARF, APEC and ASEM (Asia–Europe Meeting).

ASEAN

ASEAN has been the most affected by the economic crisis with direct and severe impacts on several of its members. Particularly important was the effect on Indonesia, which had provided much of the ASEAN leadership. That ASEAN contributed little to ameliorating the crisis is commonly seen as putting the institution under sufficient strain to diminish greatly its value.

Despite the rapid economic growth of its members, ASEAN as an economic institution had not contributed much directly to that growth. With the weakening effect of the crisis, the political influence that came from ASEAN's economic strength has clearly declined. Moreover, not only did it not have within it a country that could provide financial resources (with the exception of some help proffered by Singapore to Indonesia), but it had little by way of established processes of economic cooperation across the board that could facilitate foreign involvement in crisis management. In practice, however, expectations of its role in a financial crisis were unreal, and, despite consequent efforts to introduce changes, it is unlikely by its nature to be able to contribute significantly in similar circumstances in the future.

It has been trying to develop further its economic integration as a means of enhancing coherence and pushing forward its AFTA objectives. It also has interests in developing more of a role in the monetary field. In December 1998, ASEAN leaders directed that a study be undertaken of the feasibility of establishing an ASEAN currency and exchange rate system (ASEAN Secretariat, 1998), but initial reactions were understandably cautious.

ASEAN's objectives were never primarily economic, however, but involved security and then political influence. It was initially concerned with internal security objectives (to avoid existing territorial and border disputes or challenges to national legitimacies becoming military conflicts). Judged on its ostensible economic objectives, ASEAN's achievements were limited. As a confidence-building measure to facilitate avoidance of conflict among its members, however (and then encouraging peaceful settlement of disputes and developing confidence building more widely in the region), it was a singular success. Many of ASEAN members' past border and territorial differences are still unresolved but remain largely quiescent. Keeping the peace was an important indirect contribution to the economic success of its members. It then developed a political strength by being able to present a united front in response to external challenges. External problems such as airline rerouting, Vietnam, Cambodia, the Spratlys and China have been major challenges for the group's unity but they often provided the cement required for maintaining ASEAN's coherence.

To a degree its future importance will continue to reflect members' economic fortunes. Economic recovery therefore will be important from this perspective as well as from others. Nevertheless, more important will be its ability to maintain coherence as an institution, and in consequence to sustain its international influence, especially in the political and security fields. Many of the difficulties now and prospectively facing ASEAN arise not from the economic downturns but from the consequences of its enlargement, with different agendas likely to be followed by the new members – Vietnam, Myanmar, Laos and Cambodia – and greater difficulties to be expected in achieving common positions. Relations between Singapore and Malaysia have long been difficult, at least since Singapore broke away from Malaysia. The differences have been exacerbated by the crisis (Ahmad and Ghoshal, 1999).

ASEAN followed the logic of inclusiveness, enlarging ASEAN to encompass the whole of Southeast Asia in the belief that this would enhance security and strengthen representativeness. It also saw this as bolstering its position *vis-à-vis* China, as it may well do, but it provides difficulties for its international position overall. Nevertheless, provided the ten strategically placed states can maintain collective unity, ASEAN's potential political influence will never be negligible.

Coherence would in any case be more difficult in the post-Cold War era than during the Cold War because the anti-communist rationale, already becoming differentiated before the passing of the Cold War, has gone. US strategic interests during the Cold War, for ASEAN an element in its significant international influence, have changed. Even during the Cold War, substantial differences remained among ASEAN members, as over Vietnam and Cambodia, but a process of accommodation was realized that enabled solidarity to be maintained, and that experience will help, especially if the argued new sense of regional solidarity holds.[5]

The crisis led to more direct questioning of the policy of non-intervention in the affairs of other members. The economic crisis convinced some members that it was not possible to continue to strictly adhere to this principle, as earlier had the haze problems stemming from Indonesia's forest and peat fires. Change, however, has been strongly resisted in particular by the new members, notably Myanmar and Cambodia, who would feel vulnerable in those circumstances (Haacke, 1999). Nevertheless, without some compromise on that principle, the influence of ASEAN internationally is likely to diminish. The compromise on 'enhanced interaction' is unlikely to meet this need (Henderson, 1999: 48–55).

Nevertheless, the ability to continue to present a united front was demonstrated over the Spratlys and its reaffirmation of its 'one-China' policy in response to the Taiwanese president's 'special state-to-state' restatement of Taiwan's links to China in July 1999. While the US may have less strategic interest in ASEAN, that is only marginally related to its changed economic circumstances. This is also true of its problems, and those of the Europeans, with Myanmar's membership. The effects of the economic crisis have made a difference, however, to the substantially economics-based European interest and, if not to the Japanese government, perhaps to Japanese companies (Henning, 1999).[6] Yet China's interests in ASEAN seem not to have diminished and indeed may have been strengthened by ASEAN's support for China's position on Taiwan. Moreover, ASEAN's regional facilitating influence is likely to remain, given its role in managing ARF.

Security and the ARF

In a way not paralleled elsewhere, security for the countries of the region was, and remains, a critical internal as well as external question. This comes from the region's particular history, with problems of nation building making internal security still the prime security issue. It also responds, however, to the recognition that long-standing animosities, unresolved borders and territorial sensitivities remain that, although quiescent, could emerge as conflicts in certain circumstances.

In its early stages, ASEAN had problems reaching agreement over external security interests. The ARF reflects, however, a reasonably clear definition of security interdependence. It also responds to a broader conception of security. Economic security was a major regional concern, initially to overcome internal subversion, for nation building and to establish national resilience. It has been reinforced by the new security issues, such as drugs, transnational crime, piracy, refugees and illegal migration particularly relevant to the regional security agenda. With the economic crisis, however, this new multilateral agenda now includes questions of capital market vulnerability.

While economic influences pull Asia increasingly into the global economy, regional approaches to security have gained in salience since the end of the Cold War with bilateral and regional aspects of security more central. Yet many in the region still have alliances or military links with the US, most recently those established bilaterally between the Philippines and Thailand and the US.

Direct progress (i.e. through the ARF) has been slow in the security field but a significant buildup of CBMs is apparent on borders and in the maritime region. While progress on preventive diplomacy and conflict resolution is slow, socializing through multilateral dialogues, including not just the ARF but the economic co-operation processes of the PECC and APEC, have led to significant changes in understandings and worldviews relevant to security postures.

The Asian economic crisis has not had major traditional security impacts, but these are not the major security concerns for most countries in the region. Nation-state building – internal security – is still incomplete for most countries. While that makes the non-intervention principle in the ARF an important and sensitive issue, there are calls for its re-evaluation. Although there have been small moves in this direction (discussion of Myanmar's human rights, Indonesia's reporting on East Timor and the proposals for a code of conduct in the South China Sea), sensitivities remain. Nevertheless, while specific proposals in this context received little support, the issue and a need for stronger regional institutions has gained regional support and will remain in regional thinking. Past experience suggests some (probably modest) change will be made eventually in a form acceptable to all.

The issue of ASEAN's leadership of the ARF was already in question before the crisis on several grounds, but particularly the exclusion from any leadership role of non-ASEAN members, notably those from Northeast Asia. The crisis, and particularly Indonesia's instability and weakness, have increased concerns about the issue, as has ASEAN's enlargement. Although the disposition within ASEAN is to retain control, influential voices within ASEAN, for example, Wanandi (1998: 59), have suggested permitting a co-chair from non-ASEAN countries.

Trade and finance

Trade and APEC

The initial APEC agenda was largely the agenda of PECC, its progenitor: trade liberalization, trade facilitation (standards, regulatory and certification procedures and the like), investment protection and human resource development. It also continued the provision of the public goods of market and technical information, and transparency, that remain an important part of regional economic multilateralism not just in a static sense of reducing transactions costs but as a dynamic means of shaping members' understandings and ultimately policies.

Criticisms of APEC do not simply stem from its response to the crisis but to separate problems, notably over the Early Voluntary Sector Liberalization (EVSL) programme. Trade liberalization had gradually become a more central feature and, for the US, commonly the only criterion of its effectiveness. This limited focus was unfortunate in several respects but particularly in pursuing the EVSL, an initiative that failed to achieve its objectives. Despite this, critics linked to the region have argued the need for specific reciprocity on the grounds that domestic politics would not allow countries in the region to opt for unilateral liberalization (Moon, 1999).

The argument overlooks three considerations. Over the long period of regional economic cooperation dialogues, trade liberalization, including unilateral trade liberalization, became widely accepted as important in regional development strategies and for the domestic competitiveness benefits that result – the pressure to increase domestic efficiency is an explicit reason the Chinese are pursuing trade and investment liberalization.[7] Second, in an increasingly democratic or at least publicly responsive region, political cycles seldom coincide with trade negotiation cycles – and a steady process of liberalization as and when politically possible may be more acceptable than a larger, one-off reduction when a negotiating round requires it.

More importantly, the region has in practice pursued unilateral liberalization, accepting the diffuse reciprocity that underlies regional multilateralism. While not a precise guide to the specific contribution of APEC, unweighted tariffs of APEC economies declined from 15.4 per cent in 1988 to 9.1 per cent in 1996 (PECC, 1995). The attempt at reciprocal negotiations of the EVSL was a mistaken effort to move from diffuse reciprocity to specific reciprocity, the appropriate place for which is the WTO. APEC will have to manage the continuing difference between the US and most others on the issue of reciprocity.

The influence of regional economic cooperation dialogues on policies have included: substantial direct trade barrier reductions under the APEC programmes, particularly following the Bogor initiative; changed attitudes to where for most APEC members trade liberalization is seen as having positive benefits in itself – the exception being the US; and changes from initial distrust of the GATT to open and strong support for the GATT/WTO process and trade liberalization.

Progress in trade facilitation has also been substantial, if little publicly under-stood and less quantitatively measured. Yet given the potential gains from moving to the European Single Market (Cecchini, 1988), it is not hard to visualize consid-erable potential gain in transaction cost reductions from similar changes taking place, if more slowly and with less regulatory backing, within the APEC region.

Although North–South issues within the region did not take the shape experi-enced elsewhere, a programme of technical assistance and human resource development designed to meet the needs of developing countries as a programme in support of 'internationally oriented development strategies' (Ecotech) has gained support from developed country members of APEC, becoming more important in the light of the economic crisis.

There are often suggestions for more specific bloc arrangements within the region. ESCAP sought to push the NIEO philosophy, with import replacement and preferential trade, without finding wide acceptance in Asia. The AFTA (ASEAN Free Trade Area) was largely a response to NAFTA, the original thinking behind the EAEC (East Asian Economic Caucus) was to develop an Asian trading bloc, the US frequently presses for bilateral free trade arrangements or special investment arrangements and moves are now underway to consider a Japanese–Korean free trade area.

Moreover, the liberal agenda has its opponents. For Malaysia, Dr Mahathir has articulated strongly his concerns that international trading institutions such as WTO are at best irrelevant to, and at worst biased against, Asian countries and at times he has acted accordingly, not participating, for example, in the 1994 Bogor APEC meeting. With a history of discontent with Western markets, starting from his view of the London Metal Exchange tin market, he argued that the economic crisis was a conspiracy of the West against Asia. Such arguments have not, how-ever, become the dominant philosophy in the region, and Malaysia has in practice gone along with much of the regional action.

Given the limited role APEC could play directly in addressing the crisis, the hope was that APEC could hold the line in the trade field in the face of the down-turn by encouraging countries to resist pressures to turn inward and to avoid 'beggar-thy-neighbour' policies. Contrary to a wide expectation at the time, the line was held – and indeed in a number of countries further economic liberalization has taken place. Most fundamentally, the overall priority to an outward-looking economic policy orientation has not changed despite the crisis.

Finance in and near APEC

The institutional area of greatest pressure in the face of the Asian crisis was the financial one. APEC is not a financial institution and has no special access to funds that could be mobilized in the crisis, despite the region's large foreign exchange reserves. APEC was in any case in a weak position to respond to the financial crisis but its initial responses were even weaker – the Leaders' response at Vancouver 1997 'was banal' (Garnaut, 1999). The inability to build on a Japanese proposal in a way that, given the right circumstances would have contributed constructively to reducing the problem, was especially unfortunate.

As a result of the crisis, however, in looking to reduce financial volatility, closer links have been established between regional banks and other financial institutions, and links have been enhanced between governments and regional and multilateral organizations. Subsequent meetings of leaders and further finance ministers' meetings have improved the situation to where they can contribute positively in various ways. These include supporting or activating the IMF and World Bank, in developing new instruments that may help, in providing training in financial management, in financial market development and risk management, and in sparking new capital flows to Asia.

Although needing considerable strengthening, the regional effort in response to the crisis was not negligible. At their Shanghai meeting in July 1997, the eleven members of the Executive Meeting of East Asia and Pacific Central Banks (EMEAP) had agreed to examine a new Asian facility to supplement IMF funding. Over $10bn was committed by EMEAP finance ministries in August 1997 in Tokyo. This was especially important in putting together the Thai package in which the US did not participate; regional funds constituted three quarters of the total package, the IMF contributing the balance (Smith, 1999). These arrangements were formalized by the APEC finance ministers' meetings in November of that year under the Manila Framework (Grenville, 1998).

The establishment of the Manila Framework Group (MFG) in November 1997 was an important step in developing mechanisms for restoring financial viability, including for regional surveillance to complement the IMF's global surveillance. Under that Framework, an Asian Surveillance Group was established, meeting first in March 1998. It is enhancing economic and technical cooperation to strengthen domestic financial systems and regulatory capacities, and developing cooperative bilateral financing – this became the IMF's Supplemental Reserve Facility in late 1997, used first by Korea.

Consequently, a number of steps begun before the crisis have since become important regional building blocks for better regional financial management. These need not be formally linked with APEC but they are likely to be through the APEC finance ministers' meetings. The regional contribution to the crisis was limited. It was, at best, supplementary to the actions of the global institutions and, in the future, it will need to remain supplementary and not be competitive. Particularly if supported by APEC, however, it should be capable of being more effective in supporting the crisis management activities of global institutions. The APEC process could offer a mechanism by which an agreed set of minimum regional financial standards could be established and national performances become part of APEC's individual action plans (Garnaut and Wilson, 1999). It could also provide an improved information base and local expertise on regional economic conditions.

While Japan's proposal for an Asian Monetary Fund was given little support within the region and less from without, more considered thought suggests that if modified to include the US and designed explicitly to supplement the IMF (as the Asian Development Bank does the World Bank), this could be a valuable regional complement to the IMF (Bergsten, 1998). While opposition to a Japanese financial leadership role might have diminished, helped by the experience of the regionalization of Japan's bilateral support under the Miyazawa Plan, and a stronger Japanese leadership capability, this is where APEC's role could again be crucial.

Although not directly linked to APEC, as a reaction to the Euro, Japan has formally indicated that it will move towards making the yen an international currency. The mix of motives probably includes not just a reflection of concerns at the dominance of the dollar and the Euro but as a desire for more political influence globally (Castellano, 1999; Group 21, 1999), and perhaps also to position Japan to maintain its regional economic predominance rather than concede the field to China. It reflects a changed regionalist attitude that, rather than offer criticisms to such a suggestion, as happened some years ago, ASEAN countries have indicated their receptivity to the idea. Despite Japan's continuing strong external economic position, its economic downturn, and perhaps regulatory inertia (although capital movement restrictions are being eased), will make it at best a slow process.[8]

Overall, APEC is likely to have a greater input in the future in financial questions affecting the region. Membership of APEC has always been a contentious issue reflecting in part the competing ideas of region, and this aspect will be more important as financial issues become more central. Thus the admission of Chile was largely an effort to dilute membership and thereby make necessary a smaller group in due course. In fact Chile progressed to meet an implicit trade criterion for membership: a similar agenda to that of existing members, linked to an outward orientation in economic development. Peru, and more particularly Russia, hardly meet these criteria and Russia in particular seems to have been added under US pressure as compensation for a NATO expansion Russia did not want. Their membership will complicate APEC's coherence in the financial area, as does the US emphasis on reciprocal trade liberalization in the trade field but, in contrast to the US, Russia has little else to add at the functional level. A smaller APEC subgroup may therefore be necessary.

ASEM

ASEM, which met first in 1996, was an ASEAN initiative, supplementary to the EU–ASEAN dialogue with membership, in addition to the ASEAN countries, of Japan, China and Korea. It was scheduled to meet regularly at ministerial level with the EU to discuss political and, in particular, trade and investment issues between the two groups. From the Asian perspective it had a number of motivations, including providing an offset to the EU and NAFTA and increasing investment from Europe.[9] There are questions about how far the ASEM process could go given the reluctance of countries on both sides, but particularly in Asia, to accept a coordinated line. As an indicator of regionalism it may be seen as defining Asia more narrowly. Prime Minister Mahathir, although not the originator, is an enthusiast for ASEM.[10] His has been the principal voice opposing membership in ASEM of Australia and New Zealand.

EU's new agenda of human rights, the environment and labour rights poses problems that will continue to pose problems. Some slackening of interest on the European side seems apparent that, to the extent that it was an economic-based interest in the first place, may be ascribed to the crisis. Moreover, the European response to the crisis was limited (Bobrow, 1999).

Nevertheless, a further intensification of a narrower concept of region has emerged from the ASEM process. The coordinating meetings of the Asian members of ASEM (ASEAN plus three – Japan, China and Korea) have been developed into a process formally involving meetings of leaders of the ASEAN 10 plus 3 Northeast Asian countries annually. It is now close to Dr Mahathir's original proposal for the EAEC.

Global implications

Asian states and their institutions have been generally globally oriented. It is easy to forget that rules of diplomacy, cooperative arrangements for international collaboration in telecommunications, postal services, shipping and air transport have been mostly followed by countries in the Asia Pacific region since their inception. Thus, when able to make independent decisions, regional countries have been a cooperating part of the global system, in some cases from the late nineteenth century. Most countries in the region now participate in the global multilateral institutions and adhere to the norms, and the rules buttressing those norms. There are exceptions. Dr Mahathir's persistent efforts to reduce dependence upon the West (excluding Japan) were illustrated again by Malaysia's avoidance of IMF intervention in favour of alternative funding sources, notably Japan.

The crisis has intensified concerns at the imposition of reforms from outside the region since these are seen as in part ideologically driven, lacking a knowledge of, and sensitivity to, regional circumstances. There has at times been an increased sense of a lack of understanding of and consideration for Asian views and interests in Eurocentred 'global' institutions. EMEAP, for example, was set up in the belief that Asia was under-represented in global financial councils (Grenville, 1998).

For its part, although Asian multilateralism at the regional level has characteristics that distinguish it from regional multilateralism elsewhere, one of its strengths is that it does not in general conflict with the global multilateralist order, economic or strategic. Indeed, in the economic field it has been trying to move the international community more rapidly to achieve the community's own stated objectives in the WTO, and at times it has pressed for more rapid progress in the security area.

In Asia, multilateral institutions have clearly become embedded in the economic, political and strategic fields. Differences that exist between Asia and elsewhere in the approach to multilateralism, however, are predominantly at the regional level and especially concerned with regional security. Asian countries participate actively in global institutions, whether issue specific or concerned with international order – such as the the UN (and its norm-setting bases: e.g. the law of the sea), WTO, IMF, NPT and CTBT.

The economic crisis has not changed this. There is criticism regionally of the IMF as part of the blaming process but this has not reached major proportions. The region is seeking reforms in the international financial architecture but not the scrapping of the present architecture, merely its improvement and its modification. The positive global outcomes of regional multilateralism have not been greatly affected by the economic crisis.

Conclusion

I have looked at regionalism in multilateral terms. Among the initial motives for embracing multilateralism in the region was the objective of developing a sense of community, and a sense of region grew out of the various factors that brought them together. Multilateralism has had a number of specific economic and political objectives, but in each case the processes have had a broader underlying objective – to establish and develop networks of relations among countries in the region and to build and generate confidence within those relations.

Security has been the ultimate objective in two senses. The regional economic cooperation arrangements – in ASEAN, PECC and APEC – have been equally concerned with these confidence- and network-building purposes as well as to enhance regional economic interdependence for the same purpose. Regional economic cooperation has at the same time contributed to their other and often more substantial internal security concerns – the lack of national resilience – which threatens stability of the country or at least the regime. In so doing the region has accepted that its economic development objectives require an outward-looking market orientation.

In that sense, multilateralism and economic development have been mutually reinforcing in establishing a normative framework for the region. This consists, on the one hand, of a security framework of norms as exemplified in the region-wide acceptance of the principles of the ASEAN's Treaty of Amity and Cooperation, and notably the peaceful resolution of international conflicts; and on the other hand, the acceptance of the principles of liberal trade and the acceptance of economic interdependence as a contributor to economic growth. One strength of these two normative frameworks is the general compatibility with principles laid down in global institutions.

The global crisis has had some impacts on multilateralism in the region but perhaps less than expected, in part because multilateralism is normatively rather than functionally oriented. Weaknesses have been evident in the regional multilateral institutions themselves but only partly due to the crisis. In major respects the two major elements of the normative framework have not been significantly affected by the crisis. First, security concerns have not been accentuated by the crisis – the current crisis points involve areas relatively unaffected, namely, China-Taiwan and North Korea. Nor for that matter have the systemic political changes matched expectations. Second, despite the economic crisis, the priority given to economic development and greater economic interdependence has not changed – it may have slowed in particular contexts but the direction of liberalization is being maintained.

The push for greater regional cooperation has intensified as a result of the crisis and, while the concept of region remains flexible, the crisis has led to increased interest in regional policy consultation and development of a multilateral kind that can bring to bear a stronger regional voice globally, notably in the financial field.[11] Moreover, the region's interest has increased in addressing concerns that reforms in the region are imposed from outside. Both were seen as being countered to some extent and, in the event temporarily, through Asian membership in the G22 context; the new G20 of 'systemically significant' countries now has five regional members (Australia, China, India, Japan and South Korea). The regional concern, however, reflects in part a realization of the greater vulnerability that accompanies the economic interdependence of the region's approach to economic development; in that sense it is crisis driven. In part, however, it is an intensification of a belief already in the region about its under-representation in global institutions.

Although weak, if less than often argued, some apparent weaknesses of regional multilateral institutions were a consequence of characteristics that in other contexts would receive approval, such as their consciously supplementary role to the global institutions. Given the disposition to support global institutional arrangements, the question is what can be sensibly be done better regionally than globally. Global institutions have to set global standards and have to date provided the resources on the scale needed in major crisis situations. Yet the size of those institutions often means that they are slow to respond, lack both flexibility and knowledge of the regional circumstances to make effective contributions to the problems at the regional level. Their resource base may also be increasingly inadequate.

Garnaut and Wilson use three criteria to assess an appropriate division of labour: efficiency in terms of the level of resources needed; efficiency of expertise and information; and efficiency in terms of institutional capacity (Garnaut and Wilson, 1999). The first and third in both cases mainly but not solely point to the global level and the second increasingly to the regional level. Clearly an extensive involvement from global institutions will remain necessary. Although the region made a significant supplementary contribution to resolving the crisis on this occasion, it will need to provide stronger support, largely through regional multilateral institutions, to avoid further such developments in the future.

To return to my opening question, to some extent this was little more than a speed bump on the Asian road to progress, but it has defined a greater need for regional cooperation for the future. That immediate need is recognized regionally. The question is whether this need will be met and sustained in the longer term.

Notes

1   This chapter draws on parts of Harris and Nuttall, 1999.
2   The Shanghai Cooperation Organization involves regular meetings of heads of government of China, Russia, Kazakstan, Kyrgyzstan, Tajikistan and Uzbekistan.
3   The importance of dialogue processes and continued institutional interaction for increased adherence to established norms and compliance with international treaty obligations has also been concluded from a study of global institutions (Chayes and Chayes, 1995).
4   In practice, consensus is commonly sought in international institutions (e.g. UNCLOS, IMF, WTO and NATO), but they normally have an underlying voting process available if needed.
5   Frank Ching (1999) summarizes comments by the then Indonesian Foreign Minister Alatas and ASEAN Secretary-General Severino to this effect.
6   That report is not in accord with a report in *The Nikkei Weekly* (9 August 1999), which suggests that Japanese trading houses are moving back into Southeast Asia.
7   Naturally unilateral liberalizers expect to be given credit for their trade liberalization when formal negotiations take place.
8   For a discussion of the options of monetary integration and monetary union that are at times suggested, and the intermediate options such as common basket pegs or an Asian currency unit, see Dobson, 1999.
9   Motivations from the European perspective, which among other things saw it as a way of overcoming the EU's failure to gain membership of APEC, are described in Dent, 1998.
10   ASEM 'has been more successful than the Asia–Pacific Economic Cooperation (APEC) forum for the Asian participants' (*Sunday Star* (Malaysia), 3 March 1996).
11   Although, in the regular *Far Eastern Economic Review* survey of Asian executives, 81.7 per cent believed this was also needed in international trade negotiations (*Far Eastern Economic Review*, 30 December 1999/6 January 2000: 90).

9 Europeanisation and globalisation

Complementary or contradictory trends?

Helen Wallace

FIS
RII

For too long the debates on globalisation and on Europeanisation have been conducted in separate compartments and in different terms. Too much of the discussion on Europe and Europeanisation has been conducted as if somehow Europe were closed off from the wider international arena. And too much of the discussion of globalisation has set aside the considerable experience in Europe of dealing with 'cross-border' connections.[1] These two discussions have now begun to be drawn together, prompted by two new preoccupations. One is that of Europeanists; they are under pressure to provide a more coherent account of the relationships between global and European developments and to relate both to what happens inside individual European countries. The other concern is of commentators on globalisation; their challenge is to evaluate the regional arrangements within Europe *vis-à-vis* the emergence of a variety of other 'regional' groupings across the world. Both concerns prompt a similar requirement to compare and contrast globalisation and Europeanisation.

This chapter is a contribution to this debate. It draws in particular on an account of Europeanisation and some insights that can be gained from understanding the management of 'cross-border' connections. In what follows three main assertions are laid out. The first is that efforts to manage cross-border connections belong to the long historical experience and the geographical arrangement of the European continent. The second is that this long history has produced a set of embedded features that shape European responses to cross-border connections. The third is that the pattern of European responses has a number of specific elements that make Europe as a region different from most other regions in the world. On the basis of these three assertions I argue that Europeans encounter globalisation with particular experiences and with specific 'management' and institutional resources.

This phenomenon has, perhaps paradoxically, been accompanied by important differences between European countries in the way that both European and global influences are handled. My term for this phenomenon is 'domestication', namely, the ways in which domestic factors frame and influence the incoming impacts of Europeanisation. The combination of the two elements has provided Europeans with some leverage on the process of Europeanisation; it is a shaped process, not a passively encountered process, at least for those actors and territorial units that have had certain attributes. It seems probable that this experience of

Europeanisation provides Europeans with distinctive ways of mediating the impacts of globalisation.

One important qualification needs to be made here. The richest – and most comfortable –experience of actively shaping and managing the cross-border is found in those West European countries which have provided the architects and the artisans of Europeanisation. Europeanisation and resilient domesticity are necessarily at odds with each other, insofar as there is a 'good fit' between the two. On the other hand, some West European countries have been outliers, less at ease with Europeanisation, but none the less permeated by its impacts – Norway and Switzerland are the key current examples. In central and eastern Europe the disruptions to connections across borders have produced a contrasting long history, in which options for managing transnational relationships have been more constrained. Thus Europeanisation is not an even process across the continent, although, as will be argued below, it is not a process confined to those countries that are members of the European Union (EU).

Semantics and definitions

Globalisation and Europeanisation are both topics that lend themselves to long semantic discussions and contested definitions. In what follows I deliberately take a minimalist approach to the definition of Europeanisation. The aim is simply to preserve scope for a kind of agnosticism about outcomes, and to leave scope to examine how structures, behaviours, agency and beliefs shape, or alter, the ways in which the process of Europeanisation works out – over countries, over time and over issue areas. Thus Europeanisation perhaps overwhelms the capacity of the individual European state, and perhaps it substantially removes or reduces autonomy – but perhaps not, and perhaps it depends on the country, the period and the issues. My concern is to inject a different perspective, namely, by considering the interaction of these 'beyond the state' processes of Europeanisation (and perhaps also globalisation) with the 'within the state' processes of domestic politics.

Hence my definition of Europeanisation is as follows: the development and sustaining of systematic European arrangements to manage cross-border connections, such that a European dimension becomes an embedded feature which frames politics and policy within European states. Note here that this definition deliberately does not imply that Europeanisation connotes an inexorable erosion of the domestic; it does not presume that Europeanisation is locked to the EU; and it leaves open the possibility that within European countries some arenas of political activity may be insulated from the impacts of Europeanisation.

First, then, it is important not to prejudge the issue of whether Europeanisation is increasing and inexorable in its impacts on what happens 'within the state'. The section below on the long history indeed suggests that Europeanisation as such is not new, but rather that it may have acquired distinctive contemporary attributes. What then becomes interesting is what form of Europeanisation is promoted by those 'within the state', or, in other words, there is room for debate within and between countries about different options for dealing with Europeanisation. Thus we have to prove, not assume, transfers of loyalty, just as we have to prove, not assume, that the emergence of European regimes displaces or overrides domestic processes. Europeanisation may be pervasive, but provokes defensive responses. It may lead to the articulation of alternative and non-European modes of cross-border management. Interestingly an American congressional delegation visited the United Kingdom in March 2000 to discuss with British Eurosceptics the case for the UK leaving the EU and joining the North American Free Trade Agreement (NAFTA). If the UK were to adopt such a course of action it would not remove the impacts of Europeanisation on the UK, but it would change the way in which Britons sought to mediate the impacts.

A second deliberate feature of my definition is to avoid eliding the definition of Europeanisation with membership of the EU. On the contrary, I seek to argue the point the other way round, namely, that the creation and development of the EU are in themselves responses to Europeanisation and reflect a set of choices about ways of channelling or influencing the patterns of Europeanisation. Coming at the question this way round leaves some room for appraising the role of the EU in its broader context, as part of a wider fabric of cross-border regimes in Europe, in which other organisations and frameworks (formal and informal) also play a part. In addition, we need to pay attention to the impacts of Europeanisation on European countries that are not within the EU, both those where governments and publics have preferred to remain outside of the EU and those where the opposite decision has been taken to press for membership (Batt, 2001). Indeed, we could go further and ask questions about how far and in what ways Europeanisation impacts on Europe's 'near abroad' to the south and to the east. In other words, it would be useful to develop an appreciation of Europeanisation that would give us a handle on the awkward question of where Europe shades into non-Europe.

The third qualification to Europeanisation is that it can coexist with protected domestic political spaces. Here I take issue with those who see Europeanisation as a one-way process of intrusion. Instead I suggest that there are elements of stubborn resistance to Europeanisation, reflecting country differences of societal and political preferences and characteristics as well as of economic attributes. We can also observe empirically that sometimes new efforts are made to define protected political spaces, even in countries where other aspects of Europeanisation have been absorbed. Moreover, the scale and focus of protected domestic political spaces change over time and thus Europeanisation is in some respects an unstable process.

Two different metaphors may help to clarify my approach. The first metaphor, which I have laid out elsewhere, is that of magnetic fields (Wallace, 2000a, 2000b). Picture the domestic, the European and the global as each constituting a magnetic field of varying strength. Politics and policy will be attracted by the magnetic field with the strongest force in relation to the issue being addressed. Which is the strongest may vary between issue areas and between countries, as well as over time. In terms of the conventional discussion of Europeanisation the debate has been about whether or not the magnetic field of Europeanisation has so much gained in strength that the domestic magnetic field is emptied of attractive power. If we then add in the intrusion of globalisation as a phenomenon we might enquire whether its magnetic force is displacing the magnetic power of Europeanisation such that politics and policy are framed more by globalisation – or not.

The second metaphor is more biological – elsewhere I have described this as the Heineken test (Wallace, 1999b). Advertisements in the UK (though not in the Netherlands, the home of Heineken) for Heineken beer describe it as the beer that reaches parts of the body that other beers do not reach. Thus it might be argued that forces such as Europeanisation – or globalisation – have become so powerful that they pervade the domestic body politic. Yet every beer drinker knows that the result of beer drinking is not the same for every beer drinker. Capacities vary and reactions vary. By analogy my argument is that as processes of Europeanisation or globalisation meet with the domestic, a kind of organic interaction takes place which involves adaptive behaviour. Those who are practised handle the incoming influences more adroitly and develop strategies for controlling the impacts.

History and geography matter

A long history of 'cross-border' connections

My own starting point in studying European history was around 1200 BC, in the prehistory of Greece and Asia Minor. It was a period of intense cross-border connections and of competing international systems. Already there were evident a variety of experiments, sometimes imperial and aggressive, sometimes more confederal and cooperative. Extensive cross-border trading took place; quite how far is the subject of continuing archaelogical discovery and interpretation. Periods of antagonism were interspersed with periods of regime building. Goods and people travelled around Europe, and so did ideas. As it happens, what we now know as Europe was also deeply interconnected with, and influenced by, developments in the abutting areas of the southern and eastern Mediterranean.

Then too commercial power and military power were both part of the story of what shaped cross-border connections. Indeed, a recent intriguing volume ascribes to the two millennia before Christ a series of different versions of transnational entrepreneurship (Moore and Lewis, 1999). Thus in some senses one can write a narrative of the European political economy that starts some thousands of years ago.

The most prolonged version of a robust transnational framework in Europe was generated by the Roman Empire. Interestingly the writings of Stein Rokkan place a notable emphasis on this period in shaping European experiences of cooperation and failed cooperation, as well as in developing concepts of territory and 'liminality' (see Flora, 1999). In some respects the Romans solved (at least for a period) some problems of cross-national and cross-cultural organisation that contemporary Europeans find quite challenging. There was a lingua franca – Latin – that continued in subsequently Catholic parts of Europe for a long time to be the medium for inter-elite communication, as did Greek in parts of Eastern and religiously orthodox Europe (Garcia, 1993). The system of Roman law greatly aided the administration of the regime both within and between component territories, and the investment in an extensive physical infrastrucure facilitated communications and the ordering of societies.

This historical reminder is not intended as a nostalgic idealisation of the Roman Empire. Much of its robustness came from the exercise of military power (in the form of a multinational European army!); and much of the projection of political authority was autocratic, arbitrary, and eventually decadent. None the less, it was a multinational and transnational experience, and one in which a great deal of inventiveness was applied to the designing of wide-ranging regimes that were structured and informed by shared understandings and norms.

In subsequent periods a variety of efforts were made to produce proxies for the Roman Empire, often around the projection of authority by the Catholic Church, and later through a variety of other, more temporal empires. It was with the failure of these various attempts at empire that Europe instead became a continent organised into apparently sovereign states, some more successful than others, and some more self-sufficient than others.

The purpose of this historical digression is fourfold. First, it shows a long experience and a variety of experiments in cross-border organisation, or early forms of what we might now call Europeanisation. Some were more successful and more durable than others; it is a history of fluctuations and of competing models of transnational arrangements. Second, commercial and trading links were recurrently core preoccupations, as was the competition for exploitable resources. Thus, for example, in the fifteenth century AD alum was one of the most prized resources as the best fixative for dyes in textiles, in a period in which the European textile industry was intensely competitive. Those who controlled the supplies of alum determined a great deal of the opportunites for commercial success – just as Microsoft protocols do currently for information technology. Then much of the competition was organised by a private and transnational investment and banking sector, in those days linked to competing cities (mostly Italian) rather than countries. The crux of the point here is the extent of economic interdependence. Third, over the centuries a great deal of experience was acquired in structuring relationships between different territorial units (at varying levels). From the Roman period onward a shared legal code was a crucial component as a basis for the embedding of norms and the adjudication of disputes. Similarly, the explicit articulation of preferences about institutional arrangements was a recurrent element of transnational debate. Fourth, traffic in cultural and societal expression was a repeated feature. Two of Europe's most beautiful cathedrals – Monreale in Sicily and Kirkwall in Orkney – are outstanding examples of cross-country amalgams of different cultural traditions and migrant innovation. In more recent periods ideas and doctrines have repeatedly pervaded and invaded the borders of individual European countries, borders which in this sense have always been porous.

What can we distil from this long history? Essentially what in contemporary vocabulary we might call transnational management has been an endemic feature of European history. This is not to suggest that the transnational is the default, but rather that it has recurrently been an option for managing cross-border connections. Moreover, the invention of devices to manage the transnational has provided memories and examples of arrangements that provide alternatives to conflict and antidotes to confrontation.

Geography, borders and 'neighbourness'

It has become a surprising commonplace among economists that geography matters in the development of economic transactions, surprising only in the sense that it seems an obvious observation, perhaps particularly in Europe. The continent has natural maritime borders to the north and to the west; to the south and west it abuts Africa and Asia, neither sufficiently separate in a physical sense to make firm and clear political or economic borders. The history of the continent is tied up with the relationships to these other neighbourhoods. Within the continent that is commonly described as European, history has produced a huge number of discrete territorial units. Efforts to construct widely based zones of authority have jostled with pressures to sustain smaller national or ethnic identities. Post-Second World War Europe for fifty years produced an apparently fixed map, divided into two main zones to the west and to the east. Post-Cold War Europe has undone that map, both producing a larger number of states (a number that has not yet consolidated) and undoing the demarcation of the two wider zones.

Borders in many parts of the continent have been constructed, deconstructed and reconstructed, with two consequences. One is that borders and the management of the interfaces between neighbours have been recurrently contested. The other is that wherever the variable borders have been set over time, economic, social and political connections have travelled across the borders. Indeed, this cross-border connectedness has been one of the impulses for the periodic adjustments (whether peaceful or forced) in the definitions of political borders. Thus the management of 'neighbourness' has been a core preoccupation of those responsible for the management of the territorially defined units in Europe – countries or states, other identified groups (regions and nationalities) and cities, with their hinterlands.

This crowded and volatile political geography has thus resulted in a complex cobweb of interconnectedness across the continent, the connections more dense in some parts of the continent than others, and some of the connections radiating out into the near abroads in Africa and Asia. These connections provide multiple opportunities for interference in, and influences from, across the borders. Indeed, in contemporary Europe the management of intra-European borders has become one of the most overwhelming and challenging preoccupations. It now permeates the debate about the memberships of a string of European transnational institutions, and it poses a challenge for private entrepreneurs as they try to figure out where their markets and their competitors will be over the next ten to twenty years. In addition, the issue presses of how to deal with the several near abroads – North Africa, Russia, Turkey and the Middle East.

Thus the management of neighbourness and the channelling of cross-border connections are concerns that are inescapable at all levels from high politics and security to the day-to-day running of shuttle trade and labour markets. Indeed, if we examine the agendas of the relevant national and transnational agencies in Europe we can observe the huge increase in items promoting activities to address the management of borders. Here indeed is a growth occupation for public officials, as well as for the academic community. This is incidentally a phenomenon which makes contemporary (as well as historical) Europe very different from the United States, and it marks the ways in which Europeans address issues in wider plurilateral contexts.

One other important observation needs to be noted here. Europeans are preoccupied with borders, their positions and the challenges of managing them. But – paradoxically perhaps – Europeans seem doomed to fail to control their borders, both internal and external. All European borders are rather porous, unless they are as severely and ruthlessly controlled as they were in the period of high communism. The porousness is evident in both legal and illegal, licit and illicit movements across borders, and of both goods and persons. The nervousness that arises from the illegal and the illicit movements leads to public measures that interfere with the legal and the licit, just as the relaxation of border controls to facilitate the legal and the licit also extend the opportunities for the illegal and the illicit (Monar, 1999). This conundrum pervades much of European policy-making within the EU, in relation to both intra-EU issues and extensions to its membership. It also provides one of the most testing preoccupations for the post-communist countries in central and eastern Europe, where borders are often sensitive and the management of 'neighbourness' is complicated by history and geography.

European responses to 'cross-border' connections

Contemporary Europeans, like their historical antecedents, are thus locked into a process of managing their cross-border connections. There is a kind of path-dependency here; if cross-border management is unavoidable (Albania was an odd exception in being so effectively insulated for so long and at so great a price), then better to try to channel the process of Europeanisation. Hence the development of Europe over the past fifty years or so has been crowded with efforts to design and to cement patterns of European institutions that will bear the strain of managing interconnectedness. Moreover, as I have tried to show, the crowded geography and the complexity of cross-border connections make it difficult to be functionally discrete. It is hard, for example, to construct regimes to deal with the political economy of Europe without also dealing with the security relationships. It has proved impossible to deal with the traffic in goods, services, capital and labour (the classic four freedoms on which the original European Economic Community was focused) without dealing with the traffic in persons. Europe after all enters the twenty-first century with human-trafficking and transnational crime as pressing and daunting challenges.

It follows that those who wish to understand the complexities of Europeanisation need to pay attention not only to the EU, but also to the variety of other transnational regimes that are evident in Europe. The EU has become the most important of the institutionalised frameworks for managing the cross-border, both for its own incumbent members and for its neighbours. But it is not the monopoly channel of Europeanisation; Europe spreads much further than the membership of the EU; and non-European neighbours are in varying ways appended to, or pressures on, these various European arrangements.

The creation and development of the EU is thus in my terms the predominant contemporary choice that has been made to address European interconnectedness and to channel Europeanisation. Its evolution has been buttressed by other parallel frameworks, notably the North Atlantic Treaty Organization (NATO). Interestingly the current debate about the development of the EU is how far its reach should extend beyond the market-making functions for which it was primarily designed. The core features of the EU illustrate a particularly highly articulated approach to 'designer' Europeanisation, from which flows the argument that the EU is an example not just of a regional regime but also of deep integration. Thus the EU provides within Europe a template of ambitious cross-border management, and for global comparisons a set of 'benchmarks' to distinguish between shallow and deep integration.

These core features therefore need to be made explicit and briefly explained. They are as follows: multiple locations of governance; multiple dimensions of integration; multiple modes of interaction; and extensive institutionalisation.

Multiple locations of governance

West European experience shows a revealed pattern of governance through multiple locations. The state persists as a continuing and relatively robust political and territorial unit, but with divisions of labour within and beyond the state. Many observers of the EU have called this 'multi-level governance', which implies a kind of hierarchy that spreads across the infra-national, the national, the European (EU) and the global. This is almost certainly a picture that is too neat and tidy. Divisions of labour between levels of government vary between countries and over time; some are easily agreed, while others are repeatedly contested. Nor, as I have indicated, is the EU the only option for European governance. Hence my preference is to emphasise that west European experience since the Second World War reveals a pattern of developing alternative locations of governance at and across conventional levels of governance, formally, but also informally, constructed.

An important consequential point is that the availability of multiple locations of governance provides political, economic and social actors with choices about where to address particular issues and dilemmas, and choices about appropriate partners. Thus some European regimes are in groups smaller than, or different from, the membership of the EU. The Schengen arrangements were, for example, originally and deliberately devised as a small group experiment, not as a fall-back to failed EU coordination. A crucial issue currently is about whether or not to reduce the number of locations of collective governance so as to concentrate more through the EU, for example, by taking on some functions from NATO. The flexibility of these choices among locations, within the state as well as beyond it, is one of the assets of western Europe in adapting to changing tasks. It remains to be seen how far central and eastern European countries will acquire this habit of developing multiple locations of governance, both internally and *vis-à-vis* each other.

If we recall that Europeans are subject to the impacts of globalisation as well as of Europeanisation, then a core question is when and how Europeans configure global locations of governance as alternative frameworks for dealing with their chosen requirements or resolving their dilemmas.

Multiple dimensions of integration

Over the past fifty years or so Europeans have sought to develop cross-border arrangements along three main dimensions, set out at greater length elsewhere (Wallace, 1999a). These are the territorial, the functional and the affiliational dimensions. Briefly the territorial includes the management of security (hard and soft) and the articulation of relationships with immediate neighbours. The former have been addressed mostly through multilateral arrangements, with a few countries practising articulated non-alignment in the shadow of the multilateral regimes. The latter have been dealt with by bilateral understandings and special groupings (the Franco-German, the Nordic family and so on). Some have extended into the borderland between Europe and non-Europe, thus the inclusion of Turkey as an important NATO partner.

The functional dimension has mostly concerned issues of political economy and resource management. The EU has been the core political economy organisation, buttressed by its hub-and-spoke relationships with the other neighbours. Association agreements have been spawned in varying formats to condition the ways in which this wider European economy is regulated. Whether or not other Europeans are included as full club members within the EU has been decided, however, not only on political economy criteria, but also according to factors that relate to the territorial and affiliational dimensions of integration.

The EU does not quite monopolise the functional connections. An array of mostly single-purpose organisations exists to deal with specific functional arrangements (space policy, ennvironmental protection, civil aviation and so on). Some operate in geographically defined parts of Europe – the Baltic region, the Black Sea region and so on. The combination of single-purpose frameworks and the multi-purpose EU provides a density and intensity of interactions across borders and efforts at shared management, almost all of these in highly institutionalised and rule-bound settings.

In addition, there is an affiliational dimension to integration. Some of the European frameworks, starting from the Council of Europe in the late 1940s, exist to allow states that claim to share certain norms and values to operate collective arrangements. These include, for example, the European transnational human rights regime. More recently the Organisation for Cooperation and Security in Europe has become active on a pan-European scale in addressing some issues to do with spreading good democratic practice and building up societal connections.

The combination of these three dimensions of integration leads to the characterisation of Europeanisation as promoting deep rather than shallow integration. An increasingly marked feature of the current debate in Europe about Europeanisation is how far the EU can, or should, become the fulcrum for integration across all three dimensions. Currently the two arenas of most active policy development within the EU concern, on the one hand, defence and, on the other, a common regime for 'freedom, [internal] security and justice'. In 1999 the Cologne and Helsinki European Councils committed the EU to develop a Common European Security and Defence Policy and a recasting of the division of labour with NATO. Also in 1999 the Tampere European Council committed the EU to an ambitious programme of measures to give shape to the area of freedom, security and justice (Monar, 1999). These deal with migration, refugees and asylum, and crime, as well as the development within the EU of cross-border jurisdictions affecting individuals, both citizens and non-citizens.

Multiple modes of interaction

Europeanisation is characterised by multiple modes of interaction rather than a single predominant mode. It used to be possible to assert that the 'Community method' associated with the EU (and its precursor European Community) revealed methods of transnational organisation quite different from those found in other fora. The contemporary picture is more differentiated. The EU, as it has developed regimes in a widening range of issue areas, has come to operate in a variety of different modes, some of which resemble modes of operation found in other transnational frameworks.

At least five modes of interaction can be identified within the EU and other fora:

1   the Community method of supranational governance, especially associated with the early EU (better EC) efforts at constructing common policies, as in agriculture;
2   a European regulatory mode, chiefly associated with market-making and market-supervising activites, mainly around the single market, and extended to neighbouring countries such as those within the European Economic Area or those being drawn towards membership;
3   distributional politics, mainly located around the EU in a multi-level format involving sub-national as well as central governments in the member states;
4   benchmarking and concertation, as found originally in the Organisation for Economic Cooperation and Development (OECD) and increasingly in new areas of soft policy cooperation in the EU and in bilateral efforts to transfer policy experiences from one European country to another;
5   intensive transgovernmentalism, the knitting together of national policymakers in close and operational cooperation, but without the agency of a separate strong collective executive, a mode that is now associated with the EU's embryonic defence regime, perhaps a mirror image of NATO, as well as in the field of freedom, security and justice (see Wallace, 2000a, 2000b).

The essential point here is that there is a proliferation of different modes for managing Europeanisation. These make the EU less different from other European frameworks, while also simultaneously making the EU more accepted as the preferred framework for new areas of collective policy development. But the variety of modes also implies variation in the way in which European governance interacts with domestic politics on the one hand, and the broader global context on the other. The net effect, however, is to extend the issue arenas subject to forms of transnational management in Europe.

Extensive institutionalisation

Little needs to be said here about the extent to which Europeanisation is also a highly institutionalised process. The phenomenon is widely documented in the literature on European integration. Especially in the EU, but also in other European organisations, systematic and rule-defined arrangements have been adopted to develop cross-border cooperation. Formal procedures are buttressed by informal procedures, and behaviours seem to be significantly conditioned by the operation of, and recurrent involvement in, multilateral European arrangements. The multilateral point needs to be stressed, because participants in European institutions are accustomed to having to strike compromises on at least three levels of policy-making: the national level of defining country preferences; the European arena for establishing collective regimes; and relevant broader international arenas for developing global regimes. Legal methodologies are an important part of this institutional fabric, both the entrenching of commitments between countries and the access of individuals to a process of litigation to test the application of European legal regimes (in the human rights regime of the Council of Europe, as well as in the EU).

The combination of political and legal institutionalisation provides multiple access points for groups and individuals affected by the management of cross-border connections to seek to influence the outcomes. Governance without government is one way of characterising the resulting institutional pattern. It is a pattern which diffuses rather than focuses political leadership and political accountability. The result is to make Europeans puzzling and frustrating partners in wider international regimes. Collective European positions depend on a complex of interlocking understandings rather than on crisply defined and clearly authorised hierarchies of authority. Consent for common European positions generally depends on a series of interlocking understandings. As has been argued above, these often stretch into a variety of issue areas way beyond individual policy topics.

The domestication of the extra-national in Europe

How far then does Europeanisation spread into the domestic polities of individual European countries? The range of issues caught up in the process of Europeanisation is considerable, and latterly has come much closer to the core areas traditionally associated with state sovereignty: a single currency; European defence; and internal security and citizenship. The EU has also become more active in all of these areas, displacing to an extent the other European frameworks with which it has coexisted over recent decades. Yet at the same time EU modes of policy development have become more varied; there is not a single predominant model of supranational governance. In addition, there is a complex of arrangements linking non-EU countries to EU regimes, as well as non-NATO countries to the NATO alliance.

Several features of domestic reactions to Europeanisation need to be emphasised. First, robust differences persist between countries, even those that belong to the EU which are subject to strong collective disciplines. There are significant variations in the ways that Europeanisation is interpreted and mediated through domestic polities. Ireland and Finland, for example, represent cases of countries that have used Europeanisation to buttress far-reaching processes of domestic transformation – and without losing their distinctive characters. Thus even small and potentially vulnerable states can find a distinctive national trajectory.

Second, the autonomy of individual European states may have been compromised by the pressures of Europeanisation, but this has not prevented the emergence of new European states. Central and eastern Europe has been marked by the emergence of new states. The notion of an autonomous Scotland is not beyond the bounds of the thinkable. Conceptions of what makes for the viability of a state in Europe need to be rethought.

Third, one strong feature of the newer areas of collective European regimes is that some involve the contracting out of important policy functions to quasi-autonomous transnational agencies – the European Central Bank, to manage the single currency; Europol, to manage cross-order police cooperation; perhaps the Eurocorps, to provide an element of collective military force. This is a different picture from that of concentrated European governance or quasi-government.

Fourth, increasingly the strong European organisations and regimes – the EU, the single currency, NATO and so on – cast long shadows over neighbouring, but not member countries. Elsewhere in Europe there are patterns of unilateral adjustment to collective European rules and procedures. Candidate countries for the EU or NATO imitate and seek to pre-adapt to their operating arrangements. Several east European countries are adopting versions of the Euro through currency boards. Some south-east European countries have become virtual protectorates.

Thus Europeanisation has intensified and extended, while being accompanied by a more diffuse and variegated pattern of institutional arrangements. Those individual European states with strong and resilient domestic polities have retained considerable areas of autonomy, while the weaker ones are caught in voiceless dependence. This produces a paradoxical and uneven pattern of Europeanisation, with the issue of when and whether the main European organisations, notably the EU and NATO, will extend their memberships – and to which other countries – remaining unresolved.

The intersection of Europeanisation and globalisation

Experience and practice have made west Europeans relatively adept at managing their cross-border connections. There has been a cumulative process of institutional inventiveness in terms of European-level regime building, accompanied by adaptive behaviour within countries to retain domestic identities, even in small countries. Territoriality has not disappeared as a domain for practising political and social differentiation. This heterogeneity of local responses to Europeanisation needs further attention and examination.

How far this west European pattern will be extended across the continent remains to be seen. The evidence from the experience of western Europe suggests that it depends on both within-country developments and beyond-country patterns of connection. West European patterns of managing the cross-border connections have been shaped by transnational institutions, but built upon cross-border connections in which a variety of agents and organisations (both private and public) have become stakeholders.

One result of the extensive process of Europeanisation has been to produce a quite high degree of self-sufficiency and self-absorption in Europe. Europeans trade with each other much more than they trade with the rest of the world – the proportions are much the same as those for the US. Europeans deal multilaterally with each other much more than with the rest of the world. In the defence arena Europeans are currently seeking ways of diminishing their reliance on the US.

Thus Europe as a region exhibits a vigorous pattern of intra-regional organisation, with extending scope across multiple dimensions of integration, combined with country differentiation. How widely that Europe is cast in geographical terms remains to be settled, but the outlying countries to the east and to the south are caught in the impacts of Europeanisation. There is little evidence that Europeanisation is diminishing in impact, although its forms and modes of operation are becoming more diverse. The impacts of globalisation in Europe have to be read through this experience of Europeanisation. Where global regimes offer scope for collective European inputs, Europe as a region has a considerable capacity for collective engagement, but diffusely managed depending on the issues being addressed. Hard cooperation is achievable on many of the political economy issues, and softer, less predictable cooperation on other issues. But Europeanisation is sufficiently deeply embedded to act as a filter for globalisation.

Note

1 This article draws extensively on work currently being conducted under the ESRC *One Europe or Several?* programme, details of which can be found at <www.one-europe.ac.uk>.

10 Austria's and Sweden's accession to the European Union

A comparative neo-Gramscian analysis

Andreas Bieler

Introduction

On 1 January 1995, Austria and Sweden acceded to the European Union (EU). Historically, membership had been rejected in both countries: first, for being incompatible with their neutral status, and second, because social democratic-led governments feared that the EU, dominated by big capital and Christian democratic parties, would undermine their achievements of full employment and social equality. Thus it is a paradox that Austria and Sweden joined the EU at a moment when it had moved towards positions which contributed even further to these dangers. The Internal Market programme of 1985 and the plans for Economic and Monetary Union (EMU) in the Treaty of Maastricht of 1991 signified a combination of liberalization, deregulation and further supranational policy co-ordination and, therefore, threatened to undermine national policy autonomy even further. Moreover, the Treaty of Maastricht established first steps towards a Common Foreign and Security Policy (CFSP), which at least potentially could imply sovereignty pooling in this area in the future and thus threaten Austria's and Sweden's neutral status.

In this chapter, it is argued that the 1995 enlargement of the EU has to be analysed against the background of the structural changes since the early 1970s, often referred to as globalization. Briefly, globalization may be defined as the transnationalization of production and finance at the material level, expressed in the rise in size and numbers of transnational corporations (TNCs) and a worldwide deregulation of national financial markets, and a change from Keynesian ideas to neo-liberalism at the ideological level (Cox 1993: 259–60, 266–7). The established theories of integration are unable to account for the structural change of globalization and thus to explain the puzzle of Austria's and Sweden's accession to the EU. Neo-functionalist analyses incorrectly assume an automaticity of integration through the concept of spill-over, based on an objective economic rationale, and neglect the wider world within which integration takes place. Intergovernmentalist approaches, including the most developed liberal intergovernmentalist variant, consider states to be the most important actors at the international level, and consequently overlook the importance of supranational institutions, transnational actors and the independent role of ideas. Moreover, they incorrectly concentrate on interstate negotiations as the most important instances of integration. (For a more detailed critical analysis of integration theories, see Bieler 2000: 3–8.) In the following section a neo-Gramscian perspective is suggested as an alternative, which is then applied to Austria's and Sweden's accession to the EU in the remainder of the chapter.

A neo-Gramscian alternative to European integration

In two seminal articles in the early 1980s, Robert Cox developed a neo-Gramscian perspective as 'critical' theory, based on the work of the Italian communist Antonio Gramsci (Cox 1981, 1983). In the wake of Cox's work, a whole range of different studies along neo-Gramscian lines were published, which had mainly the task of understanding hegemony at the international level as well as the structural change of world order (e.g. Cox 1987; Gill 1990, 1993; Overbeek 1993; Rupert 1995). As a result, there has been a tendency to identify a cohesive neo-Gramscian school. According to Morton, however, a 'school' formation of this type should be resisted, since this entails the danger of simplifying internal contradictions and transforming neo-Gramscian research into an orthodoxy, which could imply the loss of its original 'critical' intentions. Here, Morton's suggestion of labelling these studies *neo-Gramscian perspectives* is adopted. The emphasis on the plural form is crucial. 'It immediately accepts the diversity of contributions within the perspectives whilst also permitting the flexibility to realize commonalities and overlaps' (Morton 1998: 8). It is in this sense that this chapter suggests a neo-Gramscian perspective, capable of understanding the processes behind Austria's and Sweden's accession to the EU against the background of globalization.

Most importantly, a neo-Gramscian perspective focuses on social forces, engendered by the production process, as the most important collective actors. The concept of class is crucial for the definition of social forces. Classes are regarded 'as social forces whose cohesion derives from the role played in a mode of production' (Holman and van der Pijl 1996: 55). Consequently, class is defined as a relation and the various fractions of labour and capital can be identified by relating them to their place in the production system. A basic distinction may be drawn between national social forces of capital and labour stemming from national production sectors and transnational capital and labour, engendered by those production sectors, which are organized on a transnational scale. The first group may be further subdivided into nationally oriented capital and labour, which stem from domestic production sectors which produce for the national market, and internationally oriented capital and labour, engendered by domestic production sectors, which produce for the international market. In short, the neo-Gramscian perspective makes structural changes such as globalization accessible, since the emergence of new social forces engendered by the transnationalization of production and finance can be incorporated. These forces are located in the wider structure of the social relations of production, which do not determine but shape their interests and identity. Moreover, globalization is not simply understood as an external force, but as a process actively pursued partly by transnational social forces.

Second, this neo-Gramscian perspective 'rejects the notion of objective laws of history and focuses upon class struggle . . . [be they intra-class or inter-class] . . . as the heuristic model for the understanding of structural change' (Cox with Sinclair 1996: 57–8). The essence of class struggle is exploitation and the resistance to it, and this confrontation of opposed social forces in concrete historical situations implies the possibility of different future developments. There are no inevitable developments in history, and instances of European integration are as much the outcome of an open-ended struggle as are other political developments. Importantly, van der Pijl (1998: 36–49) shows how a concern with the degradation of human and environmental conditions can also be understood in terms of class struggle. He distinguishes three different terrains of capitalist exploitation: (1) original accumulation and resistance to it during the initial imposition of capitalist exploitation; (2) the capitalist exploitation of labour in the workplace and the conflict between the bourgeoisie and the working class; and (3) the extension of exploitation to the process of social reproduction covering the social and natural substratum.

Class struggle on the third terrain is expressed mainly in the activities of new social movements and green parties in defence of the environment, and partly as a backlash to this progressive type of resistance, by extreme-right parties and their rallying of popular resentment around anti-immigration and nationalist themes against the disruption of life through the processes of globalization. The referendum campaign in Austria on EU membership is a good example of both types of resistance to intensified exploitation of the sphere of reproduction (see below). In short, the primary emphasis on the sphere of production does not imply that other actors are overlooked. Through the concepts of class struggle and exploitation extended into the sphere of reproduction, social movements and green and extreme-right parties are firmly linked to the capitalist mode of production and thus included in the analysis.

Third, while the state is still considered to be an important analytical category, it is regarded as a structure within which and through which social forces operate rather than as a unitary actor in its own right. There are several forms of states and the national interest, the *'raison d'état'*, cannot be separated from society, as it depends on the configuration of social forces at the state level. Forms of state are defined in terms of the apparatus of administration and of the historical bloc or class configuration that defines the *raison d'état* for that form (Cox 1989: 41). Gramsci's concept of the integral state is analytically useful for the conceptualization of the relation between state and society (Rupert 1995: 27–8). On the one hand, the integral state consists of 'political society', i.e. the coercive apparatus of the state more narrowly understood including ministries and other state institutions. Due to the internationalization of the state in the processes of globalization, Cox argues that those state institutions which are linked to the global economy (such as finance ministries, central banks) are given priority within a country's governmental set-up over those institutions which deal with predominantly national problems (for example labour ministries) (Cox 1981: 146).

On the other hand, 'civil society', made up of political parties, unions, employers' associations, churches, etc., 'represents the realm of cultural institutions and practices in which the hegemony of a class may be constructed or challenged' (Rupert 1995: 27). Thus political parties and interest associations are also considered to be important. Nevertheless, in contrast to pluralist, corporatist and policy network approaches (e.g. Lehmbruch and Schmitter 1982; Marsh and Rhodes: 1992), they are not considered to be rationalistic, unitary actors. Rather, they are regarded as institutional frameworks within and through which different class fractions of capital and labour attempt to establish their particular interests and ideas as the generally accepted, or 'common-sense', view.

Finally, the independent role of ideas is taken into account. On the one hand, ideas are considered to be a part of the overall structure in the form of 'intersubjective meanings'. Hence they establish the wider frameworks of thought, 'which condition the way individuals and groups are able to understand their social situation, and the possibilities of social change' (Gill and Law 1988: 74). On the other hand, ideas may be used by actors as 'weapons' in order to legitimize particular policies and are important in that they form a part of a hegemonic project by 'organic intellectuals' (see below). This treatment of ideas allows neo-Gramscian perspectives to take into account changes such as the shift from Keynesianism to neo-liberalism, identified above as a part of globalization.

Various social forces may attempt to form a historical bloc in order to establish an order preferable to them at the national and/or international level. 'The historical bloc is the term applied to the particular configuration of social classes and ideology that gives content to a historical state' (Cox 1987: 409), and thus consists of structure and superstructure. It forms a complex, politically contestable and dynamic ensemble of social relations, which includes economic, political and cultural aspects. The relationship between structure and superstructure is reciprocal. 'Superstructures of ideology and political organization shape the development of both aspects of production . . . [i.e. the social relations and the physical means of production] and are shaped by them' (Cox 1983: 168). The main goal of a historical bloc is the establishment of hegemony. Unlike the neo-realist notion of hegemony, in which a hegemonic state controls and dominates other states and the international order thanks to its superior amount of economic and military capabilities (Gilpin 1981: 29; Keohane 1984: 32–3), hegemony here describes a type of rule which predominantly relies on consent, not on coercion. It 'is based on a coherent conjunction or fit between a configuration of material power, the prevalent collective image of . . . order . . . and a set of institutions which administer the order with a certain semblance of universality' (Cox 1981: 139). 'Organic intellectuals' play a crucial role in achieving hegemony. According to Gramsci,

> every social group, coming into existence on the original terrain of an essential function in the world of economic production, creates together with itself, organically, one or more strata of intellectuals which give it homogeneity and an awareness of its own function not only in the economic but also in the social and political fields.
>
> (Gramsci 1971: 5)

Organic intellectuals do not simply produce ideas, but they concretize and articulate strategies in complex and often contradictory ways, which is possible because
of their class location and their proximity to the most powerful forces in production
and the state. It is their task to organize the social forces they stem from and to
develop a hegemonic project which is able to transcend the particular interests of
this group so that other social forces outside the historical bloc are able to give their
consent. Such a hegemonic project must be based on 'organic' ideas, which stem
from the economic sphere. It must, however, also go beyond economics into the
political and social sphere, incorporating 'organic' ideas related to issues such as
social reform or moral regeneration, to result in a stable hegemonic political
system. It 'brings the interests of the leading class into harmony with those of subordinate classes and incorporates these other interests into an ideology expressed
in universal terms' (Cox 1983: 168).

At first sight, this neo-Gramscian perspective is not very different from
Gourevitch's approach, which analyses the policy responses of countries to crises
in the international economy. He identifies five different factors as possible explanatory variables of economic policy choices (Gourevitch 1986: 54–68): (1) the
production profile, similarly to the neo-Gramscian identification of core social
forces, stresses the importance of the location in the production process for societal
actors' preferences; (2) the intermediate associations variable highlights the role of
interest groups and political parties, that is, the neo-Gramscian 'civil society'; (3) the
state structure explanation points to state institutions, that is, the neo-Gramscian
'political society'; (4) the economic ideology factor emphasizes the role of economic
paradigms in shaping the understanding of economic situations and political cir-
cumstance, similar to the neo-Gramscian emphasis on the independent role of
ideas; and finally (5) the international system variable stresses the impact of state
interaction on economic policy. This resembles the neo-Gramscian emphasis on
globalization, although here neo-Gramscian perspectives clearly move beyond
state-centric accounts of the international system. However, instead of arranging
these different variables in a complex theoretical ensemble, Gourevitch accords
them theoretically equal importance in a pluralist fashion. The particular relevance of each individual factor and the relationship between these factors has to
be analysed in concrete situations.[1] This is the crucial point where Gourevitch
differs from neo-Gramscian perspectives. By attributing theoretically equal
importance to different variables such as ideas and the production structure,
Gourevitch takes the separation of state and market, the political and the economic, as the implicit starting point of his investigation and restricts himself to
an analysis of the external relationships between the different factors.[2]

By contrast, neo-Gramscian perspectives attribute primary explanatory importance to the social relations of production. This allows them to realize that the
political and the economic, similar to other apparently independent factors, are
the formal expressions of the very same capitalist social relations of production.
Only by comprehending this is the analysis of the internal relationship between
the various factors possible and the consideration of developments beyond capitalism feasible. As a critical theory interested in contributing to social and political

transformation, this latter quality is absolutely essential for neo-Gramscian perspectives.

Austria's and Sweden's accession to the EU[3]

Austria: the successful pro-membership hegemonic project by the Austrian Federation of Industrialists

In accordance with the neo-Gramscian perspective outlined in the previous section, an analysis of the Austrian production structure is required to identify the core social forces. Austria's post-war production structure has been predominantly characterized by small-scale industry. In 1992, out of the 2.19 million working population, 55 per cent were employed in small-sized companies with less than 100 employees and 28 per cent in medium-sized companies with less than 1000 employees. This is a relatively high percentage in an international comparison. In general, these companies contribute only between one- and two-thirds to the overall national employment (Breit and Rössl 1992: 191). Importantly, about 50 per cent of Austrian domestic production was completely sheltered against international competition with regulated supply and production quota (Luif 1994: 26).

Siegel identified twenty-one Austrian TNCs, but only one of them, Austrian Industries, dissolved in 1993, lived up to international standards in 1990 (Siegel 1992). The twenty-one TNCs were mainly concentrated in Austria in their production structure, employing only 20 per cent of their workforce abroad (Siegel 1992: 167). The small number of TNCs and their focus on Austria signals a low degree of transnationalization of production. As a consequence, the main line of division is likely to be between nationally oriented capital and labour and internationally oriented capital and labour. While the former may reject EU membership since this implies the end of their protection against international competition, the latter most likely support accession to the EU, since this guarantees primary access to their export markets. The few transnational social forces may be expected to join forces with internationally oriented capital and labour, as they too rely on international free trade and liberalization. Importantly, this analysis of the production structure only provides a range of likely actors. How these forces acted in reality, however, needs to be established in an empirical investigation.

The main actor to start the debate was the Austrian Federation of Industrialists (VÖI). Representing the export sector of the Austrian economy and foreign TNCs, it was deeply concerned about the possible barriers implied by the EU Internal Market project. After careful consideration, it published a statement on 14 May 1987 and asked the government 'to do everything possible for Austria to become a full member of the EU as soon as possible' [translation by the author] (VÖI 1987: 42). The argument went along neo-liberal economic lines. Only membership would guarantee full participation in the dynamic process of European integration, and the required dismantling of Austria's sheltered sector would bring about restructuring and increased competitiveness. Nevertheless, the VÖI realized that the main obstacle to membership could be Austria's status of neutrality.

Consequently it commissioned a study by two experts of international law, which concluded that membership was compatible with neutrality (Hummer and Schweitzer 1987). Two more publications dealing with the economic and constitutional aspects of membership followed soon after (Breuss and Stankovsky 1988; Öhlinger 1988). The goal of these publications was to establish a basis for discussion on membership which had not existed before (Interview No.3, Vienna, 22 May 1995). The VÖI's strategy did not lead directly to membership; none the less, it provided a coherent hegemonic project around which various fractions of social forces could rally.

It was, first, supported by internationally oriented social forces of capital. In particular the textile industry declared membership to be a vital issue for its economic survival. Some textile employers even threatened to transfer production units to the EU in case of non-membership (Interview No. 5, Vienna, 24 April 1996). They gained the upper hand in the Chamber of Commerce, which demanded membership at its Annual General Conference on 9 December 1987 (BWK 1987: 457–9).

The trade unions found it more difficult to support accession to the EU. Eventually, labour in the internationally oriented sectors determined the support for application by the Chamber of Labour and the Austrian Federation of Trade Unions, the two peak organizations of labour. In talks with the employer associations, high-ranking trade union officials had realized that they were unable to suggest an alternative to membership, which would offer the same kind of economic benefits. Therefore they supported membership, but made it dependent on a range of different conditions (Interview No. 2, Vienna, 12 May 1995). Neutrality was not to be compromised, and the economic gains should be used to improve the income, employment and welfare of the general population. They further demanded a commitment to full employment as the priority of economic and social policy (AK 1989; ÖGB 1988).

Internationally oriented capital and labour had a similar success in the two main parties, the Austrian Socialist Party (SPÖ) and the Austrian People's Party (ÖVP), which formed a coalition government from January 1987 onward. In January 1988 the latter decided to push for membership (ÖVP 1988). It had already adopted a neo-liberal strategy in 1982 when it demanded budgetary cuts, tax reform, flexibility, deregulation and privatization (Meth-Cohn and Müller 1994: 162–3). Membership appeared to be a logical step along these lines. Nevertheless, the ÖVP had to overcome strong internal opposition from its agricultural wing, which was also organized in the Chamber of Agriculture. Apart from some limited exports to the EU in the area of cattle, agriculture was a totally nationally oriented sector. Austrian production prices were higher than in the EU partly due to a different agricultural structure based on small and medium-sized farms with a strong emphasis on ecological factors in contrast to large-scale agricultural production in the EU focusing on efficiency (Kunnert 1993: 82–3). In the end, the Chamber's participation in the pro-EU historical bloc could be assured only through financial restructuring help. Many farmers remained unconvinced none the less.

Although slightly later than the ÖVP, the SPÖ also accepted neo-liberal ideas against the background of economic recession. In the government's economic report to parliament in 1985, Chancellor Fred Sinowatz (SPÖ) described Keynesianism as a policy of 'diving-through', which could be used only in the short term. A departure from the budget deficit spending of the 1970s was indicated (Seidel 1993: 146). From early 1988 onward, the economic wing around the then Chancellor Franz Vranitzky and Finance Minister Lacina was convinced that membership was necessary to ensure full participation in the Internal Market and some even followed the argument that this would bring about the urgent restructuring of the sheltered sector. Opposition grew, however, within the party, mainly around the issue of neutrality. It was suggested that Austria should at least wait until it was clear whether the EU would proceed towards a CFSP, which undermined Austrian neutrality (Interview No. 6, Vienna, 08 May 1996). In view of this opposition, Vranitzky waited until the official report by the international law office in the Foreign Ministry in November 1988 had declared that membership and neutrality were compatible (Völkerrechtsbüro 1988) before he spoke out clearly in favour of membership. On 3 April 1989, the national committee of the SPÖ voted in favour of application with a majority of fifty to four. The road to application was clear, which followed on 1 July 1989.

Finally, the pro-membership course was supported by state institutions linked to the global economy such as the Austrian National Bank, the Economic Ministry and the Finance Ministry. The latter regarded austerity and a consolidated budget as necessary in order to maintain a good credit rating on the integrated global financial market in times of free capital movement, and membership was considered to be a good way of achieving these objectives (Interview No. 1, Vienna, 11 May 1995).

There had been opposition to membership. Both labour and capital related to the sheltered production sectors opposed membership. This included mainly the food-processing industry, customs' officials, transport companies and the agricultural sector, where not everybody followed the direction of the political elite of the Chamber of Agriculture. Some of the employers and employees in these sectors worked together in individual instances and tried to influence their respective Chamber. They raised their voices of opposition whenever they could, but were eventually outnumbered (Interview No. 4, Vienna, 23 May 1995).

In 1988 the first publications appeared, which criticized the argument that membership was a natural necessity and pointed to alternative strategies. Althaler *et al.*, for example, regretted the one-sided orientation towards EU membership and pointed to a range of different options such as further development of the 1972 free trade agreements between Austria and the EU or association with the EU instead of membership, which would promise similar economic gains (Althaler *et al.* 1988: 44–5). Such criticism was supported by the Austrian Green Party (GA), which vehemently opposed membership. The Internal Market programme was accused of merely aiming at economic-industrial expansion at the expense of high environmental and social standards. In addition, the GA criticized the EU's democratic deficit and perceived military component (GA 1989). Overall, however, neither the criticism of the neo-liberal economics of EU membership nor the alternatives to accession were accepted by a wider audience. They seemed to lack 'common sense' in an ideological environment, in which neo-liberalism had become part of the overall structure.

Finally, and surprisingly, the Austrian Freedom Party (FPÖ) under Jörg Haider had changed course and started opposing membership from 1992 onwards. Most importantly, the surrender of national sovereignty and the idea of a multicultural European society were rejected (FPÖ 1993: 2–3). Nevertheless, while the turn of the FPÖ strengthened the no-side quantitatively, in practice it undermined the opposition. Progressive forces such as the GA had constantly to distance themselves from the extreme-right, xenophobic rhetoric of the FPÖ instead of concentrating on the campaign itself. In the end, the yes-group won in the referendum on EU membership on 12 June 1994 with a clear majority of 66.6 per cent to 33.4 per cent.

Sweden: the delayed struggle about membership

Unlike Austria, Sweden's production structure has always been characterized by TNCs. The degree of transnationalization, however, increased dramatically in the second half of the 1980s when there was a drastic upturn in outward FDI. While inward FDI had risen from only US$396mn in 1985 to US$2,328mn in 1990, outward FDI increased from US$1783mn to US$14,136mn during the same period (Luif 1996: 208). This is even more dramatic if one takes into account that 'in 1989 for the first time ever, Sweden invested more abroad than at home' (Kurzer 1993: 133). The transnationalization of Swedish production is also expressed in the change in the Swedish and foreign share of TNCs' employees and production. In 1965, TNCs employed 33.9 per cent of their employees abroad, where they achieved 25.9 per cent of their turnover. By 1990, the situation had drastically changed: 60.6 per cent of the workforce was employed in the production abroad, accounting for 51.4 per cent of the turnover. This increased emphasis on production abroad was especially apparent between 1986 and 1990. The percentage of employees abroad rose by 11.4 per cent, i.e. 42.7 per cent of the overall increase between 1965 and 1990, and the percentage of turnover abroad by 9.1 per cent, i.e. 35.7 per cent of the overall increase between 1965 and 1990 (Braunerhjelm *et al.* 1996: 10; own calculations). In some instances, this even included the transfer of headquarters. Asea Brown Boveri moved to Zürich/Switzerland and Tetra Pak and IKEA to locations in the EU. As a result, the main line of division in Sweden is likely to be between national capital and labour on the one hand, and transnational capital and labour on the other. Internationally oriented social forces are less important, and may be considered to be allies of transnational forces and their quest for EU membership and full participation in the Internal Market.

In contrast to Austria, the main struggle between social forces about membership took place after the decision of the Swedish Social Democratic Labour Party (SAP) government in October 1990 to apply to the EU. Although a new approach was developed to ensure Swedish participation in the Internal Market, the SAP government had made it repeatedly clear that membership was not an option.

'The Government's position, as in the past, is that membership is not compatible with our policy of neutrality' (Gradin 1987: 301). The SAP's hegemonic position within the Swedish system, based on its electoral strength of 40 per cent or more since the 1930s except for 1991 (Petersson 1994: 226) and, more importantly, its organizational strength due to its close links with trade unions and other mass organizations, its long tradition of programmatic renewal and the capacity to interpret *ad hoc* measures of the past as parts of a grand strategy (Heclo and Madsen 1987: 23–45), implied that the SAP had to give the start signal.

Although capital did not pursue a political strategy towards membership, it did not remain inactive either. Swedish TNCs realized that they must be part of the Internal Market due to possible discriminations and in order to be geographically closer to the consumers of their products. As outlined above, there had been a drastic increase in outward FDI between 1985 and 1990. This increase went predominantly to the EU. 'Whereas in 1985, only 21.4 percent of all Swedish direct investments abroad went to the [EU] countries, in 1989 the share was 50.1 percent and in 1990 it even attained 70.4 percent' (Luif 1994: 209). The increased investment abroad did not complement but substituted expansion at home, and therefore indicated a shift of production units to the EU (Andersson *et al.* 1996: 126–35). While there were other reasons for the increased Swedish FDI in the EU, there is a strong indication that 'a major cause for this shift was uncertainty about a future Swedish Union membership and a fear of Fortress Europe' (Braunerhjelm and Oxelheim 1996: 114).

The transfer of production units had a significant impact on the SAP government. The exact timing of the announcement in Parliament on 26 October 1990 was due to renewed pressure on the SKr and the rumours about an imminent currency devaluation in mid-October (Interview No. 9, Stockholm, 15 November 1996; Interview No. 12, Stockholm, 26 November 1996). The longer term reasons for application were, however, the ongoing capital flight of Swedish TNCs to the EU, rising unemployment and the government's concomitant loss of economic credibility (Interview No. 8, Stockholm, 12 November 1996). The idea of application emerged as a joint effort of the Ministry of Finance and the Prime Minister's Office, both closely linked to the global economy, and was regarded as a way of regaining economic credibility, stability and budgetary discipline (Interview No. 14, Stockholm, 2 December 1996). Nevertheless, the SAP as a party was not united on the question of EU membership. While transnational social forces supported the government's position, national social forces continued to regard the EU as a threat to social democratic achievements and aligned themselves with national labour (see below) in the no-camp during the referendum campaign.

Trade unions had generally been surprised by the SAP decision. After the announcement in Parliament, a union internal discussion started. Against the background of globalization, the peak organizations, the Swedish Trade Union Confederation (LO), the blue-collar workers' union, and the Swedish Confederation of Professional Employees (TCO), the white-collar workers' union, supported the quest for membership. They argued that Sweden had to deregulate its economy in any case due to globalization. Cooperation at the European level offered a way to regain some control over capital lost at the national level (Interview No. 7, Stockholm, 11 November 1996; Interview No. 10, Stockholm, 21 November 1996). Within the unions, however, there was a split between transnational, industrial unions and unions in export-oriented sectors in favour of membership on the one hand, and national unions opposing it on the other. In particular, the LO affiliates, the paper workers' union and the metal workers' union, supported EU membership. Both sectors were heavily export dependent – the paper sector exports about 80 per cent of its products, the engineering sector more than 50 per cent – and the engineering sector is also characterized by some of Sweden's most important TNCs such as Volvo, Ericsson and Electrolux. Thus, considering that the Swedish TNCs had already established themselves on the Internal Market, it was economically impossible to remain outside of the EU (Interview No. 13, Stockholm, 29 November 1996).

On the other hand, national sector unions such as the LO affiliates, the municipal workers' union and the commercial workers' union, spoke out against membership. The jobs, in particular in the public sector, did not depend on exports or transnational production and the pressures of globalization hardly played a role. Rather, it was feared that future decisions taken in Brussels would undermine important Swedish policies. For example, the possible harmonization of tax systems within the EU could lead to cut-backs in the public sector, and therefore job losses. In short, the Swedish system with its generous welfare provisions and policy of full employment was regarded as being endangered by accession to the neoliberal EU (Interview No. 11, Stockholm, 26 November 1996).

The referendum result on 13 November 1994 was very close: 52.7 per cent voted 'yes' versus 47.3 per cent 'no', after the no-side had led from spring 1992 to shortly before the referendum (Luif 1996: 214). There are several reasons for the success of the yes-side. First, the material capabilities of the yes-side based on industrial sources were significantly larger than those of the no-side. An academic investigation found that the ratio was about twenty to one in favour of the yes-side (Interview No. 15, Stockholm, 4 December 1996). The material superiority was underlined by the direct threat of transnational capital to transfer production units to the EU in case of non-membership (Fioretos 1997: 315). Second, the no-side was predominantly united by their rejection of membership. Nevertheless, the reasons behind the rejection differed. While national labour and the green and left parties opposed the neo-liberal economic policies of the EU, the no-group of the centre party considered the neo-liberal convergence criteria of EMU and their focus on inflation instead of unemployment to be the necessary basis for a sound Swedish economy. This ideological difference precluded the formation of a historical bloc with a successful hegemonic project against membership.

Conclusion

In both Austria and Sweden internationally oriented and transnational social forces respectively were behind the drive towards membership. They were supported by those state institutions which were closely linked to the global economy, most notably the finance ministries. The particular way, however, whereby membership was achieved differed significantly. In Austria, a historical bloc in favour of application and membership was firmly established by June 1989. The hegemonic project, devised by organic intellectuals of internationally oriented capital located in the VÖI, was based on economic neo-liberalism and the idea that neutrality was compatible with membership. It provided the basis for an alliance of internationally oriented capital and labour, which gained control of the two governing parties and the main interest groups.

Similarly, in Sweden, transnational social forces of capital and labour demanded a closer relationship with the EU and Internal Market initiative. Nevertheless, it was the SAP's decision that membership was incompatible with neutrality, which prevented any debate on membership between 1987 and 1990. This hegemony was expressed in the SAP's predominant position in Parliament, its leading role in defining the public discourse, but also in the acceptance by the opposition parties and employers' associations that it was the SAP which ultimately determined whether membership was possible. When the SAP eventually decided on application in October 1990, there had been neither time nor effort to form an alliance of social forces. Of course, the representatives of transnational capital immediately supported the move, but there had been no discussion within the trade unions. The real struggle was still to come.

Another significant difference was the lack of an institution in Sweden similar to the Austrian VÖI, which provided the platform for organic intellectuals to form a pro-membership hegemonic project. The reason here too must be sought at least partly in the SAP's hegemonic position. It was difficult to mount a challenge to the predominant view that membership was incompatible with neutrality. Nevertheless, this does not suffice as an explanation. The Swedish production structure provides an additional factor. In contrast to Austria, dominated by small- and medium-sized firms, Sweden had been characterized by large TNCs. The structural pressures of globalization were consequently much stronger in Sweden. The TNCs simply did not have to bother with mounting a political challenge to the SAP's anti-membership course. They had the structural option to transfer investment and production units to the EU, and thereby counter possible threats of exclusion. Eventually, this was one of the major reasons why the SAP decided on application. The flight of capital was no longer sustainable. Austrian internationally oriented capital, on the other hand, did not have this option at its disposal due to its domestic production structure. A carefully prepared and executed political strategy was therefore the only way to achieve membership.

It is frequently argued that the real reason behind Austria's and Sweden's change of national interest in relation to EU membership was the change in the security structure after the end of the Cold War. The new insecurities in their immediate vicinity – the wars in former Yugoslavia in the case of Austria and the possible conflict between Russia and the Baltic states for Sweden – would have prompted these countries to look for the security guarantees of NATO and the West European Union through the back door of EU membership. A detailed analysis of the processes behind accession provides a different answer however (Bieler 2000: 122–37). A hegemonic project cannot solely consist of an economic rationale. Pro-EU social forces in both countries knew very well that it also needed to include a security component taking into account both countries' neutral status in order to have a chance with the population in the referenda on membership. In general, there was no perception of new insecurity, and neutrality was kept in high esteem in both countries. As a consequence, pro-EU forces redefined neutrality in both countries as its core of non-participation in military alliances and combat. This was then declared and promoted as compatible with EU membership. As outlined above, the activities of the VÖI had been crucial in Austria in this respect and the pro-EU forces in Sweden also made this claim successfully. In the end, the population in both countries accepted that the continuation of neutrality was guaranteed, and security policy did not become a prominent aspect in the referenda campaigns.

Finally, it has to be remembered that the victory of the yes-coalitions in both countries does not imply that neo-liberalism as such has gained an uncontested position. In both countries, resistance at the national level has increased since accession due to disappointment with the non-fulfilment of membership promises. Moreover, while transnational Swedish labour accepted the need for EU membership, it did not agree with capital's neo-liberal rationale of deregulation and liberalization. Membership was seen as one way of regaining some of the control over capital lost at the national level. In short, the struggle over the future form of state in Sweden has been postponed and transferred to the European level. In Austria, too, labour was hoping for the positive impact of a re-regulation of the free market at the European level in general and the further development of the social dimension in particular. To conclude, neo-liberalism continues to be contested within Austria, Sweden and the EU and the outcome of this struggle remains open.

Notes

1   I am indebted to Peter Katzenstein for this observation.
2   For a more detailed discussion of this point, see Burnham's (1994) criticism of mainstream International Political Economy approaches.
3   For a detailed discussion of the processes leading to Austria's and Sweden's accession to the EU, see Bieler (2000).

11 Discovering the frontiers of regionalism

Fostering entrepreneurship, innovation and competitiveness in the European Union

Simon Lee

FIS 030 F43
LS2 E24

Introduction: the triumph or eclipse of the Rhine?

In the aftermath of the collapse of communism, it was confidently predicted that in the forthcoming battle between the 'neo-American model' of capitalism (most characteristic of the US and the UK) and the 'Rhine model' (characteristic most notably of Germany and Japan), the Rhine model would be triumphant because of its economic and social superiority, arising from an interpenetration rather than a separation (as in the US and UK) of finance and industry (Albert, 1993). However, more recent analyses of West European political economy have been less triumphalist. For example, while focusing upon the progressive undermining of national policy-making autonomy by globalisation, Rhodes has pointed to the impact of 'subversive liberalism' upon European welfare states, i.e. the erosion of the principles of universalism and solidarity in welfare provision and the subjugation of social progress to the exigencies of economic competition (Rhodes, 1998: 100). Furthermore, the triumph of the neo-American model over rival models of capitalism seemingly has been demonstrated by recent surveys of economic performance.

The World Economic Forum's 1999 competitiveness rankings have placed the US second only to Singapore, with the major EU economies more lowly ranked (UK eighth, France twenty-third, Germany twenty-fifth and Italy thirty-fifth) (WEF, 1999: 11). In a similar vein, the International Institute for Management Development's *World Competitiveness Yearbook 2000* has ranked the US in first place for the fifth consecutive year, with the major EU economies occupying rankings ranging from eighth (Germany) to thirtieth (Italy) (IMD, 2000: 1). For its part, the European Commission's first three annual competitiveness reports have told a similar story. These have highlighted the fact that 'Europe continues to lag 20 per cent behind the United States in terms of both productivity levels and the employment rate (proportion of the working age population that is employed)', that the EU economy has generated only ten million new jobs since 1960 ('less than one fifth of those in the US') (European Commission, 1997: 7–8), and that 'Europe lags behind both the USA (33%) and Japan (13%) in its standard of living, as measured by GDP per capita in purchasing power parities of 1997' (European Commission,

1998a: 1). Moroever, the average annual growth rate of investment in the EU fell sharply during the 1990s to 0.8 per cent (compared to 2.5 per cent in the 1980s). By contrast, US investment growth in the 1990s rose to an annual average of 5.4 per cent (from 2.4 per cent in the 1980s) (European Commission, 1999: xi–xii). For its part, the third annual benchmarking report of the Union of Industrial and Employers' Confederation of Europe (UNICE) has identified an 'innovation deficit' in the EU economy which it has attributed to an environment for risk-taking, entrepreneurship and innovation less supportive than that enjoyed in the US (UNICE, 2000: 6).

This chapter explores the prospects for regionalism by focusing upon a case study of the development of industrial policy in the EC/EU during the 1990s. This is a period, as the OECD has acknowledged, which has seen industrial policy take new directions as it has mutated into an industrial competitiveness policy (OECD, 1997a). Building upon the framework provided by Sauter, who has identified four distinct phases in the development of supranational industrial policy in the period from the Treaty of Rome to the Single European Act (Sauter, 1997), two further phases in the development of policy during the 1990s are identified. The first phase, which saw the first formal definition of EU industrial policy, was marked by ambitions to cut EU unemployment through a co-ordinated programme of investment. The second and most recent phase has been marked by an increasing salience for the entrepreneurial spirit and innovation as the key drivers of employment growth in the EU. This chapter demonstrates how globalisation, and the EU's perception of the implications of globalisation for industrial competitiveness in the EU, have acted as constraints on supranational policy by steadily pushing policy closer to the North American neoliberal orthodoxy. While much of the emphasis in industrial policy has been upon the development of active supply-side measures to foster innovation (e.g. through enhancing skills, availability of risk capital, etc.), the constant and increasingly salient exhortation to cut regulation has been less of a demand for a technocratic exercise in legislative and administrative redrafting and more of an assault upon the principles underlying post-war European welfare states.

The development of EU industrial policy

Industrial policy has been chosen as a vehicle to explore the prospects for regionalism for a number of reasons. First, as Sauter has noted, because the growth of international trade and the globalisation of certain sectors of production have led to the paradox of a renewed interest in industrial policy as states have sought to identify means of promoting the international competitiveness of the businesses operating within their territory (Sauter, 1997: 57). Second, because there has been a recent and increasing emphasis on patterns of intervention more attuned to regionalism, conceptualised at the sub-national level, rather than regionalism, defined in terms of supranational integration. Detailed studies of best practice in policies to foster innovation and entrepreneurship have emphasised the importance of inter-firm and policy networks which enable clusters of small and medium-sized enterprises (SMEs) to achieve collective external economies of scale in innovation (e.g. OECD, 1996, 1997b, 1999b; Porter, 1998). The emphasis upon innovation and competitive advantage as a highly localised process dependent on networking capacity, namely 'the disposition to collaborate to achieve mutually beneficial ends' (Huggins, 1997: 102), has cast doubt on whether the supranational is the most appropriate level of intervention, and whether a common European industrial policy is either a necessary or an effective policy for enhancing competitiveness. Third, the collective resignation of the European Commission in March 1999, coupled with the decision of Martin Bangemann, the Commissioner for Telecommunications and Industry, to quit his post to become a board member with Telefonica, the Spanish telecommunications company, have added to questions of democratic legitimacy surrounding EU institutions and policy. These questions have enjoyed a particular resonance in the predominantly Eurosceptic political culture of the UK, where national and sub-national regional actors have identified the same catalytic role in industrial policy as that claimed by the EU (see e.g. DETR, 1997; DTI, 1998). The implications of the Commission's *Agenda 2000* programme have served only to heighten increasing tensions surrounding the territorial distribution of public expenditure following devolution (Lee, 1999).

Given that, by its very nature, industrial policy has to contend with a multiplicity of innovation-related information flows, which take place through both market and non-market transactions, are able to take the form of tangible and intangible assets, and involve not only private businesses but also a variety of public institutions (Archibugi and Michie, 1997: 1–2), it might be thought that the multiplication of market uncertainty by locating policy at the supranational level would hinder effectiveness. However, Nicolaides has identified three principal arguments for a common industrial policy. First, policy co-ordination at the supranational level may yet improve policy effectiveness – one of the major reasons for regional economic integration. Second, national industrial policies may themselves become ineffective as member states integrate because trade protectionism and subsidies which discriminate in favour of particular national economies or companies are no longer tolerated. Third, a supranational industrial policy may be more effective when exercised over a large single regional market than a policy operating in a smaller national or sub-national context (Nicolades, 1993: 11–12). Furthermore, Davies has pointed to the importance of the creation of the Single European Market as an instrument of industrial policy, not least because of its galvanising effect in reorganising industries and integrating markets (Davis, 1993: 42–3). At the supranational level, EU industrial policy has also been justified in terms of a variety of other broader political, economic and legal reasons relating to the process of economic integration; for example, the need to develop an EU industrial policy as a positive demonstration of the progress towards political and economic union (Sauter, 1997: 69).

The history of industrial policy at the European level has been extensively documented by Sauter. He contends that the development of policy should be understood in terms of a number of distinct phases. The first phase in policy occurred between 1958 and the mid-1960s and was characterised by the establishment of the customs union and the prevalent belief that 'competition in the newly integrated market would be adequate to foster industrial restructuring'. The second phase, from the mid-1960s to the mid-1970s, saw the creation of European-wide companies and the ineffective promotion of a single European market. The third phase, from the mid-1970s until the early 1980s, was characterised by defensive measures to restructure crisis industries. The fourth phase, culminating in the Single European Act, saw the promotion of high-technology industries (Sauter, 1997: 71). However periodised, Sauter's contention is that from the early 1970s the development of industrial policy saw Economic and Monetary Union (EMU) outlined as the context for industrial policy, an emphasis on the complementarity of supranational competition and industrial policies and the rejection of central planning as the appropriate framework for the proactive or sectoral dimension of industrial policy (Sauter, 1997: 76). This rejection of *dirigisme* was reinforced in certain member states, most notably the UK, where the trajectory of industrial policy was towards diminishing state intervention and expenditure and the restoration of an entrepreneur-driven enterprise culture. On the basis of an analysis of economic growth and national relative economic decline which had identified six principal obstacles to employment and prosperity in the UK (high state spending; high direct taxation; egalitarianism; nationalisation; a politicised and Luddite trade union movement; and the presence of an anti-enterprise culture), the Thatcher government had published its landmark 1988 White Paper, *DTI – The Department for Enterprise*. This document, which asserted that 'The keynote of future DTI policies is enterprise; its two foundations are open markets and individuals' (DTI, 1988: 2), indicated the UK government's reluctance to provide any further large-scale assistance to civil manufacturing companies. In many respects, the White Paper provided a signpost to the direction of EU industrial policy during the 1990s.

Sauter has noted how Article 130f(1) EEC of the Single European Act has frequently been regarded as the introduction of a common industrial policy because this Article stated that 'The Community's aim shall be to strengthen the scientific and technological bases of Community industry and to encourage it to become more competitive at international level' (cited in Sauter, 1997: 83). However, it was in 1990 with the production of *Industrial Policy in an Open and Competitive Environment: Guidelines for a Community Approach* that supranational industrial policy effectively entered a fifth phase when the Commission first furnished a definitive statement of the principles that should underpin its industrial policy. This statement, known as the Bangemann Communication (after Martin Bangemann, the Commissioner responsible for drawing it up), was not only based on the principle of subsidiarity, i.e. that the Community should address only those issues which could be done better at the supranational level (and therefore 'the correct mix of Community, national and local responsibilities' must be identified), but also, and more importantly, on a clear rejection of the *dirigiste* industrial policies of the 1970s and 1980s. These had 'shown that sectoral policies of an interventionist type are not an effective instrument to promote structural adaptation' because they had 'failed to make industry competitive by delaying the requirement to implement necessary adjustments, led to grave misallocation of resources and exacerbated problems of budgetary imbalances' (European Commission, 1990: 19). As an alternative, it was suggested that the experience of policies conducted in the EC during the past four to five years had largely forged a consensus that an industrial policy was necessary but that the role of public authorities should be

> above all as a catalyst and pathbreaker for innovation (rather than as the prime mover of progress) with the main responsibility for industrial competitiveness in future residing with firms themselves, but they should be able to expect from public authorities clear and predictable conditions for their activities.
>
> (European Commission, 1990: 1)

On this basis, the Commission proposed an industrial policy built around 'an adequate balance' between the laying down of 'stable and long term conditions for an efficiently functioning market economy', the provision of 'the main catalysts for structural adjustment', that is, the completion of the single market, and the development of 'instruments to accelerate structural adjustment and to enhance competitiveness'. From these elements would emerge a dynamic industrial policy 'to promote the most efficient functioning of markets' (European Commission, 1990: 5). Structural adjustment would be driven by a combination of 'prerequisites' to initiate adjustment (competition, economic context, educational attainment, economic and social cohesion), and environmental protection. Furthermore, 'catalysts' would act on the willingness of businesses to undertake adjustment in response to market pressures and opportunities (the internal market and 'accelerators' to further develop structural adjustment – R&D, technology, innovation, training, SMEs and business services) (European Commission, 1990: 7–18). Industrial problems at a sectoral or regional level 'should increasingly be resolved by horizontal measures' to improve the open market environment rather than by vertical, *dirigiste* interventions (European Commission, 1990: 21).

Although the Bangemann Communication was widely seen as marking the transition to a market-oriented industrial policy, Sauter has suggested that the new policy constituted less of a break with past interventionism than is often assumed because, like its predecessors, it embraced 'both active and passive, general and sectoral policies'. Furthermore, the new policy had taken co-operation with a subsidiarity-oriented approach as a given, when in practice co-operation might not be forthcoming. It also failed to identify clearly when the Community should intervene or how its priorities should be established. However, following the omission of reference to industrial policy in both the 1990 Rome European Council and the draft Treaty on European Union, the Belgian delegation at the 1991 Intergovernmental Conference on political union put forward a proposal advocating the creation of a Community industrial strategy wedded to the common commercial policy. Although, as Sauter has further noted, this *dirigiste* proposal was subsequently diluted by the Luxembourg Presidency, and sectoral intervention replaced by horizontal measures, these actions ensured that the Treaty on

European Union would require the EU to develop policies to strengthen the competitiveness of its industries (Sauter, 1997: 92–4).

It was not until December 1991 and Article 130 of the Treaty on European Union finalised at Maastricht that the European Community actually provided an institutional framework for industrial policy (Buigues and Sapir, 1993: 24). However, one of the central problems of Article 130(1) EC of the Treaty is that it attempted to reconcile two seemingly contradictory objectives: the promotion of competitiveness through the modification of market conditions and/or industrial structures on the one hand, and the guaranteeing of respect for the system of free competition in open markets, which thereby limits public intervention on the other. As a consequence, 'neither the legal limits to the specific industrial policy actions of the Member States and the Community, nor the degree to which the Community can take industrial policy objectives into account in its pursuit of other policies are self-evident' (Sauter, 1997: 96). Indeed, Buigues and Sapir suggested that the Treaty had created a 'no-man's land between the declining capacity of Member States to conduct national industrial policies and the growing competence of the Community in this field', thereby creating 'tensions among policy-makers and uncertainties for economic agents' (Buigues and Sapir, 1993: 33). In effect, the objective of a common industrial policy had further polarised two rival camps: those in favour of an active industrial policy and the creation of pan-European champions (a vision associated with France and the Southern European member states) and those in favour of limited sectoral intervention but a strong competition policy (a vision associated primarily with the UK).

Growth, competitiveness and employment

The principles underpinning Article 130 of the Maastricht Treaty were first expressed in the so-called 'Delors II package' which specified the objectives of promoting growth, competitiveness and employment during the five-year period following the completion of the internal market programme. Market liberalisation was to be accompanied by a supplementary programme of industrial policy measures to promote structural adjustment. These initiatives constituted the 'flanking measures' to EMU. Following the ratification of the Treaty of European Union in November 1993, the EU's strategy was spelt out in the White Paper, *Growth, Competitiveness, Employment: The Challenges and Ways Forward into the twenty-first Century* (European Commission, 1993) which began by stating that its sole *raison d'être* was unemployment. To assist the seventeen million unemployed in the EU member states, the principal aim of the White Paper was the creation of employment through the location of 'a new synthesis of the aims pursued by society (work as a factor of social integration, equality of opportunity) and the requirements of the economy (competitiveness and job creation)' (European Commission, 1993: 9). Thus, as Sauter has further suggested, supranational industrial policy was seeking to align macro-economic and structural policies by remaining consistent with the convergence criteria for EMU while also recommending structural actions to promote industrial competitiveness. The task of industrial policy was 'to create as favourable an environment as possible for company competitiveness', while the Commission's recommendation was that the Community set itself 'the objective of creating at least 15 million new jobs, thereby halving the present rate of unemployment by the year 2000' (European Commission, 1993: 9, 14, 43).

It claimed that the EU economy was characterised by 'collective solidarity mechanisms', but that 'the new model of European society' arising from the attempts to cut the costs of the welfare state now called for 'less passive and more active solidarity'. First, solidarity between those in employment and the unemployed through 'a sort of European social pact' adapted to the circumstances of each member state. Second, solidarity between generations to ensure that a sufficient number of those of working age were employed and paying towards the future costs of welfare. Third, solidarity between the rich and poor regions to confirm economic and social cohesion 'as an essential pillar of European construction'. Fourth, and most importantly, solidarity between all EU citizens to create 'neighbourly solidarity' against the social exclusion of the forty million EU citizens living below the poverty line (European Commission, 1993: 15–16).

It was at this juncture that EU industrial policy was recast as 'competitiveness policy' (Sauter, 1997: 101–2). This was somewhat ironic, and perhaps a tacit recognition of the difficulties surrounding the development of a common agenda, in that only three years before, the Bangemann Communication had condemned the notion of 'global competitiveness, often put forward as the objective of industrial policy' for being 'vague and ambiguous' (European Commission, 1990: 1). More importantly, the White Paper contended that the European social model was fundamentally sound by proposing that market failures should be addressed through 'collective solidarity mechanisms' (European Commission, 1993: 15–16). Indeed, the very rationale of promoting competitiveness was the preservation of the European social model because '[w]ith a high living-standard to preserve and improve, E.C. industry is condemned to technological, commercial and financial excellence in order to enable the necessary social and environmental expenses to be incurred' (European Commission, 1993: 3). The White Paper steadfastly claimed that the Single European Act had helped 'to restore the balance in the development of the single market by way of joining flanking policies as part of economic and social cohesion' (European Commission, 1993: 15). However, in practice, by endorsing further deregulation, liberalisation and the transfer of the tax burden from the company and entrepreneur to the individual, the 'flanking policies' incorporated within the competitiveness agenda were threatening to undermine the drive for greater social cohesion by attacking the solidaristic principles of European welfare states in order to provide a more advantageous environment for businesses to operate.

In the White Paper, the EU's poor relative economic performance was accounted for primarily in terms of two deep-seated causes, namely 'suboptimal macroeconomic management of the economy and of an insufficient effort of adaptation to the changes which have taken place in the structure of the Community's economy and in its international environment' (European Commission, 1993: 39). The 'suboptimal macroeconomic management' was held to have arisen because of 'certain fundamental imbalances', notably '[t]he current levels of public expenditure, particularly in the social field' which had become 'unsustainable and have used up resources which could have been channelled into productive investment' (European Commission, 1993: 40). The structural problems were held to have arisen from a failure to innovate in the face of new technological and market opportunities.

At the same time, the positive effects of structural policies to enhance innovation and competitiveness would become apparent and feasible only in a sound macro-economic context (European Commission, 1993: 49). As a consequence, the principal task confronting macro-economic policy-makers was the elimination of 'the conflicts among policy objectives which have plagued the Community over the last 20 years and, more acutely, over recent years' (European Commission, 1993: 50). This classic technocratic prescription appeared to imagine not only that these domestic 'conflicts' were relatively trivial, and thus could be easily surmounted by more rational concerted action at the supranational level, but also that the political and economic pressures exerted on policy-makers by vested interests beyond the economic policy-making community could also be discounted. Thus, for example, the White Paper advocated both changes in national budgetary policy to establish deficits of between zero and 1 per cent of GDP but also a reallocation of public spending towards 'those items which most directly influence growth prospects: education, R&D, infrastructure investments etc' (European Commission, 1993: 53). The immense political difficulties encountered by national governments in previously attempting such reallocation was overlooked.

The White Paper identified four overriding policy objectives to be jointly pursued by industry and public authorities if the EU's industrial competitiveness was to generate the highest possible level of employment. First, 'Helping European firms to adapt to the new globalized and interdependent competitive situation' by, for example, capitalising on the Community's industrial strengths (it was not apparent why private companies would not already have done so); developing an active policy of industrial co-operation both with Eastern Europe and the Pacific Rim; and establishing 'a coherent and concerted approach to strategic alliances' to ensure that there were European rivals to the alliances formed by US and Japanese competitors (although what should be done where European companies had already formed alliances with their American and Japanese rivals was not apparent) (European Commission, 1993: 61–2). Second, '[e]xploiting the competitive advantages associated with the gradual shift to a knowledge-based economy', for example, by adjusting the relative weight of taxation borne by 'the various factors of competitiveness' so as to reduce those taxes acting as disincentives to employment. This adjustment and the need to reallocate public expenditure from consumption to investment were presented by the White Paper as simple matters of administrative reform rather than as the almost intractable problems long confronted by national policy-makers. In a similar vein, the White Paper highlighted the EU's relatively poor business investment in R&D as a percentage of GDP and recommended that companies should bear a larger share of research spending 'In view of the current budgetary constraints in all European countries'. The policy instruments to change corporate investment patterns were not identified other than the introduction of 'appropriate regulatory and tax measures' (European Commission, 1993: 88). The possibility that businesses' investment patterns might not respond to even generous incentives, and the need for the state to recoup the lost taxation from other sources without damaging competitiveness, were again passed over.

The White Paper also placed greater emphasis upon training as 'the catalyst of a changing society', recommending 'appropriate incentives (of a fiscal and legal nature)' and improved co-ordination between public and private training opportunities (European Commission, 1993: 121). However, when addressing the question of the reforms of the labour market necessary to create more employment, the White Paper denied that this would mean mere deregulation. Instead, it was asserted that 'a remodelled, rational and simplified system of regulation and incentives' would be promoted (European Commission, 1993: 123). The White Paper did acknowledge that many member states were now calling for 'an examination of social protection systems to ensure that they actually encourage people to work, for benefits to be more closely geared to the specific market situation, and for expenditure to be targeted more accurately to concentrate the effort on those in real need' (European Commission, 1993: 125).

In other words, greater selectivity in welfare provision was unavoidable if past rigidities in the labour market were to be removed. Indeed, the White Paper suggested that 'fundamental economic and social changes' would be required, including 'a general reform of the systems of incentives which affect employment in the labour market' (European Commission, 1993: 130). In this regard, the clearest indication of the challenge posed by competitiveness policy to European patterns of welfare provision was provided when the White Paper argued that '[a] co-ordinated strategy for rekindling growth and overcoming a structural crisis cannot disregard the weight and structure of statutory charges, through which the equivalent of 40% of Community GDP is channelled'. Statutory charges were defined as the sum of taxes and obligatory social security contributions. This EU figure (the EU average of 39.6 per cent disguised the variation between a high of 47.1 per cent in Denmark and Luxembourg and a low of 34.4 per cent in the UK and Spain) was portrayed as an excessive burden when the equivalent figure was 29.8 per cent of GDP in the USA in 1990 and 30.9 per cent in Japan. Furthermore, in 1991 these tax and social security costs accounted for more than 40 per cent of overall labour costs in the EU compared with 30 per cent in the USA and 20 per cent in Japan (European Commission, 1993: 137). By highlighting these cost disadvantages, the 'subversive liberalism' of the neoliberal model of capitalism had begun to intrude into supranational industrial policy.

Benchmarking: the institutionalisation of 'subversive liberalism'

Rather than marking the start of a determined drive to remedy unemployment through concerted action at the supranational level, the 1993 White Paper actually constituted the final industrial policy action of the Commission under the stewardship of Jacques Delors. Consensus about the need for common action was accompanied by marked scepticism about the funding required by the Commission to implement such a programme, particularly in member states such as the UK (Sauter, 1997: 103). As a consequence, the publication of *An Industrial Competitiveness Policy for the European Union* (European Commission, 1994) marked the onset of the sixth and most recent phase of EU industrial policy which has been distinguished by the steady advance of Rhodes' 'subversive liberalism' into the prescriptions for enhancing competitiveness advanced by the Commission.

An increasing emphasis has been placed on the role of the entrepreneur and innovation in high growth sectors as the means to generate employment and enhance competitiveness. Action plans to foster innovation (European Commission, 1996a) and to promote entrepreneurship and competitiveness (European Commission, 1998b) have been launched. In effect, EU industrial policy has adopted the rhetoric developed by the Thatcher and Major governments in the UK during the late 1980s and early 1990s. Although the EU has been far more selective in its adoption of UK policies, it has drawn upon two UK industrial policy innovations, notably the extensive use of benchmarking and the publication of an annual competitiveness report. This methodology has enabled studies to be carried out at sectoral level as well as with regard to particular aspects of innovation, notably finance, skills, and the adoption of information and communications technologies (DG III, 1999: 7). These studies have produced many unfavourable comparisons with US economic performance and best practice in innovation policy, thereby providing the means to legitimise further movement away from a social democratic European model towards a neoliberal American model of capitalism.

One of the most contentious aspects of *An Industrial Competitiveness Policy for the European Union* resided in its assertion of 'an increasingly direct correlation between economic and social cohesion and industrial and economic performance', which could 'add strength to each other' on the basis of the externalities generated by cohesion for infrastructure, especially in health, education and research (which would in turn optimise the general level of investment) (European Commission, 1994: 20). In practice, the Commission's prescriptions for enhancing competitiveness have threatened to undermine economic and social cohesion, especially in more peripheral EU member states. The combination of the impact of the EMU convergence criteria upon member states' public expenditure programmes and the introduction of regular benchmarking exercises, which have audited the performance of the EU economy against its principal rivals, has acted to challenge rather than consolidate the viability of the European social model (as defined by the Commission), especially when set against the (perceived) superiority of the American, entrepreneur- and innovation-driven model of capitalism. In particular, the desire to increase public investment in 'productive' capital spending by an (implicit) reallocation away from 'unsustainable' social expenditure has meant that the frequent demand for regulatory reform in Commission industrial policy documentation has been less of an arid technocratic exercise in the reordering of legislation and administration and more of a tacit and creeping political attack upon the principles underlying the welfare state in Europe.

In *An Industrial Competitiveness Policy for the European Union*, the Commission recognised that the EU was experiencing 'severe levels of unemployment which endanger cohesion', and that it must therefore encourage all measures aimed at improving overall economic productivity, including 'greater privatisation, more effective regulatory methods and the new role of the public services'. Higher levels of employment would not be feasible unless based on 'an effective regulatory framework combined with a more labour-intensive development model' (European Commission, 1994: 11–13). After all, the US had created just over forty million new jobs in the past twenty years (90 per cent in the private sector), while Europe had experienced a net decline in private sector employment, with its six million new jobs having been created in the public sector (Llewellyn, 1996: 91). However, such statistics illustrated the importance of the public sector in Europe to employment creation and the potentially devastating impact that expenditure cuts (whether driven by EMU or purely domestic factors) might have on attempts to foster greater cohesion. To bolster its attempts to improve productivity, the Commission began a benchmarking exercise, suggesting that benchmarking could provide 'an understanding of the processes that create superior performance' (European Commission, 1996b: 16).

Citing the earlier findings of its own Competitiveness Advisory Group, which had highlighted infrastructure quality as the single most important factor influencing multinational investment in the EU (European Commission Competitiveness Advisory Group, 1995: 11), the Commission also identified the level and structure of public expenditure as one of the key elements determining costs and ultimately competitiveness, concluding that 'public deficits remain too high and expenditure too concentrated on transfers and consumption with insufficient levels of public investment in both infrastructure and intangible investment' (European Commission, 1996b: 20). While the provision of a social safety net was necessary in the interests of equitable distribution and the avoidance of social exclusion, direct and indirect taxation (especially of labour) was nevertheless a cost to enterprises which had risen from 34 to 43 per cent of GDP in the EU between 1970 and 1995. As a consequence, the Commission asserted that the concept of security for workers would have to be 'reformulated, focusing more on security based on employability and the labour market rather than security based on the individual work place' (European Commission, 1996b: 2–11). At no point did the Commission specify how its member states were to accomplish the huge reallocation of public resources necessary to create the neo-Listian developmental state envisaged, other than its statement that the Maastricht convergence criteria should serve as 'a model for the application of benchmarking to other areas of importance for competitiveness' (European Commission, 1996b: 2).

Innovation, entrepreneurship and 'jobless growth'

The importance of entrepreneurship and innovation to the future development of supranational industrial policy was confirmed at the November 1997 European

Employment Summit when the EU adopted a co-ordinated strategy for national employment policies. Developing entrepreneurship and encouraging adaptability in business and their employees were to be two of the four central elements of this strategy (the other two being the improvement of employability and the strengthening of policies for equal opportunities) (DG III, 1998: 7). In September 1998, the Commission published its *Action Plan to Promote Entrepreneurship and Competitiveness* as part of its response to the BEST Task Force of entrepreneurs, academics and administrators which had been established a year earlier to consider 'the existing and new legal and administrative regulations in order to improve the quality of Community legislation and reduce its administrative burden on European business, particularly SMEs' (European Commission, 1998b: 2). Among the Task Force's recommendations were that the simplification and reform of regulation should be made central to public policy at all levels in the EU in order to achieve the necessary 'change of culture', and that member states should be encouraged 'to consider the impact of the way they finance and administer social security schemes, and other ways of making social protection more employment friendly' (European Commission, 1998b: 4, 10). However, in its Action Plan, the Commission narrowed its consideration of regulatory reform to those regulations specifically affecting business rather than contemplating the much wider assault suggested by the Task Force.

Despite attempts by the Commission (especially DG III) to foster an enterprise culture for entrepreneurship and innovation, its 1998 benchmarking report, *The Competitiveness of European Industry*, confirmed that the EU's labour productivity (GDP per person employed) remained almost one-fifth lower than that in the US. Furthermore, the phenomenon of 'jobless growth' in the EU had continued as a consequence of the EU's 'inability to move quickly into new, promising sectors'. This failure to innovate, especially to create SMEs in new growth areas such as electronic commerce and business services, had been particularly damaging because such firms, which account for only 3 per cent of firms in the US, are held to have created around 80 per cent of job growth between 1991 and 1995. The report also attributed the EU's poor start-up rate to the 'lack of adequate risk capital' which meant that start-ups accounted for only 15 per cent of new investments in the EU in 1997 compared with 29 per cent in the US. The EU was deemed to have been further disadvantaged by its '*poor performance in creating lead-time in the fast moving markets*, where competitive advantage is based on intangible investment in research and marketing'.

Therefore, the report identified four implications for supranational policy. First, the importance of 'the elimination of institutional and regulatory barriers to the creative and flexible management of change'. This was shorthand for further liberalisation and deregulation of the labour, financial and product markets (because delayed privatisation and liberalisation were deemed to have caused higher prices). Second, the need to continuously upgrade European industry through 'innovation, adaptability and the upgrading of human capital'. Third, the need to pursue horizontal policies to improve the general environment for innovation and entrepreneurship, rather than to pursue vertical 'picking winners' strategies, which were held only to create expensive 'opportunity costs relative to private market-based solutions'. Fourth, the importance of the diffusion of best practice because of the great diversity in labour productivity within the EU (European Commission, 1998a: 1–6, 14). This last point alluded to the difficulty of framing supranational policy beyond simple exhortation given the diversity in European national systems of innovation (OECD, 1997b).

The Commission has subsequently suggested that globalisation is a source of opportunity for employment creation rather than a threat of further unemployment provided that the EU is able to capitalise on it by reinforcing 'the capacity to stimulate innovation and the spirit of enterprise in Europe'. Portraying globalisation as a phenomenon characterised by the internationalisation of trade, the transnationalisation of capital flows and the globalisation of information flows, the Commission has identified globalisation's driving elements as 'technological, entrepreneurial, financial and institutional'. As a consequence of their impact, it has further been asserted that accelerating globalisation and new forms of competition, especially from SMEs in dynamic sectors like electronic commerce, are transforming the very concept of competitiveness itself. Thus, the 'true yardstick for competitiveness should not be sectors, but, rather, activities and markets'; the measurement of national and regional competitiveness is becoming more difficult because of the diffusion of the boundaries of companies' geographical identity; and competitive advantage can now be based on technologies and intellectual property capable of generating high value, but of a more volatile nature. To combat the EU's competitive disadvantage, especially in the many fields where it has 'failed to develop a services mentality', the Commission has advocated a new industrial policy which will 'spread the enterprise culture and encourage risk-taking' (European Commission 1998c: 1–21).

Conclusion

Attempts to push the frontiers of supranational industrial policy further in the direction of entrepreneurship may prove problematic, since, as the OECD has recently concluded, 'the globalisation of R&D has not markedly diminished the differences in innovation systems between countries'. Each nation-state continues to provide a unique environment for innovation for which few policy recommendations are equally applicable (OECD, 1999a: 45). Furthermore, it is not yet apparent that the importance attached in recent analyses of policy and best practice to clustering and inter-firm networking for competitive advantage (e.g. OECD, 1997b, 1997c, 1997d) necessarily warrants a supranational rather than a national or (sub-national) regional response.

More importantly, the increasingly prominent exhortations in Commission documentation for further reductions in the administrative and taxation burden on business, especially SMEs, in new, dynamic sectors of the economy, in order to increase employment creation, are little more than disguised demands for member states to fundamentally reassess how their welfare states are financed and whether selectivity should displace universality as the bedrock principle of service provision.

Although business groups may continue to lobby for further cuts in government spending and the tax burden to promote entrepreneurship (e.g. UNICE, 1999, 2000), the UK should serve as a salutary reminder to other EU member states of the damaging effects which the pursuit of privatisation, liberalisation and deregulation as the basis of industrial policy can have upon economic performance and social cohesion (Lee, 1997).

In 1996, the Major government branded the UK as 'the unrivalled Enterprise Centre of Europe' on account of its possession of the second lowest tax burden on business in any major industrialised economy and one of the lowest ratios of public spending to GDP in Europe. These competitive 'advantages' had allowed non-wage costs per employee in the UK to be cut to £18 (per £100 spent by employers on wages) compared with £32 in Germany, £34 in Spain, £41 in France and £44 in Italy (HMSO, 1996: 3–16). What the Major government neglected to mention was that its reforms of the labour market had not only failed to raise the long-term growth rate of the UK economy above its post-war average of 2.25 per cent but it also dramatically reduced economic and social cohesion by increasing the proportion of the population on less than half the average national income (after allowing for housing costs) from 9 per cent when the first Thatcher government had taken office in 1979/80 to 25 per cent (or 14.1 million people) in 1992/3 (Child Poverty Action Group, 1996). Furthermore, while only Portugal in the EU was now spending a lower share of its GDP on social welfare than the UK, the attempt to restore an entrepreneur-driven enterprise culture by attacking welfare dependency had not prevented total real government expenditure on welfare from increasing by nearly 60 per cent between 1978/9 and 1994/5, outstripping the growth of GDP (Hills, 1995: 30). In other words, the net effect of creating 'the Enterprise Centre of Europe' had been to increase the share of public spending taken by 'unproductive' current welfare spending while simultaneously cutting the share invested in 'productive' capital investment – a reversal of the priorities sought by successive Commission industrial policy documents. Given that the OECD has suggested that there is only weak evidence that employment protection laws have a negative effect on unemployment, and indeed that tight regulation ensures greater stability and lower labour turnover (OECD, 1999b), the time may be ripe for a wholesale review of the likely benefits of further deregulation on both competitiveness and cohesion in the EU.

12 New regionalisms in Africa in the new millennium

Comparative perspectives on renaissance, realisms and/or regressions[1]

Timothy M. Shaw

Allegedly, in an era of globalizations, Africa is the most marginal of the continents (Hoogvelt, 1997). However, while Africa may be the least affected by contemporary instabilities in the global financial architecture, it has been profoundly and nega-tively affected by the interrelated ideological, institutional and structural changes, which are reflective of myriad dimensions of 'globalizations' (Sassen, 1996; Held *et al.*, 1999; UNDP, 1999; Germain, 2000; Scholte, 2000), especially the rise of 'neo-liberalism' since the early 1980s. Subsequently, these changes have been rein-forced by the end of bipolarity and emergence of a range of 'new' security issues since the early 1990s, manifested in the emerging 'human security' agenda and dis-course (Shaw and MacLean, 1999; Shaw and Schnabel, 1999). Paradoxically, however, even if the 'Asian' crises of the late 1990s impacted directly on this con-tinent less than on others, the contemporary African political economy may reveal more about 'new' forms of regionalisms than more integrated continents and communities.

This chapter highlights five novel features of 'new regionalisms' in Africa as the new millennium dawns: (1) 'developmental' economies and ecologies; (2) corridors and triangles, civil societies and media; (3) new security threats; (4) the rather grim and pessimistic 'war economy' which encourages and facilitates continuing conflict; and (5) more orthodox and optimistic peace-building responses, reconstruction and redirection. Is the continent anticipating renaissance and/or anarchy in the new century (Ottaway, 1999)? How compatible are these features/scenarios over time? Despite all the conversations about post-bipolar, post-industrial, post-modern local and global communities and governance (Stiles, 2000), is Africa now in the vanguard of new forms of 'realism' in both theory and practice (Shaw, 1998)?

So what are the lessons to be learned from this supposedly peripheral continent for comparative studies of 'new regionalisms' (Bøås *et al.*, 1999b) and related fields of analysis? My argument is that such meso-level regional analysis, if appropriately nuanced and informed, can throw light on the diversities of political economy and culture on the African continent which other established approaches fail to discern. Such insights carry profound policy as well as analytical implications (Payne, 1998, 1999; Grugel and Hout, 1999; van Walraven, 1999). As Hettne and Söderbaum (1998b: 4) suggest,

> Regionalism has . . . 'been brought back in' to the academic debate as well as the policy one after some decades of neglect. This renewed trend, often labeled 'the new regionalism', is characterized by its multidimensionality, complexity, flexibility, fluidity and non-conformity. It is therefore appropriate to speak of regionalism in the plural rather than the singular form.

Indeed, going beyond this type of 'new regionalisms' perspective, it may be the case that an examination of the regional or meso-level dynamics between global and local connection, or macro- and micro-level connections, is crucial in explaining the descent of a few 'failed' or 'collapsed' African regimes into 'shadow states'. The war economy requires ready cross-border exchange. Cases like Sierra Leone and Somalia suggest that the erstwhile 'franchise' state now obtains licence not only by the international financial institutions (IFIs) but also by private debt bond and security agencies. If such examples proliferate, then just as we were concerned about the prospects of 'Lebanonization' in the 1980s, so we may come to define and refine a distinctive typology of shadow regimes in the new millennium, which are exacerbated by the multiplication of mafias and other forms of transnational criminal networks at the end of the twentieth century. The analytic and policy challenges of conceptualizing as well as containing such shadow states are profound. This is especially so within the context of related global corporate and criminal connections, even if it is assumed that the era of neo-liberalism is finally passing.

Given significant changes in the character of state–economy/society relations, exacerbated by the combination of the realities of globalizations and the conditionalities of neo-liberalism (whose effects will linger long after its hegemony has peaked), this chapter takes it to be axiomatic that any local–global social relationship inevitably includes a trio of heterogeneous actors. These are not just *states* (and interstate global and regional institutions), but also *economic structures* such as multinational corporations (MNCs) and informal sectors (Shaw and van der Westhuizen, 1999) and *civil societies* from international non-governmental organisations (INGOs) to grass-roots movements (Van Rooy, 1999). To be sure, the balance among the trio of state, economy and civil society varies between regions and issue areas and over time but none of these can be excluded or overlooked in any ongoing relationship either in Africa or elsewhere (Shaw and Nyang'oro, 2000). This is especially so at the intermediate, meso-level, which is increasingly characterized by a range of heterogeneous actors, coalitions and relations, both cooperative and conflictual, as well as formal and informal, legal and illegal.

First an overview is given of the genesis and current state of new regionalisms as both analysis and praxis, with a focus on trilateral relations among states and interstate organizations, companies and civil societies in what is perhaps a 'post-neo-liberal' era. At the least, the context of the late twentieth century is one in which new scepticism about the gains and sustainability of globalizations and markets is being voiced (Bøås *et al.*, 1999b). Second, I identify a range of novel forms of regional interactions and institutions beyond established, intergovernmental regional organizations: these include most notably corridors, ecologies, triangles and new forms of meso-level governance (Shaw, 1999). In the third part, reflective of renewed conflict and related 'realist' analysis, I examine new as well as old forms of confrontation and alliance: are we moving beyond peace building to sustainable human security? The fourth section addresses the recent, critical perspective on the 'real' international political economy of lingering conflicts in cases like Angola and Sierra Leone; that is, production and accumulation for the minority in the midst of destruction for the majority, characterized by regional and global connections, especially the world of diamonds. In the fifth section, I focus on the 'other' side of new (and old) regionalisms: civil societies at the regional level (MacLean and Shaw, 1996; Shaw and MacLean, 1999). Finally, in the sixth and concluding part, I attempt to highlight some salient 'lessons' which may be learned from African cases and debates for older disciplines and discourses, as well as for future policy interventions.

'New' regionalisms and trilateral relationships post-neo-liberalism

The 'old' regional studies focused on formal, interstate economic and strategic relations, from the European Community/European Union to the North Atlantic Treaty Organization (NATO) (Hettne and Söderbaum, 1998b; Hettne *et al.*, 1999). By contrast, 'new regionalisms' attempt to capture the diversities of definition and interaction, such as the 'Europe' defined by MNCs or mafias. The latter genre's inclusion of non-state and non-formal interactions between the national and global levels enables it to treat the interconnections between more and less statist relations, as well as to transcend the official by recognizing how the latter relates to the unofficial in myriad ways. The focus is thus on the multiple conceptions of 'regions', as well as diversity of issue areas, from ecologies and ethnicities to civil societies and private armies (Bøås *et al.*, 1999b).

The 'new' – unlike the 'old' – regional studies also incorporates all three major types of actor in its purview, not just states but also companies and communities. Recognition of the trilateral character of all social relations, especially since the end of the Cold War and the concomitant hegemony of neo-liberal values, is an essential attribute (and advantage) of new regionalisms. 'States' here include official governmental organizations, both local and global (such as the IFI and UN systems). 'Economies' include informal and illegal sectors, as well as the more familiar world of MNCs. 'Societies' incorporate not only indigenous and international NGOs but also charities, cooperatives, grass-roots groups, medias, new social movements, professional associations, religious organizations and sports clubs (Lindberg and Sverrisson, 1997; Van Rooy, 1999; Aulakh and Schechter, 2000).

The old regional studies gradually extended their purview to include the South, at least in terms of formal, interstate economic institutions. By contrast, the new regionalisms literature is largely rooted in non-state or semi-state cases from the South, such as *maquiladoras* and export-processing zones (EPZs), growth triangles in Asia, corridors in Southern Africa (Gelb and Manning 1998), diasporas from the South in the North, 'track-two diplomacy', confidence-building measures (CSBMs) and peace-keeping operations (PKOs). This literature increasingly links with international political economy, development and human security perspectives. Furthermore, not only are the old and new regionalisms disparate in terms of theoretical genesis and affinity, but also they are not always or even often compatible in practice. For example, in Southeast Asia, the connection between EPZs/triangles and ASEAN is not clear: is this a relationship of compatibility/reinforcement, or incompatibility/dilution (Chen and Kwan, 1997)?

This chapter proceeds to highlight four areas derived from sub-Saharan African cases which illuminate the emerging discourse about new regionalisms and may be contrasted with some disquieting forms of formal and informal conflicts elsewhere. Together these cover the spectrum of formality and informality, West, East and Southern Africa(s), issue areas, involved actors, analytic perspectives and so on. In many ways, they return us to Samir Amin's (1972) seminal essay on the distinctive types of post-colonial regional political economies in the African continent, which he identified as the peasant economy, the mining economy and labour reserves. Today he would presumably identify the several Africas of emerging markets, transitions and reconstruction processes, peace-keeping operations and anarchies as reflected in the preliminary typology developed in this chapter.

Beyond regional organizations: corridors, ecologies, triangles and new forms of meso-level governance

The prevailing perspective about regionalism in Africa is that it is a disappointment because formal sector regional trade has failed to grow faster than at the global level, notwithstanding the essential homogeneity of the overwhelming majority of Africa's economies (McCarthy, 1996; Teunissen, 1996). However, its informal sector exchange continues to boom, in part in response to formal level constraints deriving from non-tariff barriers, both familiar (such as inefficiency) and specific (such as corruption). Moreover, official statistics only record official trade within established intergovernmental groupings such as the Common Market of Eastern and Southern Africa (COMESA), the Economic Community of West African States (ECOWAS), the Southern African Development Community (SADC) and the incubating African Economic Community (AEC) (Gibb, 1998; Nel and McGowan, 1999; Vale *et al.*, 2001). Yet, palpably, ECOWAS is characterized by a vast network of informal flows, which may yet be augmented by large-scale official schemes. One such scheme is the proposed West African Gas Pipeline, involving an agreement reached with Chevron and Shell in mid-1999 to transport natural gas from these companies' Nigerian wells to Ghana through Benin and Togo.

This section seeks to identify some contemporary regional responses to the constraints and opportunities of globalization as both praxis and ideology (Gills, 1997; Germain, 2000; Murphy, 2000; Scholte, 2000). In particular, it seeks to highlight some current indigenous reactions to globalization, as well as to privilege some of the continent's own distinctive – yet underappreciated – contributions to comparative analysis and praxis. These have developed out of a significant tradition of innovative forms of regionalism, in part in response to colonial and/or settler resistance, such as Front Line States (FLS) or Southern African Development Coordination Conference (SADCC). Such non-state or semi-state strategies were themselves developed in reaction to the settler regimes' own 'unholy alliance', which came to control a shrinking proportion of the territory and population of the remaining white-ruled states. In other words, regional groupings, state and non-state alike, do not necessarily have to include all the territory, population, communities or resources of participating countries. As we will see in the following section, complex and dynamic strategic partnerships among several state and non-state actors around the current Congo conflicts split some countries and communities in Central Africa.

Guerrilla struggles led to the emergence of the first 'corridor' in Africa in the mid-1980s: the Beira Corridor which connects Zimbabwe to global trade through the middle 'waist' of Mozambique. This has since been replicated and upgraded in current plans for some nine corridors within SADC, including three (the most advanced in terms of infrastructural and organizational development) around the perimeters of post-apartheid South Africa, particularly Gauteng, its now post-mineral/post-industrial heartland (Gelb and Manning, 1998: vi). While these corridors have been declared to exist and so advertised, their internal multi-stakeholder governance structures remain embryonic (Gelb and Manning, 1998). The question is thus: What are the divisions of labour among several levels of states, companies and civil societies in the different corridors (Shaw, 1999)?

1   The *Maputo Corridor* between Gauteng and Maputo Port, which is to advance development in the relatively impoverished Mpumalanga Province of South Africa as well as in Southern Mozambique. This is a regional project in which the private sector is in the driver's seat, but in which city and provincial author-ities and the two national regimes are also positively engaged.

2   The *Trans-Kalahari Corridor* between Lobatse in Botswana and Windhoek in Namibia, so linking Gauteng with the Atlantic coast at Walvis Bay, cutting some 500km off the trip and completing the Maputo–Walvis Bay Indian Ocean–Atlantic Oceans link. Again, this is a largely corporate initiative, albeit with more national state involvement by Botswana and Namibia.

3   The *Lubombo Corridor* linking Durban with Maputo via Northern Kwazulu-Natal and Swaziland. This is more of a South African Spatial Development Initiative (SDI) than a short-term corporate venture, and one involving more community participation given the high population densities involved (Gelb and Manning 1998).

4   The *Lesotho Highlands Water Project*, already well on the way towards completion, involving the damming and flow reversal of the Orange/Senqi River into the Vaal Dam, so that water, heat, electricity and power are delivered to Gauteng. This is a largely South African private sector corporate investment with the support of Rand Water. It is opposed by many ecological and developmental NGOs and by local Basotho communities, although it is supported by the Lesotho state, which stands to collect R6.5mn 'rent' each month as well as to gain access to some water and electricity.

5   The *Cahora Bassa Dam transmission line rehabilitation,* involving a rebuilding of the 1440km power line, largely by the South African private sector, in order not only to bring HEP to Gauteng but also to enable the regional grid to be connected from the powerful Congo River to Cape Town.

Forms of multi-stakeholder or trilateral governance have yet to be agreed, let alone effected, in all these five corridor-type projects, especially in the first three more comprehensive corridor plans (Taylor, 2000). The same goes for other, much longer term projects such as Lobito, Malange and Namibe. Thus there is a palpable 'democratic deficit' not only in SADC – which has only embryonic links outside of its state members to the local and global corporate and civil society worlds – but also in these sub-regional projects (African Development Bank, 1993). SADC, like the Economic Commission for Africa (ECA), may now seek to develop dialogue with civil society and the private sector along with its extra-regional partners, but its credibility in such links is problematic and it has yet to sustain such accountable relationships over time. It remains to be seen whether SADC will really deal as partners, if not equals, with its own NGO Coordinating Committee or ECA's embryonic Centre for Civil Society, and this carries important implications for the future of regionalism (MacLean and Shaw, 1996; Barnard, 1998).

The primary beneficiaries of corridor or triangle arrangements tend to be larger South African companies – both state-owned (such as Eskom, South African Airways (SAA) and Transnet) and privately owned (such as Anglo American and South African Breweries) – along with local and national official jurisdictions, rather than local communities or NGOs. The degree to which these sub-regional arrangements reinforce or dilute somewhat moribund interstate institutions such as SADC is quite problematic, given that the latter remains state-centric in character. However, as noted in the next section, and not unrelated to regional hierarchy and hegemony, SADC has been riven by divisions over security policies rather than development corridors (Dunn and Shaw, 2001; Vale *et al.*, 2001).

In addition to such corridor projects, both Southern Africa in particular and SSA in general have been characterized by emerging patterns of 'hubs-and-spokes'. Examples include airlines (e.g. Kenya Airways and SAA, but also Air Afrique and Ethiopian Airlines); cable TV, internet servers and websites (e.g. MNet and iAfrica); distribution or logistics companies (e.g. Avis and Unitrans); financial centres (e.g. Johannesburg Stock Exchange) (Kenny and Moss, 1998); franchises (e.g. Spur, Steers, Nandos); and think-tanks and universities, especially business and economics programmes. These tend to be replicated in the NGO world also, with Gauteng again being dominant (Barnard, 1998), as well as in other sectors of civil society such as the media (e.g. SABC and *Weekly Mail and Guardian* as well as MNet), professional associations and sports groups. Export Processing Zones (EPZs) or triangles – the icons of flexible globalization – likewise tend to be concentrated around already established economic cores like Gauteng and Cape Town. Their attractiveness is now reinforced in terms of offering not only cheap labour and infrastructure but also security through gated communities or compounds, reflecting private rather than human, and individual rather than collective forms of security (UNDP, 1994).

New and old forms of conflict and alliance: beyond peace building towards sustainable human security

Africa has not benefited from any post-Cold War 'peace dividend'. Indeed, internal and regional conflicts have proliferated and escalated in the 1990s, with profound implications for regional security and stability, especially when redefined in terms of human security (Shaw, 1999; Shaw and MacLean, 1999; Shaw and Schnabel, 1999). Although almost all African conflicts are 'internal' in origin, they invariably become regional in scale as they progress. Moreover, the declared 'Revolution in Military Affairs' (RMA) has been at best perverse on the continent, involving a return to basic strategies and technologies such as machettes, landmines and AK47s (Tomlin, 1998; Boutwell and Klare, 1999). Furthermore, such struggles never involve only national armies; rather they always include non-state actors, both conflictual and economic, short-term crisis-oriented and longer term developmental. As discussed in the following section, many are long-running since they involve competition over scarce resources, such as diamonds in Angola and Sierra Leone, control of which enables factions to continue fighting (Reno, 1998). In short, these are not really 'complex political emergencies' (Cliffe, 1999): complex definitely, but typically economic and ecological as well as political, and rarely of crisis length (Ali and Matthews, 1999). The apparent inability of states to eliminate or contain such conflicts has enhanced the privatization of security, characterized by a move away from regime forces and towards private armies, whether of the more organized corporate executive outcomes style (Howe, 1998; Shearer, 1998) or of the more chaotic child soldier variety.

As indicated in the following section, the apparent sustainability of such conflicts is apparent around Angola, Liberia/Sierra Leone and the Horn, with the first and last spilling over into the Great Lakes and Congo. Moreover, as such conflicts have sucked in a growing range of actors – from global agencies and media through mercenary forces and NGOs to non-contiguous regimes – revisionist notions of 'neo-realism' become attractive again, albeit in a post-Westphalian and post-bipolar context (Dunn and Shaw, 2000; Vale *et al.*, 2001). The salience of a focus on meso-level patterns of conflict and response – and consequently on the possibility of 'security communities' emerging on the continent – is apparent in Lionel Cliffe's analysis of continuing conflicts in the Horn, which have:

> cross-border or inter-regional dimensions . . . a pattern of 'mutual intervention'. Each government sought to deal with its own internal conflicts by some degree of support for insurgencies in neighbouring states . . . Regional stability . . . [is affected by] the role of regional bodies in combining economic cooperation, peace making and security roles.
>
> (Cliffe, 1999: 89)

Regional responses on the continent to persistent conflict have stretched from a redesigned Organisation of African Unity facility to attempts to establish confidence-building and peace-keeping structures on the part of interstate organizations such as ECOWAS, the Inter-Governmental Authority on Development (IGAD) and SADC. However, some of these may be little more than thinly disguised forms of regional hegemony appropriate to the 1990s. The ECOMOG reaction by the first, for example, is largely a Nigerian creation to force the creation of peace in Liberia and then in Sierra Leone (van Walraven, 1999). While the controversial Organ for Politics, Defence and Security in the last may be less clearly a South African initiative, its stillborn character is a reflection of simmering competition between Mugabe's Zimbabwean regime and the post-apartheid state in South Africa (Gibb, 1998; Vale *et al.*, 2000). The continuing stand-off is in stark contrast to the relatively successful and cooperative anti-apartheid and anti-destabilization Inter-State Defence and Security Committee of the FLS. Meanwhile, IGAD continues to evolve away from its initial ecological and functional emphasis towards a broader mandate to advance human security as well as human development, most obviously in protracted 'track-two' diplomacy over the long-standing interrelated tensions in Southern Sudan, the Horn and so on (*Current History*, 1999b).

The diversity of actors, interests and relations in such new regionalisms not only complicates notions of human development and security, but also opens up new possibilities for both positive and negative pressure. Sanctions and incentives are no longer the exclusive preserve of states: they may be imposed on and by non-state actors, through such mechanisms as corporate or cultural boycotts and affirmative actions. Anti-apartheid sanctions came to be imposed on and by a wide range of actors, to crucial effect (Crawford and Klotz, 1999). In this instance, as in other cases such as Burundi and Nigeria, debate continues about which types of sanctions, if any, were most effective, especially when regional consequences are factored in. Types of sanctions range across economic, financial, strategic and technological terrains. The current public debate about how to deal with the controversial role in the Southern Sudanese oilfields of a Canadian 'junior' energy company – Talisman – is symptomatic.

As well as recognizing the multiple forms of state/non-state relations in emerging forms of regionalisms, though, we need to begin to appreciate the diversity of regionalisms in Africa as elsewhere. This diversity is reflected in differences in primary issue area (e.g. economic, ecological, strategic), in the degree or sustainability of integration, and in the nature and composition of state and non-state partners. Just as NGOs have begun to recognize divisions of labour among themselves in terms of their roles in PKOs (Weiss, 1999) – such as the assumption of responsibility for health by MSF, for housing by CARE, for reconstruction by OXFAM or World Vision – so we need to identify crucial catalysts in different eras and regions (such as Makerere in the East African Community in the 1960s or South African Airways and MNet in today's SADC) (Grugel and Hout, 1999). One quite distinctive form of new regionalism in Africa is the emergence of the minerals/mafias syndrome in which scarce resources are exchanged for protection as well as the enrichment or aggrandizement of regimes (Shaw, 2000b). Alas, Kaplan's (1994: 46) simplistic, stereotypical assertion that 'West Africa is becoming *the* symbol of world-wide demographic, environmental and social stress, in which criminal anarchy emerges as the real "strategic" danger' misses the point, since 'anarchy' is not entirely unstructured or unpredictable, just unfair and unstable.

Towards a 'real' political economy of conflict: local, regional and global connections

Orthodox peace-keeping and peace-building strategies (MacFarlane, 1999) have not always been efficacious in Africa or elsewhere. They have tended to be sub-verted particularly when regional contexts facilitate cross-border trade which keeps the guns and other supplies flowing through profitable global networks. Furthermore, the ubiquity of small and weak states on the continent means that Africa has more borders than any other, the proliferation of micro-states in the Balkans notwithstanding. The emergence of seemingly sustainable 'war economies' serves to complicate any easy or ready response. Such disappointments have led to a veritable military and NGO industry of 'lessons learned'. Yet if anything is to be so learned it is that conflict is positive and profitable for some even as it is disastrous and debilitating for the majority (Smillie *et al.*, 2000). The case of Sierra Leone is symptomatic (Cilliers and Mason, 1999), and related illustrations from Angola and Somalia (Reno, 1998; Spears, 1999) lend nuance to and support for the thesis. This emblematic case not only throws recently established wisdoms into disarray, but also suggests that any 'success stories' of peace operations thus far may be the exception rather than the rule (van Walraven, 1999).

The recent 'shadow' 'states' or 'warlord' regimes in Freetown (or Abuja, Kinshasa, Luanda or even Mogadishu) are but the latest iteration of the tendency or inclination of ubiquitous transnational and local informal sectors to subvert any notion of state authority, efficiency or legitimacy (Reno, 1998). To be sure, the hold on power of such rapacious regimes is tenuous, and this is especially so in smaller states, as illustrated by the contrast between the pressures on Freetown and those on Luanda. Such cowboy or pirate economies are not new: informal markets in precious stones and minerals, energy and labour are as old as the slave trade. And as in previous centuries, the ultimate markets for Africa's cornucopias lie not on the continent itself. Instead they are processed through complex networks of 'trust', ranging from informal sector mines to formal sector traders, distributors, advertis-ers and sellers in the EU, Japan and the US. The result is their ultimate vulnerability to non-state sanctions such as consumer boycotts, corporate codes of conduct and union pressures.

Thus dramatic levels of income, profit and rent from diamond or oil sales in Sierra Leone and Angola respectively serve to perpetuate the rationale and means for the protracted struggles characteristic of war economies. Clearly, these are not familiar anti-colonial nationalist movements or liberation struggles. Rather, these 'bandits' corrupt what remains of the state for their own enrichment. In so doing, they postpone any notion of peace agreements or reconstruction plans. In this sense, conditions in Freetown, Luanda, Mogadishu and elsewhere are not so much an instance of Kaplan's 'anarchy' as a distinctive form of 'African' capitalism, exacerbated by ethnic, generational and racial tensions, complicated transitions, forms of globalization, regional opportunities, and impossible structural adjustment conditionalities (Cox, 1999: 24–25; Crawford, 2000). While continuing conflicts in Central and West Africa and the Horn may serve to 'defeat' extant PKO reactions, they may also constitute the wave of the future.

The problematic incidence and impact of such 'cowboys' constitutes a profound challenge for the continent's remaining intellectuals and think-tanks (van Walraven, 1999: 109–23). What human security response? What form of governance would transcend such an unfortunate legacy? Certainly, any informed PKO reaction would need to reassure citizens that the international community would protect lives and properties even if incumbent shadow regimes were disinclined to do so. In short, getting towards an agreed process of peace building and reconstruction is part of a protracted and inseparable undertaking of governance for and towards peace building. According to Klaas van Walraven (1999: 109–24), Nigeria's advocacy of ECOMOG was always problematic and doomed: the partisan and partial character of the 'regional' force made it less than appropriate from day one. Nevertheless, it is still vital for global and regional interests to try to work together in such complicated contexts, lest parochialism reinforce trends towards greater inequality and away from cosmopolitan forms of governance more appropriate for a new and complex century.

Alternative regionalisms: civil societies at the meso-level

In contrast to this pessimistic war economy scenario, more optimistic analyses of new regionalisms in Africa as elsewhere need increasingly to recognize the present and prospective impacts of civil societies on patterns of regional cooperation and conflict. Such transnational links are not necessarily compatible with formal interstate regional structures: they may embrace different spatial areas and be concerned about issues other than economics and strategy. While regional organizations in Africa are beginning to encourage 'dialogue' with business associations and NGOs, and even with trade unions and women's groups, they are not yet ready to share power, and such consultations consequently tend to have a formal or ritual quality to them. Effective governance has yet to begin to trickle down to sub-state levels: hence the democratic deficit in all African regional institutions, which may simplify decision-making somewhat but undermines any accountability, identity, legitimacy, transparency or support. Likewise, conversely, we need to recognize the limited degree of autonomy which some NGOs and MNCs possess in their relations with certain states. Non-state actors are rarely completely autonomous of state regimes, but the degree of autonomy is uneven between NGOs and over time. Just as the UN or World Bank may coopt certain NGOs by means of subcontracting, for instance, so regional organizations may create or cajole regional NGOs for their own purposes (Lindberg and Sverrisson, 1997; Van Rooy, 1999; Kleinberg and Clark, 2000; Murphy, 2000).

Non-state definitions of regions may reflect a variety of relations: continuing bases like ecology (such as shared geographic zones from savannah and forest to valleys and mountains), ethnicity (history, language, myths) and 'modern' cultural events (such as regional book fairs, fashion competitions, musical galas, and tourist routes and packages); NGOs, such as the proposed Southern African Development Council NGO Coordinating Committee (Barnard, 1998); professional associations; regional gatherings of kinpersons; religious congregations; and regional sports competitions. Such regional communities may also include tertiary education and training, such as the historic roles of Makerere University for East Africa and UNISA for Southern Africa, and now regional graduate programmes at the Southern African Regional Institute for Policy Studies (SARIPS) or via the African Economic Research Consortium (AERC) (Quadir *et al.*, 1999). Obviously too, both African and global companies define their own regions on the continent in terms of corporate structures including headquarters and branch plants, distribution lines, franchise licences, production chains and subcontracting (Shaw and van der Westhuizen, 1999).

Increasingly, regions – especially corridors and triangles – will be defined by contemporary infrastructures, such as electricity (and related dams and water distribution), gas and oil pipeline and telecommunications grids, and transport routes, which themselves tend to reflect established communications, community and corporate networks (Vale *et al.*, 2001). If such new regional designs continue to be effected, then in the second or third decade of the new century we may find new meso-level structures emerging, such as the Great Lakes, Nile Valley and Rift Valley communities, somewhat parallel to the embryonic Horn and Sahel groupings. These would not necessarily be mutually exclusive, especially if participation was reflective of trilateral realities, that is, involving companies and civil societies as well as states.

Nor, finally, do 'African' regions end at the shores of the continent. African countries, communities and companies are involved in sub-global groupings like Atlantic and Indian Ocean Rims, the Cairns group on agriculture in the WTO, the Conventions on International Trade in Endangered Species (CITES), the Commonwealth, *la francophonie* and the Non-Aligned Movement.

Lessons learned . . . for other disciplines/fields and future interventions

I conclude with a few more speculative reflections on some of the possible implications of such new regionalist analysis for established disciplines and debates, including discourses about globalization, interdisciplinary studies and policy options. As already indicated, the overly stark, almost stereotypical dichotomy between coming anarchy and African renaissance has been moderated somewhat by the presence or dominance of each of these trends in different regions (Shaw and Nyang'oro, 2000). This is symbolized by the apparent promise of a generation of 'New Africans', notably ex-insurgency leaders such as Issayas of Eritrea, Kagame of Rwanda, Meles of Ethiopia and Museveni of Uganda (Clapham,

1998). Yet their conversion into international statesmen has not been unproblematic: continued border skirmishes and other signs of instability in the Great Lakes and the Horn suggest that the inherently problematic process of reconstructing infrastructures and institutions is more protracted than expected.

The elusiveness of anything approaching a 'security community' (Adler and Barnett, 1998a) on the continent has encouraged my own rediscovery of 'new realism' – 'new' because the conflicting states are quite distinctive, and 'realist' as their relationships are far from being only intergovernmental and strategic – as well as new regionalism. The forms of conflict around the redefined state and its tenuous hold on territory and legitimacy cannot be downplayed or overlooked (Shaw, 1998, 2000b). Moreover, some authoritarian regimes continue to be defiant (e.g. Moi in Kenya and Mugabe in Zimbabwe) and some 'shadow' regimes remain resilient (e.g. Angola, Congo, Liberia, Sierra Leone and Somalia) (Reno, 1998).

Such new regional perspectives on the continent hold promise for a range of overlapping disciplines in the social sciences, in addition to debates over globalizations. The first of these is *political science*, which needs to re-examine assumptions about 'trilateral' state–economy–society relations. These continue at all levels – local, national, regional and global – but their content and balance have changed dramatically in the post-independence and post-bipolar eras (Baylis and Smith, 1997; Clemens, 1998). The second is *international relations*, which are no longer the monopoly of state and interstate agencies but rather include economies/companies and civil societies/NGOs, and also embrace an increasingly extensive and heterogeneous range of issues (Dunn and Shaw, 2000; Shaw and Nyang'oro, 2000), from landmines to ozone, trade to peace-building, new forms of 'rent' extracted from diamonds and oil production, AIDS to ecology, leading to broad mixed actor global coalitions (Lipschutz with Mayer, 1996; Keck and Sikkink, 1998; Maxwell *et al.* 1998). Third, *security studies* have to begin to transcend state-centric and bipolar biases in both theory and practice in order to accommodate a more catholic range of actors and strategic issues such as ecology, viruses, migrations and small arms, and especially the broad peace building spectrum from confidence building to reconstruction which involves civil societies at all stages. Any rehabilitation of a neo-realist perspective would have to incorporate a range of non-state actors and interests and non-traditional issue areas (Nel and McGowan, 1999). Fourth, the implications for *international political economy* derive from the ways in which the 'new economy' (aka globalization) has distinct forms in the South, featuring a mix of high-tech 'islands' and profitable informal sectors in a sea of poverty (Castells, 1989), which generates its own security challenges. Moreover, informal and illegal sectors continue to grow, particularly at the regional level, from basic needs to money laundering, with multiple forms of 'market responsiveness' in between. As indicated above, a new IPE of protracted conflicts is beginning to emerge treating ways in which diamond and other industries fund continuing wars in Angola, Congo and Sierra Leone, leading not only to the pathology of a new generation of child soldiers but also to considerable accumulation for a few. Such forms of exchange tend to have distinct regional dimensions.

The new regionalisms pose challenges also for a range of more applied perspectives with profound policy implications, such as for *development studies*, which are no longer concerned solely with sustainable development or structural adjustments, but also increasingly with more flexible varieties of regionalism along with the causes and consequences of increasingly protracted conflicts. This may be seen especially in the growing focus on human development and security (UNDP, 1994, 1999; Dickson, 1997; Hoogvelt, 1997; Payne, 1998). Second, new regionalist insights also pose questions for the study of *comparative transitions*, from insurgencies to regimes with profound regional implications for forms of cooperation (e.g. Museveni–Kagame 'alliance' or understanding) and conflict (e.g. patterns of alliance among non-state and state interests around the interrelated Horn/Great Lakes/Congo conflict) (Shaw, 1998). Third, they carry implications for *civil societies* and varieties of NGOs, especially at fluid new regionalist or meso-levels, augmenting and containing old regional arrangements concentrated in the economic and strategic issue areas while advancing new regionalist developments (MacLean and Shaw, 1996; Bøås *et al.*, 1999b; Holden, 2000). Fourth, they require studies of new forms of *governance* appropriate to the new regionalist context, in which each of the dominant trio of actor types is represented (Lipshutz with Mayer, 1996; Keck and Sikkink, 1998; Held *et al.*, 1999; Van Rooy, 1999; Shaw, 2000a, 2000b; Stiles, 2000). Finally, they advance a set of *alternative futures*, both existential and analytic. More anarchy and/or emerging markets? More realism and/or idealism? In short, at the start of the new millennium, will Africa's trajectory be one of reconstruction and redirection, and/or one of regression and authoritarianism?

Note

1 This and related chapters benefit immeasurably from continuing collaboration with colleagues associated with an informal transnational network around studies of 'new regionalisms' based on the Global Development Section in the ISA and Research Commission #40 in IPSA, notably Morten Bøås, Sandra MacLean, Marianne Marchand, Fahim Quadir and Fred Soderbaum. It is also informed by two weeks of debate at two research workshops at Dalhousie University in mid-August 1999 and 2000 on aspects of regionalisms, globalizations and governance in the South, co-sponsored by the Ford Foundation, SSHRC and UNU, as well as the third conference of the CSGR at Warwick University in September 1999 and a symposium on globalization and the South at the University of Georgia in April 2000.

13 Good governance or good for business?

South Africa's regionalist project and the 'African renaissance'

Ian Taylor

Globalisation, in all its varying forms and dynamics, varies in its impact. Within the developing world we are witnessing a division between the more developed developing countries, and those that seem incapable – for whatever reason – of accruing any benefit from a more global world economy. This is producing ongoing consequences for the relationship of those states that are (relatively) strong within local regions with those that are in a more subordinate position. Grugel and Hout argue that 'globalisation . . . seem[s] to presage a reconfiguration of the South . . . and to pave the way for a reconstitution of a new international order in which some of the larger, more advanced states, the semi-periphery, those with an already established productive base, play a key role' (1999: 6). It is suggested that such a reconfiguration in the developing world (however uneven this may be in practice) is spearheaded by elites in dominant states, who attempt to push for greater integration and stronger regional networks along clearly defined lines by which their position in the global political economy may be emboldened. This is particularly so as the regionalist project that is promoted invariably fits with the 'requirements' of international capital: liberalisation, deregulation, an emasculation of labour and 'good governance'.

This last ingredient is worthy of note, for it forms the rhetorical foundation of South Africa's current regional policy. As suggested, in the South it is most likely that it is the dominant state within a particular region that tends to drive the regionalist project. I need not rehearse the well-known fact that South Africa is by far the dominant state in Southern Africa (cf. Ahwireng-Obeng and McGowan, 1998). This dominance is historical and specific attempts to lessen such structural imbalance by the peripheral states in the region – in the form of the Southern African Development Co-ordination Conference (SADCC) – failed miserably, though it did perhaps foster a sense of regionalism that has outlasted apartheid.

In the post-apartheid era, Pretoria's elites have been particularly occupied with promoting a rejuvenation of the region (institutionalised now as the Southern African Development Community – SADC), while at the same time pressing for an economic and political transformation. Although initially reluctant to be seen as the dominating hegemon, anti-interventionist reluctance has been largely replaced by a more activist engagement. In doing so, the need for 'good governance' and 'democracy' alongside the discourse of 'growth' and (to a lesser extent) development – all linked to the need to develop closer regional co-operation, leading to greater integration – is frequently invoked. This is invariably wrapped up within the rhetoric of what has become President Thabo Mbeki's motif 'African Renaissance', where there is an explicit connection between governance and growth, all within the context and framework of the world economy.

This agenda has been cast as an attempt to integrate the region more closely and to increase Southern Africa's drawing power *vis-à-vis* international capital. In short, South Africa's regional efforts 'may be regarded as a strategy to lure investment and trade opportunities, suggesting as it does that Africa is a worthwhile economic prospect' (Bulger, n.d.). Already, 'we're getting to the point now where it's hard to say which of the *Fortune 500* companies are *not* here', as the United States economic counsellor in Pretoria asserted (quoted in *New York Times*, 22 April 1995). This courting of transnationl capital, Mbeki asserts, means that 'South Africa ha[s] the potential in terms of its economy, in terms of its politics, and so on, to strike out on this new African path [the Renaissance]' – leading by example and exhortation as it were (quoted in *Sunday Independent* (Johannesburg), 13 July 1997).

Indeed, an implicit part of this regionalist project is to bind the region together under South African leadership (see Lieberman, 1997). This 'integration' is likely to mean a greater penetration of South African capital as in the main the markets in Southern Africa are small and varied, being largely non-complementary and susceptible to the provision of manufactured goods from the most industrialised state in the region, while they primarily export primary products for consumption and/or processing. On the ground this has meant an activist approach to the promotion of corporate South Africa's penetration of the region, in tandem with international capital. South African mining corporations have expanded into Zambia and the Democratic Republic of Congo; South African breweries have bought up local breweries and bottling plants in Zambia and Zimbabwe; Spoornet (the rail parastatal in South Africa) is renovating lines in Tanzania; Shoprite Checkers has opened up supermarkets throughout the region; and virtually every shop in the region seems stocked with South African produce.

Mbeki himself has asserted the importance of South Africa's 'business sector, which has a critical role in continuing the African Renaissance into the 21st Century, capable of both acting on its own and in partnership with international investors' (Mbeki, 1997). Despite naive (bordering on the hagiographic) attempts to portray Mbeki's African Renaissance as an 'anti-imperialist' crusade (see Ajulu, 2000), its roots lie far more in the desire to build the region as an attractive destination for local and international capital, rather than any counter-hegemonic project. This promotion of capital as an active agent in reconstituting the region reflects the reconfiguration of power between government, business and labour, where 'globalisation . . . appear[s] to give corporate South Africa added leverage over its rival social partners in the tug-of-war over the terms of the domestic renewal' (Kornegay and Landsberg, 1998: 6).

One cannot fully comprehend this phenomenon without recognising that the ANC government has acceded to the dominant neo-liberalist agenda – perhaps most graphically illustrated when the government ditched the popular neo-Keynesian-tinged Reconstruction and Development Programme (RDP) for the neo-liberalist Growth, Employment and Reconstruction plan (GEAR) – a self-imposed structural adjustment project. This has meant the effective abandonment of any interrogation of the unequal terms of international trade – for instance, questioning why balance of payment deficits must be reduced in the South, while surplus accounts in the North face no such pressure to equalise trading regimes. Instead, a policy based on 'maximum engagement' with transnational and domestically based capital as the corporate vehicles to promote growth is pursued.

While Mbeki has taunted his critics 'to call [him] a Thatcherite', (*Business Times* (Johannesburg), 16 June 1996) an ongoing process of class formation has been taking place whereby an emergent black bourgeoisie is joining the ranks of the established (white) elites to form a nascent historical bloc. This fraction is largely outwardly oriented and derivative of money capital, and hence is fast developing and redeveloping its international linkages post-sanctions. This process inexorably draws the South African elite into the wider transnational elite. This actuality, and how such a process relates to Pretoria's regional policies and the rhetoric of 'good governance' and 'democracy', is the theme of this chapter.

Globalisation and neo-liberalism

Global capitalism is more and more ordered around and within an architecture of supranational organisations, suggesting a 'transnational process of consensus formation among the official caretakers of the global economy . . . generat[ing] guidelines that are transmitted into the policy-making channels of national governments and big corporations' (Cox, 1994: 49). These organisations include: the World Bank, the International Monetary Fund and the World Trade Organisation, acting as disciplinary agents to compel states to erect and then defend the environment necessary for untrammelled capital accumulation to occur.

These ostensibly 'purely economic' institutions form a 'G-7 nexus' with political forces in governments and with the private sector (Gill, 1994). This last element in the form of transnational corporations dominates an increasing share of the global sphere of production, exploits the biosphere's resources, profits massively from mankind's labour, and benefits from the current neo-liberalist denial of ethical considerations *vis-à-vis* economic policies (Buarque, 1993). This scenario in turn is facilitated by elites within the state administrations who, at the capitalist core and in tacit alliance with the elites based in the international financial institutions and transnational corporations, form an 'Atlantic ruling class' (van der Pijl, 1998). To these fractions may be added internationally oriented merchants and the global mass media, who 'manufacture consent' on behalf of the neo-liberalist project (Herman and Chomsky, 1988). This global elite thus comprises transnational executives and their affiliates; globalising state bureaucrats; capitalist-inspired politicians and professionals; and consumerist elites (Sklair, 1995).

Such a phenomenon of transnational class formation has spread from the North to the South, linking an emergent fraction of Southern-based elites with their

Northern counterparts at the core of a concentric circle of social, economic and political power (Hoogvelt, 1997). Those within this nascent global historic bloc increasingly possess a considerable degree of class-consciousness, and view their interests as being outwardly linked to the wider transnational sphere, rather than being beholden to the 'domestic' milieu (van der Pijl, 1989). They have come to form what one analysis has termed 'the global establishment' (Kowalewski, 1997).

This process of separating the elites from simply territorially located class power – however uneven this may be – has entailed a 'subordination of domestic economies to the perceived exigencies of a global economy. States willy nilly [have now] become more effectively accountable to a nebeleuse personified as the global economy' (Cox, 1992: 27). In a globalising world a separation can increasingly be made between the 'state' – the loci of the transnationalised elite classes' power – and the 'nation-state', a more traditional concept of spatial and politico-economic integrity (Robinson, 1996a: 618).

These elites, both in the North and the South, actively construct the domestic and external political, bureaucratic and constitutional frameworks that permit the operation of the global capitalist order, fostering what may be dubbed the 'Americanisation' of business practices (Sassen, 1996: 19). The meeting point for this elite nexus takes place through unofficial and/or non-state forums like the Trilateral Commission, the Bilderberg Conference, the World Economic Forum and the International Chamber of Commerce; and through official bodies like the Organisation for Economic Cooperation and Development (OECD), the World Bank, the IMF and the G-7. 'These shape the discourse within which policies are defined, the terms and concepts that circumscribe what can be thought and done [and] also tighten the transnational networks that link policy-making from country to country' (Cox, 1994: 49).

This overall process is conducted by a 'powerful phalanx of social forces . . . arrayed . . . behind the agenda of intensified market-led globalisation' who seek to actively promote the post-Keynesian counter-revolution (Rupert, 1997: 117). For sure, capitalism does not simply happen, and the assertion of neo-liberalism as the hegemonic discourse similarly has not just occurred. 'It is a social system that has [had] to struggle to create and reproduce its hegemonic order globally, and to do this large numbers of local, national, international and global organisations [were] established' to promote the new organising norms (Sklair, 1997: 514–15). This has involved the effective imposition of 'a uniform conception of the world on an increasingly transnational society' (Holman, 1992: 13).

As has been suggested, the agents of this increasingly integrated global economy are a new transnational elite (see van der Pijl, 1998). This elite currently inhabits the positions of power where decisions *vis-à-vis* global governance are made. Such an elite is composed of the proprietors and managers of the transnational corporations; the bureaucrats, cadres and technicians who execute the policies of the international financial institutions; and the elites located in the nation-state administrations (Robinson, 1998: 1). The power of this transnational elite class has been dramatically strengthened as global integration has accelerated in the contemporary period. Indeed, there has been a wholesale shift in the balance of forces between classes within each national state, with the outwardly linked transnational elite in each state enjoying unprecedented power. It is accurate to assert that at present it is to this transnational elite and their locally situated representatives with their specific interests (frequently postured as the 'national interest') that the administrations of nation-states respond to, with all the wider contradictions that this engenders.

This transnational elite has sought to bring into being the environment most advantageous to the unimpeded operation of capitalism on a global scale. In pushing this vision, they have been engaged in a veritable 'transnational agenda' that seeks to establish specific economic and political ingredients right across the globe (see Robinson, 1996a). Economically, this is termed 'neo-liberalism', a particular paradigm which aims to establish the appropriate setting for the lightning-quick mobility and unfettered operation of capital, but which has critically been referred to as 'an owner's revolt against the class and international compromises of corporate liberalism' (van der Pijl, 1998: 130). The 'structural adjustment programmes' which have been imposed upon the South (and Africa in particular) from the 1980s onward are an integral part of this agenda, aiming to establish 'macroeconomic stabilisation' for the movement of transnational capital, and performing an important *political* function by legitimating international capital's position within state boundaries (Bush and Szeftel, 1998: 176). Since 'capitalism encompasses the entire globe, its architects require a universal vision, a picture of a globally conceived society, to join classes in different countries . . . [in order] to institutionalise global capital accumulation by setting general rules of behaviour and disseminating a developmentalist ideology to facilitate the process' (Mittelman and Pasha, 1997: 51). Pretoria's regionalist project recognises this, asserting that the 'countries of the Southern African region can achieve their full potential only through . . . the harmonisation of trade practices' (Department of Foreign Affairs, 1996: 1). This harmonisation is within the remit of neo-liberalism and is cognisant of the ostensible need in the era of globalisation to compete for investment. In essence, this means that spatial territories have had to increasingly (re-)structure themselves as 'competition states', attracting capital while competing with rival territories for investment (Cerny, 1997). To do so requires an almost complete break from any redistributive aspirations regarding social equity, and instead concentrate on a specific notion of what constitutes 'good governance'. This has obviously intense implications for nations in Africa with deplorable structural inequalities.

The contradictions of neo-liberalism and the apparent 'good governance solution'

Such a scenario stimulates deep contradictions, for a project based on liberalisation, privatisation and representing the dislocating effects of globalisation has little chance of becoming hegemonic. Indeed, a hegemonic project in the Gramscian sense needs a 'politics of support' as well as a 'politics of power', however mighty transnational capital and its class allies may be (Gamble, 1988: 208–41). This consensual element in the neo-liberalist project is, to borrow Dahl's phrase, 'polyarchy'.

This refers to a Schumpeterian system by which an elite group rules and where popular involvement in decision-making is limited to periodic leadership choices via carefully managed elections organised by contending elites.

Polyarchy aims to soothe the social and political pressures that are created by the transnational elite-based neo-liberal order and create a state of 'low intensity democracy' (Gills *et al.*, 1993). Such an analysis echoes the assertion that 'the construction of a corporate-dominant order . . . require[s] the neutralisation of social forces precipitating persistent and effective questioning of the established order' (Harrod, 1997: 108). By its very nature, polyarchy dissipates the energies of those marginalised by the ongoing order into parliamentary procedures that in themselves are acted out by political factions whose power and prestige are dependent on the polyarchical model. In short, polyarchy expresses 'not the fulfilment of democratic aspirations, but their deflection, containment, and limitation' (Good, 1997: 253). Indeed, the promotion of polyarchy has 'been instrumental in some cases (*e.g.* Zambia) in disempowering the poor by introducing the multiparty mantra as a new political panacea, while it [has] entrenched a new, rather exclusive elite in reality' (Liebenberg, 1998: 5).

Furthermore, polyarchy is based on a separation of the economic from the political, ignoring the reality that there can be no cleavage between the so-called economic sphere and its (interlinked) political and ideological consequences. Yet such a conceptualisation is currently dominant – certainly within the burgeoning literature on 'democratisation' in the South (see Diamond *et al.*, 1988; Di Palma, 1990; Huntingdon, 1991).

In contrast to conceptualisations of popular democracy, theorisations of this kind consciously divorce 'economics' from 'politics' (at a time when neo-liberalist impulses push for a greater interpenetration of the two), for in this abstraction, the former responds only to the logic of 'the market', while the latter is restricted in its role of permitting that logic to proceed without obstruction (Neufeld, 1999: 4). This limited understanding of democracy however serves to provide protection and confidence to the established elites in countries undergoing transition from authoritarian rule. As one analysis puts it:

> The assertion that the majority of African governments are now democratic is premised on contentious notions of democracy with external origins. Apart from this, the assertion has no empirical basis. It is true that multiparty elections are now common in Africa, but this truth does not describe a fundamental development. The change is strategic, not substantive. Multiparty elections have not led to new power relations in Africa. Just look at Zambia and Malawi since the fall of Kenneth Kaunda and the late Kamazu Banda.
> (Moyo, 1998: 11)

Such a process has been actively supported by the new South African government in its intercourse with the region, where the promotion of good governance, namely 'democracy' and 'transparency', has gone hand-in-hand with a deepening penetration of neighbouring economies by South African-based externally oriented capital *and* transnational capital. Indeed, much of the impulse behind such moves views the region as a possible market, waiting to devour foreign consumer goods and soak up overseas investment. This has been pictured as presenting substantial opportunities to Pretoria, as long as 'political stability' and good governance is achieved in the region. As one commentator remarked:

> [D]ecades of destabilisation by the apartheid government, helped along by corruption and mismanagement . . . has left the continent in the role of consumers rather than producers.
>
> How do we capitalise on this? The answer has to be political stability. For Africa to be our growth market, we need to drive a shift in mindset: 'No' to corruption, despotism and mindless militarism and 'Yes' to fiscal discipline, balanced budgets and low inflation.
>
> (Pillay, 1999)

In such formulations, the call to end corruption and mismanagement (a welcome call by any standards) is explicitly linked with the dogmas of the hegemonic discourse: discipline in fiscal spending. Other notions of governance such as social justice are not even brought into the frame in this orthodox 'common-sense' notion of what constitutes good governance. This orthodox view is however currently being promoted by Pretoria's elites as part of their push for a reconfiguration of the region – a push which serves specific fractions of capital within and without South Africa.

Returning to the 'new wave of democratisation', though many of the states in the region underwent 'democratisation' before the end of apartheid (though much of this historic moment coincides with the South African transition), these projects have largely been short-lived and/or containing what can only be regarded as a democratic facade, namely polyarchy. One need only think of the type of transitions that have occurred in states such as Malawi, Mozambique and Zambia to acknowledge that little has changed for the average person.

What has occurred in these contentious transitions has been an attempt by dominant factions – with the overt support of their Northern counterparts for sure – to reconstruct hegemony via a reformulation of the mode of political rule: from the overtly coercive –apartheid, Banda and Kaunda – to a more consensually based order, namely polyarchy. The result was to pre-empt fundamental changes that may have arisen through any popular alternative to polyarchy, and instead preserve the extant economic structures dominated by the transnational elites. Co-option of the democratisation movement into the structures of polyarchical democracy performed this task, dressed up as it is within the rhetoric of good governance and democracy. Such an arrangement is the political counterpart to neo-liberalism, with the 'visible hand of the voter' working alongside the mythical metaphysical 'market'.

In an epoch of deepening global capitalism, economic harmonisation on a world scale is prevented by dictatorships and overtly authoritarian systems, because such arrangements stand in direct contrast to the 'institutional certainties of democracy' preferred by investors (Koelble, 1999: 46). Undemocratic regimes are also perceived as contributing to instability, having 'disproportionate impacts on the climate for regional co-operation and integration', whereas good governance creates the 'conditions . . . for the private sector to function as the engine of growth' (Hyden, 1997: 236). Furthermore, with the decline in the utility of sheer coercion (though, as Gramsci asserts, the 'armour of coercion' is always held in reserve as the ultimate guarantor of the status quo), authoritarian regimes are no longer 'acceptable' to international society. Nor can they be openly propped up *à la* a Mobutu Sese Seko with cynical references to the Cold War milieu.

In addition, in the context of neo-liberalism whereby the state is 'rolled back', traditional forms of social control need to be re-invented and consent secured *alongside* coercion. This consensual mechanism of social control is part and parcel of the neo-liberal economic project, adding crucial legitimacy via polyarchic political systems and good governance to a specific economic model that cannot be achieved under authoritarian regimes. With a US-centred transnational hegemony characterising the international political economy, 'support for ["good governance"] efforts in Africa is part of a global strategy to promote "Western" values and institutionalise political regimes that are likely to be non-belligerent and generally positive towards the realisation of the [neo-] liberal paradigm' (Hyden, 1977: 236).

Thus with its ingredients of elite-pacting, historic compromises and provision for the co-option of majorities, more than any other system, polyarchy, as part of a project entitled 'good governance', is better equipped to legitimise the political authority of dominant groups and to achieve the political stability necessary for capitalism to operate. In the context of our study, with the South African elite increasingly representing a faction of the transnational elite, the promotion by Pretoria of good governance and democracy must be contextualised within the framework outlined above. Accepting this, it is pertinent to turn to specifically looking at the promotion of good governance and democracy by South Africa as part of the ongoing regionalist project in Southern Africa.

The 'African Renaissance', good governance and the regionalist project

As has been mentioned, President Mbeki's motif has been the 'African Renaissance'. This theme has been associated with Mbeki from the days when he was deputy president, and has been inextricably coupled with notions of good governance, democracy, liberalised economies and regional integration – all linked as one 'package' which South Africa has sought to promote within the region. It is Mbeki, and those around him, who has been most closely associated with the push within South Africa to accede to the common-sense 'realities' of globalisation – much to the chagrin of the ANC's Leftist constituency and its tripartite allies in the Government of National Unity (the Congress of South African Trade Unions and the South African Communist Party). Mbeki has also been at the forefront of developing strong links with the dominant powers in the world order: he has been instrumental in establishing a close relationship with Washington via the US-South Africa Bilateral Commission, and has been a regular participant at transnational meeting points such as the World Economic Forum and the Partnership Africa conference where he has sought to court international capital to the region on the premise that the SADC is 'involved in negotiations to transform the subcontinent into a free trade area [to] further enhance the attractiveness of the region as an investment destination' (Mbeki, 1998b: 229).

This activist approach has been bound up with Pretoria's demand of the regional elites that they restructure their economies and domestic polities to make their own territories more attractive to 'international investment' and bring the region closer together as a more uniformed (and larger) market. This in itself has been privileged around the notion of a struggle for authentic liberation, based upon 'open markets', 'good governance' and a particular regionalist vision. A lengthy quotation from Mbeki provides a flavour of this discourse:

> What is it that makes up [Africa's] genuine liberation?
>
> The first of these is that we must bring to an end the practices as a result of which many throughout the world have the view that as Africans we are incapable of establishing and maintaining systems of good governance . . .
>
> Like others throughout the world, we too are engaged in the struggle to give real meaning to such concepts as transparency and accountability in governance . . .
>
> Our history demands that we do everything in our power to . . . encourage all other countries on our continent to move in the same direction . . .
>
> Accordingly . . . many on our continent have introduced new economic policies which seek to create conditions that are attractive to both domestic and foreign investors, encourage the growth of the private sector, reduce the participation of the state in the ownership of the economy, and in other ways seek to build modern economies.
>
> Simultaneously, we are also working to overcome the disadvantages created by small markets represented by the relatively small numbers of people in many of our nation states. Regional economic associations have therefore been formed aimed at achieving regional economic integration.
>
> (Mbeki, 1998b: 247)

This regionalist project postures Southern Africa as on the threshold of economic growth, if only the familiar ingredients of the globalisation discourse were set in place. This conception 'posits Africa as an expanding and prosperous market . . . in which South African capital is destined to play a special role through the development of trade, strategic partnerships and the like' (Vale and Maseko, 1998: 279). Indeed, the strategic partnership between the government in Pretoria, South African-based corporations *and* transnational capital is integral to the regionalist project being advanced by the South African state. Post-apartheid, Pretoria has been enthusiastic in its projection of itself as a 'bridge' between the developed world and the South across a whole range of issues, and reconfiguring the region within the globalising remit is no exception. Indeed, Mbeki has been quite explicit in his promotion of the country as an entrée for international capital wishing to penetrate Southern Africa, telling Hong Kong businessmen that they 'will find in . . . South Africa . . . a bridge to access much of the rest of the African continent' (Mbeki, 1998a: 230).

Yet, though South Africa's 'vision' of a renaissance in Southern Africa (indeed, the wider continent) is predicated upon a neo-liberalist understanding of how growth and modernisation may be achieved, this project cannot be achieved while state administrations within the region remain 'unattractive' to South African and international capital, based as they are in many cases upon authoritarian and per-sonalised rule. The facade of 'democracy' (polyarchy) and the 'rule of law', with constitutional guarantees protecting property rights and investors from arbitrary interference by the state, is deemed necessary as a precursor to any sustainable regionalist project, based upon the principles outlined above.

At this point a caveat is in order: I am not suggesting that corruption, misuse of the state and incompetence is desirable; nor am I defending anti-democratic regimes. This is not the point. Curbs on such behaviour are *of course* an advance-ment for the peoples of the region. The ability to hold the threat of a non-renewable mandate over an administration may also lessen patent undemoc-ratic behaviour. Yet polyarchy as opposed to popular democracy tends to encourage elite competition and a future predicated on winning the next round of elections. Addressing structural inequalities within a society, a long and open-ended process, fades from the agenda when democracy is reduced to periodic elections, and good governance becomes defined as a readiness to open up one's markets. As Ake argued, if we 'neglect to problematise governance in democracies, we opt for a minimalist governance performance and a very shallow democratic performance' (Ake, 1996).

Hence what is under investigation is not whether democracy (however defined) is better than autocratic despotism (of course it is), but the way a *particular* form of democracy is promoted as an integral part of the regional project by elite factions within the dominant state, to make the region more attractive to 'investors' and, by doing so, advance the position of transnational capital. Ultimately, this process aims to restructure the region and, by doing so, incorporate it more and more into the international political economy along the lines demanded by the hegemonic discourse of neo-liberalism.

This being said, it has increasingly become apparent that South Africa sees itself as the agent-on-the-ground for such a reconfiguration of the region, driven by the imperatives of Pretoria's own neo-liberal GEAR programme and the accep-tance by leading fractions within the historic bloc of the hegemonic discourse. Barely an opportunity is missed to extol the necessity to accede to the rigours of good governance and democracy. For example, when President Frederick Chiluba disenfranchised former president Kenneth Kaunda in late 1997, Pretoria appealed to him based on 'the commitment of the members of the Southern African Development Community to the promotion and maintenance of democracy, good governance and human rights'. This was intimately connected to how foreign opinion may perceive such actions – Kaunda's detention was seen as 'not serv[ing] to foster confidence in the kind of free political activity to which [we are committed] as states of this region', and appealed to a speedy resolution 'in the interest of political stability and good governance in Zambia and in our region' (Mandela, 1997). Thus not only was intercession a repaying of debts accrued by the ANC to Kaunda during the struggle period, it was also linked to the desire to project a favourable 'image' of the region to outsiders. Such appeals to good governance are coupled with the belief that only by attracting international capital may economic growth be achieved.

This is frequently invoked as a starting point for a reconfiguration – a 'renaissance' – of Southern Africa. As Mbeki told an audience in Japan: 'already, a significant number of countries have shown relatively high rates of growth as a direct consequence of changes in economic policies and, of course, the achievement of stability within our countries as a result of the establishment of democratic systems of government' (Mbeki, 1998b: 248). This 'selling' of Southern Africa overseas has been a particular feature of Pretoria's foreign policy, cast as it is within the dominant meta-narrative. Within the region, South Africa has been no less active.

Governance as 'security'

In attempting to reconfigure the region and attract capital, South Africa has not only been promoting the idea of the African Renaissance, it has also been calling for a redefinition of the role of the Organisation of African Unity (OAU) and SADC as disciplinary organisations to safeguard regional 'security'. Of particular note in this regard is the SADC Organ for Politics, Defence and Security, formed in 1996. Tensions over whether the Organ should be a separate body parallel to SADC – opposed by South Africa – or that it should operate under a separate chair (i.e. Robert Mugabe) and be largely informal – the Zimbabwean view – indicate that there is at present no real consensus on how this Organ should operate. Such confusion, particularly when one of the protagonists is Mugabe – a figure largely regarded with disdain in South Africa – has led to calls within the country to take a firmer hand in running any SADC 'security' apparatus.

Indeed, one South African newspaper has argued that the organ should be brought under 'SA's discipline' so that 'military intervention is directed at advancing democracy'. 'In pursuing this end', the report suggests, Pretoria 'must contemplate the range of economic measures [its] regional dominance presents' (*Sunday Independent* (Johannesburg), 12 October 1998). In other words, South Africa should exploit its overbearing dominance of Southern Africa to advance a particular agenda in the region. The aim seemingly promoted by Pretoria is to establish mechanisms to interfere in the internal affairs of member states in the event of a breakdown in governance. Not only is this a major break from past practice where criticism of/involvement in the domestic affairs of a member country was off limits, it also suggests a determined effort to reconstitute the effectiveness of the SADC along lines favoured by the elites from the dominant state in the region.

While such developments hold within them certain positive attributes, they are also potentially problematic, particularly if the dominant discourse regarding governance and democracy is used as a litmus test to decide intervention. Indeed, efforts to have intervention sanctioned at both the continental and regional level may simply reify the position of existing elites and contribute to ongoing social inequalities. As one critical perspective frames it:

> Concepts such as 'human rights', 'democracy' and 'peace' are not ideologically neutral. 'Human rights' tend to be reduced to political rights at the expense of equally important rights – namely, social and economic rights.
>
> . . . In the West 'democracy', as we all know by now, is used interchangeably with multi-partyism, while this concept should properly also refer to such crucial factors like popular participation in politics as well as the transparency of political institutions and the accountability of politicians.
>
> . . . It is for such reasons that we should think carefully about introducing something which could be used tomorrow against [popular] movements in Africa.
>
> (Maloka, 1997: 41).

This danger is particularly so when the elites driving the regionalist project perceive 'investor confidence' and attractiveness to international capital as perhaps the overriding factor in driving the growth of the region, and not social, political and economic empowerment for the popular classes. Hence 'stabilising' regimes may (will?) achieve precedence before a more broader concept of what constitutes good governance, acting to enhance existing administrations and thwarting popular demands for social justice.

Indeed, at the very heart of such criticism lies an engagement with the notion of what *is* good governance and democracy. According to the hegemonic discourse (a discourse that is being advanced as the regional project in Southern Africa), this is coupled with polyarchy and 'open markets'. Mbeki himself explicitly has argued for 'a more global approach [within the ongoing hegemony?] which ties together both good governance and development', while asserting that 'democracy will lead to development' (Mbeki at second Tokyo International Conference on African Development (TICAD II), cited by *South African Press Agency*, Tokyo, 20 October 1998).

Yet a more inclusive definition argues that good governance 'should be measured against the access that the public or citizenry has to the levers of economic power, strategy and distribution of wealth, as well as to the design of growth' (Liebenberg, 1998: 5). This economic democratisation currently lies buried beneath the dominant rhetoric surrounding notions of good governance, democracy and regionalism.

Conclusion

The promotion of a particular type of democracy – polyarchy – represents a fundamental shift in the tactics of the Northern-based elite classes and their junior subordinates in the South on how to advance conditions favourable to the existing global accumulation regime and reconfigure the political order. Such a shift has taken place within the wider context of an increasingly integrated world economy where the ongoing hegemonic ideology – neo-liberalism – demands a profound harmonisation and deepening of fiscal and political policies across the globe in order to facilitate the mobility of capital demanded by the transnational elite in their search for profit and capital aggregation. The ongoing regional project in Southern Africa, based as it is on notions of good governance and democracy, must be seen in this context, and helps explain why the United States' representative to SADC views the regional grouping as 'the "best game going" in the advancement of democracy, economic development, capital flows and other issues' (*Times of Zambia* (Lusaka), 17 October 1998).

This is not to say that the impulses currently energising the region towards liberalisation and common-sense assumptions *vis-à-vis* good governance and democracy, albeit temporarily (?) distracted by the conflict in the Congo, are simply top-down pressures exerted by 'big brother' south of the Limpopo, acting as an agent of transnational capital. Such reductionism would be absurd. The push for a reconfiguration of the economic and political order in the region is driven by a multiplicity of actors, not least the various elite fractions within each discrete state who hope to benefit from a region more closely integrated into the global economy – or at least not suffer greater marginalisation and a further erosion of their status.

However, I suggest that such 'democratic' impulses and calls for good governance – encouraged for sure by the dominant state (in tandem with other external actors) – represents a fundamental attempt to make the region more attractive to international capital, at the expense of real development. It is this agenda that drives the regionalist project in Southern Africa, even if at critical junctures it seems to coincide with the aspirations of other, less powerful social actors.

This understanding leads to a pessimistic assessment for the region, for despite the calls for good governance and democracy, contradictions inherent in the polyarchical system mean that the future is not as closed as it may appear at first glance. This is because:

> By its very nature, [polyarchy] is designed to prevent any interference with the workings of the free market, including state redistributive policies . . . which could counterbalance the tendency in capitalism toward a concentration of income and productive resources. The neo-liberal model therefore generates the seeds of social instability and conditions propitious to the breakdown of polyarchy.
>
> (Robinson, 1996b: 344)

Furthermore, as I have suggested, the regionalist project current in Southern Africa is elite-driven, its main promoters are the leading fractions from the dominant state – South Africa – and the regionalist project overall is predicated upon 'growth'. Yet as the South African parliamentarian Ben Turok asserts, 'the pursuit of economic growth without the simultaneous pursuit of development will lead to a dead end' (quoted in *Mail and Guardian* (Johannesburg), 2–8 July 1999).

Unless the call for good governance is renegotiated to include not only a more regionally based agenda, but one that is more inclusive of forms of popular democracy (with greater concentration on notions such as social justice and equity), the push for a reconstitution of the region based on the principles outlined above holds within it inherent contradictions which cannot but contribute to a further erosion of the everyday lives of Southern African communities. Indeed, 'regional integration must . . . go beyond trade agreements because cross-border natural resources, environment, health, social and cultural relations are equally important for sustainable development and stability' (*Sunday Independent* (Johannesburg), 29 March 1999). Only once such issues are placed on the agenda, alongside a more progressive understanding of what good governance should entail, will any regional project in Southern Africa serve the interests of all its people. As the Zimbabwean opposition MP Margaret Dongo asserts:

> In the building of democracy it must be borne in mind that it is not simply about 'winning rights and liberties from an oppressive regime', but also about 'winning the individuals from themselves' to be citizens in a democratic polity. This task involves building democracy at both the subjective and objective levels – subjective with regard to culture and ideas, objective with regard to material conditions and social positions in society.
>
> (Dongo, 1998: 34)

Whether such progressive ingredients can be filtered into a reconstituted regionalism, in an epoch where harmonising tendencies tend to act against such popular aspirations and where regional co-operation and integration are predicated upon elite-driven concepts of what constitutes 'good governance' and 'democracy', will be the greatest challenge for a people-driven regional agenda in Southern Africa.

14 South Pacific Forum[1]

Survival under external pressure

Yoko Ogashiwa

The South Pacific Forum (SPF), an organization comprising fourteen Pacific Island countries plus Australia and New Zealand, has engaged in active regional co-operation for almost three decades. Indeed, the SPF has been quite highly regarded as a sub-regional organization of developing countries. Norman Palmer mentioned the SPF as one of 'the three most important comprehensive subregional organizations in Asia and the Pacific', along with the Association of Southeast Asian Nations (ASEAN) and the South Asian Association for Regional Co-operation (SARRC) (Palmer, 1991: 34). Similarly, William Tow considered the SPF to be a 'relatively more successful' sub-regional security organization, together with ASEAN, the Gulf Cooperation Council (GCC), the Organization of East Caribbean States (OECS) and the Southern African Development Coordination Conference (at present the Southern African Development Community – SADC) (Tow, 1990: 8). Both considered the SPF to be a consistently functioning regional organization in international society.

Unlike ASEAN, a renowned 'success story' (Palmer, 1991: 64), the SPF has not been sufficiently analysed. Rather, it is often considered as 'something on the other side of the globe' which seems isolated from broader global changes. However, the SPF's regional co-operation does directly relate to global processes and shows a clear nexus of global issues and regionalism.

In fact, the SPF has constantly faced external pressure stemming from global issues. Because of the geopolitical location of the South Pacific – being remote from the centres of the world – the burden and costs of global issues have been imposed on the region. For example, the region was used as nuclear testing sites and indeed has almost been used as a nuclear waste dumping site. It also faces the danger of being submerged into the ocean because of climate change generated mainly by greenhouse gas emissions in the industrialized countries. Furthermore, global economic liberalization has put the region in a predicament and forced it to take part in apparently disadvantageous economic competition.

Therefore, a question emerges. How has the SPF maintained and developed its regional co-operation without halt or collapse, even though it has been under enormous external pressure stemming from global issues? This chapter attempts to clarify how and why SPF regional co-operation has survived without being over-whelmed by external pressure from the organization's inception to the present amid constantly changing international relations. Through such an investigation, it aims to analyse the characteristics and significance of SPF regional co-operation.

In this chapter, the term 'regional co-operation' will be used to designate regional activities of the SPF. Regional co-operation, which has generally been thought of as a synonym for 'regionalism',[2] is defined here as intentional activity, conducted according to the situation, not for ideology or slogans. It is also distinguished from spontaneous regional formation or 'regionalization'.

Characteristics of Pacific Island countries

The SPF consists of sixteen member states: fourteen Pacific Island countries (Samoa, the Cook Islands, Nauru, Tonga, Fiji, Niue, Papua New Guinea, the Solomon Islands, Tuvalu, Kiribati, Vanuatu, the Marshall Islands, the Federated States of Micronesia and Palau), along with Australia and New Zealand. Among the Pacific Island countries, Samoa, Nauru, Tonga, Fiji, Papua New Guinea, the Solomon Islands, Tuvalu, Kiribati and Vanuatu are independent states. The rest are freely associated states: the Cook Islands and Niue with New Zealand; the Marshall Islands, the Federated States of Micronesia and Palau with the United States. The freely associated states normally hold self-governing status and diplomatic rights except in defence and security matters, areas which are referred to a partner of the compact of free association. Thus although they cannot be defined as independent states in a strict sense, they can be considered as political entities with respect to regional matters.[3]

The Pacific Island countries comprise the majority of SPF member states in terms of number. Apart from Papua New Guinea, all Pacific Island countries have been generally considered as 'microstates'. Although there is a wide variety of definitions about what constitutes a 'microstate', there is broad consensus regarding population size as a major element (Boyce, 1977: 233; Boyce and Herr, 1974: 24; Dommen, 1985: 13). Unfortunately, there is no clear consensus on a population ceiling. However, it miay be possible to set the population at less than one million as one criterion defining 'microstates', a figure that has been used in both the United Nations and Commonwealth circles (Harden, 1985: 9). Apart from Papua New Guinea, which has a population of 4.4 million (based on 1996 figures), all Pacific Island countries meet this criterion, with the smallest being Niue's at 2300 (based on 1994 data). Nevertheless, it is not sufficient to define 'microstates' by population size only, since the concept of 'microstates' normally implies a smallness of land area. The report of the United Nations Institute for Training and Research uses a figure of $143,000 km^2$ (Dommen, 1985: 10). Again, Papua New Guinea, which has a land area of $460,000 km^2$, would be excluded from definition as a 'microstate'.

The second characteristic of the Pacific Island countries is insularity. Scattered across the vast Pacific Ocean, which occupies about one-third of the earth's total area, they are isolated from other regions. The exception, again is Papua New Guinea, which shares a border with Indonesia. In addition, most of the Pacific Island countries consist of relatively small islands. Furthermore, the majority are archipelago states composed of a plurality of islands.

Third, the Pacific Island countries are developing countries. Their average GDP growth rate in 1995 was −4.3 per cent. According to the Asian Development Bank (ADB), the Pacific Island countries, except Niue and Palau which are not ADB members, face economic crisis in many forms (South Pacific Forum Secretariat, 1996a: 5–6). In particular, Samoa, the Solomon Islands, Tuvalu, Kiribati and Vanuatu are categorized as the least-developed countries among the Pacific Island countries.

The vulnerability of Pacific Island countries may be thought about in three ways. First, they are at an economic disadvantage[4] compared with other developing countries with bigger population size and land area, since their market size and export scale are small. They often rely on primary industries whose products are vulnerable to natural disaster. When a natural disaster does occur, therefore, the damage might disproportionately be critical to these small island countries. Furthermore, transport costs are high because of their location in a vast ocean, far from the world's major markets. While their land area is generally small, some of these countries contain a large sea area since they are archipelago states. For example, Kiribati has only 690 km^2 of land area, but its territory also comprises 3,550,000km^2 of sea, the largest sea area among all the Pacific Island countries. It is assumed that with vast sea areas there is an abundance of marine resources, such as fish, minerals, oil and gas. However, the Pacific Island countries lack sufficient physical and human resources to develop and utilize the marine resources as a way of potentially mitigating their economic vulnerability. Second, the Pacific Island countries have little political influence and their voices are – more often than not – ignored in the international arena. Finally, they lack resilience against political/military pressure and interference from major powers. Therefore, it is possible to label the Pacific Island countries as 'weak states'; that is, underdeveloped countries that are 'consumers of security and "price-takers" in economics' and who 'share a common grievance against the Great Power systems' (Rothstein, 1977: 42–3, 59).

There is a remarkable gap between the official status of the Pacific Island countries as independent (and self-governing) states and their actual situation. For the Pacific Island countries, appealing their rights and prestige as independent (and self-governing) states to the maximum may be a vital way towards improving such an unfavourable situation. In this respect, regional co-operation is the most obvious form to carry out such efforts. Through such co-operation, their presence might be increased and their voice enhanced, despite their fundamental vulnerability. This is reflected in the fact that the SPF has allowed only independent (and self-governing) states as official members from its inception. Kamisese Mara, then prime minister of Fiji who played an important role in forming the SPF, precisely defined it as an 'organization of the leaders of the states, who take responsibility for their own matters' (*New Zealand Foreign Affairs Review* [hereafter NZFAR], May 1974: 27).

It seems a natural consequence that the Pacific Island countries tend towards regional co-operation to survive in international relations. Through regional co-operation, they can obtain collective bargaining power *vis-à-vis* external powers, a situation not available to the individual countries. Furthermore, it creates leeway for repelling interference and pressure from major powers and simultaneously prevents those major powers from ignoring their presence. In addition, regional co-operation can help reduce high costs of international action imposed on individual countries through the sharing of institutions and services.

However, it is also true that the Pacific Island countries may find it difficult to pursue such regional co-operation. It is easier, more beneficial and more effective for them to link with major powers bilaterally, rather than carrying out multilateral co-operation with countries in similar circumstances. Even if they launch regional co-operation, they will face a high risk that the co-operation will collapse because of discord among members that lack the capacity for concession and compromise that larger countries tend to possess.

In addition, their geographical situation created social and cultural diversities that might prevent mutual understanding. The Pacific Island countries can be broadly divided into three major cultural regions: Polynesia, Melanesia and Micronesia. In each cultural region, the islands hold their own distinctiveness. Because of such a geographical situation, the Pacific Island countries may be considered as an area where mutual transactions have been infrequent. Even among islands where such communication has existed, it has led to conflicts and rivalries, and not necessarily to co-operation. In short, we must not think simply that the Pacific Island countries are inevitably oriented to regional co-operation because of their characteristics. Such characteristics *might* be a reason for SPF regional co-operation, but they alone do not answer sufficiently how and why SPF regional co-operation has survived. Comparative study tells us that it is not unusual for regional co-operation to stagnate and eventually cease with time, despite a spectacular start. Regional co-operation especially among developing countries often ends up in such a situation. When we consider how and why SPF regional co-operation has survived, there should be another answer beyond the characteristics of the Pacific Island countries.

Regional co-operation on nuclear issues: the formation and consolidation of the SPF[5]

In the 1960s, about a decade prior to the 1971 formation of the SPF, there emerged a crisis in the South Pacific region. In 1963, the French government announced the construction of nuclear testing sites in French Polynesia, and in 1966 it began nuclear testing. Western Samoa (at present Samoa) and the Cook Islands, two Pacific Island countries which had already gained independence or self-governance by that time, made strong protests to the French government, only to have their protests completely ignored (*Pacific Islands Monthly* [hereafter *PIM*], July 1963: 7; *PIM*, November 1965: 23; Stone, 1967: 156–7).

At the same time, the Pacific Island countries tried to make protest meetings of the existing regional organization. Prior to the formation of the SPF, the South Pacific Commission (SPC) (at present the Pacific Community) was established in 1947 for the economic and social development of Pacific Islanders. It was founded by the countries in possession of island territories in the region: Australia, New Zealand, the United States, France, the United Kingdom (withdrew in 1995) and the Netherlands (withdrew in 1962). Although the SPC contained an auxiliary body composed of delegates from Pacific Island countries called the South Pacific Conference, there existed a tacit principle of excluding political discussion from the conference, based on the intention of the founding countries. Despite this principle, the South Pacific Conference in 1965 saw a delegate from the Cook Islands calling for a resolution asking France to reconsider its planned nuclear testing (*PIM*, August 1965: 30). However, the conference turned down his request on the grounds that it was a political issue. Other attempts were made by the delegates of Fiji and Papua New Guinea at the conference in 1970 (*Fiji Times*, 24 September 1970; *Fiji Times*, 25 September 1970). Again, the conference failed to pass a resolution condemning French nuclear testing.

These incidents increased the need of the Pacific Island countries to create a separate forum outside the SPC in which they could discuss political issues. In 1971, five Pacific Island countries – Western Samoa, the Cook Islands, Nauru, Tonga and Fiji – held the first forum meeting in New Zealand's capital, Wellington. They held the meeting in New Zealand, not on an island, because some island leaders suspected Fiji of attempting to take the reins of leadership in the South Pacific (*NZFAR*, May 1974: 27). Fiji had joined the United Nations in 1970 as the first Pacific Island member and had expressed its wish to be a spokesperson for other Pacific Island countries that were not members of the UN (Boyce and Herr, 1974: 31–2). Thus although the Pacific Island countries decided to establish a forum, this did not mean that they were united with mutual trust and understanding.

In addition to the Pacific Island countries, Australia and New Zealand also attended the forum meeting. They were invited by the Pacific Island countries because the latter expected both countries to provide funding for the forum, imbue the forum with greater diplomatic impact, and correct the impression that the forum was anti-European (Mara, 1977: 105; *NZFAR*, May 1974: 26). For Australia and New Zealand, joining the forum was beneficial, as they were 'major powers' in the region, but not in the international arena. They could exercise greater diplomatic influence on the international scene collectively with the Pacific Island countries.

The SPF was thus formed as a political forum. The first forum meeting discussed French nuclear testing and adopted a final communiqué expressing deep regret over the testing (*NZFAR*, August 1971: 7). This represented the SPF's first joint protest. Even though it is difficult to measure the weight of the SPF protest, it certainly contributed to pressure on the French government. After the forum meeting, France announced that it had called off the remaining nuclear tests planned for 1971. The French newspaper *Le Monde* stated that the decision marked the first time a nuclear power had given in to pressure from countries in the Pacific Ocean area (Johnson and Tupouniua, 1976: 214).

Since that time, the SPF has developed regional co-operation against French nuclear testing. As well as adopting a final communiqué protesting against French nuclear testing at its forum meetings, the SPF endorsed a resolution opposing all nuclear tests, which Australia, New Zealand and Fiji jointly drafted for the 1972 UN General Assembly (Fiji Ministry of Foreign Affairs, 1972: 86–7). The organization also supported three countries in their 1973 attempt to present the issue of French nuclear testing to the International Court of Justice (*NZFAR*, April 1973: 16–17). These activities impressed on the international community the presence of the SPF as a regional organization. They also created an important foundation for regional co-operation centred on the SPF, which started without a founding agreement, permanent secretariat, or even – arguably – mutual trust among its members. After establishing regional co-operation against French nuclear testing, the SPF set up the South Pacific Bureau for Economic Co-operation (SPEC) (at present the Forum Secretariat) as its official secretariat in 1975 and started intra-regional co-operation, such as regional shipping services. The SPF member countries themselves also acknowledged the significance of SPF regional co-operation through the activities against French nuclear testing, and it became natural for newly independent island countries to join the SPF soon after independence.

SPF regional co-operation faced a different kind of nuclear issue in the 1980s. In 1980, the Japanese government announced that it would dump low-level nuclear waste produced by Japanese domestic nuclear reactors in the high seas of the Pacific Ocean near Japanese waters. The Japanese plan was met with strong opposition from SPF countries. The SPF meeting in the same year adopted a resolution condemning nuclear waste dumping in the Pacific Ocean (*Fiji Sun*, 16 July 1980).

Although Japan was not specifically named in the SPF resolution, the Japanese government was concerned about the SPF protest. It sent an official mission to several SPF countries to convince them of the safety of the plan. However, the SPF countries continued to demand that the plan be cancelled (*PIM*, September 1980: 9; *PIM*, October 1980: 5; *PIM*, November 1980: 35–6). The SPF meeting in the following year adopted a resolution naming Japan specifically and urged it to reconsider its plan to dumping nuclear waste (*NZFAR*, July to September 1981: 61).

Eventually, the Japanese government decided to abandon the plan. When Japanese Prime Minister Yasuhiro Nakasone visited Fiji during an official tour in 1985, he gave his assurances that Japan had decided not to dump or store nuclear waste in the Pacific Ocean (*Fiji Times*, 16 January 1985). The decision was made partly because Japan wanted to launch new policies towards the South Pacific, such as the 'Kuranari Doctrine', which aimed at a more active Japanese commitment to the region. It was apparent, however, that SPF's strong opposition put considerable pressure on Japan to change its attitude.

Further propelled by the activities against the Japanese plan of nuclear waste dumping in the Pacific Ocean, SPF regional co-operation moved ahead. At the SPF meeting in 1983, a proposal for the South Pacific Nuclear Free Zone was tabled by Australia. In the Australian proposal, nuclear testing was prohibited in the zone, but the passage and transit of nuclear-powered and nuclear-armed vessels and aircraft were not. Since Australia was a party to the ANZUS Treaty (a security agreement among Australia, New Zealand and the US signed in 1951), it tried not to jeopardize the treaty by referring to rights over whether to allow nuclear-powered and nuclear-armed vessels and aircraft into the ports and airfields of each member country. Since the views of other SPF member countries were split on this point, it was determined at the meeting to take more time to consider the Australian proposal (*NZFAR*, July to September 1983: 39–40; *Islands Business*, October 1983: 17).

It was at the SPF meeting in 1985 that the South Pacific Nuclear Free Zone Treaty was adopted. This allowed member countries to decide whether to accept nuclear-powered and armed vessels and aircraft into ports and airfields. Among the SPF member countries, Vanuatu and Tonga did not sign the treaty, with the former criticizing it as incomprehensive and partial, and the latter concerned about inter-ference from the Soviet Union, which was expected to sign the protocol of the treaty (*Vanuatu Weekly*, 17 August 1985; *Matangi Tonga*, May to June 1987: 36).[6]

Although other member countries agreed not to include the issue of port calls of nuclear-powered and -armed vessels and aircraft into the treaty, it did not mean that they simply swallowed the Australian proposal. In fact, it was difficult for the SPF member countries to include this issue into the treaty because their stances were so divergent. For example, New Zealand banned nuclear ship visits to its ports, while Tuvalu signed the Friendship Treaty with the US, stating that the two governments would consult about any American requests to use its territory for military purposes in times of crisis. It should also be pointed out that the other member countries made a modification to the original Australian proposal. In the original proposal, the issue of nuclear waste dumping was briefly mentioned in the preamble because Australia was concerned that potential nuclear dumping states, such as the US and France, would not sign the protocol if the issue was explicitly included in the treaty itself (Laka, 1985a: 6). The Solomon Islands, Papua New Guinea and Nauru presented an amendment to include the ban of nuclear waste dumping into the treaty, and it was adopted with the support of other member countries (Laka, 1985a: 6, 1985b: 12–13, 1985c: 4). The South Pacific Nuclear Free Zone Treaty thus marked itself as the first nuclear free zone treaty banning nuclear waste dumping in the ocean.

SPF regional co-operation was founded and consolidated through the 1970s and the 1980s to deal with external pressure (nuclear issues). During this period, there emerged consensus among the SPF member countries that SPF regional co-operation was something worth maintaining despite different views, as shown in the signing of the South Pacific Nuclear Free Zone Treaty. This helped to keep up the momentum of SPF regional co-operation, even though its intra-regional co-operation was not smooth, especially in the 1970s. The international reputation of the SPF as a regional organization playing a role in nuclear issues also acted as a block on member countries from becoming fragmented.

Regional co-operation on climate change issues: the multi-channelization of the SPF

During the early 1990s SPF regional co-operation was confronted by another external pressure: climate change issues generated by the phenomenon of global warming. It has been said that global warming would cause the sea-level to rise. This would have a serious and disproportionate effect upon the Pacific Island countries, which consist mostly of small low-lying atolls. Since climate change issues intersect in complex ways with the interests of various countries, the SPF has used multiple channels concurrently to make its voice heard in the international arena.

As with regional co-operation on nuclear issues, the SPF has been a fundamental channel for SPF member countries to convey their collective voice to the outside world. However, unlike the previous case, the SPF was not a sole channel. Besides adopting resolutions at its meetings and representing member nations at international conferences, the SPF played a significant role as a co-ordinating body to a larger regional organization and an inter-regional organization.

The South Pacific Regional Environment Programme (SPREP), established in 1980, was a regional agency specializing in environmental issues. The SPREP was composed of SPF member countries, non-independent island territories and three extra-regional countries which held island territories in the region, namely France and the US (see Figure 14.1). In terms of area covered, the SPREP was a larger regional organization than SPF. However, it was short of effectiveness and autonomy because it was jointly run by the SPC, the SPEC, the United Nations Environment Programme (UNEP) and the Economic and Social Commission for Asia and the Pacific (ESCAP).

The SPF tried to transform SPREP into a genuinely effective body and to use it as a vehicle to send a voice to the negotiating process of the international regime on climate change. Forming the core group within the SPREP, the SPF succeeded in its attempt in 1991, and the SPREP became an autonomous body with an independent budget and staff. After the SPREP gained autonomy, the SPF co-ordinated the voice of member countries on climate issues at meetings, tried to make that voice heard within the SPREP, and further used the SPREP as a channel to the international regime on climate change.

The SPF has also acted as a co-ordinating body to an inter-regional organization, the Alliance of Small Island States (AOSIS), formed in 1990. The AOSIS comprised forty-three small island states (thirty-eight members and five observers) in the Pacific, the Caribbean, the Indian Ocean, the Atlantic, the Mediterranean and the South China Sea, which were concerned about the damage caused to their islands by climate change (see Figure 14.1). Although the AOSIS affiliation took place on a national basis, the AOSIS has used existing regional organizations as co-ordinating bodies. In that sense, the AOSIS was an inter-regional organization that established a network of regional organizations of small island countries. The SPF sent a representative to the AOSIS co-ordinating committee, along with representatives from SPREP, the Caribbean Community Secretariat and an institution in the Indian Ocean. The SPF has used the AOSIS as another channel to convey its voice to the international regime on climate change.

The international regime on climate change was formed at the UN Conference on Environment and Development (UNCED) in Rio de Janeiro in 1992, where the Framework Convention on Climate Change (FCCC) was adopted. What the SPF

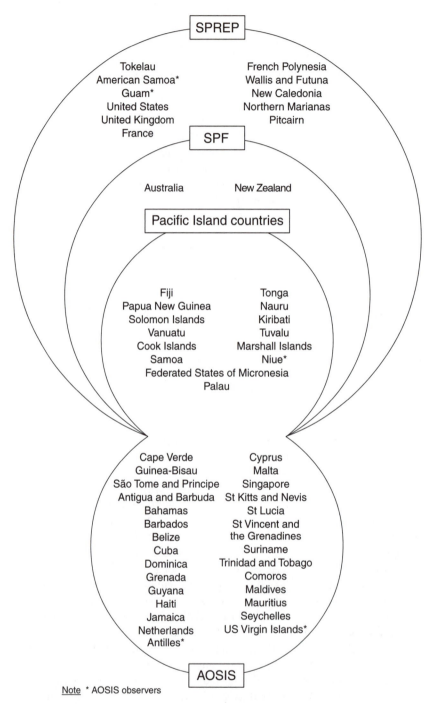

Note * AOSIS observers

Figure 14.1 Membership of the South Pacific Regional Environment Programme and the Alliance of Small Island States.

insisted upon through its three channels, namely the SPF, the SPREP and the AOSIS, was partly incorporated in the Convention. For example, reductions of industrially generated greenhouse gas emissions were mentioned in the Convention despite opposition from the US, the biggest emitter of carbon dioxide. However, the signatories were not bound to the article since the Convention itself just aimed at setting up a framework for common principles on climate change. The SPF was not fully satisfied with the result and it adopted a final communiqué at a Forum meeting which was held soon after the UNCED, urging the early commencement of negotiations of the protocol to implement and elaborate the Convention (South Pacific Forum Secretariat, 1992).

On the other hand, the SPF's request for funding and transfer of technology to the small island countries for tackling climate change was referred to in the Convention, and based on this, the Global Conference on the Sustainable Development of Small Island Developing States was held by the UN in Barbados in 1994. Again, the SPF used multiple channels in the conference to pursue its interests. The conference adopted the Programme of Action and the Barbados Declaration, stating that the international community should provide financial and technological resources to the small island developing countries which would be seriously affected by climate change (Global Conference on the Sustainable Development of Small Island Developing States, 1994a, 1994b). This encouraged the SPF to accelerate regional co-operation on climate change.

The next target for the SPF was adoption of the protocol of the FCCC. The Conference of the Parties (COP) of the FCCC had held four meetings by the end of 1998 and the protocol was adopted at the third meeting in Kyoto in 1997. Based on the initiative of the Pacific Island countries, the AOSIS presented its own proposal, the 'AOSIS Draft Protocol', requesting developed countries to reduce 20 per cent of carbon dioxide emissions based on 1990 levels by 2005 (Conference of the Parties to the United Nations Framework Convention on Climate Change, 1995; *Pacific Report*, 24 April). However, the Kyoto Protocol advocated, for the five years from 2008 to 2012, an 8 per cent reduction of greenhouse gas emissions for the EU, 7 per cent for the US and 6 per cent for Japan. Along with the AOSIS, the SPF felt that the reduction targets in the Kyoto Protocol were inappropriate (Conference of the Parties to the United Nations Framework Convention on Climate Change, 1997). To further enhance the international regime on climate change, it was expected that the SPF would continue its commitment to the regime through multiple channels such as the SPREP and the AOSIS.

The SPF responded to these 'external' climate change issues with a new style of regional co-operation using multiple channels to send a voice to the international regime. Generally, a sharp difference exists between developed countries and developing countries over these questions. While the latter insist that the former must take primary responsibility for climate change by reducing greenhouse gas emissions and providing funds and technology to them, the former believe that the latter also have a duty to reduce greenhouse gas emissions. There emerged a remarkable difference, not only between the North and South, but also within the North and South. In the North, EU and Scandinavian countries have supported the reduction of greenhouse gas emissions, while the US, Canada and Japan have been reluctant to agree to reductions. In the South, contrary to the SPF, the oil-producing countries have fundamentally taken a negative attitude towards the reduction of greenhouse gas emissions, as they are concerned about damage to their economies stemming from a decline in oil consumption. It was therefore more effective for the SPF to use multiple channels with respect to climate change issues, rather than developing a voice through only one channel in the international arena.

Regional co-operation through multiple channels also helped the SPF sustain regional co-operation despite cleavages of interest among its members. Until the adoption of the FCCC, Australia and New Zealand had kept pace with the Pacific Island countries as SPF members. However, they went along with the US, Canada and Japan – countries reluctant to reduce greenhouse gas emissions – as the negotiations of the protocol began. It was obviously difficult for them to support the reduction, especially because Australia was a major exporter of coal. Instead of persisting in unanimity at the SPF, the Pacific Island countries used multiple channels, such as the SPREP and the AOSIS, to pursue their interests. Regional co-operation through multiple channels provided a bypass for the Pacific Island countries to send their voice to the international regime, even if the two regional powers, Australia and New Zealand, were taking a different approach. This prevented both sides from developing dissatisfaction with the SPF, which kept the SPF itself intact.

Regional co-operation in global economic liberalization: the sub-regionalization of SPF

Almost at the same time as the SPF conducted regional co-operation to deal with climate change issues, it faced another external pressure: global economic liberalization. The Pacific Island countries in general had relied for their economic survival on aid from extra-regional donors and special trade treatment such as trade preferences and price-stabilization schemes. In the Cold War era the countries had a certain strategic value, although they were continuously under the 'ANZUS Umbrella', a security regime established by Australia, New Zealand and the US in 1951. They therefore received relatively large amounts of aid, mainly from Western countries. But their strategic value declined remarkably with the end of the Cold War, and accordingly the amount of aid received from donors also dropped. In addition, 'aid fatigue' of the donors caused a reduction in amount of aid.

Furthermore, economic liberalization on a global scale threatened the existence of special trade treatment on which the Pacific Island countries have also come to rely. The Pacific Island countries, as members of ACP (Africa, the Caribbean and the Pacific) countries, have enjoyed such special trade treatment offered by the EC (at present the EU) under the Lome Convention. Under the Convention, they have been allowed to export such commodities as sugar, coffee and canned fish to the EC market with preferences. The Lome Convention has also provided the Stabilization of Export Earnings System to compensate the ACP countries for fluctuations in market prices of commodities. It was expected that such special trade treatment would not remain intact due to increasing economic liberalization. The Pacific Island countries therefore had to be prepared for new economic trends and to find a way to survive economically.

Commitment to Asia–Pacific Economic Cooperation (APEC) was one solution the Pacific Island countries adopted to face global economic liberalization. The Pacific Island countries believed that by making a commitment to APEC, they could learn from the market-led policies of the Asian economies that had achieved dramatic economic growth, and diversify the international market by strengthening institutional and market linkages with Asia (South Pacific Forum Secretariat, 1995a: 4). The SPF meeting in 1991 mentioned APEC for the first time and came to an agreement that SPF member countries would enhance their relationship with APEC (South Pacific Forum Secretariat, 1991). However, among the SPF member countries, only Australia, New Zealand and Papua New Guinea maintained official membership status in APEC (see Figure 14.2). The SPF had to make contact with APEC only through the observer status it had held in APEC since the 1989 inaugural meeting, and through those SPF member countries which held full membership in APEC. Therefore, the first step for the SPF was to obtain recognition from APEC.

In 1995, the SPF indicated its position that it would adopt and implement APEC's principles of trade and investment liberalization. The SPF meeting of that year adopted a final communiqué and a plan of action for 'Securing Development Beyond 2000', stating that the SPF would adopt and implement the investment principles agreed to by APEC members, and work towards implementation of trade reform measures required by GATT/WTO (South Pacific Forum Secretariat, 1995b). Furthermore, the SPF circulated at the APEC Ministerial Meeting in Osaka in the same year a statement called 'South Pacific Forum Countries & APEC: An Important Relationship' to convey its attempts at liberalizing the economies of the Pacific Island countries through reductions in both tariff and non-tariff barriers to trade and investment (South Pacific Forum Secretariat, 1995a: 6). The SPF also started the economic ministers' meeting in 1996 and referred consideration to it regarding the next appropriate steps to maintain momentum in tariff reforms (South Pacific Forum Secretariat, 1996b).

The 1997 SPF economic ministers' meeting adopted an Action Plan which required SPF member countries to provide a policy environment to encourage private-sector development (South Pacific Forum Secretariat, 1997a). Based on the plan, the SPF meeting in the same year reaffirmed the commitment to free and open trade among the Pacific Island countries through tariff reform and ensuring investment transparency (South Pacific Forum Secretariat, 1997b). The SPF eventually decided, at its meeting in 1999, to establish the South Pacific Free Trade Area, which would be implemented over a period leading up to 2009 for developing Pacific Island countries and 2011 for the Smaller Island States and Least Developed Countries (South Pacific Forum Secretariat, 1999). Such efforts by the SPF for trade and investment liberalization aimed to gain recognition from APEC and to establish a close relationship with that organization, perhaps as one of its sub-regions, in order to survive economic liberalization on a global scale.

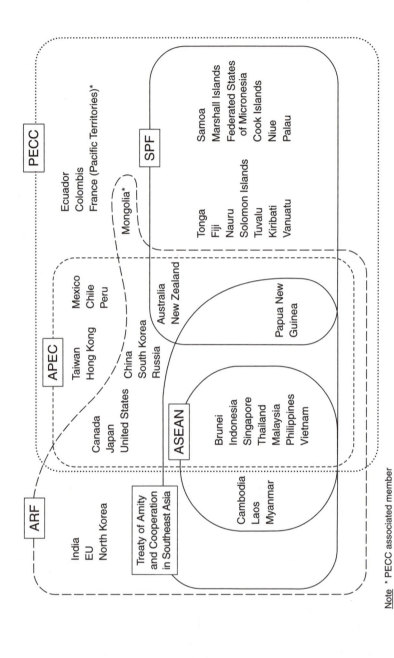

Note * PECC associated member

Figure 14.2 Multiple Regionalism in the Asia Pacific.

Nevertheless, it seemed that trade and investment liberalization was not necessarily the sole goal for the SPF in its relationship with APEC. While the SPF has been trying to follow APEC's principles of trade and investment liberalization, it also expected economic and technical co-operation from APEC, especially in the area of energy, telecommunications and information (South Pacific Forum Secretariat, 1995c). Economic and technical co-operation constituted one of the three pillars of APEC, but it has occupied less interest from APEC than trade and investment liberalization. It was not until the APEC Ministerial Meeting in Osaka in 1995 that this area began to achieve substantial progress. The meeting adopted the Osaka Action Agenda and a Japanese-initiated 'Partners for Progress' mechanism to promote economic and technical co-operation within APEC (Asia–Pacific Economic Co-operation, 1995a, 1995b). Furthermore, the APEC Ministerial Meeting in Manila in 1996 adopted the Framework for Strengthening Economic Co-operation and Development (Asia–Pacific Economic Co-operation, 1996). However, it has been observed that the development of economic and technical co-operation in APEC has stagnated in recent years because of the economic crisis experienced by Asian countries starting in 1997. Hence, it was not certain that SPF could obtain the expected economic and technical co-operation from APEC even through a close relationship.

The second problem for the SPF in its relationship with APEC was membership. The SPF has acted as a representative for Pacific Island countries that were not members of APEC. However, some countries, such as Fiji and the Solomon Islands, have shown an interest in obtaining full membership in APEC on their own terms (*Fiji Times*, 22 November 1993; *Pacific Report*, 22 May 1995). Since APEC decided in 1997 to introduce a new ten-year moratorium on the admittance of further members, the issue had been dormant in the SPF. Even if some Pacific Island countries apply to APEC for full membership after the moratorium on new membership ends, it may be difficult for them to obtain because of their small economic size. The most feasible alternative for the Pacific Island countries would be joining APEC as a collective body represented by the SPF, in the same way as they did the Pacific Economic Co-operation Council (PECC) (Papua New Guinea joined PECC as a member of the SPF) (see Figure 14.2), an international non-governmental organization for economic co-operation in the Pacific region, which was established in 1980. In that case, the SPF would be officially incorporated into APEC as a sub-region.

The third problem related to the creation of a special trade arrangement for Pacific Island countries in APEC. There was a voice among the Pacific Island countries asking for a Lomé Convention-type trade arrangement for them in APEC, including trade preferences and a trade stabilization scheme. Papua New Guinea in particular has been most vocal on this issue (*Papua New Guinea Post-Courier*, 9 February 1996; *Pacific Report*, 20 February 1996) and the idea was endorsed in 1996 at the meeting of the Melanesian Spearhead Group, a sub-group in the SPF which comprised the Melanesian Pacific Islands, Papua New Guinea, Solomon Islands, Vanuatu, Fiji, and Front de Liberation Nationale, Kanak et Socialist of New Caledonia (Melanesian Spearhead Group, 1996). Nevertheless, it was apparent that the creation of a special trade arrangement in

APEC for the Pacific Island countries was inconsistent with APEC's principles of trade liberalization. Consequently, the SPF would have to seek other possibilities rather than the creation of a special trade arrangement in APEC.

While the SPF continueds to seek a close relationship with APEC in an attempt to survive global economic liberalization, it also attempted to approach the Asian countries, like ASEAN and Japan, for the same purpose. Among the SPF member countries, Australia, New Zealand and Papua New Guinea were members of the ASEAN Regional Forum (ARF), a security forum in the Asia Pacific region, which was established at the initiative of ASEAN in 1994. Papua New Guinea also obtained special observer status in ASEAN in 1981, and signed the Treaty of Amity and Co-operation in Southeast Asia in 1987 (see Figure 14.2). While the SPF has obtained information on ASEAN through these members, it has maintained a certain relationship with ASEAN, especially in fisheries co-operation under the framework of PECC (see Figure 14.2).

Global economic liberalization accelerated SPF's commitment to ASEAN in the 1990s. When the SPF Secretary-General visited the ASEAN Secretariat in Jakarta in 1994, he proposed to send a Forum Secretariat officer to the ASEAN Secretariat to enable an assessment of ASEAN progammes that could benefit the SPF (Pacific Report, 13 June 1994). To further enhance the relationship with ASEAN, the SPF held a joint ministerial meeting with ASEAN in 1996.

Engaging Japan was another method through which the SPF sought to survive global economic liberalization. As indicated above, Japan initiated a substantial commitment to the South Pacific after launching the 'Kuranari Doctrine' in 1987. It has been one of the major aid donors to the Pacific Island countries and offered the funds to the SPF for a development programme. Because of global economic liberalization as well as increasing Japanese presence in the region, the SPF has invited Japan to the meeting for the dialogue partners which had special commitment to the region, and the Pacific Island countries/Development Partners meeting, where development and economic issues of the Pacific Island countries were discussed, to make the relationship more solid.

In response to the approach of the SPF, the Japanese government set up the South Pacific Economic Exchange Support Centre in Tokyo in 1996, which the SPF had requested since 1989 in order to enhance economic relations with Japan and promote economic development and independence of the Pacific Island countries. The centre is jointly run by the Japanese government and the Forum Secretariat. In addition, the Japanese government has conducted the Development of Unique Bio-Industries Seminar for the Pacific Island countries since 1994, focusing on their economic development with unique and sustainable bio-industries. Furthermore, it organized the Japan-SPF Summit Meeting (PALM) in 1997 and 2000, where the leaders agreed to promote Japan–SPF partnership through trade, investment, tourism, dialogue, communication, co-operation and exchanges (Joint Declaration on the Occasion of the Japan–South Pacific Forum Meeting, 13 October 1997; Miyazaki PALM Declaration, 22 April 2000).

Although the Asia Pacific region has not fully recovered from economic crises that began in 1997, it seemed that the SPF would continue to commit to APEC

and the Asian countries as a means to survive in the context of global economic liberalization. It was inevitable that the SPF would define itself as a sub-region of the
Asia Pacific macro region, and a new direction would be introduced to SPF
regional co-operation since the SPF has never formally considered itself as
attached to a higher level macro region. Put another way, the SPF has tried to
respond to global economic liberalization with sub-regionalization.

Conclusion

Let us go back to the question presented at the beginning of this chapter. How and
why has SPF regional co-operation survived even though it has been under constant external pressure stemming from global issues?

It should be stressed first that the SPF has responded to external pressure with a
flexible stance. Instead of strongly adhering to a rigid ideology of regional co-operation, the SPF has responded to external pressure by setting, and later transforming,
its style of regional co-operation according to the issues. It formed and consolidated
regional co-operation to deal specifically with nuclear issues. For climate change
issues, it has responded with multiple channels to send a 'South Pacific' voice effectively to the international regime. It has tried to survive global economic
liberalization by constructing itself as a sub-region of the Asia Pacific. This is a key
element for the survival and constant development of SPF regional co-operation,
and has thereby avoided the pitfalls that regional co-operation among developing
countries often faces. This flexible response has helped SPF regional co-operation to
adjust itself smoothly to changing international relations without being over-
whelmed by external pressure stemming from global issues.

Another important point is that the SPF has dealt with global issues in a regional
context. The SPF has perceived global issues as acute regional problems. This attitude prevented the SPF from handling issues beyond its capacity, ending with
bitter failure or losing confidence and credibility as a regional organization. For
example, the SPF has never taken an initiative in eliminating nuclear weapons in
the world while it has been active in banning nuclear testing and nuclear waste
dumping. Although SPF regional co-operation has been directly affected by global
issues, the SPF itself had no ambitions to play the role of a global actor.

It is possible to argue that SPF regional co-operation has responded to external
pressure stemming from global issues in a narrow regional perspective. Nevertheless,
it is important to note that this is the way in which SPF regional co-operation has
survived. In this respect, SPF regional co-operation surely sets a good example. It
also liberates us from stereotypical images of regional co-operation and enables us
to realize that there is a rich variety and diversity in successful regional co-operation.

Notes

1 The South Pacific Forum changed its name to the Pacific Islands Forum in 2000. An
   earlier version of this chapter appeared in *Hiroshima Peace Science* 22 (1999).
2 For discussion of the concept 'regionalism', see Hurrell (1995b: 39–45) and Hatsuse

(1997: 74–6).

3 One definition divides the Marshall Islands, the Federated States of Micronesia and Palau as independent countries from the Cook Islands and Niue as non-independent countries, since the latter have not joined the UN (Kobayashi, 1994: 107, 125). However, this chapter does not make such a distinction among them, since the Cook Islands, as well as Niue, have became party to international treaties, such as the UN Law of the Sea.

4 Exceptional among small island developing countries, Nauru has phosphate to sustain its economy. However, that resource is expected to become depleted in the near future.

5 See Ogashiwa (1991) for the details on SPF regional co-operation on nuclear issues.

6 Vanuatu signed the South Pacific Nuclear Free Zone Treaty in 1995 and Tonga signed in 1996. See Ogashiwa (1994) on the nuclear policy of Vanuatu at that time.

Bibliography

Acharya, A. (1991) 'Regionalism and regime security in the Third World: comparing the origins of the ASEAN and the GCC', in Job, Brian L. (ed.) *The (In)security Dilemma: National Security of Third World States* (Boulder, CO: Lynne Rienner).

Acharya, A. (1992) 'Regional military–security cooperation in the Third World: a conceptual analysis of the Association of Southeast Asian Nations'. *Journal of Peace Research* 29(1).

Acharya, A. (1995a) 'Regional organizations and UN peacekeeping', in Thakur, R. and Thayer, C. (eds) *UN Peacekeeping in the 1990s* (Boulder, CO: Westview Press).

Acharya, A. (1995b) 'Transnational production and security: Southeast Asia's growth triangles', *Contemporary Southeast Asia* 17(2).

Acharya, A. (1995c) *Human Rights in Southeast Asia: Dilemmas of Foreign Policy* (Eastern Asia Policy Papers no.11) (Toronto: University of Toronto – York University Joint Centre for Asia Pacific Studies).

Acharya, A. (1997a) 'Ideas, identity and institution-building: from the 'ASEAN Way' to the 'Asia Pacific Way', *Pacific Review* 10(2).

Acharya, A. (1997b) *Sovereignty, Non-Intervention, and Regionalism* (CANCAPS Paper no.15) (Toronto: Canadian Consortium on Asia Pacific Security).

Acharya, A. (1998) 'Collective identity and conflict management in Southeast Asia', in Adler, E. and Barnett, M. (eds) *Security Communities* (Cambridge: Cambridge University Press).

Acharya, A. (1999) 'Realism, institutionalism, and the Asian economic crisis', *Contemporary Southeast Asia* 21(1).

Acharya, A. (2000) *The Quest for Identity: International Relations of Southeast Asia* (Singapore: Oxford University Press).

Adler, E. (1998) 'Seeds of peaceful change: the OSCE's security community-building model', in Adler, E. and Barnett, M. (eds) *Security Communities* (Cambridge: Cambridge University Press).

Adler, E. and Barnett, M. (eds) (1998a) *Security Communities* (Cambridge: Cambridge University Press).

Adler, E. and Barnett, M. (1998b) 'A framework for the study of security communities', in Adler, E. and Barnett, M. (eds) *Security Communities* (Cambridge: Cambridge University Press).

Africa Today (1997) Special issue 'The future of regional studies' 44(2).

African Development Bank (1993) *Economic Integration in Southern Africa* (Abidjan: African Development Bank) (3 vols).

Aggarwal, V. (1993)'Building international institutions in the Asia–Pacific', *Asian Survey* 23(11).

Ahmed, Z.H. and Baladas Ghoshal, B. (1999) 'ASEAN's political evolution and the Indonesian crisis', *International Affairs* 75(4).

Ahwireng-Obeng, F. and McGowan, P. (1998) 'Partner or hegemon? South Africa in Africa', *Journal of Contemporary African Studies* 16(1).

Ajulu, R. (2000) 'Thabo Mbeki's African Renaissance in a globalising world economy: the struggle for the soul of a continent', paper delivered at the ROAPE Millennium conference, University of Leeds, 28–30 April.

AK (1989) *Europa Stellungnahme des Österreichischen Arbeiterkammertages* (Wien: AK).

Ake, C. (1996) 'How misconceptions devalue democracy', *Southern African Political and Economic Monthly* 10(2).

Albert, M. (1993) *Capitalism Against Capitalism* (London: Whurr).

Ali, Taisier M. and Matthews, Robert O. (1999) *Civil Wars in Africa* (Montreal and Kingston: McGill–Queen's University Press).

Althaler, K.S. *et al.* (1988) *AUSWEG–EUROPA? Wirschaftspolitische Optionen für Österreich* (Wien: Falter Verlag).

Amin, S. (1972) 'Underdevelopment and dependence in Black Africa: origins and contemporary forms', *Journal of Modern African Studies* 10(4).

Amsden, A. (1989) *Asia's Next Giant: South Korea and Late Industrialization* (Oxford: Oxford University Press).

Andersen, R.B. (1994) 'Inter-IGO dynamics in the post-Cold War era: the O.A.S. and the UN', paper presented at Annual Convention of the International Studies Association, Washington, DC, 28 March to 1 April.

Anderson, K. and Blackhurst, R. (1992) 'Trade, the environment and public policy', in Anderson, K. and Blackhurst, R. (eds) *The Greening of World Trade Issues* (Brighton: Harvester Wheatsheaf, 1992).

Andersson, T., Fredriksson, T. and Svensson, R. (1996) *Multinational Restructuring, Internationalization and Small Economies: The Swedish Case* (London: Routledge).

Archibugi, D. and Michie, J. (1997) 'Technological globalisation and national systems of innovation: an introduction', in Archibugi, D. and Michie, J. (eds) *Technology, Globalisation and Economic Performance* (Cambridge: Cambridge University Press).

ASEAN Regional Forum (1995) 'Chairman's statement: the Second ASEAN Regional Forum'.

ASEAN Regional Forum (1996) 'Chairman's statement: the Third ASEAN Regional Forum'.

ASEAN Regional Forum (1997) 'Chairman's statement: the Fourth ASEAN Regional Forum'.

ASEAN Secretariat (1998) *The Hanoi Plan of Action*, Kuala Lumpur, 12 December.

Asian Development Bank (1997) *Emerging Asia: Changes and Challenges* (Manila: ADB).

Asia–Pacific Economic Cooperation (1995a) 'The Osaka Action Agenda: Implementation of the Bogor Declaration'.

Asia–Pacific Economic Cooperation (1995b) Asia–Pacific Economic Cooperation Ministerial Meeting: 'Partners for Progress'.

Asia–Pacific Economic Cooperation (1996) Asia–Pacific Economic Cooperation Ministerial Meeting: joint statement.

Aulakh, P.S. and Schechter, M.G (eds) (2000) *Rethinking Globalization(s): From Corporate Transnationalism to Local Interventions* (Basingstoke: Macmillan).

Axline, A.W. (ed.) (1994) *The Political Economy of Regional Cooperation. Comparative Case Studies* (London: Pinters).

Azis, I.J. (1996) 'Resolving possible tensions in ASEAN's future trade – using analytical hierarchy process', *ASEAN Economic Bulletin* 12(3).

Bach, D. and Hveem, H. (1998) 'Regionalism, regionalization and globalization', paper presented at Third Pan-European International Relations conference and joint meeting with the International Studies Association, Vienna, 16–19 September.

Balassa, B. (1962) *The Theory of Economic Integration* (London: Allen & Unwin).

Bándi, G. (1996) 'Deregulation as an environmental policy instrument in Hungary', paper presented at workshop on 'Deregulation and the Environment', European University Institute, Florence, May.

Barnard, D. (ed.) (1997) *PRODDER: The Southern African Development Directory, 1997/8* (Braamfontein: HSRC).

Barnard, D. (ed.) (1998) *PRODDER: The South African Development Directory, 1998/9* (Braamfontein: HSRC).

Barnett, M. and Gregory Gause III, F. (1998) 'Caravans in the opposite direction: society, state and the development of a community in the Gulf Cooperation Council', in Adler, E. and Barnett, M. (eds) *Security Communities* (Cambridge: Cambridge University Press, 1998).

Bartlett, R. (1993) *The Making of Europe: Conquest, Colonization and Cultural Change, 950–1350* (New York: Penguin Books).

Batt, J. (2001) 'European identity and national identity in Central and Eastern Europe', in Wallace, H. (ed.) *Whose Europe? Interlocking Dimensions of Integration* (Basingstoke: Palgrave).

Baylis, J. and Smith, S. (eds) (1997) *The Globalization of World Politics: An Introduction to International Relations* (Oxford: Oxford University Press).

Bayoumi, T. and Mauro, P. (1999) 'The suitability of ASEAN for a regional currency arrangement', *Working Paper of the International Monetary Fund*, WP/99/162, December.

Beddoes, Z.M. (1999) 'From EMU to AMU? The case for regional currencies', *Foreign Affairs* 78(6).

Beeson, M. (1999) 'Reshaping regional institutions: APEC and the IMF in East Asia', *Pacific Review* 12(1).

Bello, W. (1999a) 'Architectural blueprints, development models, and political strategies', *Focus On Trade* 34, April.

Bello, W. (1999b) 'East Asia: on the eve of the great transformation', *Review of International Political Economy* 5(3).

Berger, M.T. (1999) 'APEC and its enemies: the failure of the new regionalism in the Asia Pacific', *Third World Quarterly* 20(5).

Bergsten, C.F. (1998) 'How to target exchange rates', *Financial Times*, 20 November.

Bergsten, C.F. (1998) 'Reviving the Asian Monetary Fund', *International Economic Policy Briefs* 98(8).

Bernard, M. and Ravenhill, J. (1995) 'Beyond product cycles and flying geese: regionalization, hierarchy and industrialization in East Asia', *World Politics* 47(2).

Bhagwati, J. (1992) 'Regionalism and multilateralism: an overview', paper presented at World Bank and CEPR Conference on 'New Dimensions on Regional Integration', Washington, DC, April.

Bieler, A. (2000) *Globalisation and Enlargement of the European Union: Austrian and Swedish Social Forces in the Struggle over Membership* (London: Routledge).

Biers, D. (ed.) (1998) *Crash of '97* (Hong Kong: Review Publishing Company).

Blecker, R. (1999) *Taming Global Finance: A Better Architecture for Growth and Equity* (Washington, DC: Economic Policy Institute).

Blomstrom, M. and Kokko, A. (1997) 'Regional integration and FDI', *NBER Working Paper W6019*, April.

Bøås, M. (1998) 'Governance as multilateral development bank policy: the cases of the

African Development Bank and the Asian Development Bank', *European Journal of Development Research* 10(2).

Bøås, M. and Hveem, H. (forthcoming) 'Regionalisms compared: the African and Southeast Asian experience', in Hettne, B., Inotai, A. and Sunkel, O. (eds) *Comparing Regionalisms: Implications for Global Development* (Basingstoke: Macmillan).

Bøås, M., Marchand, M.H. and Shaw, T.M. (eds) (1999a) 'New regionalisms in the new millennium', Special Issue of *Third World Quarterly* 20(5).

Bøås, M., Marchand, M.H. and Shaw, T.M. (eds) (1999b) 'Special Issue: New regionalisms in the new millennium', Special Issue of *Third World Quarterly* 20(5).

Bøås, M., Marchand, M.H. and Shaw, T.M.. (1999c) 'The Weave-world – regionalisms in the South in the new millennium', Special Issue of *Third World Quarterly* 20(5).

Bobrow, D. (1999) 'The US and ASEM: why the hegemon did not bark', *Pacific Review* 12(1).

Boutwell, J. and Klare, M.T. (eds) (1999) *Light Weapons and Civil Conflict: Controlling the Tools of Violence* (Lanham: Rowman and Littlefield for AAAS and Carnegie Commission).

Bouzas, R. (1999) 'Mercosur's external trade negotiations: dealing with a congested agenda', in Roett, R. (ed.) *Mercosur: Regional Integration, World Markets* (Boulder, CO: Lynne Rienner).

Bowles, P. (1997) 'ASEAN, AFTA and the "new regionalism"', *Pacific Affairs* 70(2).

Bowles, P. and MacLean, B. (1996) 'Understanding trade bloc formation: the case of the ASEAN free trade area', *Review of International Political Economy*, 3(2).

Boyce, P. J. (1977) *Foreign Affairs for New States: Some Questions of Credentials* (Brisbane: Queensland University Press).

Boyce, P. J. and Herr, R. A. (1974) 'Microstate diplomacy in the South Pacific', *Australian Outlook* 28(1).

Boyer, R. and Drache, D. (eds) (1996) *States against Markets: The Limits of Globalization* (London: Routledge).

Braathen, E., Bøås, M. and Sæther, G. (eds) (2000) *Ethnicity Kills? The Politics of War, Peace and Ethnicity in Sub-Saharan Africa* (Basingstoke: Macmillan).

Brænden, I.B. (1996) *Linking Trade and the Environment: NAFTA and the Environmental Side Agreement*, Dissertations and Theses No. 11 (Centre for Development and the Environment – University of Oslo, 1996).

Braunerhjelm, P. and Oxelheim, L. (1996) 'Structural Implications of the investment response by Swedish multinational firms to the EC 1992 Program', in Hirsch, S. and Almor, T. (eds) *Outsiders' Response to European Integration* (Copenhagen: Handelshøjskolens Forlag).

Braunerhjelm, P., Ekholm, K., Grundberg, L. and Karpaty, P. (1996) 'Swedish multinational corporations: recent trends in foreign activities', *The Industrial Institute for Economic and Social Research: Working Paper* 462.

Breit, J. and Rössl, D. (1992) 'Internationalisierung der Klein- und Mittelbetriebe', in Clement, W. (ed.) *Neue Entwicklungen – neue Formen – neue Herausforderungen. Internationalisierung Band VI* (Wien: Signum Verlag).

Breslin, S. (2000) 'Decentralisation, globalisation and China's partial re-engagement with the global economy' *New Political Economy* 5(2).

Bretherton, C. and Vogler, J. (1999) *The European Union as a Global Actor* (London: Routledge, 1999).

Breuss, F. and Stankovsky, J. (1988) *Österreich und der EG-Binnenmarkt* (Wien: Signum Verlag).

Brown, C. (ed.) (1994) *Political Restructuring in Europe: Ethical Perspectives* (London: Routledge).

Brown, L.H. (1986) 'Regional collaboration in resolving Third-World conflicts', *Survival* 28(3).

Brusco, S., Bertossi, P. and Cottica, A. (1996) 'Playing on two chessboards – the European waste management industry: strategic behaviour in the market and the policy debate', in Lévèque, F. (ed.) *Environmental Policy in Europe* (Aldershot: Edward Elgar).

Bryans, M., Jones, B. and Skin, J. (1999) 'Mean times: humanitarian action in complex emergencies – stark choices, cruel dilemmas' (Toronto: University of Toronto), *Coming to Terms* 1(3).

Buarque, C. (1993) *The End of Economics? Ethics and the Disorder of Progress* (London: Zed Books).

Buigues, P. and Sapir, A. (1993) 'Community industrial policies', in Nicolaides, P. (ed.) *Industrial Policy in the European Community: A Necessary Response to Economic Integration?* (Dordrecht: Martinus Nijhoff).

Bulger, P. (n.d.) 'Mbeki – Africa's prophet of boom'.

Bull, H. (1977) *The Anarchical Society* (London: Macmillan).

Bulmer-Thomas, V. (1999) 'The Brazilian devaluation: national responses and international consequences', *International Affairs* 74(4).

Burgueno, C. (1999) 'Mercosur Summit conclusions reported', *Ambito Financiero* (Buenos Aires) 16 June.

Burnham, P. (1994) 'Open Marxism and vulgar international political economy', *Review of International Political Economy* 1(2).

Busch, M. and Milner, H.V. (1994) 'The future of the international trading system: international firms, regionalism and domestic politics', in Stubbs, R. and Underhill, G.R.D. (eds) *Political Economy and the Changing Global Order* (Basingstoke: Macmillan).

Bush, R. and Szeftel, M. (1998) 'Commentary: "Globalization" and the regulation of Africa', *Review of African Political Economy* 76.

Buzan, B. (1991a) 'Third World regional security in structural and historical perspective', in Job, B.L (ed.) *The (In)security Dilemma: National Security of Third World States* (Boulder, CO: Lynne Rienner).

Buzan, B. (1991b) *People, States and Fear: An Agenda for International Security Studies in the Post-Cold War Era* (Hemel Hempstead: Harvester-Wheatsheaf).

Buzan, B., Waever, O. and de Wilde, J. (1998) *Security: A New Framework for Analysis* (Boulder, CO: Lynne Rienner).

BWK (1987) 'Stellungnahme der Bundeswirtschaftskammer zur Europäischen Integration; 09.12.1987 (Auszug)', in Kunnert, G. (ed.) *Spurensicherung auf dem österreichischen Weg nach Brüssel* (Wien: Verlag der Österreichischen Staatsdruckerei).

Byrnes, M. (1994) *Australia and the Asia Game* (London: Allen & Unwin).

Cahiles-Magkilat, B. (1999) 'Manila reviews position on AFTA zero tariff on imports', *Manila Bulletin*, 21 April.

Calder, K. (1996) *Asia's Deadly Triangle: How Arms, Energy and Growth Threaten to Destabilize the Asia–Pacific* (London: Nicholas Brealey).

Caporaso, J. (1978) 'Dependence, dependency and power in the international system', *International Organization* 32 (1).

Cardoso, F.H. (1999) 'Mercosur–EU: hour of decision', *Jornol do Brasil* (Rio de Janeiro) 20 June.

Castellano, M. (1999) 'Internationalisation of the Yen: A Ministry of Finance pipe dream?', *JEI Report* 23A (18 June).

Castells, M.(1989) *The Informational City* (Oxford: Blackwell).

Cecchini, P. (1988) *The European Challenge 1992: The Benefits of a Single Market* (Aldershot: Wildwood House).

Cerny, P.G. (1997) 'Paradoxes of the competition state: the dynamics of political globalization', *Government and Opposition* 32(2).

Chabal. P. and Daloz, J-P. (1999) *Africa Works: Disorder as Political Instrument* (Oxford: James Currey for IAI).

Chanwirot, P. (1998) 'Can ASEAN survive the regional crisis?', *The Nation* (Bangkok), 28 September.

Chayes, A. and Chayes, A.H. (1995) *The New Sovereignty: Compliance with International Regulatory Agreements* (Cambridge, MA: Harvard University Press).

Chen, E. and Kwan, C.H. (eds) (1997) *Asia's Borderless Economy: The Emergence of Sub-regional Zones* (St Leonards, NSW: Allen & Unwin).

Child Poverty Action Group (1996) *Poverty: The Facts* (London: Child Poverty Action Group).

Ching, F. (1999) 'ASEAN: stronger after crisis?', *Far Eastern Economic Review*, 25 February.

Christiansen, T., Jørgensen, K.E. and Wiener, A. (eds) (2001) *The Social Construction of Europe* (London: Sage).

Churchill, W. (1950) *The Hinge of Fate* (Boston, MA: Houghton Mifflin).

Cilliers, J. (1999) 'Regional African peacekeeping capacity: mythical construct or essential tool?', *African Security Review* 8(4).

Cilliers, J. and Mason, P. (eds) (1999) *Peace, Profit or Plunder? The Privatisation of Security in War-torn African Societies* (Halfway House: ISS).

Clapham, C. (1996) *Africa and the International System: The Politics of State Survival* (Cambridge: Cambridge University Press).

Clapham, C. (ed.) (1998) *African Guerrillas* (Oxford: James Currey).

Claude, I. (1963) *Swords into Plowshares: The Problems and Progress of International Organization* (New York: Random House).

Clemens, W.C. (1998) *Dynamics of International Relations: Conflict and Mutual Gain in an Era of Global Interdependence* (Lanham: Rowman and Littlefield).

Cliffe, L.(ed.) (1999) 'Special Issue: Complex political emergencies', *Third World Quarterly* 20(1).

Coleman, W.D. and Underhill, G.R.D. (eds) (1998) *Regionalism and Global Economic Integration: Europe, Asia and the Americas* (London: Routledge).

Conference of the Parties to the United Nations Framework Convention on Climate Change (1995) *Paper No. 19: Trinidad and Tobago* (on behalf of the Alliance of Small Island States).

Conference of the Parties to the United Nations Framework Convention on Climate Change (1997) *Report of the Conference of the Parties on its Third Session*.

Court, J. (1999) 'Development Research: directions for a new century', *UNU Work in Progress* 16(1).

Cox, R.W. (1981) 'Social forces, states and world orders: beyond international relations theory', *Millennium: Journal of International Studies* 10(2).

Cox, R.W. (1983) 'Gramsci, hegemony and international relations: an essay on method', *Millennium: Journal of International Studies* 12(2).

Cox, R.W. (1987) *Production, Power And World Order: Social Forces in the Making of History* (New York: Columbia University Press).

Cox, R.W. (1989) 'Production, the state and change in world order', in Czempiel, E-O. and Rosenau, J.N. (eds) *Global Changes and Theoretical Challenges: Approaches to World Politics for the 1990s* (Lexington, MA/Toronto: Lexington Books).

Cox, R.W. (1992) 'Global Perestroika', in Miliband, R. and Panitch, L. (eds) *The Socialist Register, 1992* (London: Merlin Press).

Cox, R.W. (1993) 'Structural issues of global governance: implications for Europe', in Gill, S. (ed.) *Gramsci, Historical Materialism and International Relations* (Cambridge: Cambridge University Press, 1993).

Cox, R.W. (1994) 'Global restructuring: making sense of the changing international political economy', in Stubbs, R. and Underhill, G.R.D. (eds) *Political Economy and the Changing Global Order* (Basingstoke: Macmillan).

Cox, R.W. (1999) 'Civil society at the turn of the millennium: prospects for an alternative world order', *Review of International Studies* 25(1).

Cox, R.W. with Sinclair, T.J. (1996) *Approaches to World Order* (Cambridge: Cambridge University Press).

Crawford, D. (2000) 'Chinese capitalism: cultures, the Southeast Asian region and economic globalization', *Third World Quarterly* 21(1).

Crawford, N.C. and Klotz, A. (eds) (1999) *How Sanctions Work: Lessons from South Africa* (Basingstoke: Macmillan).

Cumings, B. (1993) 'Rimspeak; or, the discourse of the "Pacific Rim"', in Dirlik, A. (ed.) *What is in a Rim? Critical Perspectives on the Pacific Region Idea* (Boulder, CO: Westview Press).

Current History (1999a) Special Issue on 'Africa's Wars' 98(628) May.

Current History (1999b) Special issue on 'Rethinking the Third World' 98(631) November.

Davis, E. (1993) 'Industrial policy in an integrated European economy', in Nicolaides, P. (ed.) *Industrial Policy in the European Community: A Necessary Response to Economic Integration?* (Dordrecht: Martinus Nijhoff).

de Melo, J. and Panagariya, A. (eds) (1993) *New Dimensions in Regional Integration* (Cambridge: Cambridge University Press).

Dean, J. (1992)'Trade and environment: a survey of the literature', in Low, P. (ed.) *International Trade and the Environment* (Washington, DC: The World Bank, 1992).

Dent, C. (1998) 'The ASEM: managing the new framework of the EU's economic relations with East Asia', *Pacific Affairs* 70(4).

Department of Foreign Affairs (DFA) (1996) *Draft Discussion Document on a Framework for Co-operation with the Countries in the Southern African Region*, Pretoria: Department of Foreign Affairs, Occasional Paper no. 1/96.

Department of Foreign Affairs and Trade (DFAT) (1998) *The APEC Region Trade and Investment* (Canberra: Department of Foreign Affairs and Trade).

Department of the Environment, Transport and Regions (DETR) (1997) *Building Partnerships for Prosperity: Sustainable Growth. Competitiveness and Employment in the English Regions* Cm. 3814 (London: Department of the Environment, Transport and Regions).

Deutsch, K.W. (1981) 'On nationalism, world regions and the nature of the West', in Torsvik, P. (ed.) *Mobilization, Center–Periphery Structures and Nation-Building: A Volume in Commemoration of Stein Rokkan* (Bergen: Universitetsforlaget).

Deutsch, K.W., Burrell, S.A. and Kann, R.A. (1957) *Political Community in the North Atlantic Area: International Organization in the Light of Historical Experience* (Princeton, NJ: Princeton University Press).

Dewitt, D. and Acharya, A. (1995) *Refugees, Security and International Politics: The Principles and Practices of Burden-Sharing* (Toronto: York University, Centre for Refugee Studies).

DG III (1998) *A Common Approach to Enhanced Competitiveness: D.G.III Work Programme 1998* (Brussels: European Commission, Directorate General III-Industry).

DG III (1999) *Work Programme 1999* (Brussels: European Commission, Directorate General III-Industry).

Di Palma, G. (1990) *To Craft Democracies* (Berkeley, CA: University of California Press).

Diamond, L., Linz, J. and Lipset, S.M. (1988) *Democracy in Developing Countries* (Boulder, CO: Lynne Rienner).

Dicklitch, S. (1998) *The Elusive Promise of NGOs in Africa: Lessons from Uganda* (Basingstoke: Macmillan).

Dickson, A.K. (1997) *Development and International Relations: A Critical Introduction* (Cambridge: Polity Press).

Dieter, H. (2000) *Monetary Regionalism: Regional Integration without Financial Crises*, University of Warwick, Centre for the Study of Globalisation and Regionalisation, Working Paper 52/00.

Dirlik, A. (1993a) 'Introducing the Pacific', in Dirlik, A. (ed.) *What is in a Rim? Critical Perspectives on the Pacific Region Idea* (Boulder, CO: Westview Press).

Dirlik, A. (1993b) 'The Asia–Pacific in Asian–American perspective', in Dirlik, A. (ed.) *What is in a Rim? Critical Perspectives on the Pacific Region Idea* (Boulder, CO: Westview Press).

Dludlu, J. (1998) 'SADC agrees on interregional free trade plan', *The Star* (Johannesburg) 20 August.

Dobson, W. (1999) 'East Asia and the international financial system', Study Group of the Trilateral Commission, Beijing, 24–25 October.

Dommen, E. (1985) 'What is a microstate?', in Dommen, E. and Hein, P. (eds) *States, Microstates and Islands* (London: Croon Helm).

Dongo, M. (1998) 'Establishing democracy in Southern Africa', in Mills, G. (ed.) *Southern Africa into the Next Millennium* (Johannesburg: SAIIA).

DTI (1988) *DTI – The Department for Enterprise* (London: Department of Trade and Industry).

DTI (1998) *Our Competitive Future: Building the Knowledge Driven Economy*, Cm. 4176 (London: The Stationery Office).

Duffield, M. (1999) 'Globalization and war economies: promoting order or the return of history?', *Fletcher Forum of World Affairs* 23(2).

Duffy, C.A. and Feld, W.J. (1980) 'Whither regional integration theory', in Boyd, G. and Feld, W.J. (eds) *Comparative Regional Systems* (New York: Pergamon Press).

Dunn, K. and Shaw, T.M. (eds) (2001) *Africa's Challenge to International Relations Theory* (Basingstoke: Macmillan).

Eccleston, B. and Potter, D. (1996) 'Environmental NGOs and different political contexts in Southeast Asia: Malaysia, Indonesia and Vietnam', in Parnwell, M.J.G and Bryant, R.L. (eds) *Environmental Change in Southeast Asia. People, Politics and Sustainable Development* (London: Routledge).

Edwards, S. (1997) 'Latin America's underperformance', *Foreign Affairs*, 76(2).

Eichengreen, B. (1998) 'Does Mercosur need a single currency?', *NBER Working Paper W6821*, September.

Eichengreen, B. (1999) *Toward a New International Financial Architecture: A Practical Post–Asia Agenda* (Washington, DC: Institute for International Economics).

Epstein, G. (1994) 'International profit rate equalization and investment', in Epstein, G. and Gintis, H. (eds) *Macroeconomics After the Conservative Era* (Cambridge: Cambridge University Press).

Esty, D.C. (1994) *Greening the GATT: Trade, Environment and the Future* (Washington, DC: Institute for International Economics).

Etzioni, M. (1970) *The Majority of One: Towards a Theory of Regional Compatibility* (Beverley Hills, CA: Sage Publications).

European Commission (1990) *Industrial Policy in an Open and Competitive Environment: Guidelines for a Community Approach* (Brussels: European Commission) COM (90) 556.

European Commission (1993) *Growth, Competitiveness, Employment: The Challenges and Ways Forward into the 21st Century: White Paper* (Brussels: European Commission) COM (93) 700.

European Commission (1994) *An Industrial Competitiveness Policy for the European Union: Communication from the Commission* (Brussels: European Commission) COM (94) 319.

European Commission (1996a) *The First Action Plan for Innovation in Europe: Innovation and Growth for Employment* (Luxembourg: Office for Official Publications of the European Communities) COM (96) 589.

European Commission (1996b) *Benchmarking the Competitiveness of European Industry: Communication from the Commission* (Luxembourg: Office for Official Publications of the European Communities) COM (96) 463.

European Commission (1997) *The Competitiveness of European Industry* (Luxembourg: Office for Official Publications of the European Communities).

European Commission (1998a) *The Competitiveness of European Industry: 1998 Report* (Brussels: European Commission).

European Commission (1998b) *Promoting Entrepreneurship and Competitiveness: The Commission's Response to the BEST Task Force Report and its Recommendations* (Brussels: European Commission) COM (98) 550.

European Commission (1998c) *The Competitiveness of European Enterprises in the Face of Globalisation: How it Can be Encouraged. Communication from the Commission to the Council, the European Parliament, the Economic and Social Committee and the Committee of the Regions* (Luxembourg: Office for Official Publications of the European Communities) COM (98) 718.

European Commission (1999) *The Competitiveness of European Industry: 1999 Report* (Brussels: European Commission).

European Commission Competitiveness Advisory Group (1995) *Enhancing European Competitiveness: Second Report to the President of the European Commission, the Prime Ministers and Heads of State* (Luxembourg: Office for Official Publications of the European Communities).

Evans, P. (1997) 'The eclipse of the state? Reflections on stateness in an era of globalization', *World Politics* 50(1).

Farer, T. (1996) 'Collectively defending democracy in the Western Hemisphere', in Farer, T. (ed.) *Beyond Sovereignty: Collectively Defending Democracy in the Americas* (Baltimore, MD: The Johns Hopkins University Press).

Fawcett, L. and Hurrell, A. (eds) (1995) *Regionalism in World Politics: Regional Organization and International Order* (Oxford: Oxford University Press).

Fiji Ministry for Foreign Affairs (1972) 'South Pacific Forum: summary record and final press communiqué'.

Fioretos, K.-O. (1997) 'The anatomy of autonomy: interdependence, domestic balances of power and European integration', *Review of International Studies* 23(3).

Flora, P. (1999) *State Formation, Nation-Building and Mass Politics in Europe: The Theory of Stein Rokkan* (Oxford: Oxford University Press).

FPÖ (1993) *Österreich Zuerst – Unser Weg nach Europa: Für ein Europa der Bürger und Völker, für ein Europa als Freiheits-, Friedens- und Wohlstandsordnung (08.05.1993)* (Wien: FPÖ).

Fraga, E. and Oliveira, F. (1999) 'Argentina's Fernadez on desire to speed up talks with EU', *O Globo* (Rio de Janeiro) 30 June.

GA (1989) 'Europamanifest der Grünen Alternative, beschlossen auf dem Europa-Kongress in Innsbruck vom 17.–19.02.1989', in Kunnert, G. (ed.) *Spurensicherung auf dem österreichischen Weg nach Brüssel* (Wien: Verlag der Österreichischen Staatsdruckerei).

Gamble, A. (1988) *The Free Economy and the Strong State: The Politics of Thatcherism* (Basingstoke: Macmillan).

Gamble, A. (1995) 'The new political economy', *Political Studies* 43(3).

Gamble, A. and Payne, A. (eds) (1996) *Regionalism and World Order* (Basingstoke: Macmillan).

Garcia, S. (ed.) (1993) *European Identity and the Search for Legitimacy* (London: Pinter).

Garnaut, R. (1999) 'APEC ideas and reality: history and prospects', paper presented at

Twenty-fifth Pacific Trade and Development Conference, Osaka, July.

Garnaut, R. and Wilson, D. (1999) 'The Asian financial crisis: regional and global responses', paper presented at Twenty-fifth Pacific Trade and Development Conference, Osaka, July.

Garrett, G. (1998) 'Global markets and national politics: collision course or virtuous circle?', *International Organization* 52(4).

Gelb, S. and Manning, C. (eds) (1998) 'Spatial development initiatives: unlocking economic potential', *Development Southern Africa* 15(5).

Germain, R.D. (ed.) (2000) *Globalization and its Critics: perspectives from political economy* (Basingstoke: Macmillan).

Ghatak, S. (1978) *An Introduction to Development Economics* (London: Allen & Unwin).

Gibb, R. (1998) 'Southern Africa in transition: prospects and possibilities facing regional integration', *Journal of Modern African Studies* 36(2).

Giddens, A. (1998) *The Third Way: The Renewal of Social Democracy* (Cambridge: Polity Press).

Gill, S. (1990) *American Hegemony and the Trilateral Commission* (Cambridge: Cambridge University Press).

Gill, S. (ed.) (1993) *Gramsci, Historical Materialism and International Relations* (Cambridge: Cambridge University Press).

Gill, S. (1994) 'Structural change and global political economy: globalising elites in the emerging world order', in Sakamoto, Y. (ed.) *Global Transformation: Challenges to the State System* (Tokyo: United Nations University Press).

Gill, S. and Law, D. (1988) *The Global Political Economy: Perspectives, Problems and Policies* (London: Harvester-Wheatsheaf).

Gills, B. (ed.) (1997) 'Special Issue: Globalization and the politics of resistance', *New Political Economy* 2(1).

Gills, B., Rocamora, J. and Wilson, R. (1993) *Low Intensity Democracy: Political Power in the New World Order* (London: Pluto Press).

Gilpin, R. (1981) *War and Change in World Politics* (Cambridge: Cambridge University Press).

Global Conference on the Sustainable Development of Small Island Developing States (1994a) *Programme of Action for the Sustainable Development of Small Island Developing States.*

Global Conference on the Sustainable Development of Small Island Developing States (1994b) 'Press release', 9 May.

Goitia, V. (1999) 'Experts warn about mercosur weakening', *Estado de Sao Paulo* (Brazil), 28 April.

Goldstein, M. (1998) *The Asian Financial Crisis: Causes, Cures and Systemic Implications* (Washington, DC: Institute for International Economics).

Good, K. (1997) 'Development and democracies: liberal versus popular', *Africa Insight* 27(4).

Gordon, L. (1961) 'Economic regionalism reconsidered', *World Politics* 13(2).

Gourevitch, P. (1986) *Politics in Hard Times: Comparative Responses to International Economic Crises* (Ithaca, NY: Cornell University Press).

Gourevitch, P. (1999) *We Wish to Inform You that Tomorrow We Will be Killed with our Families: Stories from Rwanda* (New York: Picador).

Gradin, A. (1987) 'Speech by the Minister for Foreign Trade, Ms. Anita Gradin, in the Riksdag debate on Europe (12 November)', in Swedish Ministry for Foreign Affairs (1990) *Documents on Swedish Foreign Policy 1987*, Stockholm.

Gramsci, A. (1971) *Selections from the Prison Notebooks* (edited and translated by Quintin Hoare and Geoffrey Nowell Smith) (London: Lawrence and Wishart).

Grant, W. (1996) 'Large firms, SMEs and European environmental deregulation', paper presented at workshop, 'Deregulation and the Environment', European University Institute, Florence, May.

Grenville, S. (1998) 'The Asian crisis and regional cooperation', Reserve Bank of Australia, Sydney, 21 April.

Group 21 (1999) 'Japan must introduce an Asian currency', *Japan Echo* (June).

Grugel, J. and de Almeida Medeiros, M. (1999) 'Brazil and Mercosur', in Grugel, J. and Hout, W. (eds) *Regionalism across the North–South Divide: State Strategies and Globalization* (London: Routledge).

Grugel, J. and Hout, W. (1999a) 'Regions, regionalism and the South', in Grugel, J. and Hout, W. (eds) *Regionalism Across the North–South Divide: State Strategies and Globalisation* (London: Routledge).

Grugel, J. and Hout, W. (eds) (1999b) *Regionalism Across the North–South Divide: State Strategies and Globalization* (London: Routledge).

Gurowitz, A. (1998) 'Mobilizing international norms: domestic actors, immigrants and the state', unpublished Ph.D. dissertation, Cornell University.

Haacke, J. (1999) 'The concept of flexible engagement and the practice of enhanced interaction: intramural challenges to the "ASEAN way"', *The Pacific Review* 12(4).

Haas, E.B. (1956) 'Regionalism, functionalism and universal organization', *World Politics* 8(2).

Haas, E.B. (1958) *The Uniting of Europe: Political, Social and Economic Forces, 1950–1957* (Stanford, CA: Stanford University Press).

Haas, E.B. (1964) *Beyond the Nation State: Functionalism and International Organization* (Stanford, CA: Stanford University Press).

Haas, E.B. (1968) *The Uniting of Europe: Political, Economic and Social Forces, 1950–1957* (2nd edn) (Stanford, CA: Stanford University Press).

Haas, E.B. (1973) 'The study of regional integration: reflections on the joy and anguish of pretheorizing', in Falk, R. and Mendlovitz, S. (eds) *Regional Politics and World Order* (San Francisco, CA: W.H. Freeman).

Haas, E.B. (1975) *The Obsolescence of Regional Integration Theory*, Berkeley, CA: Institute of International Studies Working Paper.

Haas, E.B. and Schmitter, P.C. (1964) 'Economics and differential patterns of political integration: projections about unity in Latin America', *International Organization* 18(4).

Hansen, R. (1969) 'Regional integration: reflections on a decade of theoretical efforts', *World Politics* 21 (2).

Harden, S. (1985) *Small is Dangerous: Micro States in a Macro World* (London: Pinter).

Harris, N. (1987) *The End of the Third World: Newly Industrializing Countries and the Decline of an Ideology* (Harmondsworth: Penguin).

Harris, S. (1994) 'Policy networks and economic cooperation: policy coordination in the Asia Pacific region', *The Pacific Review* 7(4).

Harris, S. (1997) 'China's role in the WTO and APEC', in Goodman, D. and Segal, G. (eds) *China Rising: Nationalism and Interdependence* (London: Routledge).

Harris, S. and Nuttall, S. (1999) 'The multilateralist record in Asia and Europe', paper presented at CAEC, Berlin Conference, 15–16 May.

Harrod, J. (1997) 'Social forces and international political economy: joining the two IRs', in Gill, S. and Mittelman, J. (eds) *Innovation and Transformation in International Studies* (Cambridge: Cambridge University Press).

Hatsuse, R. (1997) 'Sub, macro and mega-regionalism in East Asia and the Asia–Pacific Region' (in Japanese) *Kokusai Seiji* (International Relations) 114.

Hay, C. and Rosamond, B. (2002) 'Globalisation, European integration and the discursive construction of economic imperatives', *Journal of European Public Policy* 9(2), 147–67.

Heclo, H. and Madsen, H. (1987) *Policy and Politics in Sweden: Principled Pragmatism* (Philadelphia, PA: Temple University Press).

Held, D., McGrew, A., Goldblatt, D. and Perraton, J. (1999) *Global Transformations: Politics, Economics and Culture* (Cambridge: Polity Press).

Helleiner, E. (1996) 'Post-globalization: is the financial liberalization trend likely to be reversed?', in Boyer, R. and Drache, D. (eds) *States Against Markets: The Limits of Globalization* (London: Routledge).

Helmich, H. and Smillie, I. (eds) (1999) *Stakeholders: Government–NGO Partnerships for International Development* (London: Earthscan).

Henderson, J. (1999) 'Reassessing ASEAN', *Adelphi Paper* 328 (Oxford: Oxford University Press).

Henning, R.C. (1999) 'The exchange stabilization fund: slush money or war chest?' *Policy Analyses in International Economics* No. 57, May (Washington DC: Institute for International Economics).

Herman, E. and Chomsky, N. (1988) *Manufacturing Consent* (New York: Pantheon Books).

Hettne, B. (1993) 'Neo-mercantilism: the pursuit of regionness', *Cooperation & Conflict* 28(3).

Hettne, B (ed.) (1995) *International Political Economy. Understanding Global Disorder* (London: Zed Books).

Hettne, B. (1999) 'Globalization and the new regionalism: the second great transformation', in Hettne, B., Inotai, A. and Sunkel, O. (eds) *Globalism and the New Regionalism* (Basingstoke: Macmillan).

Hettne, B. and Inotai, A. (1994) *The New Regionalism: Implications for Global Development and International Security* (Helsinki: UNU World Institute for Development Economics Research).

Hettne, B. and Söderbaum, F. (eds) (1998a) '*The new regionalism*', Special Issue of *Politeia* 17(3).

Hettne, B. and Söderbaum, F. (1998b) 'The new regionalism approach', *Politeia*, Special Issue: 'The new regionalism' 17(3).

Hettne, B. and Söderbaum, F. (1999) 'Towards global social theory', *Journal of International Relations and Development (JIRD)*, Special Issue: 'Rethinking Development Theory' 1(4).

Hettne, B., Inotai, A. and Sunkel, O. (eds) (1999) *Globalism and the New Regionalism* (Basingstoke: Macmillan).

Hettne, B., Inotai, A. and Sunkel, O. (eds) (2000a) *National Perspectives on the New Regionalism in the North* (Basingstoke: Macmillan).

Hettne, B., Inotai, A. and Sunkel, O. (eds) (2000b) '*The new regionalism*' *and the Future of Security and Development* (Basingstoke: Macmillan).

Hettne, B., Inotai, A. and Sunkel, O. (eds) (2000c) *National Perspectives on the New Regionalism in the South* (Basingstoke: Macmillan).

Hey, C. (1997) 'Greening other policies: the case of freight transport', in Liefferink, D. and Andersen, M.S. (eds) *The Innovation of EU Environmental Policy* (Oslo: Scandinavian University Press).

Higgott, R. (1993) 'Competing theoretical perspectives on economic cooperation: implications for the Asia-Pacific', in Higgott, R. Leaver, R. and Ravenhill, J. (eds) *Pacific Economic Relations in the 1990s: Cooperation or Conflict?* (London: Allen & Unwin).

Higgott, R. (1998) 'The international political economy of regionalism: Europe and Asia compared', in Coleman, W.D. and Underhill, G.R.D. (eds) *Regionalism and Global Economic Integration: Europe, Asia and the Americas* (London: Routledge).

Higgott, R. and Phillips, N. (2000) 'Challenging triumphalism and convergence: the limits of global liberalisation in Asia and Latin America', *Review of International Studies* 26(3).

Higgott, R. and Stubbs, R. (1995) 'Competing conceptions of economic regionalism: APEC versus EAEC', *Review of International Political Economy* 2 (3).

Hills, J. (1995) 'Funding the welfare state', *Oxford Review of Economic Policy*, 11(3).

Hirst, M. (1995) 'La Dimensión Política del Mercosur: Actores, Politización e Ideología', Serie de Documentos e Informes de Investigación no. 198, FLACSO, Buenos Aires.

Hirst, P. and Thompson, G. (1996) *Globalization in Question: The International Economy and the Possibilities of Governance* (Cambridge: Polity Press).

Hix, S (1994) 'The study of the European Community: the Challenge to Comparative Politics', *West European Politics* 17(1).

Hix, S. (1999) *The Political System of the European Union* (Basingstoke: Macmillan).

HMSO (1996) *Competitiveness: Creating the Enterprise Centre of Europe* (London: Her Majesty's Stationery Office).

Hoffmann, S. (1966) 'Obstinate or obsolete? The fate of the nation-state and the case of Western Europe', *Daedalus* 95.

Hoffman, S. (1982) 'Reflections on the nation-state in Western Europe today', *Journal of Common Market Studies* 21 (1).

Holden, B. (ed.) (2000) *Global Democracy: Key Debates* (London: Routledge).

Holman, O. (1992) 'Transnational class strategy and the New Europe', *International Journal of Political Economy* 22(1).

Holman, O. and van der Pijl, K. (1996) 'The capitalist class in the European Union', in Kourvetaris, G.A. and Moschonas, A. (eds) *The Impact of European Integration: Political, Sociological and Economic Changes* (Westport, CT: Praeger).

Hoogvelt, A. (1997) *Globalisation and the Postcolonial World: The New Political Economy of Development* (Basingstoke: Macmillan).

Hook, G. and Kearns, I. (eds) (1999) *Subregionalism and World Order* (Basingstoke: Macmillan).

Howe, H.M. (1998) 'Private security forces and African stability: the case of executive outcomes', *Journal of Modern African Studies* 36(2).

Hudson, W. and Stokes, G. (1997) 'Australia and Asia: place, determinism and national identities', in Stokes, G. (ed.) *The Politics of Identity in Australia* (Cambridge: Cambridge University Press).

Huggins, R. (1997) 'Competitiveness and the global region: the role of networking', in Simmie, J. (ed.) *Innovation, Networks and Learning Regions?* (London: Jessica Kinsley with the Regional Studies Association).

Hulme, D. and Edwards, M. (eds) (1997) *NGOs, States and Donors: Too Close for Comfort?* (Basingstoke: Macmillan for SCF).

Hummer, W. and Schweitzer, M. (1987) *Österreich und die EWG: Neutralitätsrechtliche Beurteilung der Möglichkeiten der Dynamisierung des Verhältnisses zur EWG* (Wien: Signum Verlag).

Huntington, S. (1990) 'Prepared statement before the Senate Foreign Relations Committee', in *Relations in a Multipolar World* (Text of Hearings, 101st Congress, Second Session) (Washington, DC: US Government Printing Office).

Huntingdon, S. (1991) *The Third Wave: Democratization in the Late Twentieth Century* (Norman: University of Oklahoma Press).

Huntington, S. (1998) *The Clash of Civilizations and the Remaking of World Order* (London: Touchstone Books).

Hurrell, A. (1995a) 'Explaining the resurgence of regionalism in world politics', *Review of International Studies* 21(4).

Hurrell, A. (1995b) 'Regionalism in theoretical perspective', in Fawcett, L. and Hurrell, A. (eds) *Regionalism in World Politics: Regional Organization and International Order* (Oxford: Oxford University Press).

Hurrell, A. (1998) 'An emerging security community in South America?', in Adler, E. and Barnett, M. (eds) *Security Communities* (Cambridge: Cambridge University Press).

Hyden, G. (1997) 'Foreign aid and democratisation in Africa', *Africa Insight* 27(4).

IMD. (2000) 'The world competitiveness scoreboard', *IMD Press Release* (Geneva: Institute for Management Development).

IMF (1996) 'ASEAN's sound fundamentals bode well for sustained growth', *IMF Survey* (November 25).

IMF (1997) 'IMF wins mandate to cover capital accounts, debt initiative put in motion', *IMF Survey* (12 May).

Institute of Social Science (1999) *Social Science Japan: The Financial Crisis in Asia*, 13 (Tokyo: University of Tokyo).

Jackson, R. and Roseberg, K. (1982) 'Why Africa's weak states persist', *World Politics* 35(1).

Jayasuriya, K. (1994) 'Singapore: the politics of regional definition', *The Pacific Review* 7(4) pp. 411–20.

Johnson, C. (1998) 'Economic crisis in East Asia: the clash of capitalisms', *Cambridge Journal of Economics* 22(1).

Johnson, W. and Tupouniua, S. (1976) 'Against French nuclear testing: the ATOM Committee', *The Journal of Pacific History* 11(3–4).

Kao, J. (1993) 'The worldwide web of Chinese business', *Harvard Business Review* 71 (March to April).

Kaplan, R. (1994) 'The coming anarchy', *Atlantic Monthly* 273(2).

Kasfir, N. (ed.) (1998) 'Special Issue on civil society and democracy in Africa: critical perspectives', *Commonwealth and Comparative Politics* 36(2).

Katzenstein, P.J. (1993) 'Regions in competition: comparative advantages of America, Europe and Asia', in Haffendom, H. and Tuschhoff, C. (eds) *America and Europe in an Era of Change* (Boulder, CO: Westview Press).

Katzenstein, P.J. (1996) 'Regionalism in comparative perspective', *Cooperation and Conflict* 31(2).

Katzenstein, P.J. (1997) 'Introduction: Asian regionalism in comparative perspective', in Katzenstein, P.J. and Shiraishi, T. (eds) *Network Power: Japan and Asia* (Ithaca, NY: Cornell University Press).

Katzenstein, P.J. (2000) 'Varieties of Asian regionalism', in Katzenstein, P.J., Hamilton-Hart, N., Kato, K. and Ming, Y. (eds) *Asian Regionalism* (Cornell University East Asia Program, Cornell East Asia Series).

Katzenstein, P.J. and Nobuo Okawara, N. (1999) 'Japan's security policy and Asian regionalism in the 1990s', mimeo.

Katzenstein, P.J., Keohane, R.O. and Krasner, S. D. (1998) 'International organization and the study of world politics', *International Organization* 52(4).

Keating, M. and Loughlin, J. (eds) (1997) *The Political Economy of Regionalism* (London: Frank Cass).

Keck, M.E. and Sikkink, K. (1998) *Activists beyond Borders: Advocacy Networks in International Politics* (Ithaca, NY: Cornell University Press).

Keith, M. and Pile, S. (1993) 'Introduction: the politics of place', in Keith, M. and Pile, S. (eds) *Place and the Politics of Identity* (London: Routledge).

Kelly, M.E. (1993) *NAFTA's Environmental Side Agreement: A Review and Analysis* (Texas Centre for Policy Studies).

Kennedy, P. (1999) 'Sub-Saharan Africa's current plight and the threat or promise of globalisation?', *Global Society* 13(4).

Kennes, W. (1998) 'The European Union and regionalism in developing countries', in *Regionalism and Development: Report of the European Commission and World Bank Seminar*, European Commission, Studies Series no. 1 (Brussels: European Commission).

Kenny, C. and Moss, T.J. (1998) 'Stock markets in Africa: emerging lions or white elephants?', *World Development* 26(5).

Keohane, R.O. (1984) *After Hegemony: Cooperation and Discord in the World Political Economy* (Princeton, NJ: Princeton University Press).

Keohane, R.O. and Nye, J.S. (1977) *Power and Interdependence: World Politics in Transition* (Boston, MA: Little Brown).

Kingma, K. (ed.) (2000) *The Impact of Demobilization in Sub-Saharan Africa* (Basingstoke: Macmillan for BICC).

Kleinberg, R.B. and Clark, J.A. (eds) (2000) *Economic Liberalization, Democratization and Civil Society in the Developing World* (Basingstoke: Macmillan).

Kobayashi, I. (1994) *Studies for Pacific Island Countries* (in Japanese) (Tokyo: Toshin-do).

Koelble, T. (1999) *The Global Economy and Democracy in South Africa* (New Brunswick, NJ: Rutgers University Press).

Korhonen, P. (1994) 'The theory of the flying geese pattern of development and its interpretation', *Journal of Peace Research* 31(1).

Kornegay, F. and Landsberg, C. (1998) 'Phaphama iAfrika!: the African renaissance and corporate South Africa', *African Security Review* 7(4).

Kowalewski, D. (1997) *Global Establishment: The Political Economy of North/Asian Networks* (Basingstoke: Macmillan).

Kozo Kato (1998) 'Open regionalism and Japan's systemic vulnerability', Tsukuba University, unpublished paper.

Kristof, N.D. (1998) 'Japan sees itself as a scapegoat of Washington in the Asia crisis', *New York Times*, 21 September.

Krugman, P. (1999) *The Return of Depression Economics* (London: Allen Lane, The Penguin Press).

Kunnert, G. (1993) *Österreichs Weg in die Europäische Union: Ein Kleinstaat ringt um eine aktive Rolle im europäischen Integrationsprozess* (Wien: Verlag der Österreichischen Staatsdruckerei).

Kurth, J. (1989) 'The Pacific Basin versus the Atlantic Alliance: two paradigms of international relations', *Annals of the American Academy of Political and Social Science* 505 (September).

Kurzer, P. (1993) *Business and Banking: Political Change And Economic Integration In Western Europe* (Ithaca, NY: Cornell University Press).

Laka, L. (1985a) 'A report on South Pacific Nuclear Free Zone Working Group's third meeting' (Internal document of Solomon Islands Ministry of Foreign Affairs).

Laka, L. (1985b) 'A report on South Pacific Nuclear Free Zone Working Group's fourth meeting' (Internal document of Solomon Islands Ministry of Foreign Affairs).

Laka, L. (1985c) 'A report on South Pacific Nuclear Free Zone Working Group's fifth meeting' (Internal document of Solomon Islands Ministry of Foreign Affairs).

Lall, D. (1980) *The Poverty of Development Economics* (London: Institute of Economic Affairs).

Lang, T. and Hines, C. (1993) *The New Protectionism. Protecting the Future Against Free Trade* (London: Earthscan Publications).

Lawrence, R.Z. (1994a) 'Regionalism: an overview', *Journal of Japanese and International Economies* 8(4).

Lawrence, R.Z. (1994b) 'Emerging regional arrangements: building blocks or stumbling blocks?', in Frieden, J.A. and Lake, D.A. (eds) *International Political Economy: Perspectives on Global Power* (New York: St Martin's Press).

Lee, S. (1997) 'Competitiveness and the welfare state in Britain', in Mullard, M. and Lee, S. (eds) *The Politics of Social Policy in Europe* (Cheltenham: Edward Elgar).

Lee, S. (1999) 'The competitive disadvantage of England', in Cowling, K. (ed.) *Industrial Policy in Europe* (London: Routledge).

Lehmbruch, G. and Schmitter, P.C. (eds) (1982) *Patterns Of Corporatist Policy-Making* (Beverly Hills, CA: Sage).

Lévèque, F. (1996) 'Conclusion', in Lévèque, F. (ed.) *Environmental Policy in Europe* (Aldershot: Edward Elgar).

Leys, C. (1996) *The Rise and Fall of Development Theory* (Oxford: EAEP, Indiana University Press).

Liebenberg, I.(1998) 'The African renaissance: myth, vital lie, or mobilising tool?', *African Security Review* 7(3).

Lieberman, E. S. (1997) 'Organisational cloaking in Southern Africa', *Transformation* 34.

Lincoln, E.J. (1993) *Japan's New Global Role* (Washington, DC: Brookings Institution).

Lindberg, L.N. (1966) *The Political Dynamics of European Economic Integration* (Stanford, CA: Stanford University Press).

Lindberg, L.N. and Scheingold, S.A. (1970) *Europe's Would-be Polity: Patterns of Change in the European Community* (Engelwood Cliffs, NJ: Prentice Hall).

Lindberg, S. and Sverrisson, A. (eds) (1997) *Social Movements in Development: The Challenge of Globalization and Democratization* (Basingstoke: Macmillan).

Lipschutz, R.D. with Mayer, J. (1996) *Global Civil Society and Global Environmental Governance* (Albany, NY: SUNY Press).

Liska, G. (1973) 'Geographic scope: patterns of integration', in Falk, R.A. and Mendlovitz, S.H. (eds) *Regional Politics and World Order* (San Francisco, CA: W.H. Freeman).

Llewellyn, J. (1996) 'Tackling Europe's competitiveness', *Oxford Review of Economic Policy* 12(3).

Luif, P. (1994) 'Die Beitrittswerber: Grundlegendes zu den Verhandlungen der EFTA–Staaten um Mitgliedschaft bei der EG/EU', *Österreichische Zeitschrift für Politikwissenschaft* 23(1).

Luif, P. (1996) *On The Road To Brussels: The Political Dimension of Austria's, Finland's and Sweden's Accession to the European Union* (Wien: Braumüller).

McCarthy, C. (1996) 'Regional integration: part of the solution or part of the problem?', in Ellis, S. (ed.) *Africa Now: People, Policies and Institutions* (London: James Currey).

McCormack, G. (1996) *The Emptiness of Japanese Affluence* (New York: M.E. Sharpe).

MacFarlane, S.N. (1999) 'Doing good, doing wrong', *International Journal* 54(4).

MacFarlane, S.N. and Weiss, T.G. (1992) 'Regional organizations and regional security', *Security Studies* 2(1).

MacLean, B. (1999) 'The transformation of international economic policy debate 1997–98', in MacLean, B. (ed.) *Out of Control: Canada in an Unstable Financial World* (Toronto and Ottawa: James Lorimer).

MacLean, B., Bowles, P. and Croci, O. (1999) 'East Asian crises and regional economic integration', in Boyd, G. and Rugman, A. (eds) *Deepening Integration in the Pacific* (Aldershot: Edward Elgar).

MacLean, S.J. and Shaw, T.M. (1996) 'Civil society and political economy in contemporary Africa: what prospects for sustainable democracy?', *Journal of Contemporary African Studies* 14(2).

McLeod, R.H. and Garnaut, R. (eds) (1998) *East Asia in Crisis: From Being a Miracle to Needing One?* (London: Routledge).

Mace, G. and Bélanger, L. (1999) 'Hemispheric regionalism in perspective', in Mace, G. and Bélanger, L. (eds) *The Americas in Transition: The Contours of Regionalism* (Boulder, CO: Lynne Rienner).

Maloka, E. (1997) 'African renaissance: reactionary?', *African Communist* 147(3).

Mandela, N. (1997) 'Statement by President Nelson Mandela following the arrest of former president of Zambia, Dr Kenneth Kaunda', issued by the Office of the President, Pretoria, 26 December.

Manibhandu, A. (1998) 'Thailand takes up the struggle for freedom from self-reliance', *Bangkok Post* (Thailand), 31 July.

Mansfield, E.D. and Milner, H.V. (eds) (1997) *The Political Economy of Regionalism* (New York: Columbia University Press).

Mansfield, E.D. and Milner, H.V. (1999) 'The new wave of regionalism', *International Organization*, 53(3).

Mara, K. (1977) 'Speech at the Pacific Island leaders' conference', Selected speeches by Kamisese Mara, Suva.

Marchand M.H., Boas, M. and Shaw, T. (1999) 'The political economy of new regionalisms', *Third World Quarterly* 20(5).

Marks, G., Hooghe, L. and Kermit Blank, K. (1996) 'European integration from the 1980s: state-centric v. multilevel governance', *Journal of Common Market Studies* 34(3).

Marsh, D. and Rhodes, R.A.W. (eds) (1992) *Policy Networks in British Government* (Oxford: Clarendon Press).

Mathews, J.T. (1994) 'The environment and international security', in Klare, M.T. and Thomas, D.C. (eds) *World Security: Challenges for a New Century* (2nd edn) (New York: St Martin's Press).

Mattli, W. (1999) *The Logic of Regional Integration* (Cambridge: Cambridge University Press).

Maxwell, C., Lawson, R. and Tomlin, B. (eds) (1998) *To Walk without Fear: The Global Movement to Ban Landmines* (Toronto: Oxford University Press).

Mbeki, M. (1998) 'The African renaissance', in *South African Yearbook of International Affairs 1998/9* (Johannesburg: South African Institute of International Affairs).

Mbeki, T. (1997) 'Address by Executive Deputy President Thabo Mbeki to Corporate Council on attracting capital to Africa's summit', Chantilly, Virginia, 19–22 April.

Mbeki, T. (1998a) 'The African Renaissance: opportunities and challenges for Asia', address at a luncheon hosted by the Hong Kong Centre of the Asian Society and the South African Business Forum, Hong Kong, 17 April, in Mbeki, T. *Africa: The Time Has Come* (Cape Town: Tafelberg).

Mbeki, T. (1998b) 'The African renaissance, South Africa and the world', address at the United Nations University, Tokyo, Japan, 9 April, in Mbeki, T. (1998) *Africa: The Time Has Come* (Cape Town: Tafelberg).

Mearsheimer, J.J. (1990) 'Back to the future? Instability in Europe after the Cold War', *International Security* 15(1).

Melanesian Spearhead Group (1996) Tenth Heads of Government Summit: Joint Communiqué.

Meth–Cohn, D. and Müller, W.C. (1994) 'Looking reality in the eye: the politics of privatization in Austria', in Wright, V. (ed.) *Privatization In Western Europe: Pressures, Problems And Paradoxes* (London: Pinter).

Michie, J. and Grieve Smith, J. (eds) (1999) *Global Instability: The Political Economy of World Economic Governance* (London: Routledge).

Miller, L.B. (1967) 'Regional organization and the regulation of internal conflict', *World Politics* 19(4).

Miller, L.H. (1973) 'The prospect for order through regional security', in Falk, R.A. and Mendlovitz, S.H. (eds) *Regional Politics and World Order* (San Francisco, CA: W.H. Freeman).

Miller, M. and Zhang, L. (1999) *Creditor Panic, Asset Bubbles and Sharks: Three Views of the Asian Crisis*, ESRC Centre for the Study of Globalisation and Regionalisation, University of Warwick, Working Paper 35/99.

Milner, H.V. (1992) 'International theories of cooperation among nations: strengths and weaknesses', *World Politics* 44(3).

Milner, H.V. (1997) *Interests, Institutions and Information: Domestic Politics and International Relations* (Princeton, NJ: Princeton University Press).

Milner, H.V. (1998) 'Regional economic co-operation, global markets and domestic politics: a comparison of NAFTA and the Maastricht Treaty', in Coleman, W.D. and Underhill, G.R.D. (eds) *Regionalism and Global Economic Integration: Europe, Asia and the Americas* (London: Routledge).

Minassian, G. (1999) 'Bulgaria and the International Monetary Fund', unpublished paper, Institute of Economics, Bulgarian Academy of Sciences.

Ministry of International Trade and Industry (MITI) (1999) *White Paper on International Trade 1999*, English Executive Summary (Tokyo: MITI).

Mitrany, D. (1965) 'The prospect of integration: federal or functional?', *Journal of Common Market Studies* 4.

Mitrany, D. (1966) [1943] *A Working Peace System* (Chicago, IL: Quadrangle Books).

Mittelman, J.H. (1999) 'Rethinking the "new regionalism" in the context of globalization', in Hettne, B., Inotai, A. and Sunkel, O. (eds) *Globalism and the New Regionalism* (Basingstoke: Macmillan).

Mittelman, J.H. and Pasha, M.K. (1997) *Out From Underdevelopment Revisited: Changing Global Structures and the Remaking of World Order* (Basingstoke: Macmillan).

Monar, J. (1999) 'An emerging regime of European governance for freedom, security and justice', *ESRC One Europe or Several?*, Programme briefing note 2/99, November.

Moon, Chung-in (1998) 'In the shadow of broken cheers: the dynamics of globalization in South Korea', paper presented at conference on 'Coping with Globalization', sponsored by the Center for the Study of Global Change of Indiana University, Alexandria, VA (31 July–1 August).

Moon, Chung-in (1999) 'Political economy of East Asian development and Pacific economic cooperation', *Pacific Review* 12(2).

Moore, K. and Lewis, D. (1999) *Birth of the Multinational* (Copenhagen: Copenhagen Business School).

Morata, F. (1997) 'The Euro-region and the C-6 network: the new politics of sub-national cooperation in the West-Mediterranean area', in Keating, M. and Loughlin, J. (eds) *The Political Economy of Regionalism* (London: Frank Cass).

Moravcsik, A. (1993) 'Preferences and power in the European Community: a liberal inter-governmentalist approach', *Journal of Common Market Studies* 31(4).

Moravcsik, A. (1998) *The Choice for Europe: Social Purpose and State Power from Messina to Maastricht* (Ithaca, NY: Cornell University Press).

Morton, A.D. (1998) 'Labels on lapels: why there is no neo-Gramscian "school" in IPE and why it matters,' paper presented at Twenty-third Annual Conference of the British International Studies Association, University of Sussex, 14–16 December.

Moyo, J. (1998) 'The African renaissance: a critical assessment', *Southern African Political and Economic Monthly* 11(7).

Murphy, C.N. (ed.) (2000) *Egalitarian Social Movements in Response to Globalization* (Basingstoke: Macmillan).

Murphy, C.N. and Tooze, R. (eds) (1991) *The New International Political Economy* (Boulder, CO: Lynne Rienner).

Nel, P. and McGowan, P.J. (eds) (1999) *Power, Wealth and Global Order: An International Relations Textbook for Africa* (Cape Town: UCT Press for FGD).

Neufeld, M. (1999) 'Globalization: five theses', paper presented at the conference 'Globalization and Problems of Development', Havana, Cuba, January.

Neumann, I.B. (1996) *Russian and the Idea of Europe. A Study in Identity and International Relations* (London: Routledge).

Nicolaides, P. (1993) 'Industrial policy: the problem of reconciling definitions, intentions and effects', in Nicolaides, P. (ed.) *Industrial Policy in the European Community: A Necessary Response to Economic Integration?* (Dordrecht: Martinus Nijhoff).

Nonini, D.M. (1993) 'On the outs on the Rim: an ethnographic grounding of the "Asia–Pacific" imagery', in Dirlik, A. (ed.) *What is in a Rim? Critical Perspectives on the Pacific Region Idea* (Boulder, CO: Westview Press).

Nye, J.S. (1968) 'Comparative regional integration: concept and measurement', *International Organization* 22 (4).

Nye, J.S. (1971) *Peace in Parts: Integration and Conflict in International Organizations* (Boston, MA: Little, Brown).

Nye, J.S. (1988) 'Neorealism and neoliberalism', *World Politics* 40 (2).

Ocampo, J.A. (1999) 'Reforming the international financial architecture: consensus and divergence', CEPAL, Serie Temas de Coyuntura, April.

OECD (1996) *Networks of Enterprises and Local Development* (Paris: Organisation for Economic Co-operation and Development).

OECD (1997a) *New Directions for Industrial Policy*, Policy Brief no. 3 (Paris: Organisation for Economic Co-operation and Development).

OECD (1997b) *Best Practice for Small and Medium-Sized Enterprises* (Paris: Organisation for Economic Co-operation and Development).

OECD (1997c) *National Innovation Systems* (Paris: Organisation for Economic Co-operation and Development).

OECD (1997d) *Regulatory Reform for Innovation* (Paris: Organisation for Economic Co-operation and Development).

OECD (1999a) *Globalisation of Industrial R&D: Policy Issues* (Paris: Organisation for Economic Co-operation and Development).

OECD (1999b) *OECD Employment Outlook* (Paris: Organisation for Economic Co-operation and Development).

Ogashiwa, Y. (1991) *Microstates and Nuclear Issues: Regional Co-operation in the Pacific* (Suva: University of the South Pacific).

Ogashiwa, Y. (1994) 'Vanuatu's nuclear policy: evolution and prospects', in Sato, Y. (ed.) *The South Pacific in the Changing World Era* (Hiroshima: Institute for Peace Science, Hiroshima University).

ÖGB (1988) *Europa Memorandum (Dezember)* (Wien: ÖGB).

Öhlinger, H. (1988) *Verfassungsrechtliche Aspekte Eines Beitritt Österreichs Zu Den EG* (Wien: Signum Verlag).

Ohlson, T. (1993) *Conflict, Conflict Resolution, Security and Development in the Post-Apartheid Southern Africa* (Uppsala: Uppsala University Press).

Ohmae, K. (1995) *The End of the Nation State. The Rise of Regional Economies* (New York: HarperCollins).

Ohmae, K. (1996) *The Borderless World: Power and Strategy in the Interlinked Economy* (New York: HarperCollins).

Oliveira, E. (1999) 'Brazil–CAN achieve preferential tariff agreement', *O Globo* (Rio de Janeiro) 4 June.

Oman, C. (1994) *Globalisation and Regionalisation: The Challenge for Developing Countries* (Paris: OECD).

Oman, C. (1999) 'Globalization, regionalization and inequality', in Hurrell, A. and Woods, N. (eds) *Inequality, Globalization and World Politics* (Oxford: Oxford University Press).

Organization of African Unity (OAU) (1992) *Resolving Conflicts in Africa: Proposals for Action* (Addis Ababa: OAU Press and Information Service).

Orwell, G. (1948) *Nineteen Eighty-Four: A Novel* (New York: Harcourt, Brace & World).

Ottaway, M. (1999) 'Africa', *Foreign Policy* 114 (Spring).

Overbeek, H. (ed.) (1993) *Restructuring Hegemony in the Global Political Economy: The Rise of Transnational Neo-liberalism in the 1980s* (London: Routledge).

ÖVP (1988) 'Maria Plainer Beschluss des erweiterten ÖVP-Bundesparteivorstandes vom 08.01.1988 zur österreichischen Europapolitik', in Kunnert, G. (ed.) *Spurensicherung auf dem österreichischen Weg nach Brüssel* (Wien: Verlag der Österreichischen Staatsdruckerei).

Padelford, N.J. (1954) 'Regional organizations and the United Nations', *International Organization* 8(2).

Palmer, N. (1991) *The New Regionalism in Asia and the Pacific* (Lexington, MA: Lexington Books).

Park, J. (1995) 'The new regionalism and Third World development', *Journal of Developing Societies* 11 (1).

Payne, A. (1998) 'The new political economy of area studies', *Millennium: Journal of International Studies* 27(2).

Payne, A. (1999) 'Reframing the global politics of development', *Journal of International Relations and Development* 2(4).

Payne, A. (2000) 'Globalisation and modes of regionalist governance', in Pierre, J. (ed.) *Debating Governance: Authority, Steering and Democracy* (Oxford: Oxford University Press).

Payne, A. and Gamble, A. (1996) 'Introduction: the political economy of regionalism and world order', in Gamble, A. and Payne, A. (eds) *Regionalism and World Order* (Basingstoke: Macmillan).

Pazos, F. (1973) 'Regional integration of trade among less-developed countries', *World Development* 1 (July).

Pease, K. K. and Forsythe, D.P. (1993) 'Human rights, humanitarian intervention and world politics', *Human Rights Quarterly* 15.

PECC (1995) *Perspectives on the Manila Action Plan for APEC* (Singapore: PECC Secretariat).

Pempel, T.J. (ed.) (1999) *The Politics of the Asian Economic Crisis* (Ithaca, NY: Cornell University Press).

Petersson, O. (1994) *Swedish Government and Politics* (Stockholm: Publica-Fritzes).

Phillips, N. and Higgott, R. (1999) *Global Governance and the Public Domain: Collective Goods in a Post-Washington Consensus Era*, ESRC Centre for the Study of Globalisation and Regionalisation, University of Warwick, Working Paper 47/99.

Pillay, K. (1999) 'Pillay's perspective', *Cape Times* (Cape Town), 28 June.

Polanyi, K. (1944) *The Great Transformation: The Political and Economic Origins of Our Time* (New York: Rinehart).

Pollack, M. (2001) 'International relations theory and European integration', *Journal of Common Market Studies* 39(2).

Porter, M. (1998) 'Clusters and the new economics of competition', *Harvard Business Review* 76 (6).

Puchala, D.J. (1984) 'The integration theories and the study of international relations', in Kegley, C.W. and Wittkopf, E.R. (eds) *The Global Agenda: Issues and Studies* (New York: Random House).

Pyle, K.B. (1997) 'Old new orders and the future of Japan and the United States in Asia', The Edwin O. Reischauer Memorial Lecture, International House of Japan, 12 June.

Quadir, F., MacLean, S.J. and Shaw, T.M. (1999) 'Pluralisms and the changing global political economy: ethnicities in crises of governance in Asia and Africa' (Halifax: Ford Project, Dalhousie University).

Rajan, R. (1999) 'The Brazil and other currency crises of the 1990s', *Claremont Policy Briefs* 99–02.

Reno, W. (1998) *Warlord Politics and African States* (Boulder, CO: Lynne Rienner).

Rhodes, M. (1998) '"Subversive liberalism": market integration, globalisation and West European welfare states', in Coleman, W.D. and Underhill, G.R.D (eds) *Regionalism and Global Economic Integration: Europe, Asia, the Americas* (London: Routledge).

Richards, P. (1999) *Fighting for the Rain Forest: War, Youth and Resources in Sierra Leone* (Oxford: James Currey for IAI).

Robinson, W.I. (1996a) 'Globalization, the world system and "democracy promotion" in US foreign policy', *Theory and Society* 25(5).

Robinson, W.I. (1996b) *Promoting Polyarchy: Globalization, U.S. Intervention and Hegemony* (Cambridge: Cambridge University Press).

Robinson, W. I. (1998) 'Neo-liberalism, the global elite and the Guatemalan transition: a critical macro-structural analysis', paper presented at seminar on 'Guatemalan Development and Democratization: Pro-active Responses to Globalization', Universidad del Valle de Guatemala, 26–28 March.

Robson, P. (1993) 'The new regionalism and developing countries', *Journal of Common Market Studies* 31(3).

Rocasalbas, A. (1999) 'Menem cited on dollar peg, economic stability', *Telam* (Buenos Aries) 31 March.

Rocha, J. (1999) 'Experts view "worst" crisis affecting Mercosur', *Jornol do Brasil* (Rio do Janeiro) 3 April.

Rodarte, M. (1998) 'El FMI en la crisis', *El Economista* (Mexico) 7 October.

Rodrik, D. (1995) 'Getting interventions right: how South Korea and Taiwan grew rich', *Economic Policy* 20.

Rodrik, D. (1997) *Has Globalization Gone Too Far?* (Washington, DC: Institute for International Economics).

Rodrik, D. (1999) *The New Global Economy and Developing Countries: Making Openness Work*, Policy Essay no. 24 (Washington, DC: Overseas Development Council).

Rosamond, B. (2000) *Theories of European Integration* (Basingstoke: Palgrave/Macmillan).

Rosamond, B. (2001) '(European) integration theory and the sociology of knowledge', paper presented at Forty-second Annual Convention of the International Studies Association, Chicago, IL, 20–24 February.

Rosenau, J.N. (1992) 'Governance and change in world politics', in Rosenau, J.N. and Czempiel, E-O. (eds) *Governance without Government: Order and Change in World Politics* (Cambridge: Cambridge University Press).

Rosenau, J.N. (1997) *Along the Domestic–Foreign Frontier: Exploring Governance in a Turbulent World* (Cambridge: Cambridge University Press),

Rothstein, R. (1977) *The Weak in the World of Strong: The Developing Countries in the International System* (New York: Columbia University Press).

Roubini, N. (n.d.) 'What caused Asia's economic and currency crisis and its global contagion?' http://www.stern.nyu.edu/~nroubini/asia/AsiaHomepage.html

Ruggie, J.G. (1995) 'At home abroad, abroad at home: international liberalisation and domestic stability in the new world economy', *Millennium: Journal of International Studies* 24(3).

Rupert, M. (1995) *Producing Hegemony: The Politics of Mass Production and American Global Power* (Cambridge: Cambridge University Press).

Rupert, M. (1997) 'Contesting Hegemony: Americanism and far-right ideologies of globalization', in Burch, K. and Denemark, R. (eds) *Constituting International Political Economy* (Boulder, CO: Lynne Rienner).

Sanger, D.E. (1998) 'US and IMF made Asia crisis worse, World Bank finds', *New York Times*, 3 December.

Sassen, S. (1996) *Losing Control? Sovereignty in an Age of Globalization* (Boston, MA: Beacon Press).

Saunders, O.J. (1994) 'NAFTA and the North American Agreement on Environmental Co-operation: a new model for international collaboration on trade and environment', *Colorado Journal of International Law and Policy* 5(2).

Sauter, W. (1997) *Competition Law and Industrial Policy in the EU* (Oxford: Clarendon Press).

Sbragia, A. (1994) 'Thinking about the European future: the uses of comparison', in Sbragia, A. (ed.) *Euro-Politics* (Washington, DC: Brookings Institution).

Schechter, M.G. (ed.) (1999) *The Revival of Civil Society: Global and Comparative Perspectives* (Basingstoke: Macmillan).

Scheffer, D.J. (1992) 'Challenges confronting collective security: humanitarian intervention', in US Institute of Peace *Three Views on the Issue of Humanitarian Intervention* (Washington, DC: USIP).

Schmitter, P.C. (1971) 'A revised theory of European integration', in Lindberg, L.N. and Scheingold, S.A. (eds) *Regional Integration: Theory and Research* (Cambridge, MA: Harvard University Press).

Scholte, J.A. (1997) 'Global capitalism and the state', *International Affairs* 73(3).

Scholte, J.A. (2000) *Globalisation: A Critical Introduction* (Basingstoke: Macmillan).

Schulz, M., Söderbaum, F. and Öjendal, J. (eds) (2001) *Regionalization in a Globalizing World* (London: Zed Books).

Schuurman, F.J. (2000) 'Paradigms lost, paradigms regained? Development studies in the twenty-first century', *Third World Quarterly* 21(1).

Seidel, H. (1993) 'Austro-Keynesianismus – revisited', in Weber, F. and Venus, T. (eds) *Austro-Keynesianismus in Theorie und Praxis* (Wien: Dachs-Verlag).

Sender, H. (1999) 'Stemming the flood', *Far Eastern Economic Review*, 29 July.

Severino, R. (1999) 'The ASEAN way in Manila', *Far Eastern Economic Review*, 23 December.

Severinto, H.E.R.C. (1999) 'Regionalism: the stakes for South-East Asia', Address by the Secretary-General of ASEAN delivered in Singapore, 24 May.

Shaw, J. and More, G. (eds) (1995) *New Legal Dynamics of European Union* (Oxford: Oxford University Press).

Shaw, T.M. (1998) 'African renaissance/African alliance: towards new regionalisms and new realism in the Great Lakes at the start of the twenty-first century', *Politeia* 17(3).

Shaw, T.M. (1999) 'Globalisations and conflicts in Africa: prospects for human security and development in the new millennium', *ACCORD Conflict Trends* 3.

Shaw, T.M. (2000a) 'Overview: global/local – states, companies and civil societies', in Stiles, K. (ed.) *Global Institutions and Local Empowerment* (Basingstoke: Macmillan).

Shaw, T.M (2000b) 'Conflicts in Africa at the turn of the century: more of the same?', in Legault, A. (ed.) *Conflicts in the World, 1999–2000* (Quebec: IQHEI, Laval University).

Shaw, T. M. and MacLean, S.J. (1999) 'The emergence of regional civil society: contributions to a new human security agenda', in Jeong, H-W. (ed.) *The New Agenda for Peace Research* (Aldershot: Ashgate).

Shaw, T.M and Nyang'oro, J.E. (1999) 'Conclusion: African foreign policies and the next millennium: alternative perspectives, practices and possibilities', in Wright, S. (ed.) *African Foreign Policies* (Boulder, CO: Westview Press).

Shaw, T.M. and Nyang'oro, J.E. (2000) 'African renaissance in the new millennium? From anarchy to emerging markets?', in Stubbs, R. and Underhill, G.R.D. (eds) *Political Economy and the Changing Global Order* (2nd edn) (Oxford: Oxford University Press).

Shaw, T.M. and Schnabel, A. (1999) 'Human (in)security in Africa: prospects for good governance in the twenty-first century', *UNU Work in Progress* 15(3).

Shaw, T.M. and van der Westhuizen, J. (1999) 'Towards a political economy of trade in

Africa: states, companies and civil societies', in Hocking, B. and McGuire, S. (eds) *Trade Politics* (London: Routledge).

Shearer, D. (1998) 'Outsourcing war', *Foreign Policy* 112 (Autumn).

Shenon, P. (1998) 'Of the turmoil in Indonesia and its roots', *New York Times*, 9 May.

Short, I. (1987) 'The Cook Islands: autonomy, self-government and independence', in Hooper, A. *et al.* (eds) *Class and Culture in the South Pacific* (Suva: University of the South Pacific).

Sideri, S. (1997) 'Globalisation and regional integration', *The European Journal of Development Research* 9(1).

Siegel, D. (1992) 'Die Bedeutung österreichischer multinationaler Konzerne für die Internationalisierung', in Clement, W. (ed.) *Neue Entwicklungen – neue Formen – neue Herausforderungen. Internationalisierung Band VI* (Wien: Signum Verlag).

Sklair, L. (1995) 'Social movements and global capitalism', *Sociology* 29(3).

Sklair, L. (1997) 'Social movements for global capitalism: the transnational capitalist class in action', *Review of International Political Economy* 4(3).

Smillie, I., Gberie, L. and Hazelton, R. (2000) 'The heart of the matter: Sierra Leone, diamonds and human security' (Ottawa: Partnership Africa Canada).

Smith, A.D. (1992) 'National identity and the idea of European unity', *International Affairs* 68(1).

Smith, H. (1999) 'Managing international economic forces post-crisis: some implications for regional security', sixth meeting of the CSCAP Working Group on Comprehensive and Cooperative Security, Beijing, May.

Smith, S. (1998) 'New approaches to international theory', in Baylis, J. and Smith, S. (eds) *The Globalization of World Politics: An Introduction to International Relations* (Oxford: Oxford University Press).

Snitwongse, K. (1998) 'Thirty years of ASEAN: achievements through political accommodation', *Pacific Review* 11(2).

Soares de Lima, M.R. (1999) 'Brazil's alternative vision', in Mace, G. and Bélanger, L. (eds) *The Americas in Transition: The Contours of Regionalism* (Boulder, CO: Lynne Rienner).

South Pacific Forum Secretariat (1991) 'Twenty-Second South Pacific Forum: Forum Communiqué'.

South Pacific Forum Secretariat (1992)'Twenty-Third South Pacific Forum: Forum Communiqué'.

South Pacific Forum Secretariat (1995a) 'South Pacific Forum countries & APEC: an important relationship' (Statement from the South Pacific Forum to the Seventh APEC Ministerial Meeting, Osaka, Japan).

South Pacific Forum Secretariat (1995b) 'Twenty-Sixth South Pacific Forum: Forum Communiqué'.

South Pacific Forum Secretariat (1995c) 'Forum Secretariat News', April.

South Pacific Forum Secretariat (1996a) *Pacific Island Countries: Regional Economic Policy Overview* (Working Paper 96/2).

South Pacific Forum Secretariat (1996b) 'Twenty-Seventh South Pacific Forum: Forum Communiqué'.

South Pacific Forum Secretariat (1997a) 'Forum Economic Ministers Meeting: Action Plan'.

South Pacific Forum Secretariat (1997b) 'Twenty-Eighth South Pacific Forum: Forum Communiqué'.

South Pacific Forum Secretariat (1999) 'Thirtieth South Pacific Forum: Forum Communiqué'.

Spears, I.S. (1999) 'Angola's elusive peace: the collapse of the Lusaka Accord', *International Journal* 54(4).

Stiglitz, J. (1998) 'More instruments and broader goals: moving toward the post-Washington consensus', 1998 WIDER Annual Lecture, Helsinki, 7 January,

Stiles, K. (ed.) (2000) *Global Institutions and Local Empowerment: Competing Theoretical Perspectives* (Basingstoke: Macmillan).

Stone, D. (1967) 'The awesome glow in the sky: The Cook Islands and the French nuclear tests', *Journal of Pacific History* 2: 154–9.

Stone, D. (1997) 'Networks, second track diplomacy and regional cooperation: the role of Southeast Asian think tanks', paper presented at Thirty-eighth Annual Convention of the International Studies Association, Toronto, Canada, 22–26 March.

Strange, S. (1986) *Casino Capitalism* (Oxford: Blackwell).

Strange, S. (1996) *The Retreat of the State: The Diffusion of World Power in the World Economy* (Cambridge: Cambridge University Press).

Strange, S. (1999) 'The Westfailure system', *Review of International Studies* 25(3).

Streeck, W. and Schmitter, P.C. (1991) 'From national corporatism to transnational pluralism: organised interests in the Single European Market', *Politics and Society*, 19(2).

Stubbs, R. and Underhill, G.R.D. (eds) (2000) *Political Economy and the Changing Global Order* (2nd edn) (Oxford: Oxford University Press).

Taylor, I. (2000) 'Public–private partnerships: lessons form the Maputo Development Corridor toll road' (DPRU, University of Cape Town).

Tett, G. (1999) 'Special report: the hidden truth behind the mask', *Financial Times*, 18 June.

Teunissen, J.J. (ed.) (1996) *Regionalism and the Global Economy: The Rise of Africa* (The Hague: FONDAD).

Tow, W.T. (1990) *Subregional Security Co-operation in the Third World* (Boulder, Co: Lynne Rienner).

Tranholm-Mikkelsen, J. (1991) 'Neofunctionalism: obstinate or obsolete?', *Millennium: Journal of International Studies* 20(1).

UNCTAD (1998) *World Investment Report 1998: Trends and Determinants* (New York: United Nations).

UNDP (1994) *Human Development Report 1994* (New York: Oxford University Press).

UNDP (1999) *Human Development Report 1999* (New York: Oxford University Press).

UNICE (1999) *Fostering Entrepreneurship: The UNICE Benchmarking Report 1999* (Brussels: UNICE).

UNICE (2000) *Stimulating Creativity and Innovation in Europe: The UNICE Benchmarking Report 2000* (Brussels: UNICE).

United Nations, Task Force of the Executive Committee on Economic and Social Affairs (1999) 'Towards a new international financial architecture', 22 January, http://www.eclac.cl/English/Coverpage/architecture.htm.

Uvin, P. (1998) *Aiding Violence: The Development Enterprise in Rwanda* (West Hartford: Kumarian).

Vale, P. and Maseko, S. (1998) 'South Africa and the African renaissance', *International Affairs* 74(2).

Vale, P., Swatuk, L.A. and Oden, B. (eds) (2001) *Theory, Change and Southern Africa's Future* (Basingstoke: Macmillan).

van der Pijl, K. (1984) *The Making of an Atlantic Ruling Class* (London: Verso).

van der Pijl, K. (1989) 'The international level', in Bottomore, T. and Bryan, R. (eds) *The Capitalist Class: An International Study* (Hemel Hempstead: Harvester-Wheatsheaf).

van der Pijl, K. (1998) *Transnational Classes and International Relations* (London: Routledge).

Van Rooy, A. (1999) *Civil Society and Global Change: Canadian Development Report 1999* (Ottawa: North–South Institute).

van Walraven, K. (1999) *The Pretence of Peace-keeping: ECOMOG, West Africa and Liberia (1990–1998)* (The Hague: NIIR, November).

Vellinger, M. (ed.) (1999) *Dialectics of Globalization: Regional Responses to World Economic Processes: Asia, Europe and Latin America in Comparative Perspective* (Boulder, CO: Westview Press).

Verdun, A. (2000) *European Responses to Globalization and Financial Market Liberalization: Perceptions of Economic and Monetary Union in Britain, France and Germany* (Basingstoke: Macmillan).

VÖI (1987) *Europa – Unsere Zukunft. Eine Stellungnahme der Vereinigung österreichischer Industrieller zur Europäischen Integration* (Wien: Schreiftenreihe der Vereinigung österreichischer Industrieller).

Völkerrechtsbüro (1988) 'Mitgliedschaft Österreichs in den Europäischen Gemeinschaften und immerwährende Neutralität (22.11.1988)', in Kunnert, G. (ed.) *Spurensicherung auf dem österreichischen Weg nach Brüssel* (Wien: Verlag der Österreichischen Staatsdruckerei).

Wade, R. (1990) *Governing the Market: Economic Theory and the Role of Government in East Asian Industrialization* (Princeton, NJ: Princeton University Press).

Wade, R. (1998) 'From "miracle" to "cronyism": explaining the great Asian slump', *Cambridge Journal of Economics* 22(6).

Wade, R. (1999) 'Lessons from the Asian crisis', Asian Development Bank annual meeting (30 April).

Wallace, H. (1996) 'The institutions of the EU: experience and experiments', in Wallace, H. and Wallace, W. (eds) *Policy-Making in the European Union* (3rd edn) (Oxford: Oxford University Press).

Wallace, H. (1999a) 'Whose Europe is it anyway? 1998 Stein Rokkan Lecture', *European Journal of Political Research* 35.

Wallace, H. (1999b) 'The domestication of Europe: contrasting experiences of EU membership and non-membership', Hans Daalder Lecture, Department of Political Science, University of Leiden.

Wallace, H. (2000a) 'The policy process', in Wallace, H. and Wallace, W. (eds) *Policy-Making in the European Union* (4th edn) (Oxford: Oxford University Press).

Wallace, H. (2000b) 'The Institutional setting: five variations on a theme', in Wallace, H. and Wallace, W. (eds) *Policy-Making in the European Union* (4th edn) (Oxford: Oxford University Press).

Wallace, H. and Wallace, W. (eds) (2000) *Policy-Making in the European Union* (4th edn) (Oxford: Oxford University Press).

Wallace, W. (1990) 'Introduction: the dynamics of European integration', in Wallace, W. (ed.) *The Dynamics of European Integration* (London: Pinter/RIIA).

Wallace, W. (1994) *Regional Integration: The West European Experience* (Washington, DC: Brookings Institution).

Wallace, W. (1995) 'Regionalism in Europe: model or exception?', in Fawcett, L. and Hurrell, A. (eds) *Regionalism in World Politics: Regional Organization and International Order* (Oxford: Oxford University Press).

Wan, M. (1995) 'Spending strategies in world politics: how Japan has used its economic power in the past decade', *International Studies Quarterly* 39(1).

Wanandi, J. (1998) 'Boost ARF – and security', *Asiaweek*, 31 July.

Webb, C. (1983) 'Theoretical prospects and problems', in Wallace, H., Wallace, W. and Webb, P. (eds) *Policy-Making in the European Community* (2nd edn) (Chichester: John Wiley).

WEF (1999) *The Global Competitiveness Report 1999* (New York: Oxford University Press).

Weidenbaum, M. and Hughes, S. (1996) *The Bamboo Network: How Expatriate Chinese Entrepreneurs are Creating a New Economic Superpower in Asia* (New York: The Free Press).

Weiss, L. (1998) *The Myth of the Powerless State: Governing the Economy in a Global Era* (Cambridge: Polity Press).

Weiss, T.G (1999) *Military–Civilian Interactions: Intervention in Humanitarian Crises* (Lanham: Rowman and Littlefield).

Weiss, T.G. and Campbell, K.M. (1991) 'Military humanitarianism', *Survival* 33(5).

Wendt, A. (1992) 'Anarchy is what states make of it: the social construction of power politics', *International Organization* 46(2).

Whalley, J. (1996) 'Trade and environment beyond Singapore', *NBER Working Paper 5768*, September.

Wilcox, F.W. (1965) 'Regionalism and the United Nations', *International Organization* 10(3).

Williamson, J. (1990) 'What Washington means by policy reform', in Williamson, J. (ed.) *Latin American Adjustment: How Much has Happened* (Washington, DC: Institute for International Economics).

Wincott, D. (1995) 'Institutional interaction and European integration: towards an everyday critique of liberal intergovernmentalism', *Journal of Common Market* Studies 33 (4).

World Politics (1995) Special issue 'The role of theory in comparative politics: a symposium' 48 (1).

Wright, S. (ed.) (1999) *African Foreign Policies* (Boulder, CO: Westview Press).

Wrobel, P.S. (1998) 'A free trade area of the Americas in 2005?', *International Affairs* 74(3).

Young, O.R. (1995) *Global Governance: Drawing Insights from the Environmental Experience*. Occasional Paper, The Dickey Center, Dartmouth College, New Hampshire.

Yue, C.S. (1998) 'Foreign and intra-regional direct investments in ASEAN and emerging ASEAN multinations', in Fukasaku, K., Kimura, F. and Urata, S. (eds) *Asia & Europe: Beyond Competing Regionalism* (Brighton: Sussex Academic Press).

Zelikow, P. (1992) 'The new concert of Europe', *Survival* 34(2).

Zysman, J. (1996) 'The myth of a "global" economy: enduring national foundations and emerging regional realities', *New Political Economy* 1(2).

Index